The Limitation of Shipowners' Liability: The New Law

AUSTRALIA AND NEW ZEALAND
The Law Book Company Ltd.
Sydney : Melbourne : Perth

CANADA AND U.S.A.
The Carswell Company Ltd.
Agincourt, Ontario

INDIA
N. M. Tripathi Private Ltd.
Bombay
and
Eastern Law House Private Ltd.
Calcutta and Delhi
M.P.P. House
Bangalore

ISRAEL
Steimatzky's Agency Ltd.
Jerusalem: Tel Aviv : Haifa

MALAYSIA : SINGAPORE : BRUNEI
Malayan Law Journal (Pte.) Ltd.
Singapore and Kuala Lumpur

PAKISTAN
Pakistan Law House
Karachi

The Limitation of Shipowners' Liability: The New Law

London
Sweet & Maxwell
Institute of Maritime Law
1986

Published in 1986 by
Sweet & Maxwell Limited of
11 New Fetter Lane, London.
Computerset by Burgess & Son (Abingdon) Ltd.
Printed in Great Britain by
Hazell, Watson & Viney Ltd. (Member of the B.P.C.C.), Aylesbury, Bucks.

British Library Cataloguing in Publication Data

Limitation of shipowners' liability: the
new law.
1. Liability for marine accidents
341.7'5668 JX4411

ISBN 0–421–34890–9

Foreword

The Convention on Limitation of Liability for Maritime Claims will shortly have the force of law in the United Kingdom. The effect of that will be to introduce new internationally-agreed rules in place of those previously contained in The Convention Relating to the Liability of Owners of Seagoing Ships 1957. In this situation, the need for an entirely new work, dealing with the legal and commercial consequences of those new rules, is immediately apparent. That need is met, in a remarkably diverse and comprehensive way, by this present book, which the Institute of Maritime Law of the University of Southampton has so carefully and studiously compiled and which Sweet and Maxwell Limited have so timeously published.

The work consists of twenty-one chapters, written by twenty different authors from twelve different countries. Its diversity and comprehensiveness are apparent in four main ways. First, the antecedent history leading up to the 1976 Convention is fully examined. Secondly, the effect of the 1976 Convention is described from four significantly different points of view in the United Kingdom: that of academic lawyers; that of practising lawyers, both barristers and solicitors; and that of insurers of marine risks as represented by Protection and Indemnity Associations. Thirdly, the relationship between the 1976 Convention and other International Conventions, such as the Convention on Civil Liability for Oil Pollution 1969, is carefully explained. Fourthly, there are chapters written by distinguished lawyers, both academic and practising, from a large number of countries other than the United Kingdom, explaining the impact, actual or potential, which the 1976 Convention will have to each of them. Those countries are Argentina, France, German Democratic Republic, West Germany, Greece, Japan, the Nordic countries, Poland, Spain, the United States of America and Yugoslavia.

A number of significant points emerge from a reading of this book. The first point is the long interval, in this case ten years, which is bound to elapse between the making of a Convention and its coming into force after a sufficient number of states have adhered to it. The most important aspect of this is the progressive erosion of the limits of liability agreed as appropriate in 1976 by the extensive world-wide inflation which has taken place between that year and 1986. The second point is that by no means all maritime countries have yet adhered, or can be expected in the future to adhere, to the 1976 Convention. The most important aspect of this is that, however desirable it may be in theory for the 1976 Convention to be truly and completely international, there is no real prospect of this being achieved in practice, with some countries still applying earlier Conventions or their own special systems in their domestic laws. The third point is that, while the 1976 Convention was intended to deal with, and may well effectively have dealt with, a number of difficulties and inadequacies in the 1957 Convention, it seems likely that the 1976 Convention will also present its own problems of interpretation and application. That prospect is, perhaps, more appealing to lawyers than it is to ship operators and their insurers, for whom certainty of the law is of such vital importance.

As one who practised at the English Admiralty Bar for nearly twenty years, and was privileged to be the Judge of the English Admiralty Court for the twelve years which followed, I have no hesitation in commending this book to all those whose work or occupation requires that they should be as well informed as possible about the 1976 Convention when it comes into force in the United Kingdom later this year.

Brandon of Oakbrook

Preface

In September 1984 the Institute of Maritime Law, Southampton University held a one day conference on the 1976 Convention on Limitation of Liability for Maritime Claims. At that stage there was every likelihood that the Convention would enter into force very soon. In the event the necessary number of ratifications was achieved over a year later, in November 1985, enabling the Convention to come into force internationally on December 1, 1986. In view of the importance of the Convention for the maritime world and of the interest shown in the papers delivered we decided to publish them to a wider audience. At the same time it seemed a good opportunity to expand the areas covered in the original papers and to invite extra contributions from maritime lawyers, both in the United Kingdom and from abroad. It has been a failing, and a criticism, of lawyers in this country that we are too insular. Therefore, we are grateful to Sweet and Maxwell for continuing their support of the Institute by agreeing to publish the set of collected papers in this volume.

The scheme of the book is, first, to have a detailed analysis of the provisions of the Convention in PART A. This is followed, in PART B, by national perspectives on limitation of liability, generally, and on the 1976 Convention. In addition to the chapters in PART A by speakers at the original Conference there are now Chapters by Institute members David Jackson and Ralph Beddard. We were also fortunate in being able to persuade Andrew Dykes to deal with oil pollution and Erling Selvig to provide an introduction to the Convention. The PART A discussion of the detailed provisions of the 1976 Limitation Convention is not isolated from the practical realities of British law : nor would one expect it to be, with contributions from Geoffrey Brice Q.C., Richard Shaw and Robert Seward. PART B was designed to provide a non-British perspective on limitation. Of course, it is always difficult to comment on a Convention that is about to come into force, as national policies may still be in the process of formulation. But we are extremely grateful to our overseas lawyers for meeting the difficult deadline and contributing their views on what is a truly international subject. We hope that the Institute of Maritime Law can continue to encourage such international exchanges of information. Because PART A is not directed solely at domestic law we are grateful to Steven

Hazelwood for providing, in PART B, an overall view of the United Kingdom position.

This book is a collection of individual views about particular aspects of the Convention. It does not pretend to be a type of basic A to Z guide, although we are confident that in structure and content it will be of use and interest to shipowners, operators, their legal advisers and insurers as well as academics and students. To assist the book's practical value copious extracts from conventions and statutes have been included in the Appendices. As a result of the tolerance of Sweet and Maxwell, we have also been able to include reference to the latest 1986 statutory instruments giving effect to the 1976 Convention in the United Kingdom.

It is appropriate to record here our thanks to the Department of Transport for help and information given, especially by John Perrett and Frank Wall. We are particularly indebted to the former for his participation in the original 1984 conference at Southampton. Similarly, we have been very fortunate to have the continued support of Lord Brandon of Oakbrook who not only chaired the 1984 conference, but also agreed to write a foreword to this book. But it would not have been produced without the hard work of all at the Institute, particularly Richard Swatton, Richard Holt and Marian von Benko. The burden of proof reading and preparing the Index, list of cases and statutes fell on the shoulders of Robert Grime and Richard Holt.

August 1986

Nicholas Gaskell
Institute of Maritime Law
University of Southampton

Contents

PART B
NATIONAL PERSPECTIVES ON LIMITATION
AND THE 1976 LIMITATION CONVENTION

Table of Cases

xiv

Table of Statutes

(Figures in **bold** indicate the page where a section is set out.)

Table of International Conventions

(Figures in **bold** indicate the page where a section is set out.)

Table of Abbreviations

CLC	Convention on Civil Liability for Oil Pollution Damage (1969)
CMI	Comité Maritime International
CMR	Convention on the Contracts for the International Carriage of Goods by Road (1956)
ECE (CLN)	European Commission for Europe (Convention relating to the Limitation of the Liability of Owners of Inland Navigation Vessels) 1973
g.f.	Gold franc
HNS	Convention on Liability and Compensation in Connection with the Carriage of Noxious and Hazardous Substances by Sea (Draft)
IMCO	International Maritime Consultative Organisation
IMF	International Monetary Fund
IMO	International Maritime Organisation
MAP	Decree on Civil Proceedings in Maritime Affairs
MC	Maritime Codes
MLA	United States Maritime Law Association
MSA	Marine Safety Agency
MSC	Merchant Shipping Code
OECD	Organisation for Economic Co-operation and Development
OMS	Old measuring systems
PPA	Propelling power allowance
SDR	Special Drawing Rights
UMS	Universal measurement system
UNCTAD	United Nations Conference on Trade and Development

PART A

THE 1976 LIMITATION CONVENTION

I

An Introduction to the 1976 Convention

*Professor Erling Selvig**

1. THE LEGAL BACKGROUND

Principles of limitation

Legal limitation of the liability of shipowners for loss or damage arising on connection with the operation of the ship has long traditions in international maritime law. Although the legal regimes have varied with time and place, they have two principles in common:

(1) the legal limit of liability varies, generally speaking, with the size of the ship, and
(2) the shipowner is not entitled to limit his liability if the damage is attributable to his personal fault or neglect.

Historically, limits based on the *value* of the ship long prevailed. In nearly all countries this meant the value *after* the accident, the actual limit thus varying with the extent of damage to the ship itself. However, the limitation systems reflecting this principle took different forms.

In one group of countries (*e.g.* Germany and the Scandinavian states) the shipowner had no personal liability for limitable claims. Such claims were enforceable only against the ship and freight, but as a counterpart they had, by virtue of maritime liens, a priority right of recovery from such assets. This system has been named the *execution* system.

In another group of countries, such as France and later the United States, limitation of liability was implemented by the *abandonment* system. In principle, the shipowner was personally liable for the limitable claims, but he was entitled to avoid (limit) liability by abandoning the ship and freight to the claimants with the consequence that they were only entitled to recover by enforcing their maritime liens in these assets.

Two further principles were embodied in both these limitation systems:

* Scandinavian Institute of Maritime Law, University of Oslo.

(3) the limitation amount was to be distributed among the claimants according to the priority rules for maritime liens, and

(4) the limit of liability did not apply to each claim, but to the aggregate amount of claims having accrued up to the time when limitation was invoked.

English developments

In England a quite different system for limitation of shipowners' liability developed during the 18th and the 19th centuries. Even English law recognised the value of the ship and freight as the limit of liability, but contrary to the law of other countries this meant the value of the ship *before* the accident. In fact, this limit was monetary, the value of the ship being used merely for calculation purposes. In order to simplify the calculation new legislation was adopted in the 1850–60s, fixing the value of the ship to £8 per ton which, at the time, was regarded as an average for good English sailing ships. Since passenger ships had a higher value, their limit was to be £15 per ton, of which £7 was reserved for personal claims.

This legislation introduced several new principles into limitation law. The key concept is the *monetary* limit, calculated on the ship's tonnage. An important element is also the idea of an additional amount reserved for personal claims. There is a restrictive approach to the number of limitable claims. In general, only claims arising out of damage to persons of property were subject to limitation. The limitation amount was to be distributed among the claimants *in proportion to their claims* and not according to the priorities of maritime liens. Finally, a separate limitation fund would be available for claims arising on *any distinct occasion* and, thus, the extent of aggregation of claims for limitation purposes was restricted accordingly.

Without great changes this limitation system was subsequently carried over into the Merchant Shipping Act 1894.

1924 Convention

The international character of shipping suggests that substantial differences between the national laws on shipowners' liability are undesirable. Accordingly, at the beginning of the twentieth century limitation of shipowners' liability was taken up by *Comité Maritime International* (CMI) as a subject appropriate for international unification. In 1924 this work was concluded by the adoption of an international Convention which was a most unhappy compromise between the existing systems. The Convention reflects what has been termed the *option-system* because the shipowner may limit his liability to the value of ship and freight or

4

to an amount of £8 per ton. In either case an additional amount of £8 per ton is reserved for personal claims. Thus, the monetary limits were equivalent to those originating in the English legislation from the 1850–60s, and even in other respects the Convention incorporated elements of English law.

Although the 1924 Convention was once implemented in about 15 countries, it never achieved its objective, notably because the United Kingdom did not accede. Today this Convention retains some importance because it is the basis for Brazilian and Russian law.

1957 Convention

After World War II the efforts to achieve international uniformity were resumed. The result was the *1957 Convention Relating to the Limitation of the Liability of Owners of Seagoing Ships*. By this Convention the English system for limitation of liability[1] received full international recognition. Only a few elements were added to refine the system, *e.g.* claims by members of the crew or other employees on board the ship were essentially exempted from limitation. The main purpose of the additions, however, was to ensure that limitation of liability applies—and will be efficiently applied—to all liabilities in respect of damage arising out of the operation of a ship.

First, in order to solve the "Himalaya-problem,"[2] the right to limit liability, hitherto a benefit for the owner, was extended also to the charterer, manager and operator of the ship as well as to the crew and other servants thereof. The purpose was to ensure that the owner and his liability insurer would enjoy the benefit of limitation even if limitable claims were enforced against a person other than the owner. However, in order to maximise the effect of this extension the aggregation for limitation purposes of *all claims* arising on any distinct occasion (Article 2) had to be supplemented by an aggregation of *all liabilities in respect of limitable claims so arising* (Article 6). This transformed the English system into a system for *global limitation* in the sense that the limit of liability applies to *the total of all liabilities on the part of the ship for damage caused by one accident.* In view of P & I insurance practices the implication is that all such liabilities may be covered under *one insurance attached to the ship* and taken out by its owner.

Secondly, the 1957 Convention contains several Articles dealing with the procedural implementation of this global limitation.[3] A main objective of these provisions is to ensure the efficiency of the limit of liability and, particularly, to prevent holders of limitable

[1] See p. 4, *supra.*
[2] *Adler* v. *Dickson* [1955] 1 Q.B. 158.
[3] Arts. 2(2)–(4), 3(2)–(4), 4 and 5.

claims obtaining recoveries by taking separate or successive actions thus causing the total liability for one accident to exceed the applicable limit. Accordingly, Article 7 of the Convention also makes its provisions applicable as *lex fori* whenever limitation of liability is sought before a court of a contracting state.

In terms of unification of international maritime law the 1957 Convention became a success. During the 1960–70s the Convention was implemented in the national law of more than 40 countries, including most European states as well as many important countries in other parts of the world such as Australia, Canada, India and Japan.[4] However, other limitation systems continued to exist. In Italy, the United States and most Latin American countries, the old execution or abandonment systems are part of existing law and the limitation law of the Soviet Union is mainly based on the 1924 Convention. The measure of uniformity achieved is nevertheless impressive.

2. THE NEED FOR CHANGES

Risks contemplated

A remarkable feature of the 1957 Convention is that Article 3(1) essentially reflects the *same* monetary limits as those once fixed by the then 100 years old English statutes drafted for sailing vessels. The Convention was elaborated at a time of fixed and gold-based exchange rates, and it sets out the limits in Poincaré gold francs. However, at the 1957 Conference the limits were negotiated in pounds sterling. Thus, the limit for property damage of £24 (paper value) was meant to be equivalent to the £8 (gold value) of the 1924 Convention. The additional amount reserved for personal claims was agreed to £50 (paper value), *i.e.* twice the amount set out in the 1924 Convention. Realising that these limits, based on the tonnage principle, would cause particular hardship in cases involving small ships, the conference also fixed minimum limits calculated on the basis of 300 tons.[5]

In retrospect one notes with some astonishment that this old and low level of liability really was acceptable to the international community, particularly because it was combined with measures designed to ensure the efficiency of the global limitation system.[6] One likely explanation is that at that time the limits of liability were believed to be of significance mainly in cases of damage caused to *other maritime interests*, regularly covered to a great extent by own insurance. In any event the inadequacy appeared when in the late 1960s it was brought to public knowledge that international

[4] CMI Yearbook 1984–85, pp. 90 *et seq.*
[5] Art. 3(5).
[6] Art. 6(4), *supra*.

the adoption of the CLC in 1969 and the Fund Convention in 1971. The idea of a Protocol merely amending the 1957 Convention was kept alive for some time. In spite of general acceptance of the limitation system of the 1957 Convention, however, it was soon realized that the need for changes in substance, form and drafting could only be adequately addressed within the framework of a new Convention. Such a draft was finalized by CMI at its 1974 conference in Hamburg,[10] and the Draft with explanatory comments was subsequently submitted to the International Maritime Organisation (then IMCO) for consideration and further action.[11]

The preparatory work continued for another two years in the Legal Committee of IMCO,[12] but in the end the CMI draft remained basically intact. However, there were a few important novelties in the Draft submitted to the Diplomatic Conference,[13] *inter alia*, a special limit for personal claims by passengers of the ship[14] and a general limit expressed as the total of different amounts per ton for each of several tonnage intervals.[15] Also, the SDR was substituted for the Poincaré franc as the unit of account.[16]

Neither CMI nor the Legal Committee did much to solve the main problems prompting the revision of the 1957 Convention, namely the monetary limits and other issues related to the level of liability. However, a Resolution of the Hamburg conference sets out what later proved to be *the accepted approach* to these issues.[17] CMI recommended that

> "the limits should be fixed by reference to the amount of liability insurance, which having regard to the cost thereof, can reasonably be required of ships engaged in ordinary commercial shipping, since the cost of this insurance is inevitably reflected in the freight rates payable by shippers."

Recommending also the tonnage-principle and that special consideration be given to small ships, CMI stated, however, that the amount per ton "could be significantly increased." The proviso was that the privity rule be substituted by a rule of wilful misconduct. CMI also recalled the problems of insurance market capacity in relation to liability insurance for the very large ships.

[10] *CMI Documentation 1974*, pp. 304 *et seq.*
[11] *Ibid.* pp. 380 *et seq.*
[12] See the reports from the 23rd, 25th, 27th and 28th sessions of the Legal Committee.
[13] *Official Records of the International Conference on the Limitation of Liability for Maritime Claims 1976*, pp. 30 *et seq.*
[14] Art. 7.
[15] Art. 6.
[16] Art. 8.
[17] *Documentation 1974*, (*supra*, n. 5), pp. 326–29.

The issues directly or indirectly bearing upon the *level* of liability were squarely addressed for the first time during the Diplomatic Conference. At that time, however, the details of the liability system were well hammered out, and on such questions the Conference itself did little more than reject a great number of amendments proposed by individual delegations.

Exceptions

Before coming to the general limit of liability the Diplomatic Conference had to define the *global* character of the limitation system. Any exclusion of important groups of claims would mean an indirect increase of the level of liability since both excluded and limitable claims might arise out of the same accident.

The 1957 Convention excluded only one such group of claims, *i.e.* claims by members of the crew, etc.[18] From a practical point of view this exclusion covered claims in respect of loss of life or personal injury (*personal claims*). By agreeing rather expeditiously on a special limit for passenger claims, the Conference virtually excluded another important group of personal claims. Also, the limit for passenger claims, calculated on the *per capita* limit of the 1974 Athens Convention and the number of passengers stated in the ship's certificate[19] was sufficiently high to allow full compensation except perhaps in the case of a catastrophic accident involving a relatively great number of personal claims. In relation to personal claims, consequently, the general limit remained of significance only for a third group, namely persons not being on board the ship.

On the other hand, as regards *property claims* the Conference was not prepared to allow exceptions to the principle of global limitation. Obviously, the new Convention needed a provision—as proposed in the IMCO draft Article 3(b)—to eliminate any overlap with the 1969 Convention as regards the liability for oil pollution damage.[20] At the Conference, however, it was proposed to widen this exception so as to cover liability in respect of other polluting substances or hazardous cargo.[21] These efforts failed, but in order to meet the concerns of States not party to the 1969 Convention the Conference accepted a proposal to exclude all claims for oil pollution damage "within the meaning of" the 1969

[18] See Art. 1(4).
[19] Art. 7.
[20] See Art. 1(2).
[21] *Official Records*, pp. 248 *et seq.*

10

Convention instead of only those actually "subject to" that convention.[22]

The net effect of these decisions was that the concept of global limitation in the 1976 Convention will be of significance mainly for the property claims.

General limits

The discussion of the *general* limit of liability (for personal claims in respect of persons not on board the ship and for a variety of property claims listed in Article 2) was a lengthy and unusually complicated exercise.[23] As mentioned already,[24] the generally accepted point of departure was that the limit should be the *maximum* that was insurable at reasonable cost. At the Conference, however, there were quite a wide range of opinions both as to what was "reasonable cost" and as to what would be the cost effects of any change of the limit contained in the 1957 Convention. In fact, the consideration determining the attitudes seemed to be the extent to which the various delegations wanted to protect their shipping interests by keeping liability and insurance costs low.

The discussion of the general limit involved four main questions:

(1) the minimum amount for small ships, fixed either as a flat amount or calculated on the basis of a minimum tonnage,
(2) the amount per ton for medium-sized ships (c. 30,000 tons),
(3) the amount per ton in the 30–70,000 tons range, and
(4) the amount per ton for tonnage in excess of 70,000 tons.

The discussion centred around the two first questions, but all four questions were closely linked to two other issues.

First, there was almost general agreement that the old privity rule should be substituted by a rule based on wilful misconduct. However, several delegations proposed additions thereto which would have softened the effect of such a change. These delegations felt a need for a "safety valve" if the limits ultimately fixed would be too low. On the other hand, from the point of view of P & I insurers such additions were unacceptable[25] and eventually their view prevailed.[26]

Secondly, an equally important question was whether the

---

[22] *Official Records,* pp. 359–62. The proposal originally accepted contained the expression "as defined in," but as a matter of drafting this was later changed to "within the meaning of": see *ibid.* pp. 408–09, *cf.* pp. 477–78. As to the implications of Art. 3(b), see E. Selvig. "The 1976 Convention and Oil Pollution Damage." [1979] 1 L.M.C.L.Q. 21.

[23] *Official Records,* pp. 255–78, 283–93 and 362–76.

[24] See Art. 3(1), 1976 Convention.

[25] *Cf.* Art. 2(3), *ibid.*

[26] *Official Records,* pp. 263–78, 292 and 384.

11

general limit should be fixed *either* as one limit for all claims, but with a certain priority for personal claims, *or* as one limit for personal claims and one for other claims, but combined with a one-way "spill-over" system allowing (as with the 1957 Convention) unpaid personal claims to rank equally with other claims in the second portion of the limit. At the Conference, it was widely assumed that the relevant personal claims would rarely exceed the limit for such claims and, accordingly, that the choice was of consequence mainly for the level of compensation for property claims. The second alternative foreclosed the possibility that "unused" portions of the limitation amount for personal claims would increase the compensation available for property claims. When the Conference ultimately decided in favour of retaining the one-way spill-over in the 1957 Convention, the reason was precisely that such an increase should be avoided.[27]

Limitation amounts

There still remained to determine the *actual figures*.[28] A number of delegations submitted proposals with a great variety of figures and tonnage factors to be used for the purpose of calculating the general limits for the group of personal claims remaining subject to global limitation, and for the property claims. A working group was set up to study the matter, and its report reveals that the views were wide apart.[29] The discussion of the report did little to narrow the gaps.[30]

During the discussion of these issues as well as any other issue bearing upon the level of liability the conference were, generally speaking, divided in *three* groups. One group, consisting of the East European and most of the developing countries, favoured a low level of liability and also a low minimum level for small ships. Another group which included the United Kingdom, the Netherlands, the Federal Republic of Germany and other continental countries, was prepared to accept some increase of liability for small and even medium-sized ships, particularly to take account of the effects of inflation. A third group wanted a substantial increase of the level of liability for all ships, particularly a much higher minimum for small ships, and this group included Australia, Canada, France, Japan, the United States and the Scandinavian countries.

The group in the middle, led by the United Kingdom, rightly considered that its position would receive secondary support from the numerous East European and developing countries and

---

[27] *Official Records*, pp. 256 *et seq.* and 366 *et seq., cf.* p. 292.
[28] See Chapter 3.
[29] *Official Records*, pp. 134–40.
[30] *Official Records*, pp. 365–76.

apparently it did not see the need for meeting the wishes of the third group, except perhaps as regards the minimum limit for small ships. The final result, negotiated as always by a limited number of persons in a smoke-filled room, also reflected mainly the views of the group in the middle. The rest of the Conference accepted the result as the best compromise likely to obtain the required majority.[31]

The implications as regards the level of liability in respect of total exposure (T/E) and property claims (PropC) appear in the table below, setting out (1) the 1957 limit, (2) the 1957 limit adjusted for inflation during the period 1957–76, and (3) the limit of the new Convention with respect to four groups of ships. Since the limits were negotiated in millions of US dollars, the 1957 limits in Poincaré francs have been calculated into dollars at the rate of 12 to 1. The figures in the Convention were later stated in SDR's at the rate of 1 SDR = 1,20 U.S. dollars,[32] but in the table all figures are given in millions of U.S. dollars.

		Minimum for small ships (500 t)		Ships of 3.000 t		Ships of 30.000 t		Ships of 70.000 t	
		T/E	PropC	T/E	PropC	T/E	PropC	T/E	PropC
(1)	1957	0.077	0.025	0.77	0.25	7.7	2.5	18	5.8
(2)	1957 adj.	0.15	0.05	1.5	0.5	15.5	5	36	11.6
(3)	1976	0.6	0.2	2.6	0.7	19	6.3	37	12.3

The table shows that if account is taken of inflation during the period 1957–76, the new Convention meant in 1976 a substantial increase of the minimum limit for small ships and a modest and gradually falling increase of the limits for the ships in the range 3,000–70,000 tons. For ships above 70,000 tons the additional amount per ton for tonnage in excess of 70,000 tons is so low that the effect of inflation is not fully reflected in the 1976 figures. Thus, the level of liability imposed by the 1976 convention is relatively near the original position of the United Kingdom.[33] Only the minimum liability for small ships is markedly higher.

It should be added that a special limit for salvors not operating from a ship was fixed in an amount equivalent to the limit for a

[31] *Official Records,* pp. 377–84.
[32] *Official Records,* pp. 203–08.
[33] *Official Records,* pp. 148 and 372.

ship of 1,500 tons.[34] The other problems relating to the application of the limitation system to claims arising out of salvage operations[35] were solved by express provision in Article 2(1)(*a*) of the Convention.

4. THE 1976 CONVENTION—A GLOBAL LIMITATION SYSTEM FOR THE FUTURE?

Principles of the 1976 Convention

The outline given in n. 3, above suggests that the basic principles reflected in the global limitation system of the 1976 Convention are the following[36]:

(1) personal claims relating to members of the crew, passengers and other persons on board the ship should be excluded from the global limitation system,

(2) the level of liability for personal claims remaining subject to global limitation should be sufficient to ensure full compensation in most cases,

(3) the level of liability for property claims should be moderate and take into account that the property involved are usually covered by insurance, and

(4) the global limitation system should actually be "unbreakable."

The viability of the 1976 Convention will mainly depend on the extent to which the level of liability established in accordance with principles (2) and (3) actually remains unaffected by subsequent developments as well as on the extent to which the principles themselves remain acceptable to the international community. The fact that the 1976 Convention will enter into force in 1986 suggests that there are smooth waters ahead.[37] Nevertheless, the true explanation of the acceptance of the 1976 Convention in the 1980s may very well be that, for many countries, this is the only practical way of getting rid of the 1957 Convention. There are also several reasons suggesting that from the point of view of unification of international maritime law global limitation will continue to be a troublesome subject in spite of the obvious qualities of the 1976 Convention as a legal instrument.

---

[34] *Official Records,* pp. 388–90. It is interesting to note the lack of interest in this issue, but the solution was of no direct consequence for shipowners and P & I insurers.

[35] See Art. 2(3), *supra.*

[36] *Cf., e.g.* the views expressed at the conference in the main statements of the United Kingdom representative: *Official Records,* pp. 256, 263–65, 287 and 368–69.

[37] The criteria set out in Art. 17 of the Convention have now been met by the ratifications or accessions of Bahamas, Benin, Denmark, Finland, France, Japan, Liberia, Norway, Spain, Sweden and Yemen.

14

The 1957 and 1976 Conventions in context

When considering this question it would seem appropriate to look upon the 1957 and 1976 Conventions as a whole. In this perspective a certain number of main points become apparent.

First, one effect of the two Conventions is to reduce the role of global limitation with respect to personal claims. The group of claims retained within the system relates to seamen and passengers on board other ships as well as to persons on land. Seamen are usually covered by social insurance or the like, and the limit of liability will be of consequence mainly in relation to the two other categories.

Secondly, the two Conventions have made global limitation virtually "unbreakable." As mentioned already[38] the 1957 Convention contains two important measures in this regard. The last escape-route was closed by the 1976 Convention, Article 4, providing that only personal wilful misconduct is a bar to limitation.[39] The overall purpose is to prevent the right of limitation granted to shipowners, and enjoyed indirectly by P & I insurers, being frustrated one way or the other.

The net effect for injured parties, however, is that the limitation amounts become the *only* source of compensation available from the persons responsible for the various aspects of the operation of the ship causing the damage. The consequence thereof is particularly apparent in cases of damage for which insurance is not regularly taken out. Examples here are personal claims and property claims relating to non-maritime interests.

Thirdly, in terms of real value there has been no significant change in the *general* level of liability. The 1957 Convention meant an increase in the limit for personal claims, and the 1976 Convention also increased the limits for ships of low tonnage. In other respects, however, the adjustments of the limits made by the two Conventions went hardly much beyond what was required to compensate a fall in monetary values that *had* already taken place.[40]

This means, for example, that in 1976 the limits for property claims contained in the 1976 Convention were essentially on the same level as the monetary limits of the 1924 Convention and of the 19th Century English legislation from which they were taken. Of course, this observation is relevant only for ships of low or medium sized tonnage and not for the ships of much larger tonnage appearing after the Second World War. Nevertheless it is

[38] See Art. 1(4), *supra.*
[39] See Art. 2(3), *supra.*
[40] See Art. 2(1) and 3(4), *supra.*

hardly possible to maintain that the 1976 limits constitute the maximum that is insurable at "reasonable costs."[41]

The traditionally low level of liability for property claims may have been justified at a time when shipowners mainly incurred liabilities towards *other* maritime interests for which there regularly was insurance cover available. This is no longer so, nor was it the case in 1976 or in the 1960s. This explains why the 1969 Convention established a separate and higher limit of liability for oil pollution damage.[42] It also explains why, subsequently, many countries have felt that new liabilities for pollution or other damage caused by hazardous or noxious goods to non-maritime interests, usually without insurance cover for such damage, should not be subject to global limitation, at least not according to the 1976 Convention in its present form. The 1976 Conference failed to address this problem seriously in a long term perspective.

Fourthly, the 1957 and the 1976 Conventions do not establish procedures or other mechanisms for easy adjustment of the limits of liability to counter future deterioration of monetary values. At the 1976 Conference it was recognized that expressing the limits in SDRs would give little or no protection against world inflation. A number of proposals for an appropriate remedy were tabled during the Conference, but all failed to obtain the majority required.[43] In retrospect, this was most unfortunate and may lead to an early revision of the 1976 Convention.

In terms of real value the monetary limits of liability established by the 1976 Convention are not the same in 1986 as in 1976. World inflation during these 10 years has been considerable. In the OECD area inflation has been estimated at nearly 100 per cent. during this period.[44] This suggests that in 1986 the real value of the limits of liability in the 1976 convention will be approximately a mere 55–50 per cent. of their value when adopted in 1976. The use of SDR as the unit of account may mean that the reduction is not quite as much as average price indices for the whole OECD area show. The SDR value mainly depends on the extent of inflation in the few OECD countries with a currency included in the SDR basket and on the relative weight of such currencies when the SDR value is calculated. No doubt, the fall in the value of the 1976 limits is greater and has occurred much earlier than anticipated.

---

[41] See Art. 3(3), *supra.*

[42] See Art. 2(2), *supra.*

[43] *Official Records*, pp. 294–304, 420 *et seq.* and pp. 489–96.

[44] The OECD consumer price indices, using 1980 as basis year (100), show the figure of 68,7 for 1976 and 138,2 for June 1985. Although these figures are not fully representative for property in general, the implication as to the extent of the decline in monetary values is obvious. Also, the measure of damages for loss of life and personal injury follows the consumer price indices quite closely.

If the 1957 value of the limits in the 1957 Convention is taken as the point of departure, the real value thereof would be the same in 1986 only if the amounts per ton used to calculate the limits were approximately four times as high as the original amounts. The table already given[45] shows that under the 1976 Convention this will be the case only for ships with a tonnage less than 2,000 tons.

For ships more than 3,000 tons the level of liability in 1986 will be less than the 1957 value of the limits, declining proportionately with the size of the ship.

Future

What the future will bring for the 1976 Convention primarily depends on the extent to which future inflation will erode the real values of the limits of liability therein established. No other single factor constitutes a similar threat to the viability of the Convention.

Lack of foresight or of realism at the 1976 Conference prevented an adequate solution to this problem. Today this is to be regretted, particularly in light of the high qualities of the 1976 Convention as an international legal instrument.

[45] See Art. 3(4), *supra*.

II

The Scope of the Limitation Action

Geoffrey Brice, Q.C. [*]

Introduction

Limitation of liability is a privilege granted by statute to a defined class of persons to limit their liability to pay damages and certain other sums that would otherwise be payable in full provided that liability has arisen in certain defined circumstances. It is therefore necessary, in order to appreciate the scope of the statutory relief afforded, to analyse first those provisions which define *who may limit liability* (and therefore by a process of exclusion to indicate who may not) and secondly those provisions which set out the *classes of claim* in respect of which the right of limitation exists. Limitation of liability may, at first sight at least, appear to be a curious concept for it enables a wrongdoer legitimately to escape the just consequences of his wrongdoing—for example if it were contained in an exclusion clause in a contract to which both wrongdoer and wronged were parties one could more easily understand it: but the relief exists wholly independently of the consent of the parties. Its origins are to be found in the desire of governments and the legislature to protect the financial interests of shipowners so as not to discourage the ownership and operation of ships. By such a policy underwriters may in most cases be able to conduct their business with some reasonably ascertainable limit on their exposure and parties likely to be affected by the legislation may insure their interests in the knowledge of its existence.

History

The original English legislation passed in 1733[1] arose out of pressure from shipowners to limit their liability for loss arising out of the theft of the cargo by the Master and crew—a step which had already been taken in other continental jurisdictions. In 1786[2] (following a robbery from a ship on the River Thames in 1784) the relief was extended to theft by persons other than the Master and

[*] Of the Middle Temple; Member of the Panel of Lloyd's Salvage Arbitrators.
[1] 7 Geo. 2, c. 15.
[2] 26 Geo. 3, c. 86.

crew and the cases of loss by fire. However a more general provision was contained in the Responsibility of Shipowners Act 1813[3] and it is in that Act that one can see the origin of the more general provisions which were to be expanded over the next 170 years or so culminating in the convention[4] and legislation[5] presently under consideration. Indeed, whatever misgivings one may have about the existence of the doctrine of limitation of liability, it is to be noted that whenever Parliament (or the provisions of an international convention) have intervened, it has been to widen the scope of the classes of person who may limit and the class of claim in respect of which liability may be limited. The 1813 Act gave a right to shipowners to limit their liability for claims for damage to property to the value of the ship and freight. At that time there was no right to recover damages for loss of life. In 1846 Lord Campbell's Act[6] was passed to enable dependants to recover in fatal accident cases and it was this which led to the widening of the scope of the right to limit liability in the Merchant Shipping Act 1854[7] so as to include such claims. Indeed, Lord Campbell is said to have admitted that he had not envisaged the Act named after him encompassing claims for loss of life at sea which—in the days of emigrant ships—would have imposed enormous and unacceptable burdens on shipowners; his Act was really aimed (or so he believed) at claims arising from deaths due to railway accidents.

The limit of liability in 1854 remained the value of the ship and freight save that in the case of loss of life claims it was fixed at £15 per ton (minimum) reflecting the value in 1854 of a well-run British passenger ship (so as to prevent the owners of much less valuable ships benefiting as compared to the owners of the better class of ship). Procedurally, under the 1813 Act, a shipowner wishing to limit his liability could, when sued, set up limitation as a defence, or, if there was likely to be more than one claimant, he could exhibit a bill in any Court of Equity (supported by an affidavit), pay the value of the ship and freight into court and that sum (and any profits it earned) belonged thereafter to the claimants against him. This procedure is the origin of the present limitation action. There is one striking difference in that payment in was in effect obligatory; for without a payment in there was no obligation upon the claimant to plead in the limitation action and the Action could be dismissed.

Two points arise from the foregoing: first, under R.S.C., Ord. 18, r. 22, limitation may still be pleaded as a defence to the

[3] 53 Geo. 3, c. 159.
[4] Convention on Limitation of Liability for Maritime Claims 1976.
[5] Merchant Shipping Act 1979.
[6] Fatal Accidents Act 1846; 9 & 10 Vict. c. 93.
[7] 17 & 18 Vict. c. 104.

plaintiff's claim; secondly a limitation action may be brought by the party wishing to limit liability, if there are; or are potentially, several claimants, so as to enable him to obtain a limitation decree from the Admiralty Court binding upon all the claimants. Indeed although the provisions of sections 503 and 504 of the Merchant Shipping Act 1894[8] would appear prima facie to recognise that a limitation action as such was only applicable where there were several claimants it was held by the Court of Appeal in the *Penelope II*[9] that a limitation action was an appropriate remedy even where there was only one claimant who had a judgment in his favour for damages and where limitation had not been pleaded in the liability action as a defence. Whereas limitation as a defence may be pleaded in proceedings in any Division of the High Court (in appropriate cases), by R.S.C., Ord. 75, r. 2(1)(c) a limitation action must be begun in the Admiralty Court.

The Merchant Shipping Act 1854 listed four categories of claim which might be the subject of limitation of liability namely, (in summary) (1) claims by crew or passengers for loss of life or personal injuries (2) cargo damage claims (3) claims for loss of life or personal injury due to negligent navigation and (4) property damage claims arising from negligent navigation, the limit still being the value of the ship plus freight (save for the £15 minimum for loss of life and personal injury claims). By the Merchant Shipping Act (Amendment) Act 1862[10] the £15 per ton was retained as a fixed figure but the value of the ship and freight was abandoned as a basis for calculating the limitation fund and £8 per ton substituted. These two figures remained for some 96 years until the Merchant Shipping (Liability of Shipowners and Others) Act 1958[11] (enacting the Brussels Convention 1957)[12] substituted figures referable to the value for the time being of the gold figures in terms of sterling. Under the Merchant Shipping Acts 1854 and 1862 one can see in recognisable form the basis of the modern concept of limitation of liability. The right was afforded to a shipowner (registered or unregistered) including a part-owner; but not an owner-master whose negligence caused the loss. It was granted to the owners of ships British or foreign. The limitation fund was assessed by reference to a fixed method of calculation thus obviating costly litigation as to the value of the ship and freight. The Judicature Act 1873[13] conferred upon the Admiralty

[8] 57 & 58 Vict. c. 60.
[9] [1980] 2 Lloyd's Rep. 17 (C.A.)
[10] 25 & 26 Vict. c. 63.
[11] 6 & 7 Eliz. 2, c. 62: Temperley, *Merchant Shipping Acts* (7th ed., 1976), p. 524. (British Shipping Laws).
[12] Brussels Convention on Limitation 1957; Singh, *International Maritime Law Conventions* (1983), Vol. 4, p. 2967 (British Shipping Laws).
[13] 36 & 37 Vict. c. 66.

Court the same jurisdiction as the Court of Chancery possessed before the Act and by section 11 of the Judicature Act 1875[14] limitation actions were assigned to the Admiralty Court as they are now. Perhaps by an oversight no form of writ was laid down in the first Schedule to the 1874 Act nor in the Rules of Court of 1875; but the ordinary form of writ was adapted to overcome this procedural problem this being in essence the form of writ in modern limitation actions with the party seeking to limit being the plaintiff and the claimants against him being the defendants.

The scope of the right to limit was subsequently extended in three principal ways. First, the definition of owner and other persons entitled to limit was expanded; secondly the definition of "ship" was expanded and thirdly the classes of claims in respect of which limitation of liability could be obtained were expanded beyond the four categories contained in the 1854 Act. These enlargements of the scope of the Limitations Acts occurred principally in amendments to the Merchant Shipping Act 1894 culminating in the Merchant Shipping (Liability of Shipowners and Others) Act 1958. The first International Convention on the topic was the Brussels Convention of 1957 which was in substance enacted in the 1958 Act.

Effect of new provisions

Most, if not all, of the previous legislation on limitation of liability is repealed by the Merchant Shipping Act 1979 which is the statute giving effect to the International Convention of Limitation of Liability for Maritime Claims 1976. Section 17(1) of the 1979 Act gives the Convention (most of which is set out in Part I of Schedule 4 to the Act) the force of law in the United Kingdom. Part II of Schedule 4, extends or modifies in certain limited respects the 1976 Convention or adapts its provisions to other provisions of, or procedures of English Law. Section 18 provides for the English law concept of exclusion of liability in two classes of case. By section 19(4) the new regime on limitation of liability does not apply to any liability arising out of an occurrence which took place before the coming into force (by order under section 52(2)) of sections 17 and 18 aforesaid. Special commencement provisions apply to wreck removal claims, as discussed below.

Categories of claim

There are six categories of claim listed in Article 2 of the 1976 Convention as being claims subject to limitation of liability. The words used are, however, different from those appearing in earlier statutes up to and including the Merchant Shipping Act 1894 (as

[14] 38 & 39 Vict. c. 88.

amended); but include all classes of claim previously subject to limitation of liability. Article 2 further provides that liability may be limited "whatever the basis of liability may be."

(1) The first category of claims are contained in Article 2 (1)(a) namely—

> "Claims in respect of loss of life or personal injury or loss of or damage to property including damage to harbour walls, basins and waterways and aids to navigation) occurring on board or in direct connexion with the operation of the ship or with salvage operations and consequential loss resulting therefrom"

This category (which is probably the one which will most frequently be invoked) expressly covers both loss of life and personal injury claims and also property claims including consequential loss. Such claims are covered whatever the basis of liability may be. Accordingly whereas the former legislation was directed primarily at claims for damages arising out of negligence or the breach of the contract of carriage and the like, the new provisions cover any liability whatever its basis, including presumably an absolute liability arising irrespective of fault. The claim for loss or damage must however be one which occurs on board or in direct connection with the operation of the ship (or with salvage operations as discussed below). The expression "on board" will perhaps not give rise to difficulty; indeed it occurred in section 503 of the Merchant Shipping Act 1894. It gave rise to difficulty in the *Tojo Maru*[15] where a professional salvor, whose diver was working not on the salvor's salvage tug but beneath the casualty, was held not to be "on board" the tug so that the salvor was held not to be entitled to limit his liability (when the diver's negligence severely damaged the casualty). This particular problem has been overcome by special provisions in Articles 1(4) and 6(4) of the new Convention aside from those presently under consideration.

Questions may however arise as to what is meant in the Convention by the words "in direct connexion with the operation of the ship." These words are not defined. The words appearing in the Merchant Shipping Act 1894 were "navigation or management" of the ship. These latter words had been held to apply even though the act or omission complained of was also a breach of contract but not where the act or omission was *only* a breach of contract. In the *Vigilant*[16] it was held (*obiter*) by Sir Henry Duke P. (following *Wahlberg* v. *Young*[17] that if a tug in breach of contract failed to tow at all (and no towage was in progress) then the

---

[15] [1972] A.C. 242 (H.L.)
[16] [1921] P. 312.
[17] (1876) 4 Asp.M.L.C. 27n.

tugowner could not limit his liability for the damages arising out of that breach for that would not be an act or omission in the navigation or management of the tug. This is to be contrasted with the case of towing tug casting off her towline too soon so as to bring about a collision which would be in the navigation and management of the ship as well as a breach of contract. Under the new regime one has to consider whether a mere breach of contract (as illustrated above) would be "in direct connexion with the operation" of the tug. The term "operation" is a wide one and operators of ships carry out many functions in connection therewith. For example a tanker owner might send his tanker to an oil terminal where she negligently damages the jetty. In such a case he would be able to limit his liability. However, if, in breach of contract with the terminal owner, he omitted to send the tanker at all, so that the terminal owner sustained consequential financial loss, it would be perhaps surprising if a plea to limit liability succeeded even though the failure to send the tanker in a commercial sense related directly to the operation of the ship. It may be that when construed by the courts the word "operation" will be found to be close to "navigation or management" in the former repealed provisions and be held to relate to its physical use rather than to its purely commercial use or operation.

The claims in respect of which liability may be limited include not merely claims for the cost of repair of damaged property but also for the consequential losses flowing therefrom. This reflects the existing law as to the right to recover damages and to limit liability in respect of such damage. If, for example, a ship is damaged in collision the shipowner may not only recover for the cost of repairs but also for loss of use of the vessel and it is the *totality* of these claims (including interest therefrom) which constitute his damages and in respect of which limitation of liability may be invoked by the wrongdoer. Under this first heading of claim express mention is made of claims for "damage to harbor works, basins and waterways and aids the navigation." This may be thought of as an obvious example of damage to property; nevertheless it has received special mention. There are cases where a shipowner may be liable for such damage even though not caused by his negligence or that of his servants or agents: see section 74 of the Harbour Docks & Pier Clauses Act 1847[18]; *The Mostyn*.[19] Special provision is also made in the Convention in regard to wreck removal expenses as discussed below. It is to be noted that sub-paragraph (a) of Article 2(1) refers to "damage to property" and "to consequential loss resulting therefrom." It does not refer to the mere threat of damage which gives rise to

[18] 10 & 11 Vict. c. 27.
[19] [1928] A.C. 57 (H.L.)

expense: that class of claim probably more readily falls within sub-paragraph (f) as discussed below.

(2) Article 2(1)(b) gives a right to limit for "claims in respect of loss resulting from delay in the carriage by sea or cargo, passengers or their luggage." This right is an important one when one considers first who may be entitled to limit liability within the expression "shipowners" and secondly the nature of losses which may be incurred resulting from "delay" in the carriage by sea of cargo. It is not difficult to envisage a case in which a shipowner has carried perishable cargo in his ship which has been delayed in reaching the port of discharge. As a result the cargo is damaged and also the cargo owner suffers consequential financial losses due (say) to market fluctuations. For this purpose one has to assume that the shipowner is liable for the loss and damage caused by the delay and not protected by an exceptions clause. In such a case he can limit his liability in respect of both types of loss for there is no restriction on the word "loss" in sub-paragraph (b). Further, the right to limit is given "whatever the basis of liability may be" so it would include a liability in contract as well as one in tort. This express right to limit is probably not an enlargement of the right already afforded under section 503(1) of the Merchant Shipping Act 1894 (as amended) even though it refers expressly to loss resulting from delay: for it is possible to read the existing enactment as covering such a claim.

(3) Article 2(1)(c) gives a right to limit liability in respect of "claims in respect of other loss resulting from the infringement of rights other than contractual rights, occurring in direct connexion with the operation of the ship or salvage operations." The expression "other loss" probably refers to classes of loss other than the loss referred to in the two preceding sub-paragraphs (a) and (b) of Article 2(1). Further, the "infringement of rights" probably does not refer to the right of Harbour Authorities and the like to incur and recover wreck removal expenses (for the reasons given in respect of that topic, below). In summary the rights referred to must by the terms of sub-paragraph (c) be non-contractual and exclude the rights referred to in sub-paragraphs (a) and (b). It is indeed not at all easy to see what is being referred to in sub-paragraph (c). Section 503(1)(d) of the Merchant Shipping Act 1894 (as amended) referred to loss or damage to property or infringement of rights (echoing Article 1(1)(b) of the Brussels Convention 1957) but did not treat infringement of rights as being something quite independent. However one can assume a case where a ship wishes to enter a harbour relying upon a statutory right: it cannot do so because its passage is blocked by the presence of another wrongdoing ship and as a result economic loss (but no physical damage) is sustained. Assuming in the jurisdiction where suit is brought there is a right of action (for

public nuisance or in negligence or the like) to recover such losses, then the owner of the wrongdoing ship may under paragraph (c) limit his liability for damages arising out of the infringement of such rights.

(4) Article 2(1)(d) gives a right to limit for "claims in respect of the raising, removal, destruction or the rendering harmless of a ship which is sunk, wrecked, stranded or abandoned, including anything that is or has been on board such a ship." It has already been noted that the right to limit exists "whatever the basis of liability may be." Liability for the cost of wreck removal as hereinbefore referred to may arise as damages in an action for negligence (*i.e.* arise out of fault) or it may arise out of a statutory obligation to pay the costs as a debt due to a Harbour Authority (or the like) irrespective of fault. In the *Stonedale No. 1*[20] the Manchester Ship Canal Co. raised a sunken barge and, pursuant to statutory powers sought to recover the cost of raising it as a debt. The owners of the barge claimed to be entitled to limit their liability in respect of that claim but failed on the basis that the sum claimed was a (statutory) debt and not damages and that the right to limit under the Merchant Shipping Acts then in force related only to claims for damages. It would seem however that the wording of Article 2 would allow limitation of liability in respect of such a debt for the right to limit is not only in respect of damages. There have been other cases where the Harbour Authority has had a right to recover the sums due to it under a local statute without there being a right to limit under the Merchant Shipping Acts as occurred in the *Berwyn*[21]; but such claims would not presumably fall within paragraph (1)(d) above. In some instances wreck removal expenses have properly been claimed as damages; see, *e.g. The Putbus*[22] where the claim was by a foreign governmental authority for wreck removal carried out abroad. In *The Arabert*[23] the cost of wreck removal was included as part of the claim by a shipowner for damages in a collision action and, being part of the claim for damages, was (and would of course remain) subject to limitation.

In this context is is however important to note that by Schedule 4, Part II, para. 3 to the Merchant Shipping Act 1979, paragraph 1(d) above does not apply unless provision has been made by Statutory Order for setting up a fund to protect Harbour Authorities from the losses which would be sustained once it was possible to limit in respect of wreck removal expenses. This was the situation under comparable provisions contained in section 2 of the Merchant Shipping (Liability of Shipowners and Others) Act 1958 and no fund was ever set up. The result is that there is no

[20] [1956] A.C. 1 (H.L.)
[21] [1977] 2 Lloyd's Rep. 99 (C.A.)
[22] [1969] 1 Lloyd's Rep. 253.
[23] [1961] 1 Lloyd's Rep. 363.

right to limit for wreck removal expenses until such fund is set up. It would not, it is submitted, be possible to include wreck removal expenses under one of the other categories of claim in Article 2 even if it seemed possible to interpret the words used so as to include such expenses; for to include them would it is submitted defeat the whole purpose of not allowing such expenses to be the subject of limitation of liability pending the setting up of the special fund referred to above. There is in any event no right to limit if the sum claimed is remuneration under a contract with the person liable: Article 2(2).

(5) By Article 2(1)(e) claims in respect of "the removal, destruction or the rendering harmless of the cargo of the ship" are subject to limitation of liability. Unlike wreck removal expenses, this right to limit is not subject to the provisions that it does not come into force until a special fund is set up. There is no definition of "cargo" nor restriction on the ordinary meaning of cargo, *i.e.* goods carried as cargo in a ship. It would, as a matter of ordinary English, not include stores or bunkers but it is often the latter which have to be removed though as part of a "salvage operation" (which is the subject of special express in the Convention as discussed in paragraph 5 below). Claims for oil pollution damage and nuclear damage are excluded (by Article 3) from the ambit of limitation of liability under the Convention. It is often oil cargoes which have to be removed as part of an operation to minimise, or minimise the risk of, pollution damage—usually as part of a salvage operation—so paragraph (d) above is much restricted in its scope. There is no restriction on who may make the claim for the removal, etc., of the cargo for that claim to fall within paragraph (e). It presumably includes a claim by a governmental agency or authority having powers so to act. Notwithstanding the breadth of the words, one feels it would be unlikely to be held to include all claims for removal of cargo, *e.g.* a claim by a shipowner for damages for breach of a charterparty should he have to remove the charterer's cargo from the ship by reason of such breach. In any event by Article 2(2), claims under sub-paragraph (e) are not subject to limitation of liability if they relate to remuneration under a contract with the person liable.

(6) Article 2(1)(f) makes subject to limitation of liability "claims of a person other than the person liable in respect of measures taken in order to avert or minimise the loss for which the person liable may limit his liability in accordance with this Convention, and further loss caused by such measures." In practice this provision will be of limited scope. By Article 2(2) such claims are not subject to limitation of liability if they are claims for remuneration under a contract with the person liable. By Article 3 claims for salvage and oil pollution damage are not subject to limitation so it is not those matters which are being referred to in

sub-paragraph (f). One can envisage however the sort of case where (f) would be relevant. One can assume a case where a conventional general cargo ship drags her anchor and expense is incurred by another shipowner (or property owner) in taking protective measures to see that his ship (or property) is not harmed though it is clearly threatened. Such expense is probably the type of claim envisaged by sub-paragraph (f). It would not be covered by (a) for that sub-paragraph appears to envisage actual damage as opposed to the mere threat of damage.

Finally as regards all categories of claim covered by Article 2, it is to be noted that the sums in respect of which limitation may be decreed will in accordance with the ordinary principles of English law include the interest on the damages or the debt—although interest will continue to be payable on the limitation fund itself. Further there has never been a right to limit in respect of legal costs relating to the claim nor to the claimant's costs in the limitation action, and this should remain unchanged.

Claims excepted from limitation

(1) There are five classes of claim excepted from limitation. Article 3(a) provides that the rules of the Convention do not apply to "claims for salvage or contribution in general average." This provision is self-explanatory; but two particular points have to be noted. First, salvage operations shall, by Article 1(3), include the operations referred to in Article 2(1)(d) (*i.e.* cases of wreck removal, cargo removal or minimising damage by a salvor as part of a salvage operation): so there is no right to limit as against a salvor in such a case. Secondly, it is submitted that what is being referred to in Article 3(a) is the absence of a right to limit in respect of salvage *as against a salvor*. Accordingly if in (say) a collision action the salvage reward was included as part of the damages of the shipowner claiming damages, the owner of the wrongdoing ship could limit in respect of the total claim for damages (even though it included a sum for salvage payable by the other party).

(2) The second category of claim in respect of which by Article 3(b) there is no right to limit are claims for oil pollution damage within the Civil Liability Convention 1969[24] ("CLC"). It must be remembered that, by Article 1 para. 6 of CLC, "pollution damage" includes the costs of preventive measures and loss or damage caused by preventive measures. Further, CLC contains its own limitation provisions in favour of tanker owners. However it would seem that there may be pollution damage caused by a person *other than a tanker owner* to which the limitation provision in CLC would not apply. For example, a conventional cargo ship may

---

[24] Singh, *ibid.* Vol. 3, p. 2468.

collide with a laden tanker causing a massive oil spillage and pollution damage. The claim for pollution damage against the cargo ship would not fall within CLC; but the cargo ship would be liable in damages for pollution damage as envisaged by section 15 of the Merchant Shipping (Oil Pollution) Act 1971.[25] In such a case the cargo ship would have to rely, it is submitted, upon Article 2(1)(a) and (f) of the 1976 Limitation Convention in order to be able to limit for the pollution damage claims.

(3) Article 3(c) and (d) refer in summary to nuclear damage claims as being not subject to limitation of liability under the 1976 Convention.

(4) Finally Article 3(e) special provision is made to exclude from the 1976 Limitation Convention crew claims (and similar claims) if the proper law of the relevant contract of service excludes the right to limit in respect of such claim or if the right to limit is to a sum greater than that provided by the 1976 Convention. Such claims (when the relevant contract of service is governed by United Kingdom law) are, by section 35(1) of the Merchant Shipping Act 1979, excluded from the effects of the existing law of limitation of liability contained in section 503 (as amended) of the Merchant Shipping Act 1894. A similar exclusion is provided for in section 35(2) of the Merchant Shipping Act 1979 as regards the new regime under the 1976 Limitation Convention. The above exclusions cover not only loss of life and personal injury claims but also property claims. These exclusions under section 35 cover claims by a person who is on board or employed in connection with the ship in question or (by section 35(2) governing the new limitation regime) a person who is employed in connection with the salvage operations in question.

Leaving aside the above express exceptions in Article 3 of the Convention there is no reason why in any claim based upon contract the contract should not by its terms exclude the right to limit liability; see, *e.g.* the *Kirknes*.[26] In that case a claim for an indemnity under the express terms of the United Kingdom Standard Towage Conditions was held to be payable in full for the indemnity terms by implication waived the right to limit. It may be that under the 1976 Convention that case would be differently decided: for by Article 2(2) thereof there is a right to limit even if the claim is brought "by way of recourse or for indemnity under a contract or otherwise." That of course does not alter the position that it is possible by contract to waive the right to limit liability.

---

[25] 1971, c. 59: Temperley, *Merchant Shipping Acts* (7th ed., 1976), p. 670 (British Shipping Laws).
[26] [1957] P. 51.

Persons entitled to limit liability

Article 1(1) provides that "shipowners and salvors" may limit their liability in accordance with the rules of the Convention for claims set out in Article 2 thereof. (The meaning of "salvor" is considered below). However, "shipowner" is, by Article 1(2), defined as meaning "the owner, charterer, manager or operator of a seagoing ship." By Schedule 4, Part II to the Merchant Shipping Act 1979, the right to limit is extended as part of English law to cover ships whether sea-going or not and shipowner must be construed accordingly. Further, by the Merchant Shipping Act 1979, Sched. 4, Part II, para. 12, ship includes "any structure (whether completed or in the course of completion) launched and intended for use in navigation as a ship or part of a ship." By section 742 of the Merchant Shipping Act 1894 "ship" includes any description of vessel used in navigation not propelled by oars. The Merchant Shipping Act 1979, by Schedule 5, para. 4 extends the right to limit to hovercraft as if they were ships.

The expression "owner" probably still includes any owner whether legal or equitable, registered or not; "charterer" probably means any type of charterer, *i.e.* demise, time or voyage. The expression "manager or operator" is perhaps less easy to construe or define comprehensively. It already appeared in section 3(1) of the Merchant Shipping (Liability of Ship Owners and Others) Act 1958 but on the basis that such a person was "any person interested in or in possession of the ship." One can perhaps envisage a case where there are a group of companies one of which is the operator of the ship but does not charter her or own her, but otherwise arranges all matters connected with the management and operation of the ship. It may be intended to cover such an operator in the 1976 Convention even if he is not interested in or in possession of the ship.

It is provided in Article 1(5) that "the liability of the shipowner shall include liability in an action brought against the vessel herself." Assume, for example, a case where the shipowner would be liable in an action *in personam* in negligence for collision damage: a limitation decree may still be obtained by him if (as usually happens) proceedings are brought against the ship *in rem*. Further, assume a case where the shipowner is not liable *in personam*, but the ship is liable to arrest in an action *in rem* by reason of the maritime lien for damage arising prior to the purchase of the ship by the shipowner, Article 1(5) envisages a right to limit in respect of such a claim. By Article 1(6) an insurer "is entitled to the benefits of the Convention to the same extent as the assured himself." Whilst this concept may seem alien to English common law thinking (as opposed to the same concept in civil law jurisdictions) it is already to be found in the case of oil pollution damage in the Merchant Shipping (Oil Pollution) Act 1971 giving effect to CLC. If the insurer is entitled to the benefits of the 1976 Limitation Convention to the same extent as the insured himself, there would appear to be no reason under the new regime why the insurer should not himself commence the limitation action in his own name (as already happens in oil pollution cases under the Merchant Shipping (Oil Pollution) Act 1971.

It is to be noted that Article 1(7) provides that "the act of invoking limitation of liability shall not constitute an admission of liability." Whilst a similar provision appeared in the Brussels Convention 1957, the orthodox view[27] has been that liability had, under English law, to be admitted up to the amount of the limitation fund at least and prior to the limitation decree being pronounced: for the liability in respect of which limitation was sought was a liability in damages which presupposed a finding of (or admission of) liability. Under the new Convention the liability is not so restricted but there has to be a liability of some sort "whatever the basis of liability may be." (*q.v.* para. 2(1) hereof). Given the abolition by Article 4 of the convention of the doctrine of "actual fault or privity" there is, it is suggested, much to be said for a change in English procedure to enable a decree to be granted without any admission of liability at any stage.

Similar to the existing provisions contained in section 3 of the Merchant Shipping (Liability of Shipowners & Others) Act 1958 the servants and agents of the shipowner or salvor) including the master and crew are protected. Article 1(4) expressly provides that:

> "if any claims set out in Article 2 are made against any person for whose act, neglect or default, the shipowner or salvor is responsible, such person shall be entitled to avail himself of the limitation of liability provided in this Convention."

It must not be overlooked that there remain liabilities in respect of which there is a right to limit not covered by the 1976 Convention. As already mentioned there are special provisions in regard to pollution damage and to nuclear damage. Further pilots have a special right to limit their liability contained in the Pilotage Act 1983[28] as also do Harbour Authorities, dock owners and the like under the provisions of the Merchant Shipping (Liability of Shipowners and Others) Act 1900[29] which is not covered by any Convention. Under the 1900 Act it is to be noted that the right to limit is not extended to a servant of the dock owner, etc., so if sued

---

[27] See Marsden, *Collisions at Sea* (1961), pp. 165, 299: (British Shipping Laws).
[28] 1983 c. 21.
[29] 63 & 64 Vict. c. 32: Temperley, *ibid.* p. 310.

the personal liability of the servant is unlimited: *Mason* v. *Uxbridge Boat centre*.[30]

Whereas the 1976 Convention is concerned with limitation of liability, English law has long provided two classes of case where there is a statutory exclusion of liability. These are now to be found in section 18 of the Merchant Shipping Act 1979 (re-enacting section 502 of the Merchant Shipping Act 1894). The two classes of case are, in short, first cases of fire damage to property arising out of fire on board ship and secondly theft and the like of jewellery and other valuables on board ship in certain circumstances laid down in the section. (Contractual exclusions of limitation have been mentioned above.)

The Merchant Shipping Act 1979, Sched. 5, para. 3 extends the right to limit under the Convention to Her Majesty's ships as it applies to other ships. Article 15 of the 1976 Limitation Convention applies the Convention whenever any person referred to in Article 1 thereof seeks to limit his liability before the Court of a State Party to the Convention or seeks to procure the release of a ship or other property or the discharge of any security given within the jurisdiction of any such State.

As soon as the 1976 Convention comes into force the English courts will apply it. This means that save in the most exceptional cases where there is conduct barring limitation of liability under Article 4, a limitation decree will be granted. It may be that the courts of a non-contracting State either have no concept of limitation of liability or else have a limit which may be far in excess of the Convention limits (*e.g.* value of the ship plus freight). This may give rise to "forum shopping" as now already occurs when for example claimants seek to proceed in the courts of the United States rather than in the courts of the United Kingdom because of the higher financial limits in the United States. It is understood to be unlikely that the United States will adopt the Convention (as it stands).

The Salvor and limitation

A salvor who, as a shipowner, is liable for loss and damage, may seek to limit his liability as any other shipowner. If, for example, his salvage vessel or tug is involved in a collision then as regards limitation he is in the same position under section 503 of the Merchant Shipping Act 1894 (as amended) as regards claims in tort as any other shipowner. However, cases are often not as straightforward as that. His liability may arise from the act or omission of a person not on board the tug and not concerned with the navigation or management of the tug. In such a case the salvor will under the existing law be able to limit: the *Tojo Maru*. The loss

[30] [1980] 2 Lloyd's Rep. 592.

may, for example, arise from a breach of a salvage contract under which (say) the salvor undertakes to use his best endeavours but his salvage officer fails to do so: or there is a breakdown in office administration ashore. In such cases under the Merchant Shipping Act 1894 there is no right to limit liability. A liability in damages which is unlimited may be difficult or even impossible to insure and may put an established salvor out of business. Not surprisingly therefore the 1976 Convention has expressly given protection to salvors. Whilst that Convention is not yet in force it has already been incorporated by reference into LOF 1980 and may therefore already be relied upon by the salvor in respect of any claim by the person with whom he has contracted under LOF 1980 (but not otherwise).

Article 1(1) of the 1976 Convention gives the salvor the right to limit his liability for claims set out in Article 2 thereof. By Article 1(3) "salvor" means "any person rendering services in direct connection with salvage operations." "Salvage operations" are not as such defined in the Convention but they include it is submitted not only claims on a no cure, no pay basis but claims where the operations are being carried out for a lump sum or at a daily rate. By Article 1(3) however "salvage operations" shall also include operations referred to in Article 2(1)(d), (e) and (f) (each of which has been discussed above). The salvor's servants and agents for whom he is liable may avail themselves of the right to limit: this would also extend to a sub-contractor provided the salvor was liable for his act, neglect or default: *q.v.* Article 4(4).

By Article 6(4) the limit of liability for any salvor, *not operating from any ship* or for any salvor operating *solely on the ship* to, or in respect of which he is rendering salvage services is to be calculated according to a tonnage of 1,500 tons. This therefore covers the situation which arose in the *Tojo Maru* (see above) so that in such a case the salvor may now limit according to the tonnage of 1,500 tons. In cases not falling within Article 6(4) the salvor may still limit his liability as a shipowner etc., if the claim falls within one of the classes covered by Article 2 (as discussed above). There is (as already discussed) no right to limit as against the salvor for the amount of salvage remuneration: *q.v.* Article 3(c). Excluded from the concept of limitation of liability are claims by servants of the salvor whose duties are connected with the salvage operations (including claims of their heirs, dependants or other persons entitled to make such claims, if *under the law governing the contract of service* between the salvor and such servants the salvor is not entitled to limit his liability in respect of such claims, or if he is by such law only permitted to limit his liability to an amount greater than that provided in the 1976 Convention: *q.v.* Article 3(d).

III

The Amount of Limitation

Nicholas Gaskell*

1. INTRODUCTION

In the legal, shipping and insurance world hard-headed practition-ers are mainly concerned in the "bottom line"—for how much will they (or their clients) be liable? This chapter will consider the size of the limits allowed by the 1976 Limitation Convention; how they are calculated; and how much of a difference there will be between the 1976 Limitation Convention limits and those under the 1957 Limitation Convention.[1]

One crucial feature to note about the 1976 Convention[2] is that it follows the "tonnage" system of limitation as opposed to the older methods calculated according to the extent of the ship-owners interest in the adventure, mainly the value of his vessel.[3] An owner could satisfy the claim by abandoning the ship and its freight to the claimants. This is essentially still the position in countries such as the United States,[4] Greece,[5] and Italy.[6] The British Merchant Shipping Acts 1854 and 1862 provided the basis for the modern system of limitation by providing fixed limits of liability for personal and property claims calculated according to

---

* Institute of Maritime Law, Southampton University.

[1] Reference will also be made to the corresponding British legislation in order to illustrate the principles. Explanations of calculations are often confusing, but the author has attempted to provide some enlightenment by the use of Tables and Examples: see pp. 67–101, *infra*.

[2] See generally the Admiralty Law Institute, *Symposium on Limitation of Liability* (1979) 53 Tulane Law Review; A. Evans, *The Future of Limitation of Liability, Lloyds World of Shipping Conference*, Hong Kong (1981); T. Coghlin, "The Convention on Limitation of Liability for Maritime Claims 1976," in *The International Maritime Organisation*, (Ed.) S. Mankabady (1984), pp. 234–251.

[3] See Chap. 1, and J. Donovan, *The Origins and Development of Limitation of a Shipowner's Liability* (1979) 53 Tulane Law Review 999; A. Rein, *International Variations on the Concept of Limitation of Liability*, (1979) 53 Tulane Law Review 1259.

[4] Under 46 U.S.C. s.183, although personal claims are treated differently.

[5] T. Karatzas, N. Ready, *The Greek Code of Private Maritime Law* (1982). See Arts. 85 *et seq.* of the 1958 Code and Chap. 14, *infra*.

[6] P. Manca, *The Italian Code of Navigation* (1969): see Arts. 275–277, 621 *et seq.* See generally, K. Pineus, *Limited Liability in Collision Cases* (1984).

the tonnage of the ship.[7] This system was nearly always more favourable to claimants than value based systems as the limitation figures were apparently related to the average values of British passenger ships (£15 per ton) and all British ships (£8 per ton).[8]

The great disadvantage of a value based system is that where the vessel has a low value, *e.g.* after a serious marine casualty, then the limit of liability is similarly low. The *Torrey Canyon* caused about £6 million worth of pollution damage in 1969, but the owners claimed to limit $50 for a single salvaged lifeboat.[9] The *Titanic* disaster raised personal claims of £22 million and the U.S. limit (based on the value of the vessel and freight after the incident) was $91,805.[10] Under the British tonnage system the limit would have been $3,750,000.[11] On the other hand there is no doubt that

[7] See App. B.1, B.2. The previous legislation had been based on the value of ship and freight as indeed was cl. 423 of the original Merchant Shipping Bill 1854 (1854 H.C. 35 Vol. IV, 1). But the operation of Lord Campbell's Act 1846 (9 & 10 Vict. c. 93) had meant (probably unintentionally) that shipowners could be faced with large fatal accidents claims. Lord Campbell himself was in favour of extending the value based limit to such claims (1854 H.C. Vol. 135, Col. 132). After representations at the 2nd Reading (1854 H.C. Vol. 133, 574) the bill was amended in Committee (1854 H.C. 125, Vol. IV, 209) so that a *minimum* value of £15 was taken for passenger claims. But the *actual* value of the vessel was used, if it was *higher* than £15 per ton (see App. B.1). This penalised owners of more modern, expensive ships, and so the Select Committee on Shipping 1860 recommended that the £15 figure be definitive (1860 H.C. Vol. 13, 17). Accordingly, all references to value disappeared in the 1862 Act (see App. B.2).

[8] See Rein, *op. cit.*, at p. 1265. However, it is difficult to find documentary evidence in the Parliamentary Papers of why £15 and £8 were selected. The evidence given to the 1860 Select Committee showed that values varied greatly with the age and type of vessel. Most larger steam vessels seemed to have a value of about £20 per ton or more (*op. cit.*, Minutes, *e.g.* pp. 92, 97, 137, 155; 1862 H.C. Vol. 167, col. 749). Brunel's *Great Britain* had a new cost in 1843 of about £34 per g.t. (*SS Great Britain* (1985)). Many of the difficulties of estimating value stemmed from the debate about whether to use gross or net tonnage. The 1860 Select Committee reported that the £15 figure was fixed to prevent the employment of inferior ships and that vessels of the value of £15 per ton were sufficient to provide for the comfort and safety of passengers. The original 1862 Bill would have provided a uniform valuation of £15 per ton for personal and property claims. It appears that the £8 figure may have been a concession to the owners of sailing ships (1862, H.C. Vol. 166, 2220).

[9] In *Re Barracuda Tanker Corporation* 409 F. 2d 1013 (1969—2 Cir). Assuming a limitation tonnage of 55,000 the UK limit of liability at the rates then prevailing was about £1.3 million. It is said that the British and French Governments accepted a settlement of several million dollars.

[10] *Oceanic Steam Navigation Co.* v. *Mellor* 209 F. 501 (1913—2 Cir), affd. 233 U.S. 718 (1914). Interestingly the pre-accident value of the vessel was thought to be £1.5 million, albeit that her hull and machinery insurance was for £1 million (*i.e.* she was underinsured); see C. Hewer, *A Problem Shared: A History of the I.L.U. 1884–1984*, (1984), p. 29.

[11] *Oceanic Steam Navigation Co.* v. *Mellor, supra.* The USA did provide a minimum limitation tonnage for personal claims in 46 U.S.C s.184(b), but only after the later disaster to *The Morro Castle* in 1934. There the owners received $2.1 million from the hull insurers, but were obliged only to establish a limitation fund of $200,000 for *all* the claims against the vessel, see Donovan, *op. cit.* at p. 1031.

modern container and passenger vessels (along with their freight and passage monies) would often be worth much more than tonnage based limitation amounts.

Whatever the merits of the two systems it is the tonnage system that has prevailed internationally in the 1957 and, in a modified form, the 1976 Limitation Conventions. Accordingly the value of the vessel is irrelevant under the 1976 Convention.[12]

One of the crucial issues remaining concerns the rationale of limitation of liability.[13] There is no doubt that today one of the main reasons for continuing the system is to enable the shipowner to obtain insurance (and to encourage insurers to provide it).[14] It is debatable whether the 1976 limits are really related to the maximum realistic insurance cover which P. and I. Clubs can provide in 1986, as opposed to being a compromise figure somewhere between that "ideal" and the existing limits.[15] As Lord Denning said in an oft-quoted passage from *The Bramley Moore*,[16] limitation of liability,

" . . . is a rule of public policy which has its origin in history and its justification in convenience."

However, the attitude of the courts seems to vary from extreme hostility to the notion of limitation, to a recognition that the right,

" . . . is of long standing and generally accepted by the trading nations of the world. It is a right given to promote the general health of trade and in truth is no more than a way of distributing the insurance risk."[17]

Consideration will now be given to the unit of account, followed by an examination of the extent of the limits themselves.

---

[12] An exception would be where the limits are broken (see Chap. 4) and the owner does not appear, or is insolvent. For representative examples of new building prices, see Table 6. A superficial comparison with Table 3 shows that these values are much in excess of the 1957 Convention limits and many of them exceed the 1976 Convention limits. Note that Table 3 refers to limitation tons, whereas the *UNCTAD* document gives varying measurement criteria. The new P & O luxury liner *Royal Princess* cost £150 million, but her 1957 Convention limit would be about £5,325,534 and her 1976 Convention limit about £16,028,936 (see Example 7(a) and 3(7) Passengers, *infra*).

[13] See *e.g.* Rein, *op. cit.*, at p. 1272; Evans, *op. cit.* As the debates in 1854 and 1862 (n. 7–8, *supra*) illustrate, the concept was designed to protect shipowners both generally and in relation to the carriers of other countries.

[14] See Chap. 9.

[15] See Chap. 1.

[16] [1964] P. 200, at p. 220.

[17] *Per* Griffiths, L.J. in *The Garden City (No. 2)* [1984] 2 Lloyd's Rep. 37, p. 44. In the USA, courts have been particularly hostile to limitation: see Chap. 20, *infra*.

2. THE LIMITATION UNIT

Background

It is important that the financial unit by which limitation of liability is to be calculated should be uniform. In times of stable currencies this was not a matter of much importance but today's currency fluctuations demand a modern solution. The original British tonnage based limitation statutes[18] fixed the limits at £15 or £8 sterling[19] per ton. The limits in Article 3(1) of the 1957 Convention were expressed in francs which were defined in Article 3(6) as being units consisting of 65.5 milligrams of gold of millesimal fineness 900. The system was based on gold values which were thought to be stable and uniform. This has not proved to be the case and in some countries gold value was translated into national currencies at official rates and in others at market rates.[20]

In Britain the practice was periodically to issue a Statutory Instrument under the Merchant Shipping (Liability of Shipowners and Others) Act 1958, s.1(3),[21] specifying the sterling equivalent of the gold franc figures in the Convention.[22] However, it has been argued that section 1(3) was contrary to Article 3(6) of the 1957 Convention.[23] In any event, the date for conversion is crucial. Neither section 1(1) nor 1(3) of the 1958 Act specified what was to happen when an order changing the rate was made. In *The Abadesa*

[18] Merchant Shipping Acts 1854, 1862, 1894.

[19] The Hague Rules of 1924 use the expression £100 gold value as the package limitation. This has given rise to much misunderstanding as to whether £100 refers to the present value of 100 gold sovereigns or £100 sterling. In "Non vessel owning common carrier" a paper delivered at the Ocean Carriers Rights and Liabilities Conference (Hong Kong, 1981) Anthony Diamond Q.C. considered (at p. 28) that the former was the correct interpretation. To alleviate some of these problems the B.M.L.A. Gold Clause Agreement had been produced. In any event the Hague Rules provision did not make clear the weight or fineness of gold concerned; see generally, T. Asser, *Golden Limitations of Liability in International Transport Conventions and the Currency Crisis* (1973–1974) 5 J.M.L.C. 645, at pp. 647–8. This particular problem is solved in the 1957 Convention by Art. 3(6) and in the 1958 Act by s.1(2); see Apps. A, p. 293, B, p. 334.

[20] See A. Tobolowski, *The Special Drawing Right in Liability Conventions: An Acceptable Solution?* [1979] 2 LMCLQ 169 and *Hornlinie* v. *SNPA* [1972] N.J. 269, cited in Asser, *op. cit.*, pp. 652–3. Note also *Franklin Mint* v. *T.W.A.* [1984] 1 Lloyd's Rep. 220.

[21] See p. 68 *infra*.

[22] 3,100 and 1,000 gold francs, see Apps. A, p. 293, B, p. 334.

[23] Asser, *op. cit.*, at p. 649. See App. A.2. It could be argued that Art.3(6) does not specify the *method* by which the currency is converted, but concentrates instead on the *date* of conversion. As Brandon J. noted in *The Mecca* [1968] 2 All E.R. 731, 736, although it is questionable whether s.1(4) gave complete effect to Art. 3(6) it seems that it represented a clear attempt—at least partially successful—to do so. In *The Garden City (No. 2)* [1984] 2 Lloyd's Rep. 37, at p. 42, Eveleigh, LJ. was prepared to accept that *payment in* under s.1(4) was equivalent to the constitution of the limitation fund under Art. 3(6).

(No. 2)[24] it was fixed at the date of the decree of the Admiralty Registrar which fixed the amount of the limitation. The decision was followed by Brandon, J. in *The Mecca*[25] who applied the order in force at the date when ascertainment was made, but with the caveat that if a payment into court was made at an earlier date it would be adequate if calculated in accordance with the order in force at the date of such payment.[26] The owner who wished to limit could thus make a payment into Court with the certainty that if he got his calculations right he could rely on the conversion rate in force on that day and not at some future uncertain date on which judgment would be given.

Special drawing rights

To avoid the problems with gold the international community has turned to the special drawing rights (SDR) of the International Monetary Fund (IMF). The SDR is a unit of account whose value is determined daily by the IMF on the basis of a basket of currencies. The IMF publishes its rates daily but these are normally available in the press, (*e.g. The Financial Times*) on the following day. The technical details can be found elsewhere[27] but the importance from a legal viewpoint is that there is a figure, issued daily[28] and based on market exchange rates, by reference to which limitation amounts can be assessed and calculated. The SDR was first accepted in private international law conventions in the Montreal

---

[24] [1968] 1 Lloyd's Rep. 493. The collision was in February 1963; limitation proceedings were commenced by writ on February 8, 1966; devaluation of the pound sterling was on November 18, 1967; on November 24, 1967, a new statutory instrument (1967 S.I. No. 1725) was introduced; on February 21, 1968, the decree of the registrar was issued. A payment into court was made on February 25, 1963.

[25] [1968] 2 All E.R. 731. The collision was in May 1965; the statutory instrument was issued in 1967; the summons for the decree of limitation before the registrar was in February 1968.

[26] If the sum in Court was less than the figure obtained by converting at the date of payment into Court the appropriate rate was that in force at the time of its decision, *The Garden City (No. 2)* [1984] 2 Lloyd's Rep. 37 at p. 40. It followed from this decision that a shipowner satisfied s.1(4) by paying in the limitation amount calculated by reference to the gold franc and not, in addition, the simple interest that would be due in Admiralty from the date of the collision; see *e.g.* Kerr L.J. at pp. 48–49. See now the Merchant Shipping (Liability of Shipowners and Others) (Rate of Interest) Order 1986.

[27] See the articles cited in n. 19–20, *supra*, and also L. Bristow, "Gold franc—Replacement Unit of Account" [1978] 1 L.M.C.L.Q. 31; A. Mendelsohn, "The Value of the Poincaré Gold Franc in Limitation of Liability Conventions" (1973–74) 5 J.M.L.C. 125; P. Heller, "The Value of the Gold Franc—a Different Point of View," (1974–75) 6 J.M.L.C. 73; A. Tobolewski, "Limits of Liability in the Present Economic Situation" [1980] 1 L.M.C.L.Q. 47; L. Ward, "The SDR in Transport Liability Conventions: Some Clarification" (1981) 13 J.M.L.C. 1.

[28] Not every few months—as with the statutory instrument system.

Protocols to the Warsaw Convention on air carriage.[29] A Protocol to the 1957 Convention was agreed on December 21, 1979, which converted its gold franc figures into SDR.[30] The Protocol entered into force on October 6, 1984, and was brought into force in the United Kingdom by section 1 of the Merchant Shipping Act 1981.[31]

The 1976 Convention has taken the SDR as the basic unit of account.[32]

Date and method of conversion

Article 8(1) of the 1976 Convention lays down a date of conversion similar to that found in Article 3(6) of the 1957 Convention, namely the value of the relevant currency at the date (i) the limitation fund shall have been constituted, (ii) payment is made, or (iii) security is given which under the law of the State is equivalent to such payment.[33] Schedule 4, Part II para. 7(1) of the Merchant Shipping Act 1979 refers to the sterling sum fixed by the IMF as being equivalent to 1 SDR on the relevant date as mentioned in Article 8(1). This is a change from that adopted for the 1957 Convention in that there is a specific reference in the English Act to the Convention dates for conversion.

But where no limitation fund is constituted what is the relevant date? Article 8(1) of the Convention does not refer to the date on which the decree is pronounced. The only relevant date is that of (actual) payment.[34] It may be that the form of judicial order used will have to be conditional on some later adjustment, although this would seem inconvenient.

Article 8 of the 1976 Convention lays down that the conversion into national currency shall be calculated in accordance with the

---

[29] See also the Hamburg Rules 1978, and the 1979 Protocols to the Hague-Visby Rules 1968 and the Athens Convention 1974.

[30] See App. A, p. 302.

[31] See Table 1, *infra*, for equivalents, and App. B, p. 337. The date of conversion therein is the date of the "constitution of the fund", or otherwise the date of judgment, and see *The Garden City (No. 2)* [1984] 2 Lloyd's Rep. 37.

[32] See Art. 8, App. A, p. 304, *infra*: but note Art. 8(2) for non IMF members.

[33] It may be unclear what is meant by security which is "equivalent to payment." All security is by definition conditional on some event while "payment" is not. Security here presumably means a form of guarantee that will be paid out automatically on, *e.g.* judgment. But it might be arguable that the security becomes "equivalent to payment" at some later stage than when it is "given," *e.g.* when the court orders it to be paid out, or on execution.

[34] As in *The Mecca* [1968] 2 All E.R. 731. Art. 10(3) leaves questions of procedure where there is no fund constituted, to national law. Presumably, this is not meant to alter the substantive rule in Art. 8(1). S.1(3) of the Merchant Shipping Act 1981 specifically provided that if no Fund was constituted the date of judgment was to be the date of conversion. Para. 7(1)(*b*) of Part II of Sched. 4 of the Merchant Shipping Act 1979 allows the "last preceding date" to be taken if no sum has been fixed by the IMF under Art. 8(1).

method applied by the IMF in effect at the date in question for its operation and transactions.

The Merchant Shipping Act 1979, Sched. 4 Part II, para. 7 uses the same formula as section 3 of the Merchant Shipping Act 1981 by providing that the value on a particular day shall be treated as equal to such a sum in sterling as the IMF have fixed as being equal to 1 SDR (i) for that day or (ii) if no sum has been so fixed for that day for the last preceding day for which a sum has been so fixed. One difficulty is that the lawyer contacted immediately after a collision may only have available the published rate from the day before. This will normally be adequate for the purpose of making broad preliminary assessments of liability and if necessary the IMF could be contacted in New York.[35] It may be difficult for lawyers to obtain immediate information about the limitation position in countries whose currencies do not form part of the IMF basket of currencies. For instance, *The Financial Times* in the United Kingdom publishes SDR figures for a limited number of countries only. The experience of local correspondents will be important.[36]

The alternative method of calculation

The IMF was founded after the Bretton Woods Conference in 1944 and is often regarded as a creature of the Western capitalist world. For this reason it was thought appropriate to include an alternative monetary unit to the SDR for those countries who are not members of the IMF, or whose law does not allow them to use the SDR.

Article 8(2) provides a set of alternative limitation amounts expressed in the traditional gold francs.[37] The method (and presumably the date) of conversion are left to the law of the particular State, although Article 8(4) requires (rather hopefully) that the manner of conversion shall be such as to express in the national currency as far as possible the same real values for the amounts expressed in SDRs in Article 6 and 7. There is, however, an obligation on the State concerned to notify the depository (IMO) which manner of conversion is to be used.

[35] Again, this minor problem is not solved by the Treasury being able to give a conclusive certificate under para. 7(2).
[36] Australia, for instance, uses the SDR in the 1957 Limitation Convention and in the CLC 1969. See the Navigation Act 1912, Part VIII, as amended, and the Protection of the Sea (Civil Liability) Act 1981. Regulations under the 1981 Act require reference to a figure certified by the Reserve Bank of Australia as being the correct SDR equivalent for the A$. But, for example, the Reserve Bank and IMF SDR rates for February 12, 1986, differed by 0.55 per cent. (Daily Commercial News, February 17–18, 1986). Such variations in *official* and *IMF* rates could be significant. Regulations under the 1912 Act now simply refer to the IMF figures.
[37] Art. 8(3): see App. A, p. 304.

At one stage it was understood that the Soviet Union had indicated a willingness to accept the SDR for the purposes of international liability Conventions, but that now seems unlikely.

The suitability of the SDR

The SDR has been strongly criticised as a unit of account.[38] But as one commentator has said[39]

" . . . it ensures that limits of liability will be identical in terms of value at any one point in time regardless of the currency of payment or time of conversion. Daily fluctuations in the value of the SDR will however affect the value of limits of liability in terms of any given currency. Although the SDR has no inherent ability to maintain real value, in the short run, fluctuations in currency exchange rates will influence the domestic purchasing power of a fixed number of SDRs in terms of any particular currency. The decline in the real value of limits of liability over time will be exaggerated in terms of relatively strong currencies and mitigated to some extent in terms of weak currencies."

The movement of a currency can be shown by the fact that in a period from 1975 to 1985 there was a 33 per cent decline in the value of sterling against the SDR.[40]

3. THE EXTENT OF THE LIMIT

1957 Convention generally

The first point to note about the 1957 limits is that they have become seriously eroded by inflation.[41] One study of prices in England gives some indication of the buying power of the pound at various relevant dates in English limitation history.[42] Taking 1854 as the base of 100 it would have taken the following amounts to buy the equivalent goods:

---

[38] Tobolewski, *op. cit.* [1979] 2 LMCLQ 169.

[39] Ward, *op. cit.* at p. 19.

[40] The figures cited by Tobolewski, *op. cit.* at p. 176, show that in a period from 1975–1978 sterling declined 14 per cent. against the SDR, from £0.5704–£0.6496. Yet, taking into account a Consumer Price Index used by him the real value of the SDR in the UK for 1978 over 1975 was only 77 per cent.

[41] The same might be said of the period from 1976–1986.

[42] P. Smith, "Inflation before and after Keynes", Journal of Economic Affairs, Vol. 1, 3(3) April 1984. The study produced a price index for the period from 1981–1983. The table in the text is a computer extrapolation done for this author.

$$1854— \quad 100$$
$$1862— \quad 102.0$$
$$1894— \quad 77.6$$
$$1957— \quad 343.9$$
$$1976—1151.4$$
$$1983—2456.8$$

Secondly, the 1957 Convention gave extra protection to personal claimants by treating their claims differently in two respects from property claims.[43] (i) Personal claims (alone) were given a limit over three times that of property claims (alone), *i.e.* 206.67 SDRs, (3,100 g.f.) and not 66.67 SDRs (1,000 g.f.) per ton.[44] (ii) Where there were both property and personal claims then the latter were treated more favourably in that the claims were not aggregated (so that the misery was shared out rateably)[45] but, in effect, the top two-thirds of the fund was reserved solely for personal claimants and they shared rateably with the property claimants for the remaining one-third of the fund. Simple illustrations of this are given in Examples 4(a) and (b).[46]

Thirdly, the 1957 Convention provided a uniform limit whatever the size of the vessel. A ship of 500 tons had a limit of one-tenth of a ship of 5,000 tons.[47] However, it is difficult to say that it is likely to cause one-tenth of the damage. Small ships can cause great loss, especially where personal claims are concerned, yet

---

[43] "Personal" claims were used in Art. 1(2) of the 1957 Convention as a helpful way of describing death or personal injury claims. The drafters of the 1976 Convention, declined to use this simple expression and referred to "loss of life or personal injury" claims. The 1957 Convention referred to "property" claims, which is somewhat inaccurate as there may be economic loss claims. To that extent the 1976 Convention expression "other" claims is to be preferred. But the important point is that the 1957 Convention follows the distinction between "personal" and "other" claims made in Britain in the Merchant Shipping Acts. Many value based systems have had to be amended to make special provision for personal claims; *e.g.* the USA in U.S.C. s.183(b) Chap. 20, *infra*; see also Pineus, *op. cit.*

[44] *E.g.* on a 10,000 ton ship the limit was (see Table 3) for personal claims (alone)—£1,573,879, and for property claims (alone)—£507,720. Note that the *Total* fund would be available if there were personal claims alone.

[45] See Example 3(b) for an illustration of what would happen if all claims were to be paid rateably out of the total fund available, *i.e.* 3,100 g.f. (206.67 SDRs). The claimants recover about 50 per cent. of their respective claims. Compare this with the 1957 Convention method used in Example 3(a), where the personal claimants recover 63.41 per cent. of their claims while the property claimants recover only 25 per cent. of their claims.

[46] In Example 4(b) the personal claimants recover 94 per cent., and the property claimants 39 per cent., of their respective claims.

[47] See Example 1 for a simple illustration.

41

some quite sophisticated and expensive ships can have very low limits of liability under the 1957 Convention.[48]

The 1957 Convention was not wholly favourable to owners of small ships for it provided in Article 3(5) that " . . . the tonnage of a ship of less than 300 tons shall be deemed to be 300 tons." Thus, there was a minimum tonnage of 300 tons for both property and personal claims. Section 503 of the Merchant Shipping Act 1894 (as amended)[49] only applied this minimum tonnage to *personal* (and not property) claims.[50] In fact, because of the drafting[51] the position was unclear where there were *mixed* personal and property claims.[52]

1976 Convention generally

First, under the 1976 Convention the method of calculating the limits has been changed. Instead of there being a uniform figure, *e.g.* 206.67 SDRs (3,100 g.f.) multiplied by the tonnage of the ship, there is now a system of "slices" or "bands" of tonnage with differential limitation amounts for each. Article 6 provides five "slices" for personal claims and four for property claims. Example 2 illustrates how the "slicing" system works. The important point to notice is that with a ship of, *e.g.* 90,000 t there is no longer a *single* calculation—as with the 1957 Convention. In Example 2(b) one does not take the Article 6(1)(b) figure for each ton in excess of 70,000 t (83 SDRs) and multiply that by 90,000. Each of the three previous "slices" must be calculated according to the SDR equivalent for that slice. Thus, for a ship of 70,000 limitation tons

[48] See *e.g. McDermid* v. *Nash Dredging and Reclamation Co. Ltd., The Times,* July 31, 1984, where a deckhand's damages were limited to £43,893 when a tug was involved. Reversed in part, *The Times,* April 17, 1986: see also Small Ships and Tonnage Measurement, *infra.*

[49] By the Merchant Shipping (Liability of Shipowners and Others) Act 1958 (see App. B, p. 334). This is an Act which adopted the unfortunate technique of redrafting the 1957 Convention into *legal* English. Yet, in nearly all respects, the 1957 Convention is clearer. By comparison, Australia incorporated the 1957 Convention in the form of Schedule to the Navigation Act 1912 when replacing the old provisions based on s.503 of the English Act of 1894. This is by far the best method of reception and it is heartening that this technique was used with the Merchant Shipping Act 1979, *infra* (and App. A, p. 304). See also the Merchant Shipping Act 1983, s.9 (App. B, p. 355) for the treatment of small ships measured for length, or registered under the Small Ships Register.

[50] The different treatment was justified by a reservation made to the 1957 Convention; see App. A, p. 293.

[51] Which applied the 300 ton minimum to the 206.67 SDR (3,100 g.f.) figure; see App. B, p. 334.

[52] See Temperley, *Merchant Shipping Acts* Vol. 11, British Shipping Laws (7th ed. 1976), p. 525. The minimum figure could be applied to the whole calculation or to the property part alone. The two alternative positions are given in Examples 6(a) and (b). Example 6(b) should represent the position in English law under the 1894 Act, although the difference is small.

and above there will always be *four* calculations ("other" claims) or *five* calculations (loss of life/personal injury claims).[53]

Secondly, the 1976 Convention provides a significant increase[54] in the limits over those agreed in 1957. The amounts in Tables 1, 2, 3 and 5 show the order of the increases made by the 1976 Convention over the 1957 Convention.[55] The maximum fund available for personal claimants shown in Part Three of Table 2 is in every case larger than the 1957 figure of 206.67 SDRs per ton. In the case of small vessels the 1976 figure is five times as much (1,000 SDR) and even in the slices for tonnages in excess of 70,000 the 1976 figure (250 SDRs) is about 20 per cent higher. The increase in the figures is of the same order in Parts One and Two of Table 2. Table 3 illustrates the increases in limits, over the 1957 Convention, for a variety of ships.

Thirdly, the 1976 Convention maintains the special position of personal claimants under the 1957 Convention. (i) Where there are loss of life/personal injury claims *alone*, the fund available to the personal claimants will continue to be approximately three times that available when there are "other" claimants alone.[56] (ii) Where there are mixed personal and "other" claimants about two thirds[57] of the total fund is reserved entirely for the personal claimants. As example 5 shows, the Article 6(1)(a) figures[58] are reserved for them. To the extent that their claims remain

---

[53] See Example 2(d) for a model calculation. For "limitation tonnage," see Tonnage Measurement; *infra*.

[54] *Ibid.* for the effect of the tonnage calculations on limitation. For the updating of the limits, see Chap. 1, *supra* and Chap. 8, *infra*.

[55] It is a little confusing comparing Art. 3 (1957 Convention) with Art. 6 (1976 Convention) because they are structured differently. In effect the 1957 Convention has three components, (i) a limit reserved solely for personal claims (ii) a maximum limit for property claims (iii) a figure representing the total fund available for all claims. However, this breakdown will be misleading where there are both personal and property claims, as the maximum property claim *in any event* was 66.67 SDRs (1000 g.f.) per ton: the personal claimants had access to 140 SDRs (2100 g.f.) per ton and were also entitled to share rateably with the property claimants in the 66.67 SDRs (1000 g.f.) figure (see Examples 3 and 4).

Art. 6 of the 1976 Convention is structured more clearly in that it does away with the equivalent of the 206.67 SDRs (3100 g.f.) figure by directing attention first to the part of the fund directed solely to personal claims (Art. 6(1)(a)) and secondly, making it clear (in Art. 6.2) that any shortfall can be met from the "other" claims. Thus for a comparison between the 1957 and 1976 Conventions, the 1957 140 SDRs (2100 g.f.) figure is equivalent to the 1976 Art. 6(1)(a) figures: the 1957 66.67 SDRs (1000 g.f.) figure is equivalent to those in 1976 Art. 6(1)(b). There is no express equivalent to the 1957 Convention 206.67 SDRs (3100 g.f.) figure in the 1976 Convention, but for convenience Tables 1 and 2 have been divided into Parts One, Two and Three.

[56] Comparing Table 2, Part Three with Part Two: see n. 55, *supra*.

[57] With the exception of the slice from 501–3000 t where the "loss of life and personal injury" limit is three times the "other" limit.

[58] Part 1 of Table 2: see n. 55, *supra*.

unsatisfied, the personal claimants are entitled to share in the Article 6(1)(b) figures.[59]

Small ships

There is a significant change in the treatment of small ships. It was the purpose of the "slicing" system in the 1976 Convention to impose higher limits for those ships at the lower end of the tonnage scale. Thus for claims against a 500 ton ship there will be a total limit[60] of (in effect) 1,000 SDRs per ton. But for ships with larger tonnages the limits decline proportionately in succeeding tonnage slices. Between 501–3,000 t the limit is 667 SDRs per ton; between 3,100–30,000 t the limit is 500 SDRs per ton; between 30,001–70,000 t the limit is 375 SDRs per ton; from 70,000 t upwards the limit is 250 SDRs per ton. A comparison of the 1957 and 1976 limits for particular ships with tonnages varying from 250–200,000 t can be seen in Table 3.

Article 6 of the 1976 Convention lays down a minimum limitation tonnage of 500 t, which is applicable to ships whose actual tonnage is less than 500 t.[61] For instance, under Article 6, ships of 100 t, 300 t and 500 t will have the same limits of liability. Like the 1957 Convention, Article 6 of the 1976 Convention provides that the minimum tonnage figure shall apply to both personal and other claims.[62]

Article 15(2) allows a state to regulate by specific provisions of national law the system of limitation of liability to be applied to ships of less than 300 t. The United Kingdom has enacted such a provision in the Merchant Shipping Act 1979, Sched. 4, Part II, para. 5.[63]

(i) Para. 5(1) leaves the Convention position unaltered for ships with a tonnage of 300–500 t, inclusive. Thus, under United Kingdom law, ships with tonnages between those figures will have the same limits of liability.

(ii) For, ships with *less* than 300 t, Article 6 of the Convention is to have effect as if the figure in Article 6(1)(a)(i) referred to 166,667 SDRs and that in Article 6(1)(b)(i) referred to 83,333 SDRs.

Both figures are slightly less than half the 500 t minima laid

---

[59] Part 2 of Table 2: see n. 55, *supra.*

[60] See Table 2, Part 3.

[61] See Table 2, Part 3. As indicated in n. 55, *supra*, the 500,000 SDR figure does not appear in the Convention. It is arrived at by the addition of 333,000 SDRs (Art. 6(1)(a)(i)) and 167,000 SDRs (Art. 6(1)(b)(i)).

[62] See Example 6(c).

[63] See App. C. For hovercraft, see the Hovercraft (Civil Liability) Order 1986.

down in the Convention.[64] Nevertheless, the limitation figures produced are about four times those under the 1957 Convention.[65] United Kingdom law has also come into line with the Convention by making the minimum limits apply to both personal *and* property claims. This is a small, but significant, change, for a ship with an actual tonnage of, *e.g.* 50 t will now have a minimum United Kingdom property limit of £63,462,[66] as opposed to £3,385.[67] The change will be of particular relevance to the owners, and insurers, of small pleasure craft who, at present, may invoke tiny limits to defeat quite modest property claims.[68]

Tonnage measurement

The limit is calculated by multiplying the appropriate SDR amount for each slice by the "tonnage" of the ship.[69] Yet there are many different types of tonnage measurement, *e.g.* deadweight tonnage (dwt), gross tonnage (gt) and net tonnage (nt).[70] There is also the legal concept of "limitation tonnage". The Merchant Shipping Act 1854, which was the first to use tonnage for limitation purposes, made the calculation by reference to the "registered ton"—*i.e.*, the net registered tonnage.[71] The Merchant Shipping Act Amendment Act 1862, s.54, retained the nrt limitation amount for sailing ships, but for steamships introduced the concept of "gross tonnage, without deduction on account of

[64] Half of the Convention 500 t figure would be 166,500 SDRs and 83,500 SDRs, respectively (see Table 2). One odd result of the UK adopting fixed limits (for sub–300 t ships) which are, *pro rata*, equivalent to 250 t under the 1976 Convention is that ships with tonnages of 251–299 t will have the same UK limits as ships of 0–250 t. But this theoretical exercise apart, one must emphasise that there are only two relevant small ship "slices" in the UK: 0–299 t and 300–500 t (see Example 6(d) to see the workings of the small ship provisions in the Merchant Shipping Act 1979).

[65] See the ship of 250 t in Table 3 as well as the small ship entries in Tables 1 and 2.

[66] See Table 2, Part 2.

[67] See Table 1, Part 2: 1986 calculations.

[68] The Merchant Shipping Act 1894, s.503, did not restrict the right to limit to sea-going craft: the Merchant Shipping Act 1979, Sched. IV, Part II, para. 2, has the same effect. The Conventions are narrower, although allowing States the power to extend the limitation provisions in national law: see the 1957 Convention, Art. 8 and *cf.* the 1976 Convention, Art. 15.

[69] See, *e.g.* Example 2.

[70] Ships must be surveyed before registration and the particulars of gross and net tonnage will be entered in the register book: see, *e.g.* the Merchant Shipping Act 1894, ss.6, 11. Hence the use of the expressions gross, and net, registered tonnage (grt and nrt). The modern system of tonnage measurement, using tonnage as a measurement of volume, began with the Merchant Shipping Act 1854.

[71] S.504, App. B, p. 331.

engine room.""[72] This expression was repeated in the Merchant Shipping Act 1894, s.503(2). It was replaced by the words "registered tonnage, with the addition of any engine room space deducted for the purpose of ascertaining that tonnage" by the Merchant Shipping Act 1906, s.69. It was this formula which was adopted by the 1924 and 1957 Limitation Conventions.[73]

In simple terms this meant taking the net tonnage and adding to it the figure for the engine room deduction appearing on the tonnage certificate.[74] That figure is one of the deductions allowed from the gross tonnage used to calculate the net tonnage. A practical problem for lawyers has always been that it is difficult to find out the correct PPA, and thus the exact limitation tonnage, because it is usually recorded only on the Tonnage Certificate itself. This may be with the shipowners or on board the ship.[75] For many ships it was possible to estimate the PPA to be 32 per cent. of the gross tonnage, according to the United Kingdom Regulations.[76] But this was very much a working figure. As Table 4A

[72] See App. B, p. 331. This rather obscure phrasing gave rise to some uncertainty as, almost by definition, the gross figure would *include* the engine room space: see also, *Burrell* v. *Simpson* (1876) IV S.C.177, *The Franconia* (1878) 3 P.D. 165. What was clear was that powered ships were to be given a higher limitation tonnage. Moreover, the owners of large, powerful passenger ships (with large engine rooms and thus low nrt) were given more realistic limits in comparison with the owners of ordinary cargo ships.

[73] Arts. 11 and 3(7) respectively, see App. A, pp. 287, 293. See also the Merchant Shipping (Liability of Shipowners and Others) Act 1900, s.2(2), (App. B.9); the Merchant Shipping Act 1983, s.9, (App. B, p. 355); the CLC 1969, Art. V(10) (App. A, p. 315); the Merchant Shipping (Oil Pollution) Act 1971, s.4(2), (App. B, p. 348); U.S.C., s.183(c). For a general criticism, see the Report by the French Maritime Law Association, presented to the CMI 1955 Madrid Conference, in *Preliminary Reports, Minutes, Draft Convention* (1955).

[74] This may be described on the certificate as the "Deduction for propelling machinery spaces," or as "the propelling power allowance" (PPA). The Lloyd's Register of Shipping Certificate of Measurement also recorded the "propelling power (actual space)". This must not be confused with the PPA, which is the theoretical deduction calculated in accordance with the Tonnage Regulations. It is the PPA which is relevant for limitation purposes under the old limitation regimes and *not* the actual space occupied by the machinery: see *James Patrick* v. *Union S S Co of New Zealand* (1938) 60 CLR 650, *per* Dixon J. at pp. 676–7.

[75] A problem if the ship becomes a total loss! The ship's Certificate of Registration would normally only record the grt and nrt—as would the annually published *Lloyd's Register of Shipping*.

[76] The Merchant Shipping (Tonnage) Regulations 1967 (S.I. 1967 No. 172), as amended. Under Reg. 10, the PPA was deemed to be 32 per cent. for ships whose actual propelling machinery space was between 13–20 per cent. of grt. For ships with actual propelling machinery space from 1 per cent.–12 per cent. of grt, the PPA would vary from 2.46 per cent. to 29.54 per cent. Except in the case of tugs, the PPA could never exceed 55 per cent. of a figure which is (in effect) the gross (less all the other deductions used in arriving at the nrt, *e.g.* crew spaces). Tugs, which normally have relatively large engine rooms, could have a very high percentage PPA.

shows, large tankers could have a much smaller and small tugs a much bigger, percentage PPA.

However, the International Convention on the Tonnage Measurement of Ships 1969 entered into force on July 18, 1982.[77] That Convention provides for an entirely new system of tonnage measurement which removes many of the anomalies of the pre-existing systems.[78] From the above date the 1969 Tonnage Convention applies to all new ships, those which undergo major alterations and those which are voluntarily remeasured. Existing ships may retain their present tonnages, calculated under the old systems, until July 18, 1994. From that date all ships will have to be remeasured under the 1969 Tonnage Convention.

Accordingly, for the time being there are two (major) systems of tonnage measurement in use. But, the 1969 Tonnage Convention makes no provision for engine room deductions and no reference to them appears on a 1969 Tonnage Convention Certificate. This creates a problem for calculating limits of liability under, *e.g.* the 1957 Limitation Convention.[79] In an attempt to deal with this difficulty, the Merchant Shipping Act 1984 inserted a new section 503(2) into the Merchant Shipping Act 1894.[80] The intention was to provide that the old tonnage measurements would apply for limitation tonnage purposes to all ships under the "old" limitation regimes.[81] There may be liabilities incurred between May 14, 1984 and December 1, 1986, to ships measured under the 1969 Tonnage Convention. It will be necessary to remeasure such ships

[77] Enacted in the UK by the Merchant Shipping (Tonnage) Regulations 1982 (S.I. 1982 No. 841).
[78] *E.g.* under the Convention for a Uniform System of Tonnage Measurement 1947 (the Oslo Convention), or the British Regulations. See generally, A. Bole, "The Tonnage Measurement of Ships Convention 1969," in *The International Maritime Organisation, op. cit.* n. 2, *supra,* pp. 52–56; M. Corkhill, *Tonnage Measurement of Ships,* (2nd ed., 1980).
[79] App. A.2, and also under the CLC 1969, see App. A.6, App. B.12.
[80] See App. B.6. For ships measured for length, or under the Small Ships Register, see the Merchant Shipping Act 1983, s.9, (App. B.16).
[81] *E.g.* under the Merchant Shipping Act 1894, s.503. The main change brought about by the 1984 Act appears to be the facility provided by the new s.503(2)(b) to allow a surveyor to certify the tonnage of British ships which cannot be measured according to para. (a) (there was previously such a power for foreign ships). The assumption may have been that 1969 Tonnage Convention ships could not have their tonnages ascertained under para. (a) and so could be remeasured under (b). But the language used in (a) is at best obscure. Inexplicably, it introduces a new definition of limitation tonnage which is a combination of those used in the 1862 and 1906 Acts, namely, register [*i.e.* net] tonnage, without deduction of PPA. The reference to "this Act" presumably includes the Merchant Shipping Act under which the old and new tonnage regulations have been made. The difficulty is that the tonnage of a 1969 Tonnage Convention ship *has* been ascertained in accordance with the tonnage regulations; it has a register [net] tonnage; and the PPA is not a required deduction. On that basis remeasurement under (b) is not possible.

under the old measuring principles. Such remeasurement will *only* be necessary where limitation proceedings are involved. For 1969 Tonnage Convention ships incurring liabilities between July 18, 1982 and May 13, 1984, it is presumed that the United Kingdom limitation tonnage will be the net tonnage.[82]

Under the 1976 Limitation Convention, Article 6(5), the tonnage is to be used is the *gross* tonnage under the 1969 Tonnage Convention. This change will simplify the lawyers' task of discovering the limitation tonnage, because the 1969 gross figures will appear in the register book as well as *Lloyd's Register of Shipping*.

During the transitional period until 1994 some ships will retain their existing measurements under the old measuring systems (OMS). The 1976 Limitation Convention makes it quite clear that the tonnage *"shall"* be the universal measurement system (UMS) of the 1969 Tonnage Convention. Thus, OMS ships will have to be remeasured for limitation purposes, in the same way as UMS ships under the 1957 Limitation Convention. National law will have to make provision for this[83] dealing in particular with the problem of ships which cannot have their tonnages remeasured because they have sunk. In such circumstances it is usual for a Court appointed surveyor to certify what, in his opinion, the tonnage would have been.[84]

Remeasurement will not be a problem for lawyers at the final stages of litigation as, apart from the expense involved, a certain tonnage figure will emerge. But the lawyer may have considerable difficulties at an earlier stage when provisional calculations have to be made, *e.g.* to work out the amount of security required, or the jurisdiction in which to commence limitation proceedings.[85]

What has not been widely appreciated is that many ships will have a significantly higher limitation tonnage because of the change to the 1969 UMS. This is because the 1969 Tonnage Convention removed some anomalies under the OMS whereby

[82] As the unamended s.503(2) refers to the "addition of *any* engine room space deducted" to ascertain net tonnage: see App. B, p. 334. As no such deduction could have been made under the 1969 Tonnage Convention no addition to net can be made for limitation purposes. *Cf.* Art. 11(7) of the 1957 Limitation Convention which refers to *"the"* amount deducted: see App. A, p. 293.

[83] The Merchant Shipping Act 1979, Sched. IV, Part II, para. 5 and the Merchant Shipping (Liability of Shipowners and Others) (Calculations of Tonnage) Order 1986 (S.I. 1986 No. 1040) the gross tonnage is to be calculated according to the 1982 Regulations (n. 77, *supra*), if necessary using the "best evidence available" of measurements. The UMS gross is also used in the CLC Protocol 1984 (App. A, p. 320) and the Draft HNS Convention (App. A, p. 327).

[84] See *e.g.* the Merchant Shipping Act 1894, s.503(2), App. B, p. 337. Note the effect of the Crown Proceedings Act 1947, s.5(5), when ascertaining the limitation tonnage of British warships.

[85] This will be important for those countries who may continue to use a value-based system of limitation.

certain ships had abnormally low tonnages. RoRo's, container-ships, tugs and supply vessels may be particularly affected. Some large ships, such as tankers and bulk carriers, might have slightly lower gross tonnages under the 1969 UMS.[86] But in all examples seen by the author the limitation tonnages obtained by using the 1969 Tonnage Convention gross figures exceed those obtained by using the OMS "net plus PPA" figures.

Table 4D contains a sample of ships which have actually been remeasured under the 1969 Tonnage Convention, giving their OMS tonnages (*with* PPA's) and new UMS tonnages.[87] From the final column it can be seen that the percentage increase in limitation tonnage for these ships varies from 5–76 per cent. A similar exercise performed on certain of the ships in Tables 4B and 4C would show an even more dramatic increase in limitation tonnage.[88] It must be emphasised that these increases apply *before* the general increase in limits introduced by the 1976 Limitation Convention are considered.

Table 5A combines the changes introduced by the new tonnage regime with those made by the new limitation regime. The second and third columns compare the limitation tonnages under the OMS and the UMS. The final two columns compare the applicable limits of liability for the ships under the 1957 and 1976 Limitation Conventions. The limits for all ships have increased significantly: in most cases they are at least three times higher under the 1976 Convention and the Tug's limit has been increased nearly eight times. Table 5B gives a selection of ships whose limits have increased even more dramatically. The limits of the Car Carrier and the Supply ship have increased over 11 times.

Salvors

The *lacuna* in the 1957 Limitation created by the decision in *The Tojo Maru*[89] has been filled in the 1976 Limitation Convention by

---

[86] Tables 4B and 4C show comparisons between tonnages under the OMS and UMS for a variety of ships. In nearly all cases the *gross* tonnages are increased under the UMS. For further comparisons, see the tables presented to the 1976 Diplomatic Conference, LEG/Conf.5/WP.56 (November 8, 1976), LEG/Conf.5/C.1/WP.66 (November 10, 1976).

[87] The figures, obtained for the author by *Lloyd's Register of Shipping*, are taken from a cross section of ships of different sizes. They are intended to be illustrative only and cannot be taken as representative. The 1969 UMS net figures have been omitted, as they are not relevant to limitation tonnages. In nearly all cases those net tonnages are less under the UMS than under the OMS. The net tonnages of the two 33,000 t container ships were 40 per cent. less. This, perhaps, explains why they were remeasured.

[88] See *e.g.* the "RoRo Ship Open" in Table 4(a) and the "Car Carrier Open" in Table 4(b). It would be necessary to estimate OMS limitation tonnage, *e.g.* on the basis that their PPA's are 32 per cent. of OMS gross; see n. 76, *supra*.

[89] [1972] A.C. 242; see Chap. 2, *supra*.

Article 2(1)(i)(a), Article 1(3), and Article 6(4). The limits of liability of any salvor not operating from a ship or for any salvor operating solely on the ship to, or in respect of which, he is rendering salvage services shall be calculated according to a deemed tonnage of 1,500 t. This fairly high tonnage was meant to represent a large salvage vessel.[90] Table 2, Part 2 shows that the total fund appropriate to such a limitation tonnage will be about £888,720.

The 1,500 t limit would be applicable where a salvage team is helicoptered onto the casualty direct from land.[91] Where the negligence is committed by the salvage crew "operating from" the salvage vessel, the limit should be calculated according to the tonnage of the vessel.[92] It is noticeable that this wording is wider than that in Article 1(b) of the 1957 Limitation Convention which did not cover the actions of the diver in The Tojo Maru. It will be recalled that he was neither "on board" the salvage vessel, nor was his fault in the "navigation or management" of her.[93] It would now seem that he could be "operating from" the salvage vessel, even if he was not connected by any lines. Similarly, a salvage crew put on board the casualty from the salving vessel could be said to be operating from that salving vessel. If a wide definition of the words "operating from" is given, the salvors may be able to rely on a limitation figure much lower than the 1,500 t deemed limit under Article 6(4).[94] The difficulty is in drawing a distinction between those circumstances where the salvor is "operating from" a salving vessel and those where he is "operating solely on the ship to, or in respect of which, the salvage services are rendered". In the latter case the 1,500 t limit would apply.[95]

To what period of time does "solely" refer? The diver may perform some fabrication work on his own ship, e.g. by repairing a hull plate, before proceeding with it to the casualty. In general terms, he is operating on both ships but, when he negligently fits the plate, he is operating "on" the casualty.[96] The use of the word "solely" would seem to indicate a period, rather than a moment of

[90] Many salvage vessels would have lower tonnages than this. But salvors will be better off than not being able to limit at all, as in The Tojo Maru.
[91] Art. 9.1(c).
[92] Art. 9.1(b). If the salvage vessel was very small, e.g. a launch, the minimum tonnage provisions of Art. 6 would apply, see Small Ships, supra.
[93] See Apps. A, p. 293, B, p. 334; also Chap. 2.
[94] Compare the Salvor and Small Ships figures in Table 2. The Salvor's 1,500 t figure is over four and a half times as large as the UK small ship limit. Yet it is commonly assumed that the 1976 Limitation Convention was intended to give the salvors in The Tojo Maru the 1,500 t limit.
[95] Arts. 6(4), 9(1)(b).
[96] "On" could mean "in relation to which", as where he is working underwater on the hull; or physically on board the casualty. It seems that the latter alternative may be more likely.

time: it is difficult in one instant to be operating "solely" on two ships. Apart from this, the clearer approach would have been to concentrate on the place where the salvor was operating at the time when the liability arose.

Where there is more than one set of salvors who are liable, the intention of Article 9(1) seems to be that there should be one limitation fund in respect of claims against salvors operating from a salvage vessel and a separate fund for salvors not operating from a salvage vessel. There may be cases where, *e.g.* there is negligence by the crew of the salvage vessel and also by an employee of the salvor on board the casualty. In these circumstances, it would seem that the salvor would have a limit based on the tonnage of the salvage vessel alone, albeit that there might be two causes of action, as there is a claim against a "salvor . . . operating from a ship and [a] person for whose act, neglect or default [he is] responsible."[97]

More complicated would be the case of a company which has its salvage team helicoptered in to a ship, and then later sends one of its salving vessels to the scene. Initially, the salvage team would not be operating from a ship: its liabilities would be governed by the 1,500 t limit. When the team is joined by the salvage vessel, do the team members start operating from it (so as to fall within Article 9(1)(a)), or do they continue to operate solely on the casualty (so as to remain within Article 9(1)(b))? In the end this may be a matter of degree,[98] but it seems that the salvor can limit his liability either under Article 9(1)(a), *or* Article 9(1)(b).[99]

Employees

Under Article 1(4) of the 1957 Limitation Convention, claims by the master, members of the crew, servants of the owner on board the ship, or servants of the owner whose duties are connected with

---

[97] Art. 9(1) also allows a salvage company operating from a ship to limit (according to the tonnage of that ship) for the liabilities of persons for whom it is responsible. It is arguable that, once a salvage company has *a* salving vessel on the scene, that ship's tonnage will apply even where employees not operating from the ship are negligent. The matter is complicated by Art. 1(3) which includes an individual in the definition of salvor.

[98] The salving vessel may supply equipment, or provisions; it may maintain radio contact; control of the salvage operations may be directed from it.

[99] See 3(12) Aggregation, *infra*. Unless it can be said that the "or's" appearing in Art. 9(1) are conjunctive rather than disjunctive; *cf. The Huntingdon* [1974] 2 All E.R. 97. It is not clear which of the paras. applies in the event of overlap. Presumably, it is the highest limit that will be used.

the ship, are excluded from limitation if the law of their contract of service forbids limitation.[1]

The equivalent provision in the 1976 Limitation Convention is Article 3(e), which is in a slightly wider form. It refers to "claims by servants of the shipowner or salvor whose duties are connected with the ship or the salvage operations . . . " The Article clearly contemplates those persons having contracts of service with the shipowner or salvor.

The Merchant Shipping Act 1979, s.35(2), seems to go further than the 1976 Limitation Convention. It excludes the Convention in respect of a person who is on board the ship in question or employed *in connection with* that ship (or with salvage operations) if he is so on board (or employed) under a contract of service governed by UK law. The words "on board the ship in question" apply to the ship by reference to which limitation is sought. Section 35(2)(a), however, does not say expressly that the person on board has to be there by virtue of a contract with the *shipowner or salvor*. It is enough if, *e.g.* there is a:

> "liability in respect of loss of life . . . caused to . . . a person who is . . . employed in connection with that ship [the ship "in question"] . . . if . . . he is so . . . employed under a contract of service governed by the law of any part of the United Kingdom".

Does "in connection with" refer only to a contract with the shipowners or salvors? A literal reading would suggest that the section could apply to those who have a UK contract of service with *anyone*, but whose work is connected with the ship. These persons could include dockers, shiprepairers, surveyors, pilots, customs and immigration officers, the Admiralty Marshall and even marine lawyers! In effect the section could cover any UK contracted worker on board the ship for some ship-related purpose and not merely non-seamen, such as caterers, hairdressers or lecturers, on board under a contract with the owner.

Such an interpretation would be wider than that allowed under Article 3(e) of the Convention, which does not seem to exclude limitation for employees of contractors hired by the shipowner, or government officials. Conflict could be avoided by using the Convention to assist the interpretation of section 35 by reading

---

[1] The Merchant Shipping (Liability of Shipowners and Others) Act 1958, s.2(4), enacted this provision without proscribing such limitation. The Merchant Shipping Act 1979, s.35(1), filled this gap in the Merchant Shipping Act 1894, s.503, by removing limitation for claims by a person who is on board or employed in connection with the ship in question if he is on board or employed under a contract of service governed by UK law. The purpose of this exemption from limitation was presumably to equate the treatment of employees on land and sea.

"in connection with that ship" as referring to a contract of employment or service with the shipowner or salvor.[2]

One should note that injury to the employees does not have to take place while they are on board the ship. It is enough (under the Act or the Convention) if they suffer loss and are employed in connection with the ship. Thus, a crew member would not be faced with limitation if his cause of action against the shipowner arose during a transfer to the ship by launch.

It follows that it will be in the interests of crew members to find causes of action against their *own* employers. The owner of a colliding ship will be able to rely on the limits in Article 6.

Passengers

Article 7 of the 1976 Limitation Convention introduces a new and separate limit of liability where there is loss of life or personal injury to a passenger carried in a ship. This limit, which applies to claims made by passengers against the carrying ship, is 46,666 SDRs multiplied by the number of passengers that the ship is authorised to carry, up to a maximum of 25 million SDRs.[3] Passenger property claims, *e.g.* for lost luggage,[4] will be subject to the general property limit in Article 6(1)(b).

Article 7 does not create any *liability* for passenger carriage. That will be decided according to the existing law. Reference should be made to the Athens Convention Relating to the Carriage of Passengers and Their Luggage 1974.[5] This does create a regime of liability and limitation for passenger carriage.[6] It also provides a limit of liability for death or personal injury per

---

[2] See, *e.g. Buchanan* v. *Babco* [1978] A.C. 141. The problem is that s.35(2) could easily have said exactly that. It may be that reasons of industrial relations policy favoured the wider exclusion.

[3] See Table 2. The maximum is reached for ships carrying 536 or more passengers.

[4] See, *e.g. The Stella* [1900] P. 161, treating passenger luggage as "property" under the Merchant Shipping Act 1894.

[5] With its Protocol of November 19, 1976. The Convention is expected to come into force in 1986 or 1987. Pending its international entry into force, it has been substantially enacted in the UK. Originally, the enactment was indirect, through the Unfair Contract Terms Act 1977, s.28. From January 1, 1981 the applicable provisions are the Merchant Shipping Act 1979, s.16, the Carriage of Passengers and Their Luggage by Sea (Interim Provisions) Order 1980 (S.I. No. 1092) and the Carriage of Passengers and Their Luggage by Sea (Interim Provisions) (Notice) Order 1980 (S.I. No. 1125). See generally, R. Grime, "The Carriage of Passengers and the Athens Convention in the UK" in *The International Maritime Organisation, op. cit.* pp. 252–276.

[6] Rather in the same manner that the Hague and Hague-Visby Rules operate as a separate regime for the carriage of goods. The passenger and goods rules do, however, differ.

passenger of 46,666 SDRs.[7] Like the Hague and Hague-Visby Rules, this operates as a first stage of limitation in relation to each contract of carriage before any question of global limitation is considered.

At first sight the Athens Convention limit might seem identical to the 1976 Limitation Convention limit, but there are two major differences. First, the 1976 Convention limit is *not* applied in relation to *each* passenger claim (as under the Athens Convention), but is multiplied by the *theoretical* number of passengers that the ship is authorised to carry according to her certificate.[8] This is important, because if the ship is half full the *whole* 1976 Article 7 limit will be available to those passengers. The fewer passengers actually carried, the greater will be the proportionate limit available to them. Secondly, the 1976 Convention has the overall maximum limit of 25 million SDRs, whereas there is no equivalent figure in the Athens Convention.[9]

Example 7 illustrates these principles for three passenger ships, the *Royal Princess*, the *Mikhail Lermontov*,[10] and the *Queen Elizabeth II*. The existing Athens Convention limits per passenger of about £35,538 are very low, particularly when they are combined with the global limits of the 1957 Limitation Convention. Thus, under the Athens Convention (alone) the maximum exposure of the owners of a fully loaded *Queen Elizabeth II* would be about

[7] Under the 1976 Protocol; 700,000 gold francs under the 1974 Convention. There have been proposals to increase these very low limits, see IMO LEG 54/5/1.

[8] Under the Merchant Shipping Act 1979, Sched. 4, Part II, para. 6, this certificate will be the passenger steamers certificate issued under s.274, Merchant Shipping Act 1894, but only for passenger steamers within the meaning of Part III of the 1894 Act. These are ships carrying more than 12 passengers: see the Merchant Shipping (Safety Convention) Act 1949, s.26(2), the Merchant Shipping Act 1964, s.17(2), and the cases cited n. 16, *infra*. It is unclear what is to happen when, for some reason, ships do not have a certificate. A literal reading of Art. 7(1) could indicate that the 25 million SDR limit would apply, but this would be surprising in the case of small vessels.

[9] This is because the Athens Convention (like the Hague and Hague-Visby Rules) is itself subject to "international conventions relating to the limitation of liability of owners of seagoing ships": see Art. 19. These would include the 1957 and 1976 Limitation Conventions. Countries not party to the Limitation Conventions, such as Greece, would not be advised to ratify the Athens Convention unless they wished to have no maximum for passenger claims.

[10] The latter sank on February 16, 1986 off New Zealand, while reportedly carrying 409 passengers and 330 crew. Example 7(b) is based on the assumption that all the passengers were personal injury or death claimants (there were no passenger deaths). It is understood that under Art. 275 of the Soviet Maritime Code there would be no limit for personal claims, while property claims would have faced a tiny limit as, under Art. 276, the limit would be based on the value of the ship after the incident: she was a total loss. Example 7(b) is, therefore, entirely hypothetical. The limitation tonnages for all three ships in Example 7 have been estimated, with the exception of Example 7(a)(iv) where the UMS gross of the *Royal Princess* is known. Ship details from *Lloyd's Register of Shipping 1985–1986*.

£61,836,327. But the 1957 Limitation Convention would reduce this to about £9,239,141—equivalent to £5,310 per passenger. The 1976 Limitation Convention, Article 7 limit will improve matters, as the maximum would be increased to about £19,038,550, equivalent to £10,942 per passenger.[11] As the *Mikhail Lermontov* example shows, a ship carrying less than her full complement of passengers will still have to make available the same amount under Article 7 as if she had been full.[12] It is also apparent that passenger ferries with much smaller tonnages, but with a high carrying capacity, will face significantly greater global limits under the 1976 Limitation Convention.[13]

The separate Article 7 limits only apply where there are claims for loss of life or personal injury to "passengers." According to Article 7(2) a passenger is any person carried in that ship:

"(a) under a contract of passenger carriage, or
(b) who, with the consent of the carrier, is accompanying a vehicle or live animals which are covered by a contract for the carriage of goods."

A passenger includes one who has a contract of carriage and is being carried under it. This would exclude stowaways, visitors, guests of the owners or crew and those working on the ship under a contract of employment with somebody else, (*e.g.* dockers).[14] It might be possible for a Court to imply a simple contract in the case of certain visitors. But, although the Convention does not specify the level of formality required for there to be a "contract of

[11] Assuming in both examples that all claims were equal. It should be remembered that the 1957 Convention fund must also be shared with other personal (and property) claimants: see pp. 40–42, *supra*. The 1976 £19,038,550 limit would stand alone and, as already noted, would be available if the ship was part loaded.

[12] See Example 7(a)(ii), (b)(ii), (c)(ii). Examples 7(a)(iv), (b)(iv) and (c)(iv) give some idea of the total exposure of the owners of the three ships.

[13] Many of the Cross-Channel ferries have gross tonnages (OMS) of around 6,000 t, yet can often carry between 1,200–1,800 passengers. In the event of a disaster the 1957 Limitation Convention would have allowed them ludicrously small limits. When the comparatively large ferry *Olau Brittannia* (14,996grt, 13,779nrt) was involved in a collision with the RoRo *Mont Louis* (4,210grt, 1,405nrt) on August 25, 1984 she was carrying 935 passengers, although having the capacity for 1,600. Had there been a disaster the passengers would have faced 1957 Limitation Convention limits, from both ships combined, of about £2,677 *each* passenger (assuming all the passengers had equal claims). That sum would certainly have been lower if property claims were taken into account. Under the 1976 Limitation Convention, Art. 7, the equivalent limit could have been about £19,585 each. This is not exactly generous, but is an improvement. The Art. 7 maximum of 25 million SDRs would, of course, have been available if only one passenger had been killed. It should also be recalled that many passenger ferries will have their limitation tonnages increased dramatically by the change to the UMS gross tonnage: see pp. 47–49, *supra*.

[14] And see Employees, *supra*.

passenger carriage," it would seem that a constructive contract was not intended.

The claim has to be made by or on behalf of a person "carried" in "that" ship. Cruise ship passengers sometimes have to make ship to shore transfers in small launches. These may, or may not, belong to the shipowner. If the ship's boat sinks there is almost certainly a claim, " . . . in direct connection with the operation of the [mother] ship" under Article 2(1)(a). But are the passengers "carried" in the mother ship under Article 7? It would seem that they probably are so carried, at least where the contract of passenger carriage covers such feeder services. Article 7.2 does not say that the claim must *arise* while they are actually on board the ship. It is enough that there is a liability in direct connection with the operation of the ship—a phrase in Article 2 which was intentionally broad. Where wholly independent feeder vessels are selected and used by passengers, issues of liability and limitation will presumably be directed at the owners of such vessels.[15]

Article 7(2)(b) includes in the definition of passenger certain persons accompanying vehicles or live animals. It is intended to cover persons such as truck drivers using RoRo ferries (even where no separate payment has been made for the driver[16]) and veterinary surgeons. In both cases the consent of the "carrier" is required. This could include a charterer as well as the shipowner. In many cases express consent may not have been obtained before the person goes on board. A Court might be entitled to imply consent in some circumstances, *e.g.* where an assistant accompanies the driver or vet, intending to go ashore before sailing. The test would be whether the carrier would have consented, if asked.

A traditional "supercargo" would not fall within the definition of passenger, unless he was accompanying vehicles or animals, and not goods generally. Nor would it extend to visitors who come on board ferries or cruise ships to say farewell to friends or relatives. Although there might be implied consent to them coming on

---

[15] There may be cases where it is unclear whether the services are independent or not, particularly where the shipowner appears to act as an agent, and/or requires an extra payment. Courts will no doubt be wary of legal devices, purporting to insulate owners of large cruise ships from liability, which are designed to force passengers to sue owners of small launches certified to carry comparatively few passengers.

[16] *Cf. Clayton* v. *Albertson* [1972] 2 All E.R. 364. Where school children pay to participate in an excursion on a yacht, it would seem that they do not cease to be passengers and become employees merely by signing a booking form acknowledging their presence on board as "unpaid crewing participation": see *The Biche* [1984] 1 Lloyd's Rep. 26, (decided under the Merchant Shipping (Safety Convention) Act 1949). See also *Temperley*, para. 231.

board, they have no contract of passenger carriage themselves. Nor are they accompanying vehicles[17] or live animals.

It is important to clarify the definition of passengers as, although they are treated less favourably than employees, they are usually placed in a better position than ordinary personal claimants in limitation actions. This is because the Article 7 limit is entirely separate from the Article 6 limits. Article 6(1) makes it clear that its limits apply to claims "other than those mentioned in Article 7." Moreover, Article 7(1) is phrased imperatively, "the limit . . . of liability of the shipowner . . . *shall* be an amount of 46,666 [SDRs]." This division is reinforced by Article 9, dealing with the aggregation of claims. Article 9(1) regulates the aggregation of claims under Article 6 and Article 9(2) regulates those under Article 7.

This separate treatment of passengers will ensure that they will not have to share in the general limitation fund. However, there may be rare cases where the 1976 limitation Convention is disadvantageous to passengers. Example 7(d) is an illustration of the Convention working to the advantage of passengers in the event of a disaster to the *Queen Elizabeth II*, also involving catastrophic loss of life elsewhere.[18] Example 7(d)(i) assumes that the ship sinks in circumstances not involving third party personal claimants, *e.g.* where she founders.[19] With a ship as large as the *Queen Elizabeth II*, her total Article 6 limit could be greater than the separate Article 7 limit. There would be a smaller fund available to the claimants as passengers than as non-passengers. It would then be to the advantage of an individual to assert that he was not a passenger as defined by Article 7(2).

Docks and harbours

The Limitation Conventions were designed with the aim of protecting the owners and operators of ships. Neither the 1976 nor the 1957 Conventions refer to the possibility of the owners of docks or harbours limiting *their* liabilities. Where they incur liabilities as shipowners, (*e.g.* in the operation of tugs) they will be entitled to limit in the ordinary way. Otherwise, their liabilities will be regulated by national law.

It is appropriate here to mention one of the curious relics of British maritime legal history, the Merchant Shipping (Liability of

---

[17] A Court would not be impressed with the argument that they were "accompanying" the vehicle of the friends or relatives, at least where they were not travelling in it.
[18] The example is rather unlikely, but collision with an offshore accommodation platform could raise large third party personal claims.
[19] As with the *Mikhail Lermontov*.

Shipowners and Others) Act 1900.[20] This Act made, in section 1, certain amendments to the Merchant Shipping Act 1894, s.503, which have since been repealed.[21] But the 1900 Act contained, in section 2, a system of limitation of liability parallel to, but separate from, section 503. The owners of any dock or canal, or harbour or conservancy authority[22] are allowed to limit *their* liabilities for loss or damage caused *by* them to vessels or their cargoes. The 1900 Act must have been considered relevant and necessary, because it is to continue, with modifications, when the 1976 Limitation Convention comes into force.

Although this system has been exported to countries deriving their law from the UK, such as Australia, it is not known whether similar provisions are widespread internationally. It seems most peculiar to allow harbour authorities to limit their liabilities to vessel owners, but not, *e.g.* to owners of cargo damaged on wharfs.[23] None of the usual justifications would seem to apply to such bodies.[24] Moreover, the limit is calculated in a bizarre way which appears to have little to do with the extent of the interest of the dock owner or harbour authority in their operations, or their ability to obtain insurance cover. The category of persons entitled to benefit is surprisingly wide,[25] as is the definition of dock.[26] Shiprepairers are a major beneficiary of the Act[27] and there may be many owners of vessels (pleasure and commercial) who are unaware of this extra-contractual UK limit on a shiprepairer's liability.

[20] Although, by s.5, it has to be construed as one with the Merchant Shipping Acts, it did not form part of the Merchant Shipping Act 1894, Part VIII, and therefore had to be read separately from s.503. This has had a number of consequences, largely unforeseen (see *e.g. Mason* v. *Uxbridge Boat Centre and Wright* [1980] 2 Lloyd's Rep. 592). When the Australian Navigation Amendment Act 1979 repealed Part VIII of the 1894 imperial legislation, it left untouched the 1900 Act.

[21] By the Merchant Shipping (Liability of Shipowners and Others) Act 1958, s.8.

[22] As defined in s.742, the Merchant Shipping Act 1894. For the text of s.2 of the 1900 Act, see App. B, p. 344.

[23] This result might be achieved by local Regulations or by contract.

[24] See n. 13, p. 35, *supra*. There seems no historical foundation for such limitation. It would have a marginal influence on the international trade of a country, although it may serve to reduce the operating costs of ports and hence their relative trading position. Many of the claimants may be foreign shipowners. There are few risks particular to operating harbour services that would justify a distinction being made from other large industrial concerns. There may be an influence on insurance rates, although s.2 does not apply to liabilities to persons and property *not* on board vessels.

[25] It applies to owners of docks and canals and persons or authorities having control and management: see s.2(4). It includes lessees of wharves: see *e.g. The Neapolis II* [1980] 2 Lloyd's Rep. 369.

[26] It includes wet docks and basins, tidal locks and basins, locks, cuts, entrances, dry docks, graving docks, grid irons, slips, quays, wharves, piers, stages, landing places and jetties: see s.2(3).

[27] See *e.g. Mason* v. *Uxbridge Boat Centre and Wright* [1980] 2 Lloyd's Rep. 593.

The limit is calculated by reference to the tonnage of the largest British ship which has visited the area in the five years prior to the loss or damage.[28] It may be difficult to discover the ship by reference to which to apply the limit. Most harbour authorities will have records of the ships visiting their areas, although ship repairers and private dock owners might not. The records must also be maintained for longer than five years to take into account the effect of the statutory time bar.[29] The area which the ship has to have visited, under section 2(1), is that over which the defendant "performs *any* duty or exercises any powers." This seems to suggest a geographical area,[30] although its extent could be unclear, causing particular problems for private organisations which are not under a duty to keep records.

The amount of the limit was fixed at 66.67 SDRs for each ton of the British ship selected by the above method.[31] The Merchant Shipping Act 1979, Schedule 5, paragraph 1(2), will replace the 66.67 SDRs by the method specified in Article 6(1)(b) of the 1976 Limitation Convention.[32] The result is that a minimum tonnage for property claims will apply to the 1900 Act for the first time. That tonnage will be the UMS tonnage of the 1969 Tonnage Convention. Harbour authorities may face particular difficulties, in ascertaining what *was* the largest registered British ship that has visited the area, where there have been visits by ships measured under the old and new tonnage regimes. The Act was not specific as to whether it was the largest gross, net, or limitation tonnage that was relevant. But when the 1979 Act changes are brought into force the 1969 UMS gross figure will be used. Many ships recorded as having visited the area will have been measured under

---

[28] Presumably, this formula is meant to reflect the size of the dock or harbour operations. It seems rather anomalous to exclude foreign ships, although doing so reduces measuring problems.

[29] Six years under The Limitation Act 1980. The Maritime Conventions Act 1911 two year limit would not usually apply unless the liability arose out of the operation of the defendant's ship. In that case the ordinary Limitation Convention rules would apply. In any event, the information about the relevant ship will often be under the entire control of the defendant harbour authority. A plaintiff shipowner will presumably be able to offset any concealment of information by applying for an order for discovery.

[30] See *The Ruapehu* [1927] A.C. 523; *The Ruapehu (No.2)* [1929] P. 305. The remainder of s.2(1) excludes certain ships which are in the area casually, *e.g.* passing through: see App. B.9.

[31] Originally £8. This was replaced by 1,000 g.f (see s.1(1)(*b*), Merchant Shipping (Liability of Shipowners and Others) Act 1958), which itself was replaced by the SDR amount (see s.1(4), Merchant Shipping Act 1981). The limit was available only for property, not personal, claims. Neither in the original Act, nor in the amendments made by s.1(1) of the 1958 Act, was there any provision for a minimum tonnage, *e.g.* of 300 t.

[32] Read together with para. 5(1) and (2) of Sched. 4, Part II of the 1979 Act. This means that the limits shown in Table 2, Part Two will apply, subject to the UK small ship rules: see, Small Ships, *supra*.

the old system. There is no method of comparing directly UMS and OMS tonnages: OMS ships may have larger or smaller UMS gross tonnages.[33] Is an authority to organise remeasurements for every OMS ship because of the chance that it might have a higher UMS tonnage? The problem might be dealt with by Regulations.[34]

It does not appear that the 1979 Act has cured existing defects in the 1900 Act.[35] Perhaps a future revision might replace the cumbersome method of ascertaining the limit by adopting some fixed limit, as has been done for salvors in Article 6(4) of the 1976 Limitation Convention.[36]

Pilotage

Although the 1976 Limitation Convention makes no direct reference to pilots, they could, presumably, be entitled to limit under Article 1(4) as persons for whom a shipowner is responsible.

However, for many years in the United Kingdom licensed pilots and pilotage authorities were entitled to separate limits of liability under the Pilotage Act 1913 and the Pilotage Authorities (Limitation of Liability) Act 1936.[37] The relevant provisions have been substantially re-enacted in the Pilotage Act 1983 and the limits have not been increased.[38] The 1983 Act distinguishes between the liability of a pilotage authority as shipowner, *employer* of pilots and otherwise.

As a shipowner the authority can limit in the ordinary way.[39]

[33] See Tonnage Measurement, *supra*, and Table 4.
[34] Under the Merchant Shipping Act 1979, Sched. 4, Part II, para. 5.
[35] *E.g.* revealed by *Mason* v. *Uxbridge Boat Centre and Wright* [1980] 2 Lloyd's Rep. 592. Sched. V, para. 1(1) of the 1979 Act applies the new limitation breaking provisions of Art. 4 of the 1976 Limitation Convention only to owners or authorities and not to their employees; see Chap. 4, *infra*.
[36] Admittedly, it would be difficult to know at what level to set the limit, in view of the differing sizes of organisations involved, but the system would be easier to operate and probably less arbitrary in its results.
[37] S.35 of the 1913 Act stated that a licensed pilot who had given a bond (for £100) should not be "liable for neglect or want of skill beyond the penalty of the bond and the amount payable to him on account of pilotage in respect of the voyage in which he was engaged when he became so liable". S.1 of the 1936 Act provided that a pilotage authority was not to be liable where:
"loss or damage is caused to any vessel or vessels or to any goods, merchandise or other things whatsoever on board any vessel or vessels or to any other property or rights of any kind, whether on land or on water or whether fixed or moveable, . . . to damages beyond the amount of £100 multiplied by the number of pilots holding licences from the pilotage authority . . . at the date when the loss or damage occurs."
[38] See the Pilotage Act ss.42, 55, App. B, p. 356. Note that an order will be made under s.55(4) to apply the new limitation breaking provisions of the 1976 Limitation Convention to the 1983 Act. Curiously, in the interim, the test is "fault or privity" and not "actual fault or privity": see Chap. 4, *infra*.
[39] Pilotage Act 1983, s.58: *i.e.* either under the 1894 or 1979 Merchant Shipping Acts. See the Pilotage Act 1983 (Appointed Day No. 1) Order 1986 (S.I. 1986 No. 1051).

Where an employed pilot has been negligent, or *e.g.* where the authority has negligently engaged an incompetent pilot, the limit is the total pilot's limit of £100 plus the amount of the pilotage charges in respect of the voyage during which the liability arose.[40]

Where the authority incurs liabilities for property damage, other than through the negligence of its pilots, it is entitled to limit to £100 multiplied by the number of pilots holding licences from the pilotage authority for the pilotage district of the authority at the date when the damage or loss occurs.[41] This formula is reminiscent of that applied to dock owners and harbour authorities,[42] although it is calculated differently and is likely to produce a lower limit. It may also provide uncertainty, *e.g.* where a pilotage authority is responsible for more than one pilotage district.[43]

Towage flotillas

When a tug with one or more tows is involved in a collision with a third party an issue always arises concerning the applicable limitation fund. Under the 1957 Limitation Convention, tugs have very small limits of liability. Although these limits will be increased by the 1976 Limitation Convention it may still be important for the third party to have access to the limitation fund applicable to the tow. Behind much of the litigation on towage related collisions lies this need of the third party to be able to sue the tow in *addition* to the tug. In some of the cases there is confusion between two

---

[40] Pilotage Act 1983, s.42(1). After the *Mikhail Lermontov* sinking in 1986 there was apparently a dispute as to whether the pilot was on leave at the time he navigated the liner aground. Casual employment arrangements, particularly in small districts, could cause legal uncertainty as to the authority's liability. Note that there is no liability for *licensing* a pilot; see s.17.

[41] *Ibid.* s.55. It is assumed that ss.42(1) and 55 are mutually exclusive, although the Act is by no means clear on this.

[42] See Docks and Harbours, *supra.* A harbour authority might also be a pilotage authority. S.60 stops funds belonging to an authority in one capacity from being attached to meet liabilities incurred in the other. But the Act does not say which limitation fund will apply, that under s.55, or that under the Merchant Shipping (Liability of Shipowners and Others) Act 1900, s.2. As s.55 is drawn widely, the authority could argue that it should apply (as it might give a lower limit), although the inference of s.60 is that one must ask in which capacity the liability was incurred.

[43] It would seem from the wording of s.55(1) that reference should be made only to the district in which the pilot held his licence. See generally, F. Rose, *The Modern Law of Pilotage*, (1984), pp. 45–47: G. Geen, R. Douglas, *The Law of Pilotage*, (2nd ed., 1983), pp. 79–80.

quite separate issues, namely: who is liable for the collision; and which vessel or vessels should be taken as the limitation unit.[44]

The 1957 Limitation Convention did not deal specifically with this "flotilla" issue nor, unfortunately, does the 1976 Limitation Convention. Once again there is a question of policy: how high should the limits be? Where the tug and tow are in common ownership there is every reason in logic and principle to treat the two vessels as one. Not only are they connected and navigated as one, but they are often treated commercially by their operators as an alternative to a single vessel.

The legal position in British law is apparently the same whether tug and tow are in common or separate ownership. The leading case, *The Bramley Moore*,[45] will still be good law in the absence of any contrary intention in the 1976 Limitation Convention, or the Merchant Shipping Act 1979. Each owner is entitled to limit his liability according to the tonnage of his own vessel. The first stage is to decide the liability of the owner by seeing whether the tug or tow, or both, are at fault.[46] In simple terms, where there is fault of the tug alone, the tug's limit applies (even where the tow is in the same ownership as the tug).[47] Where there is fault of the tow alone, the tow's limit applies. Where there are faults of both tug and tow, each owner can limit according to the tonnage of his own vessel. Where tug and tow are in common ownership and both are at fault, the limitation amounts of both ships will be available. Although in Admiralty law it is usual to speak of the faults of the vessel, it seems more accurate to ask whether there is an

---

[44] See generally, L. Kovats, "Limitation of Liability: the Flotilla Issue" [1977] 1 L.M.C.L.Q. 19; A. Hyndman, "Tug and Tow Limitation of Liability under Canadian Law," in *Law of Tug and Tow* (Continuing Legal Education Society of British Columbia, 1979); N. Gaskell, "Towage", in D. Jackson (ed.) 2 *World Shipping Laws* (1982), IIID/5; A. Parks, *The Law of Tug, Tow and Pilotage* (2nd ed., 1982) pp. 334 *et seq.*

[45] [1964] P. 200.

[46] That raises the difficult issue of the nautical "control" or command of the towage operation: see *e.g. The Panther* [1957] P. 143. Where a tug is towing barges it will normally have nautical control and it alone will usually be responsible for a collision with a third party (although the barge crew may also be negligent in failing to steer correctly or to cast off tow lines). A tow having on board a pilot or master will often be at fault for their failure properly to control the tug: the tug may also be at fault in negligently performing the orders. However, some countries, such as Norway, are believed to make the tow automatically responsible for the faults of the tug.

[47] *The Sir Joseph Rawlinson* [1972] 2 All E.R. 590.

independent cause of action against the vessel, as the fault may not occur on board.[48]

National law may differ on the flotilla issue, in the absence of any clear guidance in the Convention. In the United States the position where a tug is sued by a third party appears to be broadly the same.[49]

Distinct occasion

It is necessary to decide what happens when there are several incidents caused by a ship, each of which result in loss. One of the earliest ideas was to fix the limit by reference to the voyage, so that each voyage provided one limitation fund. An example can be seen in Article 3(1) of the 1924 Limitation Convention. This conforms to a theory which allows an owner to limit his liability according to his interest in the adventure, namely the particular ship on a particular voyage.

The formula used by the 1976 Limitation Convention, Article 9, is to make the limits apply to claims which arise on any "distinct occasion."[50] The expression "distinct occasion" has been interpreted a number of times, although not in recent years. There is no difficulty where one collision occurs at the start of the voyage and another at the end: each is a distinct occasion and there will be two funds. Problems arise where a ship is successively involved in a number of incidents. The crucial issue seems to be that of causation: *i.e.* whether two or more incidents were the result of the same act of negligence. Thus, in *The Rajah*[51] a ship struck a tug and also the tow, to which the tug was passing a line. It was held that

---

[48] In *The Smejli* [1982] 2 Lloyd's Rep. 74 some platform supporting towers were being taken by ocean towage from Rotterdam to Yugoslavia on a barge owned by the tug owner. There were navigation faults by the tug master (in allowing a fuse wire to part and failing to take shelter). There was also negligence in the management of the tow (by allowing it to leave when there was a poor weather forecast and by using an inadequate towing wire), so that a cause of action could be maintained against the tow—whoever owned the tug. It was held that the limitation amounts applicable to both vessels should be available.

[49] *Liverpool* v. *Brooklyn* 251 US 48 (1919), but not where the owner is sued on a contractual basis, *e.g.* by the tow, *Sacramento* v. *Salz* 273 US 326 (1929). See generally, Parks, *op. cit.* and K. Volk, "US limitation of Liability and Tug and Tow," in *Law of Tug and Tow, op. cit.*

[50] Following Art. 21 of the 1957 Limitation Convention, which itself was based on the Merchant Shipping Act 1894, s.503(3). Although a new s.503(3) was inserted by the Merchant Shipping (Liability of Shipowners and Others) Act 1958, s.8(2), it is thought that the change did not make any alterations of substance. See also the Merchant Shipping (Liability of Shipowners and Others) Act 1900, s.3, (App. B, p. 344) and the Pilotage Act 1983, s.56, (App. B, p. 356), which are both technically separate from the 1976 Limitation Convention test. *Cf.* the expression "incident" in the pollution Conventions: the CLC 1969 (App. A, p. 315), the Fund Convention 1971 (App. A, p. 322).

[51] (1872) L.R. 3 A. & E. 539.

there was one act of negligence, one distinct occasion and thus one limitation fund. By contrast, in *The Schwan*[52] a ship collided with another by reason of a negligent helm order, but then, having failed to take sufficient avoiding action, hit a second ship. It was held that there were two distinct occasions. In effect, the Court found that there was a *novus actus interveniens* between the first navigational error and the second collision. It was not the passage of time that was crucial, but whether the second loss resulted from the same act of negligence.

That approach is reasonably straightforward when a Court feels able to draw a clear line between the two acts of negligence. There may be cases where it is not able or prepared to draw such a line. In *The Calliope*[53] Brandon J., as he then was, refused to accept that he was forced to adopt an approach which meant that one incident, out of a set of successive incidents, must be categorised as the sole legal cause of any resulting damage. The alternative, favoured by him, was to adopt a more flexible approach and to allow a finding that an earlier act of negligence might combine with a later negligent act to be a *partial* cause of any resulting damage. If such an approach, involving a sub-apportionment, is correct, it raises the question in limitation actions of whether there would be two distinct occasions, or one.

In that case, as a result of the faults of the *Carlsholm* and the *Calliope* there was a collision and the *Calliope* grounded suffering the "first grounding damage" ("damage 1").[54] The grounding occurred in the River Seine. Because of the size of the *Calliope* in relation to the river, the state of the tide and the weather, it was decided that she must return upriver to await the ebb tide. This necessarily involved a difficult turning manoeuvre and, despite towage assistance, she grounded for a second time, suffering new "second grounding damage" ("damage 2"). The case concerned the apportionment of responsibility for damage 2. *Calliope* was undoubtedly negligent during the turning manoeuvre and the *Carlsholm* owners argued that this was a *novus actus interveniens* and that they were not responsible for damage 2. However, Brandon J. sub-apportioned the liability, finding that damage 2 was partly caused by *Calliope*'s negligence in making the turn, but *also* by those responsible for damage 1.[55]

The facts of the case were unusual, because of the crucial

---

[52] [1892] P. 419.

[53] [1970] 1 All E.R. 624.

[54] The liability for damage 1 was apportioned *Carlsholm* 45 per cent.: *Calliope* 55 per cent.

[55] He apportioned liability for damage 2 on a 50:50 basis. *i.e.* 50 per cent. of damage 2 was caused by *Calliope*; 50 per cent. was caused by the faults of the two vessels in bringing about the original collision. As noted above, *Carlsholm* was responsible for 45 per cent. of the collision, and thus for 22.5 per cent. of damage 2.

finding that the effects of the first acts of negligence were still *continuing* when the turn was made.[56] In many, if not most, of the cases raising issues of *novus actus interveniens* this continuing factor will not be present.[57]

Were there two distinct occasions or one?[58] There were 12 hours between the two incidents and a layman would be inclined to say there were two "occasions." But were they "distinct?" The passage of time alone is not decisive, as the wording requires an examination of the causation issue. One consequence of *The Calliope* is to say that, as a general principle, a second incident may not be *wholly* distinct from the first. On that basis there would only be one distinct occasion for which the *Carlsholm* would be liable. This could be important where a third party is involved, *e.g.* if the *Calliope* had damaged a bridge while turning. It might seem hard to require the *Carlsholm* to put up two funds. It could be equally hard on the third party to allow the *Calliope* to say that the third party should proceed against the single limitation fund set up to satisfy claims resulting from the original collision.[59] For there was *also* "distinct" negligence by *Calliope* in the turn.

It appears that the onus of showing that the damage did not arise on distinct occasions rests on the ship that is seeking to limit its liability (to a single occasion).[60] Courts might use this reasoning to allow two (or more) limitation funds where the "occasions" are separate, but the causative acts of negligence are not wholly "distinct." Alternatively, it could be said that the second incident is a distinct occasion unless it resulted *wholly* from the first act of

---

[56] There was a difficult manoeuvre involving risks that would not normally have been undertaken in good weather, let alone the dense fog that existed. This "continuing" element will normally turn on the absence of choice, or the ability to act without restriction, as a result of the negligence. "Was the hand of the negligent navigator still heavy on the other ship?" *per* Brandon J. [1970] 1 All E.R. 624, at p.640.

[57] A case like *The Fritz Thyssen* [1967] 1 All E.R. 628, [1967] 3 All E.R. 117 would still be decided the same way. A master refused salvage assistance after a collision. He was in continuing difficulty in that his ship was leaking as a result of the collision. But he was not under a continuing difficulty about making a decision whether to accept or reject salvage services. His repeated rejections of help did completely break the "chain" of causation.

[58] The limitation issue was not raised in the case, perhaps because of the size of the sums at stake.

[59] Cargo on the *Calliope*, damaged in the first and second incidents, could be affected by the question as to whether there were one or two distinct occasions. Negligence in navigation would probably be excepted under the bill of lading or the Hague (or Hague-Visby) Rules, although deviation might deprive the owner of this protection: *Hain* v. *Tate & Lyle* [1936] 2 All E.R. 597. The Hamburg Rules 1978, Art. 5, would remove the protection completely and one can envisage circumstances in which there are two incidents causing loss to a valuable cargo where either the whole cargo is lost, or part is lost in each incident.

[60] See Marsden, *Collisions at Sea*, (11th ed., 1962), p. 157, citing the Scottish case of *The Lucillite* v. *The R. Mackay* [1929] S.C. 401.

negligence. But, unless such an approach is adopted, it would seem that in a case like *The Calliope* the owners of both ships would be able to assert that there was one distinct occasion. It would be in the interests of the *Calliope*, if faced with third party claims from the second incident, to argue that there had been continuing negligence from the first incident. Then, the third party would have to share the fund with the collision claimants.

Aggregation

The limits of liability under Article 6 are not available in respect of each defendant against whom there is a cause of action. For instance, an injured party cannot, by suing the owner, charterer, master, helmsman and lookout, claim to have (in effect) five limitation funds. Under Article 9(1), the limits apply to the *aggregate* of all claims that arise on any distinct occasion against: (a) shipowners[61] (and those for whom they are responsible); or (b) shipowners and salvors[62] (and those for whom they are responsible) providing salvage services from a ship; or (c) salvors (and those for whom they are responsible) not operating from a ship.

There is also a separate aggregation, under Article 9(2) of the passenger claims subject to the limits of Article 7. It seems that once a person is defined as a passenger he cannot seek to share in that ship's Article 6 funds to the extent that he has claims unsatisfied because of the limits in Article 7. But, it would appear from Article 9(2) that he would be entitled to sue a non-carrying ship (which collides with the passenger ship) to the extent of that ship's Article 6 limits. The passenger would have to share with any other claimants against that fund.

Claimants subject to limits under any of these four heads will have their claims met *pro rata*.[63]

Counterclaims

It was an established part of English Admiralty Practice that where, as a result of a collision, there were counterclaims, the correct procedure was to set them off so that the shipowner who was a net debtor was entitled to limit his liability on the balance.[64] The 1957 Limitation Convention, Article 1(5), followed the English practice and Article 5 of the 1976 Limitation Convention provides likewise.[65]

---

[61] As defined in Article 1(2).
[62] As defined in Article 1(3).
[63] See Article 12(1).
[64] *The Khedive* (1880) 5 App.Cas. 876. This may have some significance where one ship has a large limit and the other a small one, as Example 8 shows.
[65] Accordingly, the procedure under the Convention will be identical to that adopted in Example 8(b) and *not* 8(a).

TABLES

Table number

TABLE 1

1957 LIMITATION CONVENTION

(With examples of sterling conversions)

		£ [1894][1]	£ 1958[2]	£ 1984[3]	£ 1985[4]	£ 1986[5]
PART ONE Reserved solely for Personal Claims	2,100 gold francs per ton (140 SDR's per ton)	[7]	49.75	99.11 108.50	106.42	106.62
PART TWO Other Claims	1,000 gold francs per ton (66.7 SDR's per ton)	[8]	23.69	47.20 51.67	50.68	50.77
PART THREE Total Fund Available	3,100 gold francs per ton (206.67 SDR's per ton)	[15]	73.44	146.31 160.17	157.10	157.39
SMALL VESSELS[6] Minimum 300t	930,000 gold francs per ton (62,001 SDR's per ton)	[N/A]	22,032	43,893 48,050	47,130	47,216

NOTES TO TABLE 1

[1] Figures in square brackets were the limitation amounts in force under the (unamended) Merchant Shipping Act 1894, s.503.

[2] Gold franc calculation under S.I. 1958 No. 1287 (in force from August 1, 1958).

[3] Gold franc calculation under S.I. 1983 No. 582 (in force from May 9, 1983). SDR calculation £0.774989: August 13, 1984 (*Financial Times*, August 14, 1984), corrected to two decimal places. Note that the 1979 Protocol (introducing SDR's to the 1957 Convention) did not enter into force until October 6, 1984 (see Special Drawing Rights, pp. 37–38, *supra*.).

[4] SDR calculation £0.760157: September 13, 1985 (*Financial Times*, September 16, 1985), corrected to two decimal places.

[5] SDR calculation £0.761542: January 17, 1986 (*Financial Times*, January 18, 1986), corrected to two decimal places.

[6] The small vessels calculation is based upon claims under Part Three, on January 17, 1986. See Example 6.

TABLE 2

1976 Limitation Convention
(With examples of sterling conversions)

	TONNAGE[1]	SDR	£ 1984[2]	£ 1985[3]	£ 1986[4]
PART ONE Reserved for Loss of Life/ Personal Injury Claims Only (Art. 6(1)(a))					
tonnage not exceeding	500t	333,000 SDR [=666 SDR per ton]	258,071 [=516.14]	253,132 [=506.26]	253,593 [=509.96][5]
and for each ton	501 to 3,000t	500 SDR	387.49	380.08	380.77
,,	3,001 to 30,000t	333 SDR	258.07	253.13	253.59
,,	30,001 to 70,000t	250 SDR	193.75	190.04	190.39
,,	70,001t upwards	167 SDR	129.42	126.95	127.18
Salvor (off salvage vessel)	Fixed tonnage 1,500 tons	833,000 SDR	645,566	633,211	634,364
Small Ships (U.K.)	Tonnage under 300 tons	166,667 SDR	129,940	126,693	126,924
PART TWO Other Claims (Art. 6(1)(b))					
tonnage not exceeding	500t	167,000 SDR [=334 SDR per ton][5]	129,423 [=258.85][5]	120,946 [=253.89][5]	127,178 [=254.36][5]
and for each ton	501 to 30,000t	167 SDR	129.42	126.95	127.18
,,	30,001 to 70,000t	125 SDR	96.87	95.02	95.19
,,	70,001t upwards	83 SDR	64.32	63.09	63.21
Salvor (off Salvage vessel)	Fixed tonnage 1,500 tons	334,000 SDR	258,846	253,892	254,355
Small Ships (U.K.)	Tonnage Under 300 tons	83,333 SDR	64,582	63,346	63,462

TABLE 2 (contd.)

	TONNAGE[1]		SDR	£ 1984[2]	£ 1985[3]	£ 1986[4]
PART THREE Total Fund Available	tonnage not exceeding	500t	500,000 SDR [=1,000 SDR per[5] ton]	387,494 [=774.97][5]	380,079 [=760.16][5]	380,771 [=761.54][5]
(Art. 6(1)(a) and Art. 6(1)(b))	and for each ton	501 to 3,000t	667 SDR	516.91	507.02	507.95
	,,	3,001 to 30,000t	500 SDR	387.49	380.08	380.77
	,,	30,001 to 70,000t	375 SDR	290.62	285.06	285.58
	,,	70,001t upwards	250 SDR	193.74	190.04	190.39
	Salvor (off salvage vessel)	Fixed tonnage 1,500 tons	1,167,000 SDR	904,412	887,103	888,720
	Small Ships (U.K.)	Tonnage under 300 tons	250,000 SDR	194,522	190,039	190,386
Passengers (Art. 7)	For each passenger (certified capacity)		46,666 SDR	36,166	35,473	35,538
	Maximum		25,000,000 SDR	19,374,725	19,003,925	19,038,550

NOTES TO TABLE 2

[1] All references to tonnage are to limitation tonnage.

[2] SDR calculation £0.774489: August 13, 1984 (*Financial Times*, August 14, 1984). Smaller sums corrected to two decimal places: larger to nearest whole number.

[3] SDR calculation £0.760157: September 13, 1985 (*Financial Times*, September 16, 1985). Smaller sums corrected to two decimal places: larger to nearest whole number.

[4] SDR calculation £0.761542: January 17, 1986 (*Financial Times*, January 18, 1986). Smaller sums corrected to two decimal places: larger to nearest whole number.

[5] Figures in square brackets indicate the theoretical limit per ton in the first "slice." They are included *only* by way of comparison with the succeeding figure per ton in order to illustrate the decline in relative limits for ships with higher tonnages.

70

TABLE 3

COMPARISON OF LIMITS UNDER 1957 AND 1976 LIMITATION CONVENTIONS

SHIP SIZE[1]	TYPE OF CLAIM[2]	£ 1957 CONVENTION[3]	£ 1976 CONVENTION[3]
150,000t	Personal	15,992,382	25,842,166
	Other	7,615,801	12,743,263
	Total	23,608,183	38,585,429
80,000t	Personal	8,529,270	16,939,740
	Other	4,061,760	8,318,704
	Total	12,591,030	25,258,444
10,000t	Personal	1,066,159	2,980,675
	Other	507,720	1,335,364
	Total	1,573,879	4,316,039
5,000t	Personal	533,079	1,712,708
	Other	253,860	699,476
	Total	786,939	2,412,184
1,000t	Personal	106,616	443,979
	Other	50,772	190,766
	Total	157,388	634,745
500t	Personal	53,308	253,593
	Other	25,386	127,178
	Total	78,694	380,771
250t[4]	Personal	31,985	253,593 [126,924][5]
	Other	15,232	127,178 [63,462][5]
	Total	47,216	380,771 [190,386][5]

NOTES TO TABLE 3

[1] "Ship size" relates to limitation tons. No allowance is made for the differing tonnage regimes: see Table 4.
[2] For explanations of the categories of claim, see pp. 40–44, *supra*.
[3] Calculations based on the SDR conversion rate of 0.761542 (January 17, 1986) and corrected to nearest whole number for convenience. This explains the apparent distortion in the first digit of the 250t/Total/1957 Convention figure.
[4] 250t ship will attract the minimum tonnage provisions of the 1957 Convention (300t) and the 1976 Convention (500t).
[5] Calculations in square brackets are those under the Merchant Shipping Act 1979, Sched. 4, Pt. II, para. 5. See pp. 44–45, *supra*.

TABLE 4A

Comparison of Limitation Tonnages Using the Propelling Power Allowance (PPA) in Pre-1969 Convention Tonnages (OMS)[1]

SHIP TYPE	GROSS	NET	P.P.A.	P.P.A. AS PERCENTAGE OF GROSS	LIMITATION TONNAGE
REEFER	(1,463)	811	458)	31.31	1,269
	(695	370	160)	23.02	530
REEFER	4,527	2,194	1,179	26.04	3,373
REEFER	2,485	950	795	31.99	1,745
REEFER	7,729	4,445	2,473	32.00	6,918
REEFER	4,696	2,115	1,196	25.44	3,311
TUG	347	NIL	260	74.93	[260]
TUG	391	NIL	252	64.45	[252]
SUPPLY SHIP	821	314	354	43.12	668
SUPPLY SHIP	1,598	635	511	31.98	1,146
CELLULAR	(6,807	3,928	2,178)	32.00	6,106
CONTAINER	(3,583	1,990	1,049)	29.28	3,039
CELLULAR	(6,783	3,918	2,170)	32.00	6,088
CONTAINER	(3,527	1,945	1,059)	30.03	3,004
RO/RO FERRY	5,465	2,485	1,749	32.00	4,234
RO/RO FERRY	6,376	2,896	2,040	32.00	4,936
VEHICLE CARRIER	9,354	4,917	2,993	32.00	7,910
GAS CARRIER	994	529	168	17.80	697
BULK CARRIER	3,893	2,406	932	23.94	3,338
BULK CARRIER	4,334	2,228	1,051	24.25	3,279
BULK CARRIER	17,939	10,173	3,435	19.15	13,608

TABLE 4A (*cont.*)

SHIP TYPE	GROSS	NET	P.P.A.	P.P.A. AS PERCENTAGE OF GROSS	LIMITATION TONNAGE
BULK CARRIER	16,421	11,410	3,609	21.98	15,019
BULK CARRIER	37,913	29,427	7,242	19.10	36,669
BULK CARRIER	87,132	68,026	17,721	20.34	85,747
BULK CARRIER	16,023	10,173	3,435	21.44	13,608
PRODUCT TANKER	18,954	11,974	6,065	32.00	18,039
PRODUCT TANKER	18,959	12,811	4,257	22.45	17,068
PRODUCT TANKER	19,249	11,888	6,159	32.00	18,047
TANKER	637	549		DECK MOUNTED ENGINES	[549]
TANKER	126,260	109,484	14,956	11.85	124,440
TANKER	163,448	110,126	20,227	12.38	130,353

NOTES TO TABLE 4A

[1] Gross, net and P.P.A. figures provided for the author by Lloyd's Register of Shipping. Figures in round brackets represent alternative tonnages for the ships in question. Square brackets indicate a presumed total in the absence of a net or P.P.A. figure.

73

TABLE 4B

APPLICATION OF THE REGULATIONS OF THE 1969 TONNAGE MEASUREMENT CONVENTION TO MODERN SHIP TYPES[1]

Type	No. in Sample	Gross Tonnage			Net Tonnage		
		Mean[2] Existing (OMS)	Mean[2] 1969 (UMS)	Ratio	Mean[2] Existing (OMS)	Mean[2] 1969 (UMS)	Ratio
Tankers	26	36,825	35,017	0.951	23,291	23,795	1.022
Bulk Carriers	36	17,132	16,532	0.965	10,257	8,640	0.842
Ore Carriers	12	11,820	10,948	0.962	5,191	3,591	0.691
Singledeckers Closed	24	629	723	1.150	383	389	1.019
Shelterdeckers over 3,000 g.r.t. Closed	36	8,523	8,796	1.032	4,883	4,505	0.923
Shelterdeckers less than 3,000 g.r.t. Open	7	797	821	1.030	NOT AVAILABLE		
Shelterdeckers over 2,000 g.r.t. Open	39	5,926	8,319	1.404	3,340	3,685	1.103
Shelterdeckers less than 2,000 g.r.t.	12	332	821	2.473	217	310	1.428

74

TABLE 4B (*cont.*)

Type	No. in Sample	Gross Tonnage			Net Tonnage		
		Mean[2] Existing (OMS)	Mean[2] 1969 (UMS)	Ratio	Mean[2] Existing (OMS)	Mean[2] 1969 (UMS)	Ratio
Ro/Ro ship closed	8	2,802	3,794	1.354	NOT AVAILABLE		
Ro/Ro ship open	8	968	3,794	3.919	478	1,149	2.404
Passenger ships	6	15,231	15,319	1.006	8,292	6,604	0.796
Ferries	4	1,844	2,948	1.599	824	1,038	1.260

NOTES TO TABLE 4B

[1] Figures from International Chamber of Shipping and International Shipping Federation, ICS/27: see M. Corkhill, *The Tonnage Measurement of Ships* (2nd ed., 1980), p. 49.

[2] Arithmetic mean used to give idea of size of vessel considered.

TABLE 4C

APPLICATION OF THE REGULATIONS OF THE 1969 TONNAGE MEASUREMENT CONVENTION TO INDIVIDUAL "OPEN SHELTERDECK" TYPE VESSELS[1]

Ship Type	Length BP metres	Gross Tonnage			Net Tonnage		
		Existing (OMS)	1969 (UMS)	Ratio	Existing (OMS)	1969 (UMS)	Ratio
General cargo—open shelterdeck (below 200 g.r.t.)	41.2	199	550	2.764	135	253	1.874
General cargo—open shelterdeck (below 500 g.r.t.)	66.5	499	1,368	2.74	324	479	1.478
General cargo—open shelterdeck (below 1,600 g.r.t.)	82.0	1,502	2,839	1.87	763	1,285	1.684
General cargo—open shelterdeck (above 1,600 g.r.t.)	120.7	4,112	6,633	1.613	1,907	2,896	1.519
Ro/Ro cargo ferry—open shelterdeck	68.8	982	2,462	2.50	488	739	1.514
Ro/Ro passenger ferry—open shelterdeck	97.3	4,082	7,450	1.822	1,850	3,710	2.00
Car carrier—open shelterdeck	145.6	5,353	19,927	3.72	2,586	5,978	2.310
Supply ship—open shelterdeck	49.3	496	928	1.871	165	278	1.685

NOTES TO TABLE 4C

[1] Figures from International Chamber of Shipping and International Shipping Federation, ICS/27, and see M. Corkhill, *The Tonnage Measurement of Ships* (2nd ed., 1980), p. 50.

TABLE 4D

Comparison Between Limitation Tonnages for Ships Measured both under the 1969 Tonnage Convention (UMS) and Old Measurement Systems (OMS)[1]

Ship Type	Pre-1969 Convention tonnages (OMS)				1969 Convention (UMS) Gross	Increase UMS/OMS	
	Gross	Net	P.P.A.	Limitation Tonnage		Tonnage	Percentage
TUG	558	163	200	363	642	279	76.86%
CARGO	1,599	1,157	293	1,450	1,935	485	33.45%
CARGO	9,754	5,716	2,536	8,252	10,097	1,845	22.36%
TANKER	17,559	10,769	5,049	15,818	16,595	777	4.91%
TANKER	19,593	12,595	5,040	17,635	18,092	457	2.59%
TANKER	19,763	11,520	6,099	17,619	18,654	1,035	5.87%
TANKER	39,280	22,894	7,338	30,232	36,865	6,633	21.94%
TANKER	70,790	44,684	10,655	55,339	66,024	10,685	19.31%
TANKER	159,647	125,057	17,270	142,327	150,806	8,479	5.96%
BULK CARRIER	36,341	26,371	6,626	32,997	36,284	3,287	9.96%
BULK CARRIER	69,903	44,473	12,483	56,956	67,914	10,958	19.24%
BULK CARRIER	78,531	55,600	12,888	68,488	80,624	12,136	17.72%
CONTAINER	24,216	14,424	7,538	21,962	24,889	2,927	13.33%
CONTAINER	24,820	15,214	7,425	22,639	24,699	2,060	9.10%
CONTAINER	31,035	17,657	7,413	25,070	30,817	5,747	22.92%
CONTAINER	33,761	21,257	9,348	30,605	32,534	1,929	6.30%
CONTAINER	33,758	21,298	9,406	30,704	32,534	1,830	5.96%
OBO	39,059	30,043	7,565	37,608	45,025	7,417	19.72%

77

TABLE 4D *(cont.)*

Ship Type	Pre-1969 Convention tonnages (OMS)				1969 Convention (UMS) Gross	Increase UMS/OMS	
	Gross	Net	P.P.A.	Limitation Tonnage		Tonnage	Percentage
OBO	57,526	46,269	9,742	56,011	61,055	5,044	9.01%
OBO	90,846	63,747	14,624	78,371	90,747	12,376	15.79%

NOTES TO TABLE 4D

[1] Figures on tonnages of a cross section of ships (of varying nationalities) provided for the author by Lloyd's Register of Shipping. The ships have been actually remeasured to obtain 1969 Tonnage Convention (UMS) tonnage. Accordingly the figures are exact and not in any way hypothetical. UMS net tonnages have not been shown as they are irrelevant to limitation. See generally, pp. 45–49, *supra*.

TABLE 5A

Comparison Between Limits of Ships in Table 4D, calculated under: the 1957 Limitation Convention, using Old Measurement System (OMS) tonnages; and the 1976 Limitation Convention, using 1969 Tonnage Convention Universal Measurement System (UMS).

SHIP[1] TYPE	LIMITA-TION[1] TONNAGE (OMS)	LIMITA-TION[1] TONNAGE (UMS)	TYPE OF[2] CLAIM	£ LIMIT UNDER[3] 1957 CONVENTION (USING OMS)	£ LIMIT UNDER[3] 1976 CONVENTION (USING UMS)
TUG	363t	642t	Personal	38,702	307,663
			Other	18,430	145,237
			Total	57,132	452,900
CARGO	1,450t	1,935t	Personal	154,593	615,326
			Other	73,619	247,996
			Total	228,212	863,322
CARGO	8,252t	10,097t	Personal	879,794	3,005,274
			Other	418,971	1,347,700
			Total	1,298,765	4,352,974
TANKER	15,818t	16,595t	Personal	1,686,450	4,653,124
			Other	803,112	2,174,100
			Total	2,489,562	6,827,224
TANKER	17,635t	18,092t	Personal	1,880,171	5,032,754
			Other	895,364	2,364,484
			Total	2,775,535	7,397,238
TANKER	17,619t	18,654t	Personal	1,878,465	5,175,273
			Other	894,552	2,435,958
			Total	2,773,017	7,611,232*
TANKER	30,232t	36,865t	Personal	3,223,211	9,359,542
			Other	1,534,939	4,532,412
			Total	4,758,151*	13,891,953*
TANKER	55,339t	66,024t	Personal	5,900,016	14,910,992
			Other	2,809,672	7,308,138
			Total	8,709,688	22,219,130
TANKER	142,327t	150,806t	Personal	15,174,318	25,944,671
			Other	7,226,227	12,794,208
			Total	22,400,545	38,738,879
BULK CARRIER	32,997t	36,284t	Personal	3,518,004	9,248,928
			Other	1,675,324	4,477,105
			Total	5,193,328	13,726,033
BULK CARRIER	56,956t	67,914t	Personal	6,072,414	15,270,820
			Other	2,891,770	7,488,052
			Total	8,964,184	22,758,873*
BULK CARRIER	68,488t	80,624t	Personal	7,301,908	17,019,099
			Other	3,477,273	8,358,146
			Total	10,779,180*	25,377,244*
CONTAINER	21,962t	24,889t	Personal	2,341,498	6,756,429
			Other	1,115,055	3,228,910
			Total	3,456,553	9,985,339
CONTAINER	22,639t	24,699t	Personal	2,413,677	6,708,246
			Other	1,149,427	3,204,746
			Total	3,563,104	9,912,992
CONTAINER	25,070t	30,817t	Personal	2,672,860	8,208,090
			Other	1,272,854	3,956,687
			Total	3,945,714	12,164,776

SHIP[1] TYPE	LIMITA- TION[1] TONNAGE (OMS)	LIMITA- TION[1] TONNAGE (UMS)	TYPE OF[2] CLAIM	£ LIMIT UNDER[3] 1957 CONVENTION (USING OMS)	£ LIMIT UNDER[3] 1976 CONVENTION (USING UMS)
CONTAINER	30,605t	32,534t	Personal	3,262,979	8,534,982
			Other	1,553,877	4,120,133
			Total	4,816,856	12,655,114
CONTAINER	30,704t	32,534t	Personal	3,273,534	8,534,982
			Other	1,558,904	4,120,133
			Total	4,832,438	12,655,114*
OBO	37,608t	45,025t	Personal	4,009,610	10,913,087
			Other	1,909,434	5,309,185
			Total	5,919,044	16,222,272
OBO	56,011t	61,055t	Personal	5,971,662	8,634,173
			Other	2,843,791	4,169,728
			Total	8,815,453	12,803,900
OBO	78,371t	90,747t	Personal	8,355,953	18,306,516
			Other	3,979,053	8,998,000
			Total	12,334,645*	27,304,517

NOTES TO TABLE 5A

[1] Ship types and tonnages taken from Table 4D. As a result, the figures are not estimates.
[2] For explanation of the categories of claim, see pp. 40–45, *supra*.
[3] Calculations based on the SDR rate £0.761542: January 17, 1986 (*Financial Times*, January 18, 1986) and corrected to the nearest whole number for convenience. This explains why the final digit in eight (marked *) of the "Total" examples appears to be one number out.

TABLE 5B

Comparison Between Limits of Ships with large increase in limitation tonnage, calculated under: the 1957 Limitation Convention, using Old Measurement Systems (OMS); and the 1976 Limitation Convention, using 1969 Tonnage Convention Universal Measuring System (UMS).

SHIP TYPE	LIMITATION[3] TONNAGE (OMS)	LIMITATION[4] TONNAGE (OMS)	TYPE OF[5] CLAIM	LIMIT UNDER[6] 1957 CONVENTION (USING OMS) £	LIMIT UNDER[6] 1976 CONVENTION (USING UMS) £
RO/RO SHIP[1] (open shelterdeck)	788t	3,794t	Personal	84,013	1,406,874
			Other	40,008	546,100
			Total	124,022	1,952,974
RO/RO CARGO FERRY[2] (open shelterdeck)	802t	2,462t	Personal	85,506	1,000,666
			Other	40,719	376,700
			Total	126,225	1,377,366
CAR CARRIER[2] (open shelterdeck)	4,299t	19,927t	Personal	458,342	5,498,098
			Other	218,269	2,597,855
			Total	676,611	8,095,953

TABLE 5B *(cont.)*

SHIP TYPE[1]	LIMITATION[3] TONNAGE (OMS)	LIMITATION[4] TONNAGE (OMS)	TYPE OF[5] CLAIM	LIMIT UNDER[6] 1957 CONVENTION (USING OMS)	LIMIT UNDER[6] 1976 CONVENTION (USING UMS)
SUPPLY SHIP[2]	324t	928t	Personal	34,544	416,563
			Other	16,450	181,609
			Total	50,994	598,173*

NOTES TO TABLE 5B

[1] Ship taken from Table 4B. Note that it is a mean figure, rather than being the tonnage of a particular ship.

[2] Ships taken from Table 4C.

[3] Limitation tonnage *estimated* on basis of 32 per cent of gross plus net. See p. 46, *supra.*

[4] Limitation tonnage is UMS gross.

[5] For explanations of the categories of claim, see pp. 40–44.

[6] Calculations based on the SDR rate £0.761542: January 17, 1986 (*Financial Times*, January 18, 1986) and corrected to the nearest whole number for convenience. This explains the apparent distortion in the final digit (marked *) of the "Total" figure for the "Ro/Ro Ship" and the "Car Carrier."

TABLE 6

Newbuilding Prices[1]

(U.S. $ Millions)

Type and size of vessel	$m 1980	$m 1982	$m 1983
30,000 dwt bulk	16.7	19.2	15.0
32,000 dwt tanker	18.7	27.7	24.0
70,000 dwt bulk	23.6	29.9	22.5
80,000 dwt tanker	28.3	34.1	30.0
120,000 dwt bulk	32.2	41.3	32.0
250,000 dwt tanker	75.0	75.0	73.0
125,000 m3 LNG	200.0	249.1	200.0
75,000 m3 LPG	77.0	70.0	55.0
1,200 TEU ro/ro	43.7	43.7	40.0
15,000 dwt general cargo ship	13.9	14.0	13.0
1,600 TEU full containership	31.5	34.7	28.0

NOTES TO TABLE 6

[1] Source: the UNCTAD Review of Maritime Transport 1983 (TD/B/C.4/266, p.25, April 25, 1984). It gives representative examples taken from various issues of *Lloyd's Shipping Economist*.

EXAMPLES

Example number

1. *1957 Limitation Convention*

1(a) Personal Claims Alone
1(b) Property Claims Alone
1(c) Total Fund Available

2. *1976 Limitation Convention*

2(a) Personal Claims Alone
2(b) Other Claims Alone
2(c) Total Fund Available
2(d) Model Tables

3. *Mixed personal and property claims 1957 Limitation Convention examples*

3(a) Correct Calculation
3(b) Incorrect Calculation—Rateable Allocation

4. *Mixed personal and property claims 1957 Limitation Convention sterling examples*

4(a) Small Personal and Large Property Claims
4(b) Equal Personal and Property Claims

5. *Mixed personal and property claims 1976 Limitation Convention*

6. *Small Ships*

6(a) 1957 Limitation Convention
6(b) U.K. Merchant Shipping Act 1894, s.503
6(c) 1976 Limitation Convention
6(d) U.K. Merchant Shipping Act 1979

7. *Passenger ship limits*

7(a) Royal Princess
7(b) Milkhail Lermontov
7(c) Queen Elizabeth II
7(d) Comparison of Article 6 and Article 7 Limits
　　　1976 Limitation Convention
　　　Queen Elizabeth II

8. *Counterclaims*

8(a) Incorrect Method: Claims Limited Separately
8(b) Correct Method: Claims Set Off Before Limitation

EXAMPLE 1

1957 Limitation Convention

(a) Personal claims alone

Assume 90,000 (limitation) ton ship
        Conversion date—January 17, 1986
        Conversion rate —1 SDR=£0.761542
        Limit   —140 SDR's per ton[1]

90,000t×[140 SDR's×£0.761542]   = £9,595,429

(b) Property claims alone

Assume 90,000 (limitation) ton ship
        Conversion date—January 17, 1986
        Conversion rate —1 SDR=£0.761542
        Limit   —66.67 SDR's per ton[2]

90,000×[66.67 SDR's×£0.761542]   = £4,569,480

(c) Total fund available

Assume 90,000 (limitation) ton ship
        Conversion date—January 17, 1986
        Conversion rate —1 SDR=£0.761542
        Limit   —206.67 SDR's per ton[3]

90,000t×[206.67 SDR's×£0.761542]   =£14,164,909

---

[1] See Table 1, Pt. One.
[2] See Table 1, Pt. Two.
[3] See Table 1, Pt. Three.

EXAMPLE 2

1976 LIMITATION CONVENTION

2(a) "Personal"[4] claims alone

Assume 90,000 (limitation) ton ship
  Conversion date—January 17, 1986
  Conversion rate —1 SDR=£0.761542
  Limit[5]:

Tonnage Slices	Tons SDR Rate	SDR Total
0– 500t	[fixed slice]	333,000 SDR
501– 3,000t	2,500t×500 SDR	1,250,000 SDR
3,001–30,000t	27,000t×333 SDR	8,991,000 SDR
30,001–70,000t	40,000t×250 SDR	10,000,000 SDR
70,001–90,000t	20,000t×167 SDR	3,340,000 SDR
		23,914,000 SDR
		TOTAL LIMIT
		£18,211,515

2(b) "Others"[6] claims alone

Assume 90,000 (limitation) ton ship
  Conversion date—January 17, 1986
  Conversion rate —1 SDR=£0.761542
  Limit:[7]

Tonnage Slices	Tons SDR Rate	SDR Total
0– 500t	[fixed slice]	167,000 SDR
501–30,000t	29,500t×167 SDR	4,926,500 SDR
30,001–70,000t	40,000t×125 SDR	5,000,000 SDR
70,001–90,000t	20,000t× 83 SDR	1,660,000 SDR
		11,753,500 SDR
		TOTAL LIMIT
		£8,950,784

2(c) Total fund available

Assume 90,000 (limitation) ton ship
  Conversion date—January 17, 1986
  Conversion rate —1 SDR=£0.761542
  Limit:[8]

Tonnage Slices	Tons SDR Rate	SDR Total
0– 500t	[fixed slice]	500,000 SDR
501– 3,000t	2,500t×667 SDR	1,667,500 SDR
3,001–30,000t	27,000t×500 SDR	13,500,000 SDR
30,001–70,000t	40,000t×375 SDR	15,000,000 SDR
70,001–90,000t	20,000t×250 SDR	5,000,000 SDR
		35,667,500 SDR
		TOTAL LIMIT
		£27,162,299

---

[4] Including personal injury and death claims.
[5] See Table 2, Pt. One.
[6] Including property claims, *e.g.* by cargo owners.
[7] See Table 2, Pt. Two.
[8] See Table 2, Pt. Three.

2(d) Model Tables

Personal claims alone (Article 6(1)(a))

Tonnage Slices	Tons SDR Rate	SDR Total
0– 500t	[fixed slice]	333,000 SDR
501– 3,000t	2,500t×500 SDR	1,250,000 SDR
3,001–30,000t	27,000t×333 SDR	8,991,000 SDR
30,001–70,000t	40,000t×250 SDR	10,000,000 SDR
70,001– ?t	?t×167 SDR	? SDR
		TOTAL LIMIT
		£?

Other claims alone (Article 6(1)(b))

Tonnage Slices	Tons SDR Rate	SDR Total
0– 500t	[fixed slice]	167,000 SDR
501–30,000t	29,500t×167 SDR	4,926,500 SDR
30,001–70,000t	40,000t×125 SDR	5,000,000 SDR
70,001– ?t	?t× 83 SDR	? SDR
		TOTAL LIMIT
		£?

Total fund available (Article 6(1)(a) and (b))

Tonnage Slices	Tons SDR Rate	SDR Total
0– 500t	[fixed slice]	500,000 SDR
501– 3,000t	2,500t×667 SDR	1,667,500 SDR
3,001–30,000t	27,000t×500 SDR	13,500,000 SDR
30,001–70,000t	40,000t×375 SDR	15,000,000 SDR
70,001– ?t	20,000t×250 SDR	? SDR
		TOTAL LIMIT
		£?

EXAMPLE 3

MIXED PERSONAL AND PROPERTY CLAIMS
1957 LIMITATION CONVENTION: THEORETICAL EXAMPLES

3(a) Correct calculation

Assume personal claims	4,100 g.f. per ton
property claims	2,000 g.f. per ton[9]
total claims	6,100 g.f. per ton

personal claimants obtain:

2,100 g.f. [that part reserved for personal claims, being the difference between 3,100 g.f. and 1,000 g.f.[10]

Unsatisfied personal claims   2,000 g.f.

Unsatisfied property claims   2,000 g.f.

Unsatisfied claims must share the 1,000 g.f. per ton[11] rateably:

Personal $\frac{2,000}{4,000} \times 1,000 = 500$ g.f.

Property $\frac{2,000}{4,000} \times 1,000 = 500$ g.f.

Result

Personal claimants receive [2,100 g.f. + 500 g.f.] = 2,600 g.f. per ton

i.e. 63.41% of claim

Property claimants receive   = 500 g.f. per ton

i.e. 25% of claim

3(b) Incorrect calculation: rateable allocation[12]

Assume personal claims	4,100 g.f. per ton
property claim	2,100 g.f. per ton
total claims	6,100 g.f per ton

---

[9] Gold francs are used because the calculation is easier to follow than that with SDR figures (273.34 SDR's and 133.34 SDR's respectively), although the principles are the same.

[10] *i.e.*, Table 1, Pts. Two and Three.

[11] See Table 1, Pt. Two.

[12] This example is illustrative *only* of what would happen *if* the total funds were to be allocated rateably between personal and property claimants. It does *not* represent the actual legal position under the Convention.

A rateable division would give the following results:

Personal $\dfrac{4,100}{6,100} \times 3,100$ g.f. $= 2,084$ g.f.

Property $\dfrac{2,000}{6,100} \times 3,100$ g.f. $= 1,016$ g.f.

Result

Personal claimants receive $\qquad = 2,084$ g.f.

i.e. 50.82% of claim

Property claimants receive $\qquad = 1,016$ g.f.

i.e. 50.8% of claim

EXAMPLE 4

MIXED PERSONAL AND PROPERTY CLAIMS:
1957 LIMITATION CONVENTION—STERLING EXAMPLES

4(a) Small personal and large property claims

Assume	personal claims	£200,000
	property claims	£1,000,000
	total	£1,200,000

10,000 (limitation) ton ship
Limit (total)   £1,573,879[13]

personal claimants obtain:

£200,000 [from the 140 SDR's (2,100 g.f.) reserved for personal claims[14]]
i.e. recover in full

property claimants obtain:

£507,720 [from the 66.67 SDR's (1,000 g.f.) available for property claims[15]]
i.e. bear own loss of £492,280

4(b) Equal personal and property claims

Assume	personal claims	£1,200,000
	property claims	£1,200,000
	total	£2,400,000

10,000 (limitation) ton ship
Limit (total)[16]   £1,573,879

personal claimants obtain:

£1,066,159 [the 140 SDR's (2,100 g.f.) reserved for personal claims[17]]

Unsatisfied personal claims	£133,841
Unsatisfied property claims	£1,200,000

Unsatisfied claims must share the 66.67 SDR's (1,000 g.f) per ton, *i.e.* £507,720, rateably:

---

[13] See Table 1, Pt. Three; and Table 3.
[14] *i.e.* £1,066,159, see Table 1, Pt. One.
[15] *i.e.* £507,720, see Table 1, Pt. Two; and Table 3.
[16] See Table 1, Pt. Three; and Table 3.
[17] See Table 1, Pt. One.

personal $\dfrac{133,841}{1,333,841} \times 507,720 = 50,946$

property $\dfrac{1,200,000}{1,333,841} \times 507,720 = 456,774$

Result

Personal claimants receive [£1,066,159 + £50,946] = £1,117,105

i.e. 93.09% of claim

Property claimants receive = £456,774

i.e. 38.04% of claim

EXAMPLE 5

MIXED PERSONAL AND PROPERTY CLAIMS: 1976 LIMITATION CONVENTION

Assume "personal" claims	£20,000,000
"other" claims	£20,000,000
total claims	£40,000,000

90,000 (limitation) ton ship	
Conversion date	January 17, 1986
Conversion rate 1 SDR=	£0.761542
Limit (total)[18]	£27,162,299

personal claimants obtain:

£18,211,515 [*i.e.* that sum reserved for personal claims[19]]

Unsatisfied personal claims   £1,788,485

Unsatisfied other claims   £20,000,000

Unsatisfied claims must share the 11,753,500 SDR figure[20], *i.e.* £8,950,784, rateably:

personal $\dfrac{1,788,485}{21,788,485} \times 8,950,784 = 734,716$

other $\dfrac{20,000,000}{21,784,485} \times 8,950,754 = 8,216,068$

Result

Personal claimants receive [£18,211,515+£734,716]=£19,946,231

i.e. 94.73% of claim

Other claimants receive   = £8,216,068

i.e. 41.08% of claim

---

[18] See Table 2, Pt. Three.

[19] See Example 2(a), *supra*, and Table 2, Pt. One.

[20] See Example 2(b), *supra*, and Table 2, Pt. Two.

EXAMPLE 6

SMALL SHIPS

6(a) 1957 Limitation Convention[21]

Assume personal claims	£50,000
property claims	£100,000
total claims	£150,000

250 (actual limitation) ton ship
Conversion date   January 17, 1986
Conversion rate   £0.761542
Limit (total)   £47,216[22]

personal claimants obtain:
£31,985 [the 140 SDR's (2,100 g.f.) reserved for personal claims[23]]
Unsatisfied personal claims   £18,015
Unsatisfied property claims   £100,000
Unsatisfied claims must share the 66.67 SDR (1,000 g.f.) per ton figure of £15,232[24], rateably:

personal $\dfrac{18,015}{118,015} \times 15,232 = 2,325$

property $\dfrac{100,000}{118,015} \times 15,232 = 12,907$

     Result

Personal claimants receive	[£31,985+£2,325]	=£34,310
	i.e. 68.62% of claim	
Property claimants receive		=£12,907
	i.e. 12.91% of claim	

---

[21] Note: (i) Personal claims alone   —300t minimum tonnage
           (ii) Property claims (alone)   —300t minimum tonnage
           (iii) Mixed claims   —300t minimum tonnage
[22] See Table 1, Pt. Three; and Table 3.
     300 (minimum tonnage)×206.67 SDR's (3,100 g.f.)=£47,216.
[23] See Table 1, Pt. One.[23]
[24] See Table 1, Pt. Two; and Table 3.

6(b) Merchant Shipping Act 1894, s.503[25]

Assume personal claims	£50,000
property claims	£100,000
total claims	£150,000

250 (limitation) ton ship	
Conversion date	January 17, 1986
Conversion rate	£0.761542
Limit (total)	£44,678[26]

personal claimants obtain:

£31,985 [the 140 SDR's (2,100 g.f.) reserved for personal claims[27]]

Unsatisfied personal claims	£18,015
Unsatisfied property claims	£100,000

Unsatisfied claims must share the 66.67 SDR's (1,000 g.f.) per ton figure of £12,693[28], rateably:

$$\text{personal} \quad \frac{18,015}{118,015} \times 12,693 = 1,938$$

$$\text{property} \quad \frac{100,000}{118,015} \times 12,693 = 10,755$$

Result

Personal claimants receive [£31,985+£1,938] =£33,923
i.e. 67.85% of claim

Property claimants receive =£10,755
i.e. 10.76% of claim

---

[25] Note: (i) Personal claim (alone) —300t minimum tonnage
(ii) Property claim (alone) —actual limitation tonnage
(iii) Mixed personal and property claims —Unclear whether as in Example 6(a), fn. 21 *supra*, or, as assumed here, with actual tonnage for the "property" figure.

[26] See Table 1, Pt. Three and Table 3.
300t×140   SDR's×£0.761542=£31,985
50t×66.67   SDR's×£0.761542=£12,693

£44,678

[27] See Table 1, Pt. One; and Table 3.
[28] See Table 1, Pt. Two; and Table 3.

6(c) Limitation Convention[29]

Assume personal claims of	£300,000
other claims of	£600,000
total claims of	£900,000

280 limitation) ton ship[30]	
Conversion date	January 17, 1986
Conversion rate	£0.761542
Limit (total)	£380,771[31]

personal claimants obtain:
£253,593 [the 333,000 SDR's reserved for personal claims[32]]
Unsatisfied personal claims   £46,407
Unsatisfied other claims   £600,000
Unsatisfied claims must share the 167,000 SDR's, *i.e.* £127,178[33], rateably:

personal $\dfrac{46,407}{646,407} \times 127,178 = \quad 9,130$

other $\dfrac{600,000}{646,407} \times 127,178 = 118,048$

  Results
Personal claimants receive [£253,593 + £9,130] = 262,723
                    i.e. 85.57% of claim
Other claimants receive   = £118,048
                    i.e. 19.67% of claim

---

[29] (i) Personal claims (alone)   —500t minimum tonnage
   (ii) Other claims (alone)   —500t minimum tonnage
   (iii) Mixed claims   —500t minimum tonnage.
[30] But under the Convention the minimum limit is, in effect, 500t.
[31] See Table 2, Pt. Three.
   500,000 SDR's × £0.761542 = £380,781.
[32] See Table 2, Pt. One.
[33] See Table 2, Pt. Two.

6(d) Merchant Shipping Act 1979[34]

Assume personal claims	£300,000
other claims	£600,000
total claims	£900,000

280 (limitation) ton ship[35]	
Conversion date	January 17, 1986
Conversion rate	£0.761542
Limit (total)	£190,386[36]

personal claimants obtain:

£126,924 [the 166,667 SDR's reserved for personal claims[37]]

Unsatisfied personal claims	£173,076
Unsatisfied other claims	£600,000

Unsatisfied claims must share the 83,333 SDR's, *i.e.* £63,462[38], rateably:

personal $\dfrac{173,076}{773,076} \times 63,462 = 14,208$

other $\dfrac{600,000}{773,076} \times 63,462 = 49,254$

   Result

Personal claimants receive [£126,924 + £14,208] = £141,132
                                                i.e. 47.04% of claim

Other claimants receive   = £49,254
                          i.e. 8.21% of claim

---

[34] (i) personal claims (alone)   = 166,667 SDR's
   (ii) other claims (alone)   = 83,333 SDR's
   (iii) mixed claims (alone)   = 250,000 SDR's

   Note that the calculation technique is the same as that under the 1976 Convention itself (see Example 6(c)). Thus:

   (1) for ships of 300–500t, the limits will be the same as those fixed under the Convention, but

   (2) for ships of 0–299t the United Kingdom limits are those given in (i)–(iii), above.

[35] But under the Convention the minimum limit is, in effect, 500t.

[36] See Table 2, Pt. Three.

   250,000 SDR's × £0.761542 = £190,386.

[37] See Table 2, Pt. One,

[38] See Table 2, Pt. Two.

EXAMPLE 7

Passenger Ship Limits

7(a) Royal Princess

Tonnage[39]
         44,348 grt
         19,646 nrt

Capacity   1,260 passengers
Conversion date   January 17, 1986
Conversion rate   £0.761542

(i) Athens Convention 1974 passenger limit
Maximum for each passenger 46,666 SDR's =   £35,538
Total Limit for owners (fully loaded):
 46,666 SDR's×1,260=58,799,160 SDR's

               =£44,778,029

(ii) 1976 Limitation Convention: Article 7 limit
46,666 SDR's×1,260 (theoretical Capacity)=58,799,160 SDR's
But maximum limit is 25,000,000 SDR's   =£19,038,550
 therefore, (assuming 1,260 equal claims),
 equivalent to £15,110 per passenger[40]
(iii) 1957 Limitation Convention: Total Limit[41]
 Limitation tonnage (estimated)[42]   33,837t
206.67 SDR's×33,837=6,993,093 SDR's = £5,325,534
 therefore, (assuming 1,260 equal claims),
 equivalent to £4,227 per passenger[43]
(iv) 1976 Limitation Convention: Article 6 Total Limit[44]
 Limitation Tonnage   44,348t
 [fixed slice]   500,000 SDR's
2,500t×667 SDR's= 1,667,500 SDR's
27,000t×500 SDR's= 13,500,000 SDR's
14,348t×375 SDR's= 5,380,500 SDR's
        ——————
    21,048,000 SDR's   =£16,028,936

---

[39] Assumed to be UMS tonnages under the 1969 Tonnage Convention.
[40] The total of £19,038,550 would be available if only one passenger was a casualty.
[41] 206.67 SDR's per ton, see Table 1, Pt. Three.
[42] Assuming that OMS and UMS tonnages would be broadly comparable (but see Tonnage Measurement, pp.44–49):
 19,646 (nrt)
 14,191t(32% of grt)
 ——————
 33,837t
 ——————

[43] The total fund of £5,325,534 would have to be shared with other personal and/or property claimants.
[44] See Table 2, Pt. Three and Example 2. These limits are not strictly relevant to passengers, but are included to give some overall idea of the exposure of the shipowner.

7(b) Mikhail Lermontov

Tonnage[45]	20,352 grt
	10,740 nrt
Capacity	700 passengers
Actually carrying	409 passengers[46]
Conversion date	January 17, 1986
Conversion rate	£0.761542

(i) Athens Convention 1974 passenger limit

Maximum for each passenger 46,666 SDR's $=$ £35,538

Total Limit for owners (as actually loaded)$=$
46,666 SDR's$\times$409$=$21,746,356 SDR's

$=$£14,535,090

(ii) 1976 Limitation Convention: Article 7 limit
46,666 SDR's$\times$700 (theoretical capacity)$=$32,666,200 SDR's
But maximum limit is 25,000,000 SDR's $=$£19,038,550
therefore, (assuming 409 equal claims),
equivalent to £46,549 per passenger[47]

(iii) 1957 Limitation Convention: Total Limit[48]

Limitation tonnage (estimated)[49] 17,253t

206.67 SDR's$\times$17,253$=$3,356,678 SDR's $=$£2,715,414
therefore, (assuming 409 equal claims),
equivalent to £6,639 per passenger[50]

(iv) 1976 Limitation Convention: Article 6 Total Limit[51]

Limitation Tonnage (estimated)[52] 20,352t

[fixed slice]	500,000 SDR's	
2,500t$\times$667 SDR's$=$	1,667,500 SDR's	
17,351t$\times$500 SDR's$=$	8,675,500 SDR's	
	10,843,000 SDR's	$=$£8,257,400

---

[45] Assumed to be OMS tonnages.

[46] And 330 crew. Figures from contemporary reports after her sinking on February 16, 1986. See p. 54, n. 10, *supra*.

[47] The total of £19,038,550 would be available if there was only one passenger claimant.

[48] 206.67 SDR's per ton, see Table 1, Pt. Three.

[49] See Tonnage Measurement, pp. 40–44, *supra*. Estimated on the following basis:
10,740t(nrt)
6,513t (32% of grt)

17,253t

---

[50] The total fund of £2,715,414 would have to be shared with other personal and/or property claimants.

[51] See Table 2, Pt. Three and Example 2. These limits are not strictly relevant to passengers, but are included to give some overall idea of the exposure of the shipowner.

[52] On the basis that the OMS and UMS gross tonnages are broadly similar, see, *e.g.* the passenger ships in Table 4(b).

7(c) Queen Elizabeth II

Tonnage[53]	67,140 grt
	37,218 nrt
Capacity	1,740 passengers
Conversion date	January 17, 1986
Conversion rate	£0.761542

(i) Athens Convention 1974 passenger limit

Maximum for each passenger 46,666 SDR's   =   £35,538

Total Limit for owners (fully loaded)=
46,666 SDR's×1,740=81,198,840 SDR's

$$=£61,836,327$$

(ii) 1976 Limitation Convention: Article 7 limit

46,666 SDR's×1,260 (theoretical Capacity)=81,198,840 SDR's

But maximum limit is 25,000,000 SDR's   £19,038,550

therefore, (assuming 1,740 equal claims),
equivalent to £10,942 per passenger[54]

(iii) 1957 Limitation Convention: Total Limit[55]

Limitation tonnage (estimated)[56]   58,703t

206.67 SDR's×58,703=12,132,149 SDR's   =£9,239,141

therefore, (assuming 1,740 equal claims),
equivalent to £5,310 per passenger[57]

(iv) 1976 Limitation Convention: Article 6 Total Limit[58]

Limitation Tonnage (estimated)[59]   67,140t

[fixed slice]	500,000 SDR's	
2,500t×667 SDR's=	1,667,500 SDR's	
27,000t×500 SDR's=	13,500,000 SDR's	
37,139t×375 SDR's=	13,927,125 SDR's	
	29,594,625 SDR's	=£22,537,549

---

[53] Assumed to be OMS tonnages.

[54] The total of £19,038,550 would be available if there was only one passenger claimant.

[55] 206.67 SDR's per ton, see Table 1, Pt. III.

[56] See Tonnage Measurement, pp. 40–44, *supra.* Estimated on the basis that:
37,218t(nrt)
21,485t(32% of grt)

58,703t

[57] The total fund of £9,239,141 would have to be shared with other personal and/or property claimants.

[58] See Table 2, Pt. Three and Example 2. These limits are not strictly relevant to passengers, but are included to give some overall idea of the exposure of the shipowner.

[59] On the basis that the OMS and UMS gross tonnages are broadly similar, see, *e.g.* the passenger ships in Table 4(b).

7(d) Comparison of Article 6 and Article 7 Limits of 1976 Limitation Convention:
Queen Elizabeth II

(i) Collision

Passenger claims	£19,000,000
Third party personal claims	£25,000,000
No other claims	
Article 7 limit[60]	£19,038,550
therefore passenger claims satisfied in full	
Article 6 limit[61]	£22,537,549

therefore third party personal claimants
must share this amount rateably

(ii) Foundering

Passenger claims	£20,000,000
No third party personal or property claims	
Article 7 limit[62]	£19,038,550
therefore passenger claims satisfied in full	
Article 6 limit[63]	£22,537,549

therefore persons on board who are not
"passengers"[64] could share this amount

---

[60] See Example 7(c).
[61] *Ibid.*
[62] *Ibid.*
[63] *Ibid.*
[64] See 3(7) Passengers.

EXAMPLE 8

COUNTERCLAIMS

8(a) Incorrect method: claims limited separately

Assume a collision where:
Ship A (1,000 limitation tons) suffers £400,000 property damage
Ship B (10,000 limitation tons) suffers £800,000 property damage

Liability apportioned:

Ship A—50% to blame
Ship B—50% to blame

1976 Limitation Convention limits[65]:

Ship A— £190,766
Ship B—£1,335,364

(i)	A claims 50% of its damage from B	=£200,000
	B's limit is £1,335,364, so A recovers in full	=£200,000
(ii)	B claims 50% of its damage from A	=£400,000
	A's limit is £190,766, so B recovers only	£190,766
	Result	
	B pays A [£200,000−£190,766]	£9,834

8(b) Correct method: claims set off before limitation

Assume a collision where:
Ship A (1,000 limitation tons) suffers £400,000 property damage
Ship B (10,000 limitation tons) suffers £800,000 property damage

Liability apportioned:

Ship A—50% to blame
Ship B—50% to blame

1976 Limitation Convention limits[66]:

Ship A— £190,766
Ship B—£1,335,364

(i)	A claims 50% of its damage from B	=£200,000
(ii)	B claims 50% of its damage from A	=£400,000
(iii)	Therefore net claim by B for [£400,000−£200,000]	=£200,000
(iv)	A limits liability to	=£190,766
	Result	
	A pays B	£190,766

[65] See Table 2, Pt. Two; and Table 3.
[66] *Ibid.*

101

IV

The Loss of The Right to Limit

Professor Robert Grime*

1. THE DEMISE OF ACTUAL FAULT OR PRIVITY

For as long as global limitation of liability has been permitted to British shipowners, it has been subject to the qualification that it be not available if the loss was in some direct way the fault of the defendant shipowner (or other entitled to limit). For the last 130 years, that principle has been expressed by requiring that the loss should take place "without the actual fault or privity" of the shipowner. The only exception to that requirement has been the provision of Article 6(3) of the 1957 Limitation Convention that limitation be allowed to masters or members of the crew "even if the occurrence . . . resulted from the actual fault or privity of one or more of such persons." This was translated into legislation in the United Kingdom by the Merchant Shipping (Liability of Shipowners and Others) Act 1958, s.3 as "notwithstanding his actual fault or privity in that capacity." The last three words have given rise to some problems.[1]

---

* Institute of Maritime Law, Southampton University

[1] The phrase "in that capacity" in s.3 has no correspondent in the Convention. In *Coldwell-Horsfall* v. *West Country Yacht Charters Ltd, The Annie Hay* [1968] 1 Lloyd's Rep. 141, Brandon J held that when the owner of a motor launch made it available as a patrol boat for the use of officials during a power boat race off Falmouth and while navigating it for that purpose negligently struck and sank a larger motor-cruiser, he could limit liability, since his navigational fault arose in his capacity as master, not owner, of his vessel. In this, the English Admiralty Court reached a conclusion different from that reached by the Exchequer Court of the New Brunswick Admiralty District in *The Gloucester No. 26* [1964] 2 Lloyd's Rep. 554 where on similar facts it was held that an owner/skipper could not avail himself of the exemption from the actual fault or privity rule if he was sued as owner. The 1961 amendment to the Canadian Navigation Act, passed to give effect to the 1957 Convention, does not contain the additional phrase "in that capacity". In *The Alastor* [1981] 1 Lloyd's Rep. 581 the English Court of Appeal applied the reasoning of *The Annie Hay* to an owner who carried out the maintenance of his yacht so negligently that the engine controls failed and a collision occurred. So long as the owner was acting in a crew member's capacity when the fault occurred, he could limit liability despite his apparent "actual fault or privity". Clearly, without the added words, the Convention would equally well support the "procedural" analysis—that the exemption from the actual fault or privity rule is available only to a defendant sued as a master or crew member.

Article 4 of the 1976 Convention replaces this tried formula with a new phrase:

"A person liable shall not be entitled to limit liability if it is proved that the loss resulted from his personal act or omission committed with intent to cause such loss or recklessly with knowledge that such loss would probably result."

The background to this change is described elsewhere.[2] It may be an over-simplification to regard it as a *quid pro quo* for higher limits, but it can be said that the interpretation of "actual fault or privity," particularly in North American jurisdictions, had rendered it relatively easy to "break" limitation.[3] The new formulation is clearly protective of defendant shipowners.

The form of words was used in Article 13(1) of the Athens Convention on the Carriage of Passengers and Their Luggage in 1974, a document which loomed large in the debate on the Limitation Convention. Before the Athens Convention, a similar formulation had appeared in 1955 in the Hague Protocol to the Warsaw Convention on Carriage by Air where it serves the same function. Similar language is also used in the Hamburg Rules.[4]

When the formulation was introduced to the Warsaw Convention by the 1955 Hague Protocol, the task before the Conference had been particular. The words in the French text of the original Warsaw Convention were "dol ou d'une faute qui . . . est considerée comme équivalente au dol." "Wilful misconduct or such default as is . . . considered to be equivalent to wilful misconduct" had been offered as an English translation but over the years that had not achieved universal respect.[5] The debate centred on the question of whether the French or the English term did or did not import a degree of malice or otherwise wrongful activity in addition to knowledge of the consequences of one's actions, together with willingness to see those consequences carried through. There were many views and little international comity.[6]

Thus the language of the Hague Protocol to the Warsaw Convention was intended to clarify a situation very different from that currently existing in the limitation of maritime claims. The words "actual fault or privity" do not raise any questions with

[2] See Chap. 1.
[3] See Chaps. 9, 19.
[4] United Nations Convention on the Carriage of Goods by Sea, 1978, Art. 8.
[5] As it stands the second part of the formulation has no clear meaning. The Irish text, by translating "dol" as "malice" obtains a comprehensible result, but perhaps a narrower rule.
[6] For French commentators the question was whether the formulation included the French concept of "faute lourde", or gross negligence, which might involve a level of malice or moral reprehensibility. See generally, *Shawcross & Beaumont on Air Law*, (4th ed.), Chap. 7, p. 210. The case law has also been confused.

regard to malice or reprehensible conduct. "Fault" does not necessarily imply bad behaviour: that is to say, in legal terms, the purposive breach of some generally binding obligation. It can also encompass carelessness, lapse of attention, or simple inefficiency. Nor was there a problem with regard to knowledge of the consequences.

Although "privity" may in many cases be satisfied by proof of the knowledge of the shipowner of the fault of others, it does not seem ever to have been suggested that knowledge of the consequences of that fault is a necessary part of "privity." And, of course, fault or privity are alternative grounds for breaking limitation. So non-malicious, non-reprehensible inattention without giving thought to the morrow did not present a problem in maritime law. It could provide grounds for breaking limitation.

So what was used in 1955 to clarify an existing position and to deal with problems that have never arisen at sea was adopted in 1976 to introduce a radical change. In this context it would seem less than usually useful to examine the case law surrounding the forerunner to the new formulation. Nevertheless, if we are to offer opinion on the meaning of "personal act or omission committed with intent to cause such loss or recklessly and with knowledge that such loss will probably result," then we must in part look to that authority. The formulation will be taken phrase by phrase.

2. PERSONAL ACT OR OMISSION

Article 4 of the 1976 Convention speaks of the "*personal* act or omission" of the person otherwise entitled to limit liability. In so doing it immediately parts company with its forebears[7] which speak of "act or omission" simply. In the case of the Warsaw Convention on Carriage by Air the reason is clear. In that Convention, the carrier is made liable for the fault or neglect of his servants or agents and equally loses the right to limit if either he or they commits an act or omission with the requisite intent or recklessness.[8] Under the Athens Convention for the Carriage of Passengers and their Luggage by Sea, 1974 the situation is a little more complicated. As in the Warsaw Convention, the carrier is made liable for the fault or neglect of his servants or agents[9] but the right to limit is lost only when the carrier commits an act or

---

[7] See the Athens Convention 1974, Art. 7, Hague Protocol to Warsaw Convention 1955, Art. 25. See also Hamburg Rules 1978, Art. 8.
[8] Art. 25 states this in terms.
[9] Art. 3(1).

omission within the definition.[10] It might, however, be expected that the more general phraseology of the description of conduct barring limitation could be interpreted so as to include some at least of the range of acts or omissions which were not strictly the act of the person otherwise entitled to limit, but for which that person was legally responsible.

The 1976 Convention adopts a third position. It contains no provision affecting the vicarious liability of the shipowner for the fault of those in his employ.[11] That is left to be decided by the general principles of the law applicable to the claim. The right to limit is not, however, to be lost on proof of a reckless or intentional act or omission on the part of a servant or agent. The use of the word "personal" strongly reinforces this. In this, the Convention appears to be maintaining in general terms a position adopted with regard to maritime claims under the previous law. Put simply, the old language ("actual fault") would permit limitation of claims founded on vicarious liability, but rarely when direct liability was established. As Viscount Haldane once said, the words imported: "something personal to the owner, something blameworthy in him, as distinguished from constructive fault . . . such as the fault . . . of his servants or agents."[12]

There seems little doubt, then, that the words "personal act or omission" were introduced with the intention of effecting a result not dissimilar from that achieved by the use of the words "actual fault." The question is, therefore, what acts or omissions were accounted the "actual fault" of the shipowners (invariably a company) under the old law, and how far those conclusions would be altered when the new formulation "personal act or omission" is applied.

The leading case on the point is the *Lennards Carrying Co* case and the phrase used therein is *"alter ego."*[13] That phrase was particularly apt to the facts of the case, since the fault was that of Mr. Lennard and Lennards Carrying Co Ltd was in every practical

---

[10] Art. 13. The article does not even in its terms cover its "performing carriers" who may effect the carriage on behalf of the contracting carrier. By Art. 11, a servant or agent, if sued personally may "avail himself of the defences and limits of liability which the carrier or the performing carrier is entitled to invoke."

[11] Art. 1 describes those entitled to limit liability, including under Art. 1(4) "any person for whose act, neglect or default the shipowner . . . is responsible." Compare this formulation with that in Art. 3 of the 1957 Convention. App. A, p. 293, and fn. 1, *supra*.

[12] In *Lennards Carrying Co Ltd* v. *Asiatic Petroleum Co Ltd* [1915] A.C. 705.

[13] *Ibid.* Viscount Haldane, who gave the only speech, said at p. 715 "I should be inclined to think there was enough known about Lennard to show that, to use the appellant's learned counsel's own phrase, he was the *alter ego* company. He was a director of the company. I can quite conceive that a company may by entrusting its business to one director be as truly represented by that one director as, in ordinary cases, it is represented by the whole board."

sense a "one man" company. The *alter ego* analysis has been, as is well known, devastatingly attacked by Lord Reid in *Tesco Supermarkets* v. *Nattrass*,[14] a case which might be regarded as the leading modern authority on the criminal liability of corporations. Lord Reid's memorable comment was: "the person who speaks and acts as the company is not *alter*. He is identified with the company."

If we are to adopt Lord Reid's approach we must then ask who speaks and acts as the company in actual fault or privity cases. The matter has received attention on several occasions. Three cases are of particular significance: *The Lady Gwendolen*[15]; *The Garden City*[16]; *The Marion*.[17]

In the *Lady Gwendolen* the collision was caused by a vessel owned by Arthur Guinness & Co proceeding at too high a speed through fog. The Court of Appeal held that the collision had not occurred without actual fault on the part of the owners. The fault which effectively caused the collision was in the management of the navigation—*i.e.* in the control and instruction of Captain Meredith, the Master, in terms of speed and the use of radar—a notion to which we shall return.

The owners were brewers of stout and had in truth delegated the management of the navigation of their ships to Mr. Robbie, their Marine Superintendent. He reported to Mr. Boucher, the Traffic Manager, whose expertise lay with railway trains. Mr. Boucher reported to Mr. Williams, the Assistant Managing Director, a member of the Board who was in origin a Chief Brewer.

Where did fault lie? Clearly with Mr. Robbie. Possibly also with Mr. Boucher. Less easily with Mr. Williams.

In the Court of Appeal, Willmer, LJ, at least, was prepared to hold that the fault of Mr. Boucher was the fault of the Company[18] although all agreed that fault could be found at Board level (that is to say with Mr. Williams). There is also support to be found for two further propositions:

(a) That he who speaks and acts for the company need not be a board member[19]; and

(b) That delegation of obligation may either of itself amount to a fault, if improperly made, or it may make the fault of the person to whom the delegation has been properly made the "*alter ego*," whose fault is the fault of the company.[20]

The Garden City also concerned excessive speed in fog. The

---

[14] [1972] A.C. 153, at p. 174.
[15] [1965] 2 All E.R. 283.
[16] [1982] 2 Lloyd's Rep. 382.
[17] [1983] 2 Lloyd's Rep. 156 (CA); [1984] 2 Lloyd's Rep. 1 (H.L.).
[18] [1965] 2 All E.R., at p. 295 H.
[19] [1965] 2 All E.R., at pp. 295 A (Willmer L.J.), 303 B (Winn L.J.).
[20] See particularly the judgment of Willmer L.J., *passim*.

vessel in question, the *Zaglebie Dabrowski*, was owned by Polsteam, the Polish State shipowning organisation. The faults alleged were in essence similar to those alleged in *The Lady Gwendolen*: failure to check on the navigational habits of the master of the vessel. The Chief Navigator of Polsteam—a post somewhat similar to the post of Marine Superintendent in English practice—was at fault, but Staughton J held that his fault was not the fault of Polsteam. The duties he carried out, negligently, had been delegated to him. The only relevant issue was whether the system of management adopted by the Director of Technical and Investment Affairs, including that delegation, was faulty. It was not, and there was no actual fault on the part of Polsteam.[21]

Thus it would seem that the decision in the *Garden City* would support the view that where authority has been delegated, there can only be actual fault if the system of delegation was itself a faulty one. The negligence of the delegate would not of itself amount to actual fault of the delegator.

There was however one further point in the *Lady Gwendolen*. Willmer LJ pointed out that Mr. Boucher was the registered ship's manager.[22] If the formal legal managership of a vessel is handed to an·identifiable person, it may be argued that the fault of that person must be the actual fault of the owner. The delegate is, as it were, the statutory *alter ego* of the company. In taking this point, Willmer LJ appeared to affirm a decision of Hill, J in *The Charlotte*,[23] where the management of a ship had been delegated by its owners, a company, to a managing partnership. Fault by those partners was held the actual fault of the owners.

This same proposition, that the fault of an identifiable person to whom the management of a ship had been wholly delegated amounted to the actual fault of the owners, was accepted, apparently without argument, in *The Marion*.[24] In this case management of the ship had been carried on by a separate company: the attention of the court was shifted from the owning company to the managing company.

To sum up, it would seem that the "actual fault" of a shipowning company included: a fault brought home to the Board of Directors; the fault of a proven "*alter ego*," who need not be a Board member; and the fault of a person, partnership or company which is either a registered ship's manager or to whom management has been wholly delegated. Faults of others will not be the

---

[21] [1982] 2 Lloyd's Rep. 382.
[22] [1965] 2 All E.R. at p. 295 B: Willmer L.J. was presumably referring to a "ship's husband" under s.59(2) of the Merchant Shipping Act 1984.
[23] (1921) 9 Lloyd's Rep. 341.
[24] [1983] 2 Lloyd's Rep. 156 (CA); [1984] 2 Lloyd's Rep. 1 (HL). There could be no question of the management company being a registered ship's husband under the Merchant Shipping Act since the vessel was Liberian registered.

actual fault of the company, but if the delegation of responsibility to another was improper, faulty or not sufficiently supervised, then the act of delegation might itself be accounted the actual fault of the shipowning company.

What effect will the change to "personal act or omission" have?

First, the voice of the company must be more tightly identified. If anything of the "*alter ego*" theory survived the *Nattrass* decision, then it cannot survive "personal act." In ordinary language, the word "personal" must import the act of the person, in this case the legal person, itself. The occasions when fault outside the board-room is held to be the fault of a company may be few. The occasions when such fault can be held to be the personal act of the company must be many fewer.

It also follows that there can be no room for two interpretations of the significance of delegation. If duties have been delegated, the only personal act which is relevant must be the act of delegation. The fault of the delegate cannot be significant. This must be true even on the narrow facts of *The Charlotte* and *The Lady Gwendolen*, where there is a registered ship's husband, as it is on the wider formulation assumed in *The Marion*. If the management of a ship has been delegated to a managing partnership or company, the fault of that company or partnership cannot be the personal act of the owner. It follows from this that an owner can never have limitation broken in a case of fault in navigation if the management of the vessel has been properly delegated to apparently competent managers.

Since in practice fault in the management of navigation is a fault most commonly alleged in the context of the breaking of limitation, and since the modern practice largely supports the employment of professional ship managing companies, it would seem that the practical consequence of the shift from actual fault to personal act is to make limitation safer.

3. THE DISAPPEARANCE OF PRIVITY

If "personal act or omission" is different from and narrower than "actual fault," what is the significance of the dropping of the "privity" of the shipowner as an alternative ground for breaking limitation?

The central and most compelling case of privity to the fault of another must be the circumstance when the owner of a vessel has connived at the faulty operation of the vessel by the master or other member of the crew. But the word in its dictionary definition does not have the connotation of connivance. To be privy to another's action means to have private knowledge of it, to be in the secret. Thus "privity" in the phrase "actual fault or privity" needs to mean no more than that the shipowner was aware of the fault. The argument inevitably centres on the extent to which it is proper to take an objective view of such knowledge. Will a shipowner be held privy to a fault of which he ought to have known or of which he wilfully failed to take notice? As Lord Denning put it in the leading case of *The Eurysthenes*[25]:

"When I speak of knowledge, I mean not only positive knowledge, but also that sort of knowledge expressed in the phrase 'turning a blind eye.' If a man, suspicious of the truth, turns a blind eye to it, and refrains from enquiry—so that he should not know of it for certain—then he is to be regarded as knowing the truth. This 'turning a blind eye' is far more blameworthy than mere negligence. Negligence in not knowing the truth is not equivalent to knowledge of it."

The word "privity" would seem of itself to provide few opportunities to break limitation. Even objectively construed to the extent allowed by Lord Denning, it is hard to see how the factual circumstances which amount to privity would not also usually amount to fault. An owner who knew of or who wilfully shut his eyes to a fault must run the risk of being held actually at fault himself as well as privy to the fault of others. Knowledge of poor practice usually implies an omission to do something about it. There is left only the unusual circumstance when the owner is made aware of the failing on the part of the master or member of the crew and it is unreasonable to expect the owner to do anything about it. Such bare knowledge would make him privy to the fault of another without himself being at fault.

The new formulation, "personal act or omission," cannot include cases of mere knowledge of the fault of others. A failure to act by the owner may however amount to a "personal omission" but it cannot have been intended to cover such cases when there is no legal power to act and when it is not reasonable to expect action. Inaction in such circumstances can hardly be described as an "omission." It must also be remembered that in such cases the requisite intent or degree of recklessness must also be proved.

4. THE INTRODUCTION OF INTENTION AND RECKLESSNESS

The most significant change in this area of the law wrought by the 1976 Convention is the introduction that the "personal act or

[25] *Compania Maritima San Basilia SA* v. *The Oceanus Mutual Underwriting Association (Bermuda) Ltd, The Eurysthenes* [1976] 3 All E.R. 243, at p. 251 F. The case concerned the application of s.39(5) of the Marine Insurance Act 1906 implying into contracts of marine insurance for time policies a warranty that the vessel be not sent to sea in an unseaworthy state with the privity of the assured. However the Court of Appeal drew the analogy in the use of the word "privity" with limitation.

omission" be committed "with intent to cause such loss or recklessly with knowledge that such loss would probably result." This is clearly narrower than "actual fault or privity" in two respects. First, it specifies in precise terms the mental element which must be proved of the person entitled to limit. Second, it applies that mental element—intention or recklessness—not to the negligent act but to the consequences, that is to say the loss ensuing. This too may be regarded as narrowing the circumstances in which the right to limit may be lost since it is entirely possible that a person may intend or be reckless about the act but be legitimately neutral about the consequences of that act.

There is little authority from the private law on these words. They have their most obvious use in the criminal law.

Intention received much attention from the Law Commission in its Report on the Mental Element in Crime.[26] That report gave rise to a Draft Criminal Liability (Mental Element) Bill which proposed a test of intention which contained two elements: that the propositus intend to produce the result or have no substantial doubt that the result in question would ensue. However the need to spend much time on the possible objective extension of "intention" is avoided when, as here, recklessness with regard to the result is also expressly included.

Recklessness has been the subject of close attention by the HL in two criminal cases. R. v. Stephenson[27] offered a definition which concentrated on an appreciation of a risk of damage resulting from the act and an unreasonable decision to take that risk. In Metropolitan Police Commissioner v. Caldwell[28] however, Lord Diplock in the House of Lords would have included within the designation "reckless" those who fail to give thought to the possible consequences of their acts.

Much of this may be obviated by the particular formulation of the requirement adopted in the 1976 Convention. Recklessness, in terms of Article 4 also requires that the actor has "knowledge that such loss would probably result." It would seem to follow that the person who acted in even unreasonable ignorance of a risk of loss would not be deprived of the right to limit. This analysis would seem to be supported by a decision of the Court of Appeal in Goldman v. Thai Airlines[29] which concerned a piece of deliberate risk-taking involving flying a passenger aeroplane through an area of clear air turbulence without illuminating the "fasten seat belts" sign. It was accepted that the test of knowledge was subjective and that it was not sufficient to show that another, perhaps more

---

[26] Law Commission Report No. 89 (1978).
[27] [1979] Q.B. 695 (CA).
[28] [1982] A.C. 341 (HL).
[29] [1983] 3 All E.R. 693.

reasonable, pilot, would have considered the consequences.[30] The provision of Article 25 of the Warsaw Convention is, as we have seen, similar to the provision of the 1976 Convention.

In one respect, however, these provisions differ. The Warsaw Convention requires intention or recklessness with regard to "damage." The 1976 Convention speaks of "such loss." It would seem likely that the right to limit is not lost under the 1976 Convention simply because the person otherwise entitled to limit was aware of the risk of some damaging consequences if the result that actually occurred was not considered.[31]

The formulation of intent and recklessness contained in Article 4 of the 1976 Convention would seem to produce a result extremely favourable to limitation. There is good grounds for the view that the test is subjective and in its own terms requires proof of a degree of knowledge which is likely to be difficult to establish.

5. BURDEN OF PROOF

Under the old law the burden of proof lay upon the person seeking to establish the right to limit. So it was the defendant shipowner who had to establish that the loss occurred without his actual fault or privity.[32] There seems no doubt that in its terms the 1976 Convention places the burden of proof on the other side. In practice this may turn out to be the most significant change. Many cases have failed on burden of proof in the past.[33]

6. INSURANCE

Finally it should be noted that there is a close connection between

---

[30] See *per* Eveleigh J, at p. 699 d. It should be pointed out that there is some variation in the interpretation of this provision of the Warsaw Convention. See *Shawcross and Beaumont on Air Law, op. cit.*, at p. 132. All but France would appear to tend to a subjective analysis.

[31] *Goldman* v. *Thai International Airlines* [1983] 3 All E.R. 693. The Court of Appeal reached the opposite conclusion in a case involving the Warsaw Convention.

[32] Although the Convention is neutral on the point—*e.g.* Art. 1 of the 1957 Convention states simply that "the owner of a seagoing ship may limit his liability . . . unless the occurrence . . . resulted from the actual fault or privity of the owner"—the UK statutes have always been clear. s.503 of the Merchant Shipping Act 1894 states "The owners of a ship . . . shall not, where all or any of the following occurrences take place without their actual fault or privity . . . be liable . . . " This formulation was not altered by the Merchant Shipping (Liability of shipowners and Others) Act 1958, which gave effect to the 1957 Convention.

[33] *Lennards Carrying Co Ltd* v. *Asiatic Petroleum Co Ltd* [1915] AC 705, *The Charlotte* (1921) 9 Lloyd's Rep. 341, *The Lady Gwendolen* [1965] 2 All E.R. 283 are all cases decided on the burden of proof: in all the court concluded that the defendant to the damage claim had failed sufficiently to demonstrate that loss occurred "without his actual fault or privity" without deciding what degree of fault or privity had to be established. Hence the unsatisfactory nature of the authority for analytical purposes.

the loss of the right to limit and the operation of the so-called "warranty of seaworthiness" in policies of marine insurance. Most vessels are insured under time policies on their hull and machinery and are entered in Protection and Indemnity Associations, which membership is also treated as a time policy.[34] Liabilities in respect of collisions and other occurrences which may give rise to limitable claims are split between the two.[35] For time policies the matter is governed by section 39(5) of the Marine Insurance Act 1906, which enacts " . . . where, with the privity of the assured, a ship is sent to sea in an unseaworthy state, the insurer is not liable for any loss attributable to unseaworthiness."[36] Where the unseaworthiness relates to a fault in the navigation or management of the vessel, such as poor maintenance or inadequate manning, if limitation is broken under the "actual fault or privity" regime, it is possible that the underwriters might repudiate liability under section 39(5). The fault which led to the breaking of limitation might amount to unseaworthiness up to which the owner was privy for the purpose of that section. That indeed was the case in *The Eurysthenes*.[37]

With the abandonment of the word "privity" such obvious overlap has disappeared. Although there may now be many more cases in which section 39(5) could be used by underwriters unwilling to pay in which the shipowner will still be able to limit liability, there will be very few in which limitation is broken under the 1976 Convention where section 39(5) will not apply. If a shipowner is guilty of a personal act or omission committed with intention or recklessness in respect of the navigation or management of his ship, it is hard to see how he could not also be "privy" to its consequential unseaworthy state.

[34] This was the first point decided by the Court of Appeal in *The Eurysthenes* [1976] 3 All E.R. 243. See generally Chap. 9 on insurance.

[35] Generally the hull and machinery policy covers ship-to-ship collision liabilities up to $\frac{3}{4}$ of the insured value of the vessel and the P & I Club covers the balance of such claims, cargo claims, personal injury claims, contact with fixed and floating objects, wreck-raising costs and much else besides. Other regimes are of course possible.

[36] Voyage policies, which are rarer than time policies, and almost unheard of for P & I risks, contain a warranty that the ship be seaworthy at the commencement of the voyage. Such policies may contain clauses reducing the absolute nature of the warranty.

[37] [1976] 3 All E.R. 243.

V

Practice and Procedure

1. INTRODUCTION

Limitation of a Shipowner's Liability is an esoteric subject familiar only to a small band of maritime lawyers. The practising solicitor whose client has an apparently good recoverable claim may be forgiven his bewilderment when faced with a pleaded defence of limitation of liability or, worse still, service of a writ in a limitation action. In an era of so called consumer rights and the widespread notion that if you have suffered loss or damage, there must be somebody you can sue, the notion of statutory protection of rich shipowners seems strange. But such notions, like general average, are the stuff of which marine insurance law is made, namely the sharing of the risks of the unexpected, and the losses suffered when an unexpected risk becomes a reality.

Any reader of this volume who has penetrated thus far must have a genuine interest in such intricacies and, by now at least, some notion of the rationale behind limitation of a shipowner's liability. This paper, written by a solicitor practising in the field of admiralty law in England, will, of necessity, assume that measure of familiarity with the general concepts to permit a rewarding study of the practical effects of the 1976 Convention.

With two noteworthy exceptions, the 1976 Convention is not yet in force and the comments which follow are therefore to some extent conjecture. No amendments to the Rules of the Supreme Court have yet been published to give effect to the workings of the 1976 Convention, although it is understood that the Admiralty Registrar and his colleagues are already working on this.[1]

The most noteworthy circumstance in which the 1976 Convention has come into force is its incorporation into the 1980 edition of Lloyd's Form of Salvage Agreement (No cure—No pay). The draftsmen of this revision of Lloyd's Form, led by Mr Gerald Darling, Q.C., introduced a number of bold innovations, the most notable being the "safety net" provisions whereby the salvor of a laden tanker can recover his expenses plus a reasonable profit

---

* Solicitor, Partner, Messrs. Shaw and Croft.
[1] O.S.C., p. 158.

margin, even if the casualty is not successfully salved. Clause 21 of the 1980 edition also provides, however:–

> "21. The Contractor shall be entitled to limit any liability to the Owners of the subject vessel and/or her cargo bunkers and stores which he and/or his Servants and/or Agents may incur in and about the services in the manner and to the extent provided by English Law and as if the provisions of the Convention on Limitation of Liability for Maritime Claims 1976 were part of the law of England."

It is believed that at the time of writing[2] no salvor has found himself in a position requiring him to invoke the provisions of this clause. This is probably just as well since the procedural rules to give effect to the provisions of the 1976 Convention have not yet been published and the salvage arbitrator hearing such a case might thus be forced to make up his own.

A second notable exception is the domestic law of Japan where the provisions of the 1976 Convention are already in force. Thus in cases where no non-Japanese parties are concerned, it is understood that the Convention will be applied. What happens where foreigners bring claims which are submitted to the Japanese Courts appears still to be uncertain.[3]

2. PRINCIPAL CHANGES

The principal changes brought about by the 1976 Convention compared with previous limitation regimes are twofold, namely:–
- (a) Increased limitation funds.
- (b) It will be much more difficult to defeat the owners' right to limit.

To the practitioner these developments will be doubly welcome. The decisions in *The Lady Gwendolen*[4] and *The Marion*[5] have cast considerable doubts on the extent to which an independent shipowner trading for profit (as distinct from a major public shipowning corporation or a state owned company) will ever succeed in limiting his liability. An English solicitor may be forgiven some twinge of regret as he is forced to advise clients against agreeing to English jurisdiction if there is a serious risk that he will need to invoke limitation of liability. The result is that, unselfishly, he will recommend the client to bring proceedings in Germany, Netherlands or France where the "fault or privity" requirements of the 1957 Limitation Convention are more liberally interpreted.

[2] August 1985.
[3] See further, Chapter 16, *infra*.
[4] [1965] 1 Lloyd's Rep. 335; [1965] P. 294.
[5] [1984] 2 Lloyd's Rep. 1.

However correct may have been the principles applied by the House of Lords in *The Marion*, those principles are not easy to apply in the heat of the busy hours following a major casualty, when strategic decisions as to choice of jurisdiction have to be made. No legal advisor will now give confident advice as to the right to limit without a detailed analysis of the organisation of the shipowning client and the degrees of supervision exercised by those in charge of its direction.

It is far from easy to decide at what level in the hierarchy the *alter ego* of the owning company is to be found. In the case of *The Garden City*[6] Staughton, J. took a five week hearing and a judgment occupying 16 pages of Lloyd's law reports to give the answer in the case of one Polish shipping company. It is therefore to be hoped that the implementation of the 1976 Convention will reintroduce a measure of certainty which will enable the practitioner to recommend English jurisdiction again—or another jurisdiction in which the 1976 Convention is applied—with recovered confidence.

This is not to say that the right of limitation of liability can simply be taken for granted. The lawyer investigating a marine casualty will ignore this subject at his peril.[7] It is to be hoped, however, that the new test involving "personal act or omission" and "recklessness" will equate with the comparable provisions in section 39(B) and section 55 of the Marine Insurance Act 1906. These provisions have not in practice given rise to anything like the difficulties which have been generated by the "fault or privity" requirements of the 1957 Convention and its predecessors.

3. SUBORDINATE CHANGES

These may be summarised as follows:–
1. Tonnage—gross tonnage under the new provisions of the 1969 Tonnage Convention in place of the old "limitation tonnage" (net tonnage plus engine space deduction).
2. The amount per ton of the limitation fund will be calculated by reference to SDRs instead of gold francs.
3. The Convention will apply to salvors.
4. There are more detailed provisions as to the administration and distribution of limitation funds.

The advent of limitation based on gross tonnage must be welcome to all practitioners. The engine space deduction, a fictitious tonnage contrived to reduce the tax liabilities of the owners of motor ships with small engine rooms (as they began to take over from cumbersome steam engines) is ascertainable only

---

[6] [1982] 2 Lloyd's Rep. 383.
[7] See further, Chap. 4, *supra*.

by reference to the vessel's international tonnage certificate. This document is rarely to be found in the owners' office and even on board the ship herself must sometimes be tracked down in a bottom drawer of the desk in the master's cabin. It is not published with the particulars of the ship in standard works of reference such as Lloyd's Register of Ships. Practitioners have their own rules of thumb for making intelligent guesses at the limitation tonnage, but in the case of specialised vessels, such as trawlers, rig supply ships, or passenger vessels, these may be wide of the mark. It will be some time before Lloyd's Register itself revises the tonnage of every vessel listed to accord with the 1969 Tonnage Convention and indeed the Merchant Shipping Act 1984, has brought in special transitional provisions to cover the period until the 1969 Tonnage Convention applies universally.[8]

The adoption of the SDR as the standard unit of account has preceded the coming into force of the 1976 Convention. The 1979 protocols adopted at the final meeting of the Standing Diplomatic Conference were brought into effect in November 1984.[9] With effect from November 29, 1984 the fixing of the sterling amount per ton to which a shipowner may limit his liability has been calculated by reference to the value of the SDR on the date of constitution of the limitation fund. The value of the SDR is published daily and thus the periodic adjustments to the sterling amount of the vessel's limit of liability by Sterling Equivalent Orders of the Secretary of State are no longer necessary. If, as is intended, the SDR remains a reasonably consistent unit of value, this will avoid the necessity for the "tactical" deposit of a limitation fund in Court in order to constitute the fund when the sterling parity is particularly advantageous. This will, it is hoped, also avoid the arguments which have been advanced in some jurisdictions that the limitation fund constituted under the 1957 Convention should be based on the free market value of gold, as distinct from the inter-governmental gold value fixed by the Bretton Woods Agreement.

The application of the 1976 Convention to salvors, which has been touched on earlier in this paper, is clearly intended to amend the effect of the decision of the House of Lords in *The Tojo Maru*.[10] It is worthy of note that the solicitor whose enthusiastic efforts contributed so much to the decision of the House of Lords

[8] This requires a vessel which has not yet been measured under the 1969 Tonnage Convention to be measured specially for the limitation action in accordance with the rules of that Convention. This will mean that the practitioner will not know the amount of the ship's limitation fund until the measurers report comes in. He may well be surprised. See further, Chap. 3.

[9] In England by the Merchant Shipping Act 1981 (Commencement No. 3) Order 1984 (S.I. No. 153).

[10] [1971] 1 Lloyd's Rep. 341.

in favour of the owner of *The Tojo Maru* (and against the salvors), Mr Robert Elborne, should have devoted so much time and effort at the 1974 Conference of the CMI which produced the draft text of the 1976 Limitation Convention.

The salvor is, of course, entitled to limitation of liability under the present law provided that he can bring himself within the terms in the UK, of the Merchant Shipping Act 1894, s. 503(1)(c) and (d). That is where injury or damage is caused through the act or omission of any person (whether on board the salving vessel or not) in the *navigation or management* of the salving vessel, or through any other act or omission of any *person on board* the salving vessel. As the House of Lords decided in *The Tojo Maru*, the act of a salvor's employee working on or under a casualty is not a person on board a salving vessel nor is he acting within the navigation or management of the salving vessel, and it is these gaps which the 1976 Convention has set out to close, by giving a salvor the protection of Limitation of Liability based on a theoretical tonnage of 1500 tons.

4. CHOICE OF JURISDICTION

In tort cases involving international maritime claims, the practitioner may well be faced with the need to advise his client as to the most appropriate jurisdiction in which the matter may be resolved. A collision on the high seas is of course the classic example of such a choice.

Limitation of liability is frequently a significant factor in the final recommendation. If the initial appraisal of the casualty indicates that his shipowning client is likely to be the paying party, then he will seek a jurisdiction in which the limitation fund of the vessel is as small as possible and the prospects of maintaining the right to limit are as good as possible. If, on the other hand, the appraisal indicates the reverse,—that his client is likely to be the recovering party—then clearly a jurisdiction should be sought where limits of liability are larger, or where there is a reasonable prospect of defeating the opponents' right to limitation.

At the present time the world may broadly be divided into those countries which apply the "abandonment" principle, *i.e.* the value of the vessel after the casualty, usually plus pending freight—the classic example being the U.S.A.—and those applying the "tonnage" principles of the 1957 Limitation Convention.

The 1957 Convention is now applied in three different ways:–

1. By fixing the limit by reference to SDRs—the position in England at the present time.
2. By fixing the limit in gold francs, valued by reference to the inter-governmental value of gold under the Bretton Woods Agreement—*e.g.* the Netherlands.

3. By fixing the value of the gold franc by reference to the market value of gold, *e.g.* Egypt.

The coming into force of the 1976 Convention will add yet a fourth choice. It is to be hoped, however, that the higher limitation funds and the greater certainty of the right to limitation of liability will offer attractions to both the paying party and the recovering party. Maritime lawyers the world over, and marine insurers, will watch this development with keen interest.

In this context a distinction must be drawn between maritime contract claims and maritime torts. In the case of most maritime contracts, such as charter-parties or contracts for the sale and purchase of ships, provisions are contained by which the parties make an express choice of governing law and jurisdiction. In the case of maritime torts (of which the collision at sea is the classic example[11]) the choice of jurisdiction lies with the parties.

The choice of jurisdiction in such cases is a very complex subject, but as has been noted limitation of liability inevitably plays an important role in the exercise of that choice. Thus, the real proof that the draftsmen of the 1976 Limitation Convention have "got it right" will be if jurisdictions where it is applied are chosen by parties who have the freedom to make such a choice.

5. ADMINISTRATION AND DISTRIBUTION OF THE LIMITATION FUND

The 1957 Limitation Convention contained no detailed provisions whatsoever as to how the principles embodied in that Convention should be applied in practice. Article 4 of that Convention expressly stated that the constitution and distribution of the limitation fund and rules of procedure shall be governed by the national law of the state in which the fund is constituted.

This provision has led to wide variations of practice between the states in which the 1957 Convention has been ratified, particularly concerning such matters as the nature of the fund itself (cash deposit or guarantee), whether the fund carries interest, and the procedure for disputing the right to limitation of liability.

The 1976 Convention on the other hand contains in Articles 10, 11, 12 and 13 detailed provisions on these matters which will, it is hoped, produce greater consistency between states in the application of the principles of limitation of liability.

---

[11] Although there are others, such as contact with fixed and floating objects and personal injury claims.

6. LIMITATION WITHOUT CONSTITUTION OF A LIMITATION FUND: (ARTICLE 10)

It has always been possible in English law to plead limitation of liability as a defence to a claim brought in the English Courts. In such circumstances no Limitation Fund as such is constituted, but the issues as to entitlement to limitation of liability and as to the amount of the limitation fund are pleaded between the parties and decided at the hearing of the action or arbitration. Such a procedure is clearly appropriate only where an incident gives rise to one sole claim—as for example in the case of damage to a bulk cargo on board the limiting vessel.

Article 10 of the 1976 Convention provides that a State party may provide in its national law that the right to limitation of liability may only be invoked if a limitation fund has been constituted in accordance with the Convention. This provision is permissive rather than mandatory and it is noteworthy that the draftsmen of the 1979 Merchant Shipping Act have not seen fit to modify the practice of English Law in this respect.

Other jurisdictions, *e.g.* Japan, now require the constitution of a limitation fund before the right to limitation of liability may be invoked in the substantive proceedings. It will be interesting to see whether the Japanese legislation giving effect to the 1976 Limitation Convention has modified this practice.

7. CONSTITUTION OF THE FUND: ARTICLE 11

This provides that the fund shall be constituted in the amounts specified in Articles 6 and 7 "with the Court or other competent Authority in any State party in which legal proceedings are instituted in respect of claims subject to limitation."

By paragraph 11 (A) of Part II of Schedule 4 to the Merchant Shipping Act 1979 "the Court" is specified to be the High Court in England and Wales and the Court of Session in Scotland.

The opening sentence of Article 11(1) raises interesting questions of jurisdiction. At a first reading it would appear that the limitation fund may only be constituted in a jurisdiction where a claimant against the limiting shipowner has already instituted legal proceedings.

In England and indeed in many other jurisdictions the right of limitation of liability is invoked by the institution of a separate limitation action independently of any claim on the merits. In theory, at least, it is possible to commence a limitation action in a jurisdiction in which no proceedings have been brought against the limiting party. For example, if a legal action on the merits has been commenced in England it is still possible for the defendant to commence a limitation action in Holland in respect of the same distinct occasion. The writer is aware that one of Her Majesty's judges practising in admiralty has expressed the opinion that there must be either a judgment or an admission of liability against a shipowner before that shipowner may commence a limitation action,[12] but it is submitted that there is no express provision in the Merchant Shipping Acts, nor in the Rules of the Supreme Court, to this effect.

An interesting question arises as to whether the commencement of a limitation action in England would itself be sufficient to fall within the phrase "Legal proceedings ... instituted in respect of claims subject to Limitation." A literal reading of this phrase would suggest that it would, but it is submitted that the true meaning of this phrase in the Convention is that the legal proceedings in question must be commenced by claimants against the limiting party, in respect of the merits of claims arising out of the incident in question.

The result of such a conclusion, it is appreciated, would be to prevent pre-emptive action by a shipowner, such as was taken by the Polish owners of *The Wladyslaw Lokietek*.[13] The construction of this sentence which has been adopted above would, in such circumstances, require the limiting shipowner to wait until a claimant had commenced proceedings before he could invoke limitation of liability. If this sentence is to be interpreted literally the possibility might arise whereby the limiting shipowner would provoke an action, for example, by a member of the crew of his vessel, simply to invoke the provisions of Article 11.

The 1976 Convention provides that a fund may be constituted either by depositing the sum in question, or by producing a guarantee acceptable under the legislation of the State party where the fund is constituted and considered to be adequate by the Court.

The current English practice is for the amount of the limitation fund, plus interest, to be paid into court in cash, but there is in fact no statutory provision or Statutory Instrument requiring this to be so.[14]

Once, however, the 1976 Convention comes into force in England, it will clearly be open to a party seeking a decree of limitation of liability to offer a guarantee in lieu of a cash deposit. At the present time the only form of guarantee which is acceptable to the court is bail in the form prescribed by the provisions relating to arrest. It remains to be seen, however, whether in interpreting Article 11, the court will be prepared to extend the scope of such guarantees to include letters of guarantee custom-

---

[12] This is no longer necessary under the 1976 Limitation Convention, see Art. 1(7).
[13] [1978] 2 Lloyd's Rep. 520.
[14] See Rules of the Supreme Court, Ord. 75, r. 37 and the notes thereto in *The White Book*.

arily treated as acceptable in the city of London, such as those of a P & I Club, or of a substantial insurance company.[15]

It is of the essence of such an arrangement that the limitation fund should be available on short notice, but it is submitted that to tie up valuable cash resources of the owners of a limiting vessel or his underwriters while all claims against the fund are proved or disputed is inappropriate in current financial conditions.

8. DISTRIBUTION OF THE FUND: ARTICLE 12

This article does not specify how or by whom the fund shall be distributed, this being left to the rules established by the State Party in which the fund is constituted in accordance with article 14. In England this is carried out by the Admiralty Registrar, in the Admiralty Court. In several continental systems of Law an independent *dispacheur* is appointed by the Court to perform this function.

Article 12(1) contains the general statement that the fund should be distributed among the claimants in proportion to their established claims against the fund. Thus, no lien or privilege to which a claimant may be entitled will enable that claimant to priority over the other claims against the fund. This has been spelt out in paragraph 9, Part II, Sched. 4 of the Merchant Shipping Act 1979 and reflects the equivalent provisions in the 1967 Convention on Liens and Mortgages.[16]

Article 12(2) and 12(3) enable a limiting shipowner or his insurer to settle claims against the fund and to stand in the shoes of the Claimant as regards priorities. This principle is in accord with the principle applied by the English Admiralty Court in *The Giacinto Motta*.[17] It is submitted that the phrase "has settled a claim against the fund" in paragraph 2 must be interpreted broadly. In circumstances such as those which prevailed in the case of *The Giacinto Motta*, where the limiting shipowner had settled a claim in another jurisdiction (in which the principles of the 1957 and 1976 Convention did not apply) that claim had never been made "against the Fund" since the claimants had chosen to pursue their claim in a non-convention country. Nevertheless it would be wholly unjust if the literal meaning of this phrase in Article 12(2) were to deprive the owner of his right of subrogation.

Article 12(4) has the practical advantage of enabling a provisional distribution of the limitation fund to be made to deserving claimants whose claims have been properly established, while

---

[15] See also the comments of Brandon, J on the subject of Letters of Guarantee in *The Wladyslaw Lokietek* [1978] 2 Lloyd's Rep. 520, 533.

[16] Art. 14.—This Convention is not in force and has not been widely ratified, but this provision confirms the existing English Law.

[17] [1977] 2 Lloyd's Rep. 221.

reserving part of the fund to cover other claims which are anticipated.

9. BAR TO OTHER ACTIONS: ARTICLE 13

This Article, although new in drafting, is a successor to Article 5 of the 1957 Convention, incorporated into English law by section 5 of the Merchant Shipping (Liability of Shipowners and Others) Act 1958. The Courts have had considerable difficulty in applying this section and, indeed, in *The Putbus*[18] Lord Denning described it as:

"...not a piece of English. It is only a collection of word-symbols."[19] Later in the case of *The Wladyslaw Lokietek*, Brandon, J, as he then was, analysed the section in meticulous detail and then proceeded to render it virtually ineffective by requiring the limiting shipowner to prove his right to limit (*i.e.* the absence of fault or privity) to the satisfaction of an English Court before his vessel could be released from arrest.[20] Despite the strictures of the Court of Appeal in *The Putbus* that the section should be construed liberally in order to give effect to the provisions of Article 5 of the 1957 Convention, the Admiralty Court has, for the moment at least, declined to give up its privilege of requiring any shipowner seeking limitation of liability, whether in England or elsewhere, to prove the absence of fault or privity to its own satisfaction.

It appears that the draftsmen of Article 13 of the 1976 Convention have sought to mitigate the rigours of *The Putbus* and *The Wladyslaw Lokietek* decisions.

Article 13(1) is clear enough. A party who has made a claim against the fund where it has been constituted shall not be entitled to exercise any right against other assets of the limiting shipowner: the rationale being that the fund itself shall act as security for all claims against it.

Under article 13(2), however, *The Putbus* and *The Wladyslaw Lokietek* problems are dealt with head on. Once a limitation fund has been "constituted" in accordance with Article 11, any ship belonging to the limiting shipowner may be released from arrest and *must* be released if the limitation fund has been constituted in the four places specified.

Article 11 does not define "constituted" and Article 14 merely states that the constitution and distribution of the limitation fund shall be governed by the law of the State Party in which the fund is constituted. Does "constituted" mean simply the deposit of the Limitation Fund, either by cash or guarantee, with the appropriate

[18] [1969] 1 Lloyd's Rep. 253.
[19] *Ibid.*
[20] Or, in that case, the security provided to procure her release.

authorities, or does it also require a legal declaration that the limiting shipowner is entitled to limitation of liability, and is not guilty of conduct barring limitation within the meaning of article 4? Both constructions can be deduced from the wording of the 1976 Convention and, alas, different jurisdictions may adopt different approaches. Viewed simplistically, Article 11(2) explains how "a fund may be constituted" by depositing cash or guarantee acceptable under the legislation of the State Party where the fund is constituted.

This wording does not contain any suggestion that a ruling as to entitlement to limitation or as to the absence of conduct barring limitation is a prerequisite to constitution of the fund. Similarly, the wording of Article 14, which confers jurisdiction on the State Party in which the fund is constituted to make rules relating to the constitution and distribution of the limitation fund, would be meaningless if a formal declaration of entitlement to limit was necessary before the fund is constituted. This would leave an apparent hiatus until such a declaration had been obtained with no provisions in the Convention as to which State Party is competent to rule on such an important issue.

On the other hand, if mere deposit of the amount of a limitation fund is to be sufficient to "constitute" the fund this equally means that the principal point decided in *The Wladyslaw Lokietek* by Brandon, J has been reversed, and that once a limitation fund has been "constituted" a ship or other property which has been arrested or attached within the jurisdiction of a State Party, or any security given, may be released and must be released in the four instances specified.

Where does this leave the confused limiting shipowner, and his equally confused legal adviser? If it is legitimate to compare the wording of Article 5 of the 1957 Convention, "Where a Shipowner is entitled to limit his liability under this Convention" with the words in the 1976 Convention, "After a limitation fund has been constituted in accordance with Article 12," one is driven to the view that indeed the draftsman of the 1976 Convention sought to mitigate the rigours of *The Wladyslaw Lokietek* decision, and that once a Limitation Fund has been constituted by cash deposit or guarantee in accordance with Article 11(2) it will not be necessary for the limiting shipowner to prove his entitlement to limitation of liability to the satisfaction of every other Court in the world where his ships may be arrested.

An interesting procedural point arises as to the meaning of "at the port" in Article 13(2)(a), (b) and (c). By Schedule 4, Part II to the Merchant Shipping Act 1979 (which contains provisions having effect in connection with the Convention) references in the Convention to the Court are, in relation to England and Wales, references to the High Court. By the Rules of the Supreme

Court,[21] every limitation action shall be assigned to the Queen's Bench Division and taken by the Admiralty Court. Strictly speaking, therefore, deposit of a limitation fund with the Admiralty Registry of the High Court, which is where such funds will ordinarily be deposited, it is not literally "at a port" at all. It will be left to the judges of other jurisdictions to decide whether, in the event of a casualty occurring in, for example, Southampton, the deposit of a limitation fund at the Admiralty Court in London is to be treated as having been constituted at the port where the occurrence took place.

Article 13(3) is clearly intended to meet the argument raised in *The Wladyslaw Lokietek*, although not necessary for the final decision of the Court, namely that a limitation fund must be actually available and in a currency freely transferable internationally.

10. CONCLUSIONS

The 1976 Limitation Convention has proved a comprehensive review of the subject. It is to be hoped that the higher limitation funds and the removal of the old "fault or privity" precondition to the right to limitation will add certainty to the law and promote widespread acceptance of this Convention among seafaring nations around the world.

In the intervening period while it gradually gains acceptance after coming into force, the life of a practising maritime lawyer will be that much more complicated as he has to compare the limitation regimes of countries which apply three different measures of Limitation of Liability, namely:

(a) The abandonment principle.

(b) The 1957 Convention principles.

(c) The 1976 Convention principles.

He will have to wait patiently for the spread of general acceptance of the 1976 Convention before it can be said that the law on this subject has been harmonised internationally. That may indeed be a pious hope. It is reported that the maritime law policy makers in the United States have taken the view that the limits fixed by the 1976 Convention are too low to justify ratification, while conversely the Greeks have taken the view that the limits are too high.[22] We can only hope that the policy makers in both countries will see the advantages of international uniformity in such matters as finally overcoming the initial reservations which they have expressed.

It is clear, however, that the debate will go on for some time, and that the subject of limitation of liability will provide the

[21] R.S.C., Ord. 75, r. 2(b).
[22] See Chaps. 21 and 14 respectively.

practising maritime lawyer, and the Courts, with interesting and challenging problems to resolve.

VI

The 1976 Convention and International Uniformity of Rules

*Professor David Jackson**

1. INTRODUCTION

The purpose of a Convention is uniformity of approach. Such uniformity depends first on the Convention itself, secondly on the manner of its implementation into national laws and on its national effect as against other national laws and thirdly on the consistency with any other Convention which may touch on identical topics. The question of the relationship of the 1976 Convention with other Conventions and national laws is relevant not only to other rules of limitation of liability but the assessment of the liability to which limitation is attached and jurisdictional and choice of law rules. The 1976 Convention is concerned primarily with rules which are to be applied in limiting liability; those rules must be fitted into the national structures for the hearing of disputes and the law to be applied.

2. THE 1976 CONVENTION

The Convention provides a uniform structure for limitation of liability in respect of persons entitled to limit, claims subject to limitation and rules concerning the constitution and distribution of the limitation fund. It sets out rules concerning the release of security given in one contracting state once a limitation fund is set up in that state or any other. Once a claim is made against the fund the claimant is prohibited from making any other like claim against the assets of the person setting up the fund. The Convention is, therefore, largely focused on uniform rules of national internal law *i.e.* rules by which the questions of limitation of liability and consequential security issues are to be resolved. It contains no express jurisdictional provisions, its choice of law provisions are confined to the constitution and distribution of the limitation fund

* Institute of Maritime Law, Southampton University

and there are no provisions relating to recognition in one state of a judgment in limitation proceedings given in another.[1]

Jurisdiction

(1) Limitation proceedings

Unlike, for example, the Athens Convention 1974,[2] the 1976 Convention contains no express jurisdictional provisions. There are, therefore, no restrictions on limitation proceedings on the basis of domicile, nationality, place of claim or events on which the claim is based or any other connection.

The Convention does, however, affect the establishment and exercise of jurisdiction by imposing in specified circumstances an obligation to release security obtained. The Convention provides that the courts of a contracting party must release a ship or other property arrested, if a limitation fund is established in a jurisdiction linked to the proceedings in any one of specified ways. Article 13(2) provides[3]:

> "After a limitation fund has been constituted in accordance with Art. II, any ship or other property, belonging to a person on behalf of whom the fund has been constituted, which has been arrested or attached within the jurisdiction of a State Party for a claim which may be raised against the fund, or any security given, may be released by order of the court or other competent authority of such State. However, such release shall always be ordered if the limitation fund has been constituted:
>
> (a) at the port where the occurrence took place, or, if it took place out of port, at the first port of call thereafter; or
> (b) at the port of disembarkation in respect of claims for loss of life or personal injury; or
> (c) at the port of discharge in respect of damage to cargo; or
> (d) in the State where the arrest is made."[4]

A claimant in a court other than one specified in Article 13(2)

---

[1] As, *e.g.* the Convention on the Contracts for the International Carriage of Goods By Road 1956 (CMR). For the relevance of the CMR to limitation under the 1976 Convention: see 4(1)(a), *infra*.

[2] Art. 17. See also the Hamburg Rules 1978, Arts. 21, 22; the Multimodal Convention 1980, Arts. 26, 27.

[3] The Article also provides for discretionary release in respect of funds set up in other jurisdictions.

[4] It appears from the Conference proceedings that it was intended that mandatory release should apply whether the fund is established before or after the arrest. There were proposals for amendment to ensure that this meaning was clear but the text unfortunately remains as it was originally. Some doubt must remain.

and in which the fund is established runs the risk, therefore, of lack of security. Further, insofar as any jurisdiction on the merits of a court releasing the security is founded on arrest, such jurisdiction would be removed. There is no indication in the Convention or Conference Proceedings that this provision is intended to restrict merits jurisdiction and, therefore, it is open for a national law which bases jurisdiction on arrest to provide for an alternative.[5]

A proposal at the International Conference to add the place of the shipowner's business was rejected, failing to obtain the required two thirds majority. It was agreed both that a claimant may be subjected to heavy expense in that the place may have no connection with the accident and that in practice such a place would have exclusive jurisdiction.[6] Under the Collision Civil Jurisdiction Convention 1952[7] collision proceedings not based on a collision in inland waters or on arrest must be brought in an agreed Court or the Court of the defendant's habitual residence. It appears from Article 11 that the shipowner cannot force a claimant into that jurisdiction by setting up a fund, unless another claimant starts proceedings there.[8] Bearing that in mind, it is difficult to appreciate the defensibility of mandatory release once a fund is established in a jurisdiction specified, but not if established in the shipowner's residence. The exclusion perhaps shows a certain lack of confidence in the impartiality of the courts of contracting states.

(2) Limitation and liability proceedings

There are no provisions in the Convention directly linking jurisdiction over limitation proceedings to jurisdiction in liability proceedings; or indeed any direct prohibition on multiplicity of liability or limitation proceedings. However, the mandatory provision limiting the ability to claim independently of the fund controls multiplicity of proceedings. Although national laws may provide that limitation may be invoked without the setting up of a fund, as has been said, it appears that a fund may be set up in a

---

[5] As to the provision in English law see fn. 10 and text.
[6] *Conference Proceedings*, pp. 481–483.
[7] The International Convention on Certain Rules Concerning Civil Jurisdiction in Matters of Collision 1952 (reflected in English law in the Supreme Court Act 1981, ss. 20–22).
[8] A fund may be constituted "in any State Party in which legal proceedings are instituted in respect of claims subject to limitation" (Art. 11(1)). It is perhaps possible to read this as including an action to limit liability in respect of that claim; and the phraseology perhaps leaves open the question of whether a conservatory arrest would be institution of legal proceedings within it. *Cf.* Chapter 5.

jurisdiction only when liability proceedings have been instituted there. Once a claim is made against a fund no other claim based on the same right may be made against the assets of the person setting up the fund; payments made in respect of claims which are within the scope of aggregation in respect of any occasion in relation to which the fund is established are to be brought into the distribution of the fund.[9]

Subject to national laws, therefore, liability proceedings arising out of the same "occasion," in respect of which the Convention will operate to create a limit, may be brought in different jurisdictions. Likewise, national laws may permit limitation proceedings independently of, or in answer to, liability proceedings—the Convention imposing no control. However, if it be right that Article 11 sees the setting up of a fund only as a response to the bringing of liability proceedings this severely restricts the ability of a defendant to force claimants into a jurisdiction of his choice through limitation proceedings. Indeed, it is entirely defensible not to allow the defendant in practice to control the choice of jurisdiction in this way.

However, the Convention does indirectly affect jurisdiction over liability proceedings based on the maintaining of a ship under arrest. The effect of the mandatory release provisions would be to remove the foundation in the jurisdiction in respect of which they operated.

In English law this effect is countered by the provision in the Merchant Shipping Act 1979 that where release is ordered the applicant for release "shall be deemed to have submitted to" English jurisdiction to adjudicate in the claim for which the property was arrested.[10] Whether such a provision as it applies to a collision claim is consistent with the Collisions Civil Jurisdiction Convention 1952 (which if jurisdiction is not based on arrest or habitual residence requires agreement) seems dubious.

Further, even if jurisdiction is maintained despite the release, the provision may have an effect on the choice of jurisdiction by a claimant. In selecting a jurisdiction not specified in Article 13 there is the risk of lack of security, although it should be said that even selection of one of the specified jurisdictions will not ensure security. Once liability proceedings are started in one of the specified jurisdictions the setting up a fund may in effect focus the security on *that* jurisdiction—and the mandatory release will operate whether the other jurisdictions are or are not specified in Article 13.

[9] See Arts. 12, 13.
[10] See Schedule 4 Part II, para. 10.

129

(3) Jurisdictional agreements

It is possible to envisage a jurisdictional agreement relating solely to limitation proceedings entered into after the events creating the liability to be limited. It is more likely that any jurisdictional agreement affecting limitation proceedings would relate directly to liability proceedings—either in the case of a collision action entered into after the event creating liability[11] or as part of a contract of carriage, liability under which is subject to the 1976 Convention limitation rules.[12]

The 1976 Convention directly affects reliance on a jurisdictional agreement only insofar as it provides uniform limitation rules for contracting states. Therefore, it could be argued on general principle that any clause opting for a jurisdiction in a contracting state other than the forum be upheld on the basis of enforcement of contract or, conversely, that there is no reason to uphold it as the law will be the same. The approach will depend on the force given to jurisdictional clauses by the national law.

Where England is the forum and there is a jurisdictional clause opting for a non-contracting state it is arguable that, the 1976 Convention being mandatory, a jurisdictional clause should not be upheld insofar as it would lead to the application of a different limitation structure. In 1984 in *The Benarty*[13] the Court of Appeal held that a jurisdictional clause in a bill of lading was not defeated even though the consequence was the application of an Indonesian tonnage limitation statute in assessing liability for damage to cargo. The Court considered that although the Hague-Visby Rules were mandatory as to limitation[14] by their own provisions[15] they were subject to national tonnage limitation statutes. Therefore, the Rules, as applied in English law, *permitted* derogation from package limitation in this respect. The question was, therefore, whether according to general principles the clause should be upheld. On several undertakings given by the shipowners (including apparently that any issue as to liability could be tried in England) the Court upheld the clause. No argument was put that the English statute enacting tonnage limitation[16] was mandatory.

In the light of the enactment of the text of the 1976 Convention into English law (as distinct from the method of implementing the 1957 Convention) it may be thought arguable that it would be

---

[11] As is provided for in respect of liability proceedings by the Collisions Civil Jurisdiction Convention 1952 Art.
[12] As to Conventions concerning such contracts see 4(1)(a), *infra*.
[13] [1984] 2 Lloyd's Rep. 244.
[14] See *The Morviken* [1983] A.C. 565.
[15] Art. III r. 8.
[16] *i.e.* The Merchant Shipping (Liability of Shipowners and Others) Act 1958 enacting the provisions of the 1957 Convention.

contrary to policy to allow evasion through choice of jurisdiction. The purpose of the Convention, it may be said, is to create a uniform system. In *The Morviken*[17] the House of Lords held that the obligation in the Hague-Visby Rules Article III r. 8 not to derogate from the carriers' liability provisions could not be avoided by opting for jurisdiction in a non Hague-Visby Rules state. At the International Conference leading to the 1976 Convention, Liberia proposed the insertion of a clause avoiding any contractual provision depriving a person of the benefits of the Convention.[18] The proposal received little support, there being some feeling that to prevent waiver of the Convention provisions would be to favour shipowners to an unacceptable degree. Such evidence as there is, therefore, points against any international Convention mandatory principle, and it would seem unlikely that lacking such principle national laws would adopt a mandatory approach. The validity of jurisdictional clauses having the consequence of application of a different limit or limitation process would not, therefore, be affected by that factor: it has to be said, however, that the attitude of a contracting state may be different if a selected jurisdiction imposed a lower limit of liability.

In English law it is said that, presumptively, a jurisdiction clause will be upheld although the consistency of application in practice is questionable: identity of English and foreign law could well work either for or against staying proceedings in England to uphold a clause. In the United States since the Supreme Court decision in *The Bremen*[19] a jurisdictional clause will weigh heavily in favour of staying proceedings. In *The Bremen* itself neither the initiation of limitation proceedings in the United States, as a defensive measure, nor the fact that the amount recoverable in England was considerably less than that in the United States prevented the upholding of an English jurisdiction clause in towage liability proceedings.

The validity of a jurisdiction clause will, therefore, be affected by the Convention only to the extent that a national law sees the Convention as mandatory (which is unlikely) or, in the case of a clause opting for a contracting state the effect given by the forum to the uniformity of the applicable law.[20]

---

[17] [1983] A.C. 565.

[18] *Conference Proceedings*, pp. 142, 247.

[19] 407 U.S. (1971). At p. 519, fn. 8, reference is made to a theoretical English "limitation fund" of £80,000 in comparison with a U.S. limit of $1,390,000. The English limitation figure, of course, would have been irrelevant if the exculpatory clauses were upheld. See *The Chaparral* [1968] 2 Lloyd's Rep. 158 for the English proceedings.

[20] See, *e.g. The Morviken* [1983] A.C. 565 for an English court relying on this principle as regards the Hague-Visby Rules in refusing to uphold a jurisdictional clause opting for a non contracting state.

(4) *Forum non conveniens*

Apart from the Convention the plea of *forum non conveniens* may be relevant in limitation proceedings, as such, on the basis that limitation proceedings should accompany liability proceedings. Conversely in liability proceedings a plea of *forum non conveniens* may be based on the desired place of claiming limitation.

As with jurisdictional agreements, the 1976 Convention affects the issue of *forum non conveniens* as between contracting states only in the creation of uniform rules of limitation. It is arguable that *forum non conveniens* is inapplicable to a Convention which either expressly or impliedly provides for restricted or unrestricted jurisdiction.[21] At the International Conference the United States sought to introduce a clause expressly empowering a State court to decline to allow the initiation of limitation proceedings on the grounds of inconvenience to other parties to the proceedings.[22] The suggestion received little support, it being stressed that in many legal systems there was no such doctrine as *forum non conveniens* and that such a doctrine was hardly consistent with the desirability of the bringing of liability and limitation proceedings in the same place, in particular the linking of the establishment of the fund to the bringing of such proceedings. The operation of *forum non conveniens* among contracting States is, therefore, dubious. As between a contracting State and any other State, as has been said, it is unlikely that the limitation rules of the 1976 Convention will be applied mandatorily to any case within it. A plea of *forum non conveniens* will, therefore, be affected by the Convention only to the extent that as between contracting states the plea itself is thought inappropriate.

Choice of law

Insofar as the 1976 Convention provides a code of rules governing the issue of limitation of liability in its national implementation it forms the law to which reference must be made by the courts of contracting states. However, in respect of some matters the 1976 Convention bows to other Conventions and refers others to national laws. Further, the interpretation of the 1976 Convention "code" will always be subject to variation of national approaches.

---

[21] See in particular the EEC Jurisdiction and Judgments Convention 1968, *infra* 4(2)(d).
[22] *Conference Proceedings*, pp. 325–326.

(1) National Implementation

The text of the 1976 Convention constitutes the law of a contracting state only to the extent it is implemented in that State. There is no Convention provision specifying parties' obligations to introduce the Convention into national law; but there is also no reservation permissible such as in the 1957 Convention that the Convention may be implemented "either by giving it force of law or by including in national legislation, in a form appropriate to that legislation, the provision of this Convention."[23] Implicitly, therefore, the obligation is to give the Convention "the force of law" and arguably thereby to make it mandatory to any proceedings, within its scope. As a consequence, subject to permitted restrictions,[24] the 1976 Convention would apply in a contracting state whenever any person entitled to claim limitation "seeks to limit his liability or seeks to procure the release of a ship or other property or the discharge of other security given in the jurisdiction of the State." However, as has been said, it appears that the Convention is not intended to be mandatory in the sense that it cannot be waived. It is unlikely that it cannot be avoided through jurisdictional agreement. Such an approach leaves open, however, the question of whether a court of a contracting state would apply a choice of law which avoids the Convention.

(2) References to conventions[25]

By its own provisions the 1976 Convention is fitted into the increasingly complex shipping Convention structure through the exclusion of claims for oil pollution damage within the International Convention on Civil Liability for Oil Pollution Damage 1969, and "claims subject to any international convention or national legislation governing or prohibiting limitation of liability

---

[23] 1957 Convention, Protocol of Signature, para. 3. Presumably reading this as authorising a national version of the international text the United Kingdom implemented the 1957 Convention through the Merchant Shipping (Liability of Shipowners and Others) Act 1958, the provisions of which do not entirely coincide with the Convention.

[24] Art. 15(1) A State may limit the application of the Convention to persons having either habitual residence or place of business there, or to ships flying the flag of that State, *ibid*. For further restrictions see Arts. 15(2)–(4), 18(1). As to references to national law, see *infra* 2(2)(c). For restrictions on claims subject to limitation see Art. 3 and Chapter 2.

[25] As to the provisions of other Conventions affecting the 1976 Convention see, 4, *infra*. For pollution, see Chapter 8, *infra*. The difficulties caused by failure to provide for potential conflicts are illustrated by the present IMO negotiations for a Convention concerning liability for damage caused through the carriage at sea of hazardous or noxious substances (the HNS Convention): See, *e.g.* IMO, LEG SS/S August 1, 1985.

for nuclear damage."[26] The tonnage which is the basis of the Convention's limitation is to be calculated according to the Tonnage Measurement Convention 1969; and drilling ships are to be excluded by any State to the extent that it has entered into an international Convention "regulating the system of liability in respect of such ships."[27]

(3) References to national laws

As indicated above, the Convention provides that in a number of aspects a contracting state may opt to restrict its application. In addition the Convention, on occasion, confers a discretion on national courts or directly refers to national laws.[28] Most importantly it leaves matters relating to the constitution and distribution of a limitation fund to the law of the State in which the fund is constituted.

(4) General[29]

The more the available restrictive options are taken by State parties the less effective is the Convention. Further, the Convention may be optional because the Convention is not imposed on national laws mandatorily. Thirdly, it may lack uniformity of application if interpretation of it differs. Ironically, perhaps the introduction of uniform rules for resolution of disputes, as distinct from uniform choice of law rules, may actually create divergencies. Whereas, apart from a Convention, issues may be referred to one law, the same issues forming part of a Convention may be interpreted according to the law of the forum.[30]

(5) Validity and priority of claims

Article 12 provides that subject to Convention provisions for

[26] Art. 3. See *e.g.* the Convention on Third Party Liability in the field of Nuclear Energy, 1963 (the Paris Convention).
[27] Or imposes a higher limit by national law.
[28] In respect of the acceptability of a guarantee as an alternative to the deposit of a sum establishing the limitation fund (Art. 11(2)): the setting aside from the fund of a sum sufficient to meet a future claim (Art. 12(4)), and (apart from circumstances of mandatory release) the release of a ship after the establishment of a fund: (Art. 13(2)).
[29] A limited reference to national law is made in respect of the value of a national currency when the contracting state is not a member of the International Monetary Fund, see Art. 8(1), (4). For a further limited reference to national law see fn. 33.
[30] See *The Wladyslaw Lokietiek* [1978] 2 Lloyd's Rep. 520 (construing the 1957 Convention).

the limit for claims[31] and for priority of claims[32] the fund is to be distributed in proportion to the claim; that a person liable or his insurer who has settled a claim acquires by subrogation[33] the rights which the person compensated "would have enjoyed under the Convention"; that part of the fund may be set aside for future payments.

Article 14 provides that subject to the provisions of the 1976 Convention relating to the limitation fund "the rules relating to the constitution and distribution of a limitation fund, and all rules of procedure in connection therewith, shall be governed by the law of the State Party in which the fund is constituted."[34] The scope of this provision seems unclear. By its express wording it extends beyond the procedural rules of constitution and distribution of the fund. Its placing within, and reference to, the provision of the chapter of the Convention dealing with rules of priority and "established claims" indicates a substantive role. Even accepting such a role it remains uncertain whether the provision is a direction that the internal law of the State referred to applies or whether the issue of the law to be applied is left to that law.

Reading Article 14 as directing that the internal law of the State in which the fund is constituted is to decide on the distribution of the fund, it is further arguable that the Convention directs that it is that law which by Convention provision decides on the *validity* of the claim. It is unlikely, however, that the Convention would be seen as providing a choice of law rule for any issue concerning liability as such. Any choice of law direction for limitation claims, therefore, may mean that "validity" for liability and validity for limitation purposes is governed by different laws.

If Article 14 is seen simply as an indication that national internal law controls distribution the result in English law at least would be identical with present doctrine insofar as proceedings for distribution would be taken in the State where the fund is. There are, however, a number of different national approaches to the question of the law to govern limitation issues. Any approach other than reference to the internal law of the forum will be

---

[31] Arts. 6, 7.

[32] Art. 6(2), (3). A national law may provide that claims in respect of damage to harbour works, basins and waterways and aids to navigation may have priority over claims other than those for loss of life or personal injury, see Art. 6(3).

[33] The right of subrogation may be exercised by other persons to the extent subrogation is permitted by national law, see Art. 12(3).

[34] Art. 10(3) provides that national law may permit limitation to be invoked without the establishment of a fund. In that case all questions of procedure are to be governed by that law.

affected if (whatever its scope) the Convention is seen to provide a choice of law rule.[35]

The 1976 Convention may, therefore, be read as directing that any aspect of the distribution of the fund be referred to the law of the State in which the fund is established and, in effect, approving the rather crude English approach. It is more likely, however, that Article 14 will be read as a negative exclusion of distribution rules from the Convention and leaving the different national law approaches to develop in their own way.

Recognition of judgments of contracting states

Save for the reference to future compulsion to pay compensation the 1976 Convention contains no provision relating to the recognition of judgments. At the International Conference, Australia sought to introduce a comprehensive clause imposing a duty to recognise a judgment "in respect of a claim enforceable under this Convention"[36] given in courts of the state of the defendant's residence or place of business or to the jurisdiction of which the defendant submitted.[37] It received minimal support, primarily on the basis that there were Conventions concerned with the enforcement of judgments and there was some indication that under such Conventions liability judgments would be recognised. The United Kingdom delegate indicated that the proposal was not acceptable—"the question was a highly complicated one and could not be dealt with in the present context."[38] Such a reaction is perhaps not the most helpful—for it is difficult to appreciate a context more suitable for discussion of enforceability of judgments in limitation proceedings. Any future Convention concerned generally with the recognition of judgments could take into account provisions of a Convention dealing with a particular matter, such as limitation.[39]

It is clear, however, that acceptance of the proposal would have radically changed English law. In *The "Wladyslaw Lokietek"*[40] Brandon, J clearly thought that in many countries and in most cases a plaintiff would have to prove his claim in the country in which the fund against which he was claiming was established. It

---

[35] From answers to a CMI questionnaire it appears that in 1965 there were nine countries applying the law of the forum, four applying the law of the flag and seven the *lex loci* if a collision was the basis of the claim and it occurred in foreign territorial waters.

[36] For the text, see *Conference Proceedings*, pp. 93–96.

[37] Later amended (see *Conference Proceedings*, p. 192) to provide that "if necessary" a contracting state should ensure that a judgment given in another contracting state should be enforceable against a limitation fund in the first state.

[38] *Conference Proceedings*, p. 352.

[39] As, *e.g.* the EEC Convention on Jurisdiction and Judgments 1968 (see 4(2)(d) *infra*).

[40] [1978] 2 Lloyd's Rep. 520.

would help the plaintiff not at all to have established his claim elsewhere.

3. NATIONAL CHOICE OF LAW APPROACHES IN LIMITATION PROCEEDINGS

In English law a person who seeks payment for a claim must establish the claim in those proceedings. To receive credit for payments previously made the person liable must establish that the payment reflects liability under English law. So in *The "Giacinto Motta"*[41] following a collision shipowners had settled a claim by cargo owners made in the United States on the basis of a liability under that law leading to a payment of double the amount recoverable in English law. They were held entitled to have taken into account in distribution of a fund in England only such sum as the cargo owners could have claimed against the fund, and that was the sum which was recoverable under English law.

The reasoning of Brandon, J in *The Giacinto Motta*[42] follows the conclusion of the learned judge in *The Wladyslaw Lokietek*[43] on the lack of effect of the right of recovery declared in liability proceedings on the right to a share in a limitation fund. A right declared in liability proceedings, he said, is not *res judicata* in respect of limitation proceedings. Whether in English law this means that, lacking admission of liability, the whole question of liability is open to argument despite a finding on liability seems unclear. For the general proposition Brandon, J relied on *C.A. Van Eijk and Zoon* v. *Somerville*[44]—a case concerned only with challenge in limitation proceedings to the value of the ship assessed in liability proceedings. The value of the ship, it may be argued, lies at the heart of limitation proceedings affecting the amount available for all claimants—but, it may also be argued, so does the liability of the shipowner to each claimant.

While, therefore, in limitation proceedings an English court may approach a claim unsullied by any finding in liability proceedings it is clear that a court has the power to decide liability in limitation proceedings. The power is emphasised by the ability conferred by statute to enjoin claimants from taking other proceedings.[45] In Canada, the Federal Court of Appeal has

---

[41] [1977] 2 Lloyd's Rep. 221.
[42] [1977] 2 Lloyd's Rep. 221. See also *The Bethelehem Steel* case [1978], I F.C. 476 in the Canadian Federal Court. Addy, J. expressed the view that as regards torts committed in Canada, only claims held valid under Canadian law by a Canadian court would lie against a limitation fund established in Canada.
[43] [1978] 2 Lloyd's Rep. 520.
[44] [1906] A.C. 489.
[45] Merchant Shipping Act 1894, s.504—to be replaced in similar terms in respect of the 1976 Convention, by the Merchant Shipping Act 1979, Sched. 4, Part II, para. 8(2).

stressed that this power to stay should not be used to prevent a claimant establishing liability if the shipowner does not admit it, particularly if the claimant challenges the shipowner's right to limit.[46]

The judgment in *The Giancinto Motta* did not raise any possibility that any aspect of a limitation claim (including liability) would be referred to any law other than the English law; and the matter seems untested. Even as regards liability proceedings the relevance of foreign law is unclear.[47] On generally applicable tort rules any reference, at most, would be confined to "substantive issues," and would be relevant only to cross the threshold of foreign liability as a prerequisite for the application of English law.

The issue of liability is a substantive issue; that of limitation, while "procedural" in that the amount recoverable is limited, may have substantive characteristics in limiting a right. However, in accordance with present practice English courts would apply English law as the *lex fori* to limitation issues (these being seen as procedural). It may be that it is because English law as the *lex fori* plays such a large part in tort liability in English conflict rules that the courts have focused neither on the relevance of foreign law nor on the possible substantive aspects of limitation and connected issues.

In the United States liability in respect of an event occurring in territorial waters would presumptively be referred to the law of the State in which the waters are. The United States Limitation of Liability Act is applied to all limitation proceedings within the United States in respect of limiting the amount recoverable. However, subject to the limit under that Act, insofar as a foreign limitation of liability statute attaches to the right rather than simply limiting the sum recoverable as damages the United States courts will apply it. So the ability of a time charterer to limit liability or a restriction on a right so that a sum recoverable is less in amount than recoverable under United States law may be referred to foreign law.[48]

It does not necessarily follow from the doctrine that a settled claim is admissible against the fund only to the extent of its validity in English law that a foreign adjudication on a claim would not be recognised.[49] The justification for the present applicability of

---

[46] See *Nishin Kisen Kaishen Ltd.* v. *Canadian National Railway Co.* [1982] I F.C. 530. Where the right to limit is admitted, however, it may be thought pointless to establish liability in proceedings other than the limitation proceedings if such a decision is of no account in those limitation proceedings.

[47] See, *e.g.* as to the applicability of the Collision Regulation through foreign law, *The Esso Brussels* [1973] 2 Lloyd's Rep. 73. See, generally, D. C. Jackson, *Enforcement of Maritime Claims*, (1985), Chapter 18.

[48] See, *e.g.*, *The M/V Swibon* [1985] A.M.C. 722; *The Arctic Explorer* [1984] A.M.C. 2413.

[49] As occurs *e.g.*, in tort cases generally.

English law despite a foreign judgment must lie in the need as seen by the English forum for forum control. It might be thought that the 1976 Convention (providing uniform rules) necessarily implies reduction of such control; but, as has been seen,[50] the contracting states emphatically rejected a proposal that the Convention should provide for recognition of judgments as between themselves.

4. THE 1976 CONVENTION AND OTHER CONVENTIONS

Conventions specifically subject to the 1976 Convention

(1) Conventions relating to carriage by sea

The Hague Rules 1924, the Hague-Visby Rules 1968, the Hamburg Rules 1978 and the Athens Convention 1974 each provide that their limitation schemes do not affect the rights and duties under any Convention relating to the limitation of liability concerning seagoing ships. The Convention on the Contracts for the International Carriage of Goods by Road 1956 (CMR) applies to the road carrier the liability structure of (*inter alia*) the Hague or Hague-Visby Rules to a contract falling within it if the goods are carried in a vehicle and the damages occur during sea carriage. It follows, presumably, that insofar as the 1976 Convention qualifies the limitation of liability under the Hague or Hague-Visby Rules it will do so for the purpose of the CMR.

(2) Conventions relating to mortgages and liens

The International Conventions for the Unification of Certain Rules Relating to Maritime Liens and Mortgages 1967 each refer to limitation of liability. The Convention of 1967 provides that any party may reserve the right to apply the 1957 Convention. The Convention of 1926 provides simply that no sum apportioned to a creditor may exceed the sum due under limitation of liability rules.[51]

These Conventions are relevant to the 1976 Convention insofar as they create or recognise liens based on claims subject to limitation and provide for priority between them. The limitation of liability necessarily imposes a limitation on the amount secured by a lien and the establishment of the fund in essence provides an alternative security to that to which the lien would attach. Further the provision in the 1976 Convention Article 12(1) that subject to the Convention priority provisions . . . "the fund shall be distri-

---

[50] See 2(3), *supra*.
[51] See the Convention of 1926, Art. 7; Convention of 1967, Art. 14(2).

buted among the claimants in proportion to their established claims against the fund" is clearly inconsistent with the priority rules set out in the Lien and Mortgage Conventions. The overriding effect of the 1976 Convention is reflected in English law through the statutory provision that "no lien or other right in respect of any ship or property shall affect the proportions in which . . . the fund is distributed among social claimants."[52]

Conventions not specifically subject to the 1976 Convention

(1) Arrest Convention 1952[53]

The Arrest Convention provides a structure for arrest of ships in relation to the maritime claims specified in it and to a less comprehensive extent jurisdiction over the merits on such claims. Neither aspect is directly affected by the 1976 Convention but the provisions of the 1976 Convention relating to release from arrest impinge on the scope of the Arrest Convention. Particularly is this so in relation to the provisions for mandatory release which must be taken to qualify any permissive release provisions of the Arrest Convention.

(2) Collision Civil Jurisdiction Convention 1952

This Convention restricts collision jurisdiction to the courts of the residence or domicile of the defendant or the place of arrest unless there is agreement, the collision takes place in internal waters or there is a connected dispute already being litigated. It is perhaps surprising that there seems to have been little connection made between this Convention and the jurisdictional conse-quences of Article 13 of the 1976 Convention.

The policy of the Collision Jurisdiction Convention is clearly to restrict jurisdiction to a place where security is acquired or to the shipowner's residence. The policy of the 1976 Convention is to provide for security through the limitation fund. Yet the latter Convention does not provide for mandatory release of security even though security is provided in the jurisdiction favoured by the Collision Jurisdiction Convention.[54] Further applying both Conventions it may not be possible to bring liability proceedings in

---

[52] Merchant Shipping Act 1979, Sched. 4 Part II, para. 9.
[53] Enacted into English law (in terms of jurisdiction over the merits) now in the Supreme Court Act 1981, ss.20, 21.
[54] As to the consistency between the provision in English law that an application for release is deemed to be submission to jurisdiction in respect of a claim and the Collision Jurisdiction Convention, see *supra* 2(2)(b).

a jurisdiction in which the establishment of a fund would require the release of security obtained elsewhere.

(3) Hamburg Rules 1978

Articles 21 and 22 provide for jurisdiction of claims within the rules.[55] The port of discharge is common to liability proceedings under the rules and the favoured jurisdictions under the 1976 Convention; but as with the Collision Jurisdiction Convention it is possible for liability jurisdiction to be created according to Convention rules and a limitation fund, therefore, established but security obtained elsewhere not to be released.

(4) The EEC Civil and Commercial Jurisdiction and Judgments Convention 1968

The Convention which all EEC member states are obligated to join[56] provides for sweeping common rules relating to jurisdiction and enforcement of judgments in civil and commercial matters. As to jurisdiction the Convention applies where a defendant is "domiciled" in an EEC State and provides for a general rule that any action must be brought in the State in which he is domiciled. That rule is subject to specific exceptions (as in insurance or consumer transactions) alternatives in certain cases (*e.g.*, in a tort action the State in which the harmful event occurred) jurisdictional agreements, submission to jurisdiction, rules based on the Arrest or other Convention dealing with a particular matter, arrest of cargo or freight by a salvor and rules applicable to multiple defendants.

Limitation of liability is within the scope of the Convention. Subject to a specific Convention provision a limitation action by a person liable must, therefore, be brought in the country of the domicile of the liability claimant or in such other jurisdiction as will qualify under the exceptional rules. The specific provision to preserve the link between liability and limitation action was introduced as part of the amendments to the original Convention made on the accession of Denmark, Ireland and the United Kingdom. It provides "Where by virtue of this convention a court of a Contracting State has jurisdiction in actions relating to liability arising from the use or operation of a ship, that court, or any other court substituted for this purpose by the internal law of

---

[55] See also The Multimodal Convention 1980, Arts. 25, 26.
[56] Greece, Portugal and Spain will in due course become parties.

that State, shall also have jurisdiction over claims for limitation of such liability."[57]

The problems of limitation of liability jurisdiction (and indeed the general problem of jurisdiction over maritime claims) appears to have been of expressed concern only on the proposed accession of Denmark, Ireland and the United Kingdom. It is, therefore, perhaps not surprising that no reference was made to the relationship between the 1976 Convention and the EEC Convention at the Diplomatic Conference in 1976. The emphasis on the shipowner's domicile in the EEC Convention makes the omission of this jurisdiction from Article 13(2) of the 1976 Convention even more questionable.

The EEC Convention may well impose an obligation as between member states to recognise limitation judgments. Article 26 provides that a "judgment given in a Contracting State shall be recognised in other Contracting States" unless (*inter alia*) such recognition is contrary to public policy. In a sense it is public policy which refuses recognition of foreign limitation decrees in that the English practice is to allow English law to govern. However, it is doubtful whether the concept of "public policy" envisaged by the EEC Convention would encompass such a wide application: it seems more akin to the narrower sense of affecting fundamental national interests.

5. CONCLUSION

The 1976 Convention establishes a uniform structure for the application of rules of limitation of liability. However, it is essential first to stress that the Convention does not stand alone, and in taking its place in an increasingly complex maritime Convention structure there is the need to assess its consistency with, and effect on, other Conventions. Secondly, while uniform rules reduce the importance of choice of jurisdiction and choice of law, jurisdiction to consider limitation issues remains a prerequisite for the application of those rules and choice of law remains insofar as the Convention permits it or restricts its operation. Through its security provision the Convention indirectly affects jurisdiction. Through reference to national law, and lack of reference to validity of claims, choice of law remains a live issue. Finally, whatever the extent of the Convention structure, recognition of Convention judgments would appear a fundamental element of it. Yet there is no relevant provision.

The uniformity introduced by the 1976 Convention depends, therefore, not only on its application within national law, but the

---

[57] Article 6A. For the background to this article see Schlosser Report (O.J. 1979 C59/71) at pp. 109, 110.

extent of recognition of its application by other national laws. On that matter the Convention is largely silent.

VII

Limitation and Oil Pollution

*Andrew Dykes**

The intention of the 1976 Limitation Convention is to provide a uniform international framework within which shipowners can, in most circumstances, limit their liability to a known figure and in which claimants can know the maximum recovery which they can expect to make on a shipowner. Nevertheless certain classes of claim, including claims for oil pollution damage, are excluded from the Convention under Article 3. The purpose of this chapter is to examine the reasons for this exception and the practical consequences of it.

The international arrangements providing compensation for oil spills from tankers are relatively modern. The emergence of supertankers in the late 1960's, coupled with concern over the potential environmental consequences of casualties involving such ships, led to a widespread desire for an agreed international standard for liability together with ample compensation to be provided for the victims. It was felt that the existing provisions of the 1957 Limitation Convention did not provide an adequate level of compensation; if claims for oil pollution damage were pooled within that Convention's limitation fund, the compensation available for pollution victims might be arbitrarily reduced, depending on the circumstances of the casualty and the size of other claims against the shipowner which would rank ratably against the limitation fund. Consequently, the decision was taken to separate such claims from all others; two separate but closely interrelated Conventions resulted.

The first was the International Convention on Civil Liability for Oil Pollution Damage, 1969 (the CLC). This Convention, which is now in force in 56 countries, imposes strict liability upon the registered owner of a ship actually carrying persistent oil in bulk as cargo for pollution damage resulting from a spill of oil from that ship.[1] This liability is subject only to very limited defences: act of war, act of God, sabotage, or negligence of a Government or other authority in the upkeep and maintenance of navigational aids.[2]

---

* Director, Thomas Miller, London.
[1] Art. 3(1).
[2] Art. 3(2).

Substantially higher limits of liability were imposed on the shipowner than under the 1957 Limitation Convention—2,000 gold francs per ton, or 210,000,000 gold francs, whichever is smaller.[3] These limits were the maximum which it was felt the shipowners' liability insurers could accept, as in addition to the novel concept of strict liability for the owner, a direct right of action against a shipowner is provided under the CLC up to the shipowners' limit of liability.[4] It was considered at the time that to make more compensation available from the shipowners might lead to an unacceptable (and at that time uninsurable) increase in claims. However, because this might be inadequate fully to protect victims in the event of a catastrophic oil spill, a second tier of compensation was established by the International Convention on the Establishment of an International Fund for Compensation for Oil Pollution Damage, 1971. This established the International Oil Pollution Compensation Fund as a legal entity in contracting States (now 33), with the purpose of providing supplementary compensation in respect of pollution damage in a contracting state if any person has been unable to obtain full and adequate compensation from the shipowners under the CLC.[5] The Fund is financed by a levy on qualifying oil imports into contracting states, and the maximum compensation presently available from it is 675,000,000 gold francs, including any sums payable by the shipowner.[6] This Convention operates as an adjunct to the CLC, and it is the latter which is important when making a comparison with a shipowner's other limitation rights; the Fund will not come into effect if the shipowner loses the right to limit under CLC because the incident occurred with his actual fault or privity.[7]

Thus, in an incident involving claims for both oil pollution damage and other claims, it was envisaged that the shipowner would have two distinct and cumulative limitation funds, one under the CLC for pollution damage, and one under the 1957 Convention for all other claims (this fund itself being divisible into property claims and personal claims). These funds are, except in size, very similar. The test for breaking the owners' right to limit is the same: the actual fault or privity of the party seeking the right to

[3] Art. 5(1). A Protocol of November 19, 1976 substituted the SDR equivalents of 133 SDR per ton and 14 million SDR, but allowed States who are not members of the IMF to continue using the gold franc figures. The Protocol entered into force on April 8, 1981.

[4] Art. 7.

[5] Art. 4.

[6] Art. 4(4)(a) as amended by the Fund's Assembly in April 1979. A Protocol to introduce the SDR (as with the CLC, fn. 3, *supra*) was agreed on November 19, 1976, but is not yet in force. The equivalent SDR figure would be 45 million SDR.

[7] Art. 4(1)(c).

limit.[8] The procedure for the establishment of the limitation fund is, broadly speaking, the same.[9] The tonnage on which the limitation amount is based is the same,[10] and the procedure for division of the limitation fund among completing claimants is also the same.[11] In this way it was felt that the respective rights of pollution victims and other claimants would best be protected while still permitting the shipowner to limit his liability at an acceptable level. One practical difference does remain, however, concerning the jurisdiction in which the two limitation funds are to be established. For obvious reasons, neither the 1957 nor the 1976 Convention attempts to impose standards of liability or jurisdictional rules over the claim itself. Therefore the establishment of a limitation fund under either Convention does not give the court in question exclusive jurisdiction over claims subject to it (although it may indeed have extra jurisdictional consequences in respect of security). Similarly, although once a limitation fund has been established under the CLC the court in question has exclusive power to determine questions arising from the distribution of the fund,[12] the CLC specifically states that all countries party to it are to ensure that their courts have jurisdiction to entertain a claim made under it, regardless of the State in which the cause of action accrued.[13] Thus it is perfectly possible, and indeed quite usual, for a CLC limitation fund to be established in one country and other claims against the shipowner in respect of other matters arising out of the same incident—for example, cargo loss—to be brought in another jurisdiction, in which a conventional limitation fund would be established. This multiplicity of jurisdictions and proceedings in respect of the same facts is probably unavoidable, but it can in practice lead to bizarre and contradictory results.

In addition, the 1957 Convention was drafted before the CLC was conceived and a number of difficulties were caused by the imposition of a new tier of liability on an already existing framework which made no allowance for it. The earlier Convention makes no distinction between claims for pollution damage and other claims in respect of property damage. In order, therefore, to impose on a shipowner the higher limits of the CLC, the provisions of the 1957 Convention must be excluded by the municipal law of a contracting State insofar as they conflict with the CLC. In the United Kingdom, this apparently simple concept gave rise to a number of difficulties.

[8] Art. 5(2) of the CLC: and see Chap. 4, *supra*.
[9] Art. 5.
[10] Art. 5(10).
[11] Art. 5(4).
[12] Art. 9(3).
[13] Art. 9(1) and (2).

Section 4(1) of the United Kingdom Merchant Shipping (Oil Pollution) Act 1971 (the enabling Act for the CLC) originally excluded the provisions of the 1957 Convention for all claims arising under the CLC. However, it was subsequently realised that the United Kingdom was still bound by the provisions of the earlier Convention in respect of countries party to it who had not ratified the CLC. Ships flying the flag of such countries were entitled to the lower limits of the earlier Convention, and the United Kingdom could not unilaterally impose upon them the higher limits of the CLC. Correcting legislation was hurriedly drafted and embodied in Section 9 of the Merchant Shipping Act 1974, which now provides that, although the strict liability provisions of the CLC may apply to such an owner, the owner of a ship registered in a State party to the 1957 Convention but not the CLC is only entitled to limit his liability under the provisions of the earlier Convention.

This has the advantage for the shipowner domiciled in such a country that, if indeed he is entitled to limit, his single limitation fund for all claims is much smaller than the two he would otherwise have been liable to provide (exactly what the CLC was intended to rectify). However, the 1957 Convention only provides the owner with the right to limit in certain circumstances,[14] which are much narrower than the strict liability imposed by the CLC, and therefore there remains in English law a gap through which a shipowner could fall without any right whatsoever to limit his liability. One such example would be a laden tanker innocently involved in a collision resulting in an oil spill from that ship; the strict liability provisions of the CLC would apply, but on the presumption that the collision was caused solely by the negligence of the crew of the other ship, the tanker owner would not be entitled to limit under the 1957 Convention.[15] In addition, having been found liable to third parties for the pollution, the tanker owner might well find that his claim for an indemnity from the negligent ship would be subject to limitation in the normal way. Thus the combination of the 1974 Act and the interaction of the two Conventions leaves the wholly innocent shipowner exposed to possibly substantial claims. It might perhaps have been better to permit such shipowners the benefit of the CLC limitation provisions under English law if the 1957 Convention did not apply for such a reason.

Another omission from the existing Conventions which must be

[14] Art. 1.
[15] Because the collision, ex hypothesi, would not have been "caused by the act, neglect or default of any person on board the ship . . . " etc. within Art. 1(1)(b) of the 1957 Convention, as far as the tanker is concerned. However this would be the case for the other ship which could, accordingly, limit under the 1957 Convention.

remedied by national law involves incidents where both the owner and the charterer may bear some liability in respect of oil pollution. The CLC provides that "no claim for compensation for pollution damage shall be made against the owner otherwise than in accordance with this convention. No claim for pollution damage under this convention or otherwise may be made against the servants or agents of the owner."[16] However, it omits to exclude a claim against a charterer, who may thus be liable under the *lex fori* for pollution damage, for instance in negligence. In these circumstances the charterer would be entitled to the benefit of the 1957 Convention, but as both he and the owner would have separate limitation funds,[17] the effect would be that greater compensation would be available from them combined in respect of oil pollution than it was thought proper to impose under the CLC—where, as so often in the case, both owner and bareboat charterer are insured together under one policy this may produce the enlarged claim thought to be uninsurable in 1969. Again, it is left to municipal law in contracting States to correct the omission in the CLC, and in the United Kingdom this was done by Section 7 of the Merchant Shipping (Oil Pollution) Act 1971, which provides that, if an owner is liable under the CLC, and on the facts of the case both the owner and another party, including the charterer, would be entitled to limit their liability under the CLC and the Merchant Shipping (Liability of Shipowners and Others) Act 1958 respectively, the other person is exempt from liability for the pollution damage.[18]

Have these problems been solved by the 1976 Convention? This was drafted after the CLC came into force, and Article 3 provides:

"The rules of this Convention shall not apply to . . .
(b) Claims for oil pollution damage within the meaning of the International Convention on Civil Liability For Oil Pollution

---

[16] Art. 3(4). And see *The Amoco Cadiz* [1984] 2 Lloyd's Rep. 304.

[17] *i.e.* the owner under the CLC and the charterer under the 1957 Convention. Art. 6 of the 1957 Convention would not apply to reduce the total liability of owner and charterer in the UK because s.4(1) of The Merchant Shipping (Oil Pollution) Act 1971 excludes its application to the owners' own liability.

[18] It is beyond the scope of this paper to discuss in full the effects of the 1984 Protocols to the CLC and Fund Convention, which are not yet in force and will probably not be for a number of years. However, in this case, the CLC Protocol amends Art. 3(4) of the CLC to exclude a claim for pollution damage made against a charterer; so this defect will eventually be cured if the Protocol comes into force. The Protocol will also bring the test for breaking the right to limit into line with that of the 1976 Convention. See further, A. Popp., "Liability and Compensation for Pollution Damage Caused by Ships Revisited—report on an important International Conference," [1985] 1 LMCLQ 118; R. Ganten, "Oil Pollution Liability: Amendments Adopted to Civil Liability and Fund Conventions" Oil and Petrochemical Pollution 2 (1985) 93.

Damage dated November 29, 1969 or of any Amendment or Protocol thereto which is in force; . . . "

This exclusion, by limiting the scope of the 1976 Convention, should remove the first conflict referred to above. Unfortunately, the wording is far from clear. It was drafted by a working group which was unable to agree on an acceptable wording—or indeed on exactly what claims should be excluded.[19] A number of States took the view that only those claims actually governed by another International Convention should be excluded; on the other hand, a number of States were concerned that such a limited exclusion would unacceptably restrict their ability to provide their own legislation for oil pollution claims, and thus hinder ratification of the 1976 Convention. Indeed, so strong was this feeling—no doubt as a result of the political sensitivity of the pollution issue—that the conference even failed to adopt a proposal made by the German Democratic Republic which would have involved adding, at the end of the wording quoted above, the words "provided that such claims are subject to these provisions or any national legislation (equivalent thereto) (having the same effect)."[20]

Thus States party only to the 1976 Convention are not restricted in their ability to introduce their own limitation provisions in respect of claims for oil pollution damage. However, the wording of the exclusion gives rise to difficulties in countries which have ratified both the 1976 Convention and the CLC or a Protocol to it. Does it refer to all claims for pollution damage, as pollution damage is defined in the CLC, or does it apply only to claims against the registered shipowner for oil pollution damage for which liability under the CLC may arise? If the former wide interpretation is preferred, the second example of the conflict between the 1957 Convention and the CLC given above (that of claims against a charterer for pollution damage) is in fact exacerbated. Whereas previously the charterer would at least have been entitled to the benefit of the 1957 Convention, now he would not be entitled to limit at all and would slip through the gap between the 1976 Convention and the CLC.[21] In the United Kingdom, this question is the more critical because the repeal of the Merchant Shipping (Liability of Shipowners and Others) Act 1958 deprives the charterer of his exemption from such claims under section 7 of the Merchant Shipping (Oil Pollution) Act 1971. Similarly, on a wide construction of the exclusion, a ship which, through its own fault, collides with a tanker causing oil to be spilt from the latter resulting in pollution damage would not be

[19] LEG/CONF. 5/C.1/WP. 64/Rev. 1.
[20] LEG/CONF. 5/C.1/WP. 73.
[21] Until the gap is closed by the CLC Protocol: see fn. 18 *supra*.

entitled to limit its liability in an action brought directly against it for pollution damage by a third party. A narrow construction of the exclusion is surely preferable, to limit it only to claims against the registered owner for oil pollution damage for which liability under the CLC may arise. It is unfortunate that it was not possible at the conference to find a wording to put this beyond doubt and it was indeed accepted then that some claims for pollution damage would not necessarily be covered either by the CLC or by the 1976 Convention.[22] As far as the United Kingdom is concerned the Merchant Shipping Act 1979 does not clarify the issue, which must therefore be left to the common sense of the courts.

On a practical level, there is a strange inconsistency in the provisions regarding the security obtainable by a claimant in actions under the CLC and those subject to the 1976 Convention. Although both the latter and the 1957 Convention envisage limitation of liability being invoked without the constitution of a limitation fund, the CLC provides that

> "For the purpose of availing himself of the benefit of limitation . . . the owner shall constitute a fund for the total sum representing the limit of his liability with the court or other competent authority of any one of the contracting states in which action is brought."[23]

This fund may be established either by a cash deposit or by a bank or other guarantee, provided that this is acceptable to the court in which the fund is constituted.[24] This is a somewhat illogical distinction because of the direct right of action against the shipowners' liability insurer under the CLC. The purpose of this is of course to ensure that pollution victims have security for their claims up to the ship's CLC limit even in the event that the shipowner himself is not available, by reason of bankruptcy or otherwise, to satisfy the claims. It therefore seems somewhat strange that, since there is no general right of direct action against an insurer for liabilities which would be subject to the 1976 Convention, the defendant in a CLC action is treated more harshly than a defendant in any other action. This is presumably a result of the CLC being "claimant orientated"—a view which is borne out by the existence of the rules in Article 6 of the CLC dealing with the release of the assets of the owner from arrest when he establishes his limitation fund. Clearly, therefore, the direct action against the insurer is not intended to be the sole security available. A claimant under the CLC thus has the benefit of direct action against the insurer, the possibility of seizure of the shipowner's

---

[22] LEG/CONF. 5/C.1/SR. 14.
[23] Art. 5(3).
[24] *Ibid.*

assets, and the security of knowing that in order to invoke limitation of liability the shipowner must also physically establish his limitation fund. Of these, only the possibility of seizure of assets is available to non-pollution claimants.

Thus on examination it appears that, despite the purpose of International Conventions being to produce uniformity in the law, there remain areas in which the various Conventions supposed to operate in conjunction with each other are inconsistent, and areas in which practical difficulties will occur when an incident gives rise to claims under both regimes.[25] From an insurance viewpoint, however, the most serious difficulty must remain the defective wording of Article 3 of the 1976 Convention. The availability of the right to limit liability in all but the most extreme circumstances is of paramount importance in ensuring the availability to the shipowner of adequate insurance at reasonable cost. The two conventions fail to dovetail exactly together to provide a "seamless web" and it is unfortunate that, through no fault of his own, an owner or charterer may incur liability in circumstances where he is not entitled to limit. It remains to be hoped that States in ratifying the 1976 Convention will use appropriate language with which to seal these illogical gaps.

---

[25] The problem of overlapping Conventions will recur when further consideration is given at IMO to the Draft Convention on Liability and Compensation in Connection with the Carriage of Noxious and Hazardous Substances by Sea (the Draft HNS Convention). Agreement could not be reached on this Draft at the Diplomatic Conference in 1984 which produced the Protocols to the CLC and fund (fn. 18, *supra*). It should be noted that the legal Committee decided on a dual system of liability, with the shipowner liable up to one limit and the shipper assuming liability for the excess up to a further limit. One of the continuing difficulties is whether to establish a completely separate set of limits for the shipowner or to link HNS liability to the 1976 Convention limits. The 1976 Convention, unfortunately, made no provision in Art. 3 for a future HNS Convention. See generally, IMO LEG SS/S, August 1, 1985.

VIII

The Implementation of the Convention

*Dr. Ralph Beddard**

1. INTRODUCTION

A major factor in the limitation of liability is the need to recognise and be sensitive to the nature and extent of the risks involved in modern specialist areas of shipping. With this in mind, three major conventions dealing with the limitation of liability in specialised areas or aspects of shipping have been concluded during the last 24 years. The International Convention on the Liability of Operators of Nuclear Ships was signed in 1962, the International Convention on Civil Liability for Oil Pollution Damage, in 1969, while the third, the International Convention relating to the Carriage of Passengers and their Luggage by Sea was concluded in Athens in 1974.

As far as general shipping matters were concerned, global limits had already been set by the 1957 Brussels Limitation Convention and its predecessor of 1924. The limits laid down in these two Brussels conventions were comparatively modest, even allowing for the particular categories of risk covered in the later conventions and especially because of the erosive effect of inflation on the traditional gold franc levels.

It was decided to embark upon a new convention to replace those of 1924 and 1957. The Legal Committee of IMCO (as it then called itself) produced a questionnaire on the possible revision of the 1957 Convention, taking as a basis draft Articles prepared by CMI. The 1976 Convention can be seen as a further step in the harmonization of the various systems which commenced with the 1924 Convention.

CMI and now IMO have between them established procedures for consultation and discussion which, probably more succinctly than in any other area of international law, exemplify the modern approach to international law making by formal agreement and render those organisations, more than many, to being described as legislative bodies. The drawback to such a description, however, lies in the process of implementation of the products of their decision-making. For instance a national legislature is able to

* Institute of Maritime Law, Southampton University.

determine, with a reasonable amount of certainty, subject perhaps to the vagaries of domestic political or economic life, the date of coming into force of a legislative instrument. Similarly, exceptions and immunities are immutably laid down in domestic statutes, and the process of amendment, while not always politically easy or feasible, is clearly regulated by the instrument or under the provisions of the general law.

The impediment to characterising formal international law-making procedures as legislative is, basically, that the consent of those to be bound by the law is owed not, as in domestic law, to the legislative body or parliament but to the other Contracting Parties of each individual treaty or agreement. International conventions are often termed "law-making" but procedures for entry into force, the lodging of reservations and the proposal and implementation of amendments always, by the consensual nature of international treaties, fall back on the Contracting Parties and sometimes even may involve signatory states which have not even accepted obligation under the Convention.

An area of international law involving, as do questions of financial liability, private rights of citizens, needs certainty and security. What are the rules to which the vessels of country X are bound?

Entry into force following the lodging of a stated number of ratifications with the depository organisation or government is now accepted as a standard procedure in international law and does indeed satisfy the criterion of certainty of obligation. The question of reservations is troublesome. International law has attempted, over the last three or four decades, to discourage the lodging of reservations which impedes the universality of treaty laws. This in its turn has led to some confusion in the minds of governments and lawyers and the proscription of reservations is becoming more common. It will be seen that attempts to do so in the case of the 1976 Convention were met with petulant cries from those States with over-zealous regard for their sovereignty.

Major amendments to a convention invariably end in the conclusion of a new, replacement treaty and the consequent expense in time and money which that incurs. At such amendment conferences there is always the risk that unwilling parties to the original treaty may use the opportunity to escape from the treaty régime altogether.[1] The sensible implementation of a treaty may, however, need flexibility and a means to make minor amendments. The necessity for a new limitation convention lay partly in the fact that time and inflation had rendered the rigid 1957 Convention

---

[1] For an excellent account of the treaty law problems of implementing the Protocols to the CLC and Fund—with their differing provisions on limitation of liability, see the United Kingdom Note, IMO LEG 55/10, September 5, 1985.

unworkable. It is sad to see that enterprising attempts to simplify amendment of the 1976 Convention were unsuccessful.

The discussion will be restricted to the 1976 Convention but it is submitted that the following discussion reveals a need on the part of the shipping industry for certainty linked with flexibility and adaptability, while the Governments, protecting what they see as their interests at diplomatic conferences, make symbolic gestures of state sovereignty which must be out-dated.

2. SCOPE OF APPLICATION

The scope of application of the 1976 Convention extends more or less in line with the 1957 Convention. It does not apply mandatorily to ships of less than three hundred tons or to ships intended for navigation on inland waterways. The 1957 Convention gave each State the right to decide what other classes of ship other than sea going should be included; the present Convention, on the other hand, lays down in the less laconic way of modern treaties, that States may regulate limitation of liability in these cases by provisions of their national law.[2] Some discussion arose as to the need to include within the Convention the term "sea going" in Article 1(2), while at the same time providing for exclusion of ships intended for[3] navigation on inland waterways in a later Article.[4] The UK has always applied the international rules to inland waterways vessels and has opted similarly under the new Convention. This country also stated at ratification that the limits of liability of ships under 300 tons shall be half those applicable to ships of 500 tons.

Under Article 18, headed "Reservations," States may exclude the application of the Convention in the cases of claims in respect of the raising, removal, destruction or the rendering harmless of wreck,[5] and those arising in respect of removal, destruction or rendering harmless of cargo.[6] A reservation was lodged by the UK[7] in respect of wreck removal[8] thus providing for unlimited liability in this respect, although the position would be changed if and when a fund to compensate harbour authorities for any loss of revenue is established under the Merchant Shipping Act 1979, Sched. 4, Pt. II, para. 3 which incorporates the Convention into United Kingdom law.

[2] Art. 15(2).
[3] "Intended for" was inserted to replace "used for."
[4] Third meeting of the Committee of the Whole Conf. 5/C1/SR 3, *Official Records* pp. 223 *et seq.* Discussion also raged over the definition of inland waterways.
[5] Art. 2(1)(d).
[6] Art. 2(1)(e).
[7] France and Japan reserved the right to exclude the application of Art. 2(1)(d) and (e).
[8] *i.e.* Art. 2(1)(d). A reservation to Art. 2(1)(e) was made only in respect of Gibraltar.

Interestingly, the original draft of Article 18 forbade all reservations other than those expressed but, following a complaint from the Soviet Union delegate that this lay uneasily with the general principles of treaty law, the Article was amended to read "No other reservations shall be admissible to the *substantive provisions* of this Convention." Since the rules of treaty law apply, it would seem that the scope for reservations is only narrowly extended by the change, but the gesture to State sovereignty has been made.

The 1976 Convention does not apply to air cushion vehicles or floating exploration platforms.[9] Nor does it apply to ships constructed for, or adapted to, and engaged in drilling when a State has established a national scheme providing for a higher limit of liability[10] or has become a party to any international Convention regulating the liability of such ships. The Norwegian proposal to exclude such drilling ships was resisted until it was pointed out that the limits of liability for such vessels were likely to be higher than those envisaged in the general scheme. Thus, the above condition for the exclusion was laid down in the Convention.

A final option under Article 6(3) allowing states to give priority to claims for damage to harbour works, basins and waterways and aids to navigation has not been taken up by the United Kingdom.

3. AMENDMENT

Both the 1924 and the 1957 Conventions provided for a conference to consider amendment of the Treaty to be convened at the behest of any party. The 1976 Convention follows the pattern of recent IMO conventions requiring a request for revision or amendment to come from at least one third of the Parties.[11] Any amendment would be subject to acceptance on the part of the contracting states, but once adopted by a two thirds majority of those present and voting at a revision conference, the text would replace that of the present convention for any States wishing, after that date, to become a party.

4. REVISION OF THE LIMITATION AMOUNTS

An early observation by the United Kingdom on the Draft Final Clauses[12] pointed out that one of the reasons for preparing the proposed convention was that the limits of liability contained in

---

[9] Art. 15(5).

[10] Art. 15(4). Norway and Sweden notified IMO of higher liabilities established by their legislation for such vessels.

[11] Art. 20, see also the Athens Convention 1974, Art. 26; the Fund Convention 1971, Art. 45; the CLC, Art. 18.

[12] September 27, 1976, LEG/CONF. 5/5, *Official Records*, p. 427.

the 1957 Convention no longer had the same purchasing power as they did at the time, and furthermore, the capacity of the insurance market had increased. Indeed the limits could be said to be already out of date by the time that the 1957 Convention came into force in 1968. Since similar developments could be expected in the future and to avoid having to hold a revision conference soon after the entry into force of the new convention, the United Kingdom Government called for an additional article making provision for ready amendment of the limits of liability. Such an amendment might be adopted by the Legal Committee of the IMO by a two thirds majority and could come into force when accepted by a similar majority of the parties.

The idea of simple revision of limitation amounts was taken up by France in a proposed article submitted on November 4, 1976.[13] This provided for the convening of a Revision Conference, to which all contracting parties should be invited, to be called at five year intervals. The sole purpose of such a conference would be the determination of new limitation amounts should this appear necessary. The amendments, taken by a two thirds majority would be communicated to all the contracting parties and would be considered as accepted after six months unless, during that period, at least one third of the contracting parties lodge an objection.

Although a large majority of states recognised the need for an accelerated revision procedure, debate in the Committee of the Whole revealed a diversity of views as to how this should best be done. Many states felt that periodic review conferences might not be the most efficient mode of revision since inflation and the insurance market had a tendency not to fluctuate in this convenient manner. Similarly, the British delegate was against Revision Conferences because, if the method of calculating limitation amounts proposed in the draft were extended to the other IMO Convention, this would lead to the inconvenience of organising four revision conferences each time. The United States delegation, associating itself with the British and the French views, suggested a line which followed the 1971 Guatemala Protocol to the Warsaw Convention. It therefore proposed[14] periodic Review Conferences with a power by a two thirds majority vote to increase the limitation amounts up to an agreed maximum, but with a fall-back regular increase laid down in the Convention. A Japanese proposal put forward at the same time,[15] recognised the widely voiced dislike of a tacit acceptance régime. Many Eastern bloc states had spoken out against such a procedure, while the delegate

[13] Cl/WP 39.
[14] Cl/WP 62.
[15] Cl/WP 63, November 9, 1976.

for Ghana revealed problems of a constitutional nature for his country if automatic application without approval were to be adopted. The Japanese proposal suggested a two thirds' acceptance of a revised amount before entry into force.

The Committee on Final Clauses, meeting three days after the debate in the Committee of the Whole, proposed[16] that a conference for revision of limitation amounts should convene at the request of not less than one quarter of the states parties. A decision to alter the amounts should be taken by a two thirds majority of parties present and voting. These amendments would come into effect following formal acceptance by states within 90 days, and under paragraph 5 of the Draft would be applicable vis-à-vis nationals and vessels of states which were not prepared to lodge such acceptances. The French delegation was still not content. Paragraph 5 of the Draft, it felt, would be unacceptable to many delegations as it was contrary to the fundamental rules on the effect of treaties and purported to modify the relationship between two States at the request of one. A new French proposal[17] abandoned both tacit acceptance and periodicity, which had not formerly been well received. It noted the general desire for an accelerated procedure for revision of the value of the unit of account, and proposed the setting up of a committee of financial experts appointed by the contracting parties. If at least three states considered the real value of the unit of account used to establish the limitation amounts had fallen by more than ten per cent, the Committee should be convened to examine the situation on a factual basis provided by official international statistics. Any proposals adopted by this committee should be reported to the parties, a quarter of whom could then request a Revision Conference. Although some states' delegates were worried by the formality of an expert committee and the consequential "indexing" which might lead to a proliferation of revision debates, the French proposal was referred to a Working Group of representatives of France, Switzerland, Belgium and Norway. The Working Group drafted Article 20 bis, which gave effect to the procedure contained in the French proposal.

In the Plenary Committee the Netherlands representative seemed to voice the general view that the procedure was "superfluous and complicated," and the proposal failed to achieve the two thirds majority vote necessary for inclusion in the Draft Convention. The French proposal had concerned itself with variation of the amount of the unit of account and not with the substitution of the unit by another, which it saw as a political rather than a financial matter. Article 21 of the Draft which was

16 CONF. 5/WP. 3.
17 CONF. 5/WP. 4, November 17, 1976.

now left for discussion did not distinguish between these two functions and, of course, the notions are so inextricably mixed that no Revision Conference, even if considering the views of experts, could separate political from other matters.

Paragraph 6 of the Draft Article 21 read as follows:

> "After entry into force of an amendment a Party which has accepted the amendment is entitled to apply the amended Convention vis-à-vis vessels and nationals of a Party which has not accepted the amendment."

Although it was argued that in the context of the Convention this provision was compatible with the Vienna Convention on Treaties, there was much concern expressed that states would find themselves bound by provisions which they had specifically not accepted. The Netherlands and Federal Republic representatives pointed out that if paragraph 6 were not retained, it would be difficult for states parties which had not accepted certain amendments to apply different amounts to different ships and chaos might ensue. Nevertheless paragraph 6 failed to receive the necessary two thirds majority.

Final agreement was eventually reached on Article 21 for revision of the limitation amounts and of unit of account or monetary limit. A conference may be called for either of these purposes at the request of not less than one quarter of the states parties, and alteration of limitation amounts may only be made following a *significant* change in their real value. A decision of this conference is taken by a two thirds majority of those states present and voting. The Plenary Committee having rejected proposals for formal acceptances to be required to amendments, it would seem that any revision accepted by the Revision Conference is directly binding on those states voting in favour but not on others. These others could presumably at a later stage indicate their wish to be bound.

It can be seen then that attempts to accelerate and maybe encourage revision of limitation amounts have succeeded only in so far as the number of states seeking revision has been reduced from the one third of Article 20 to one quarter. Brave attempts to write into the convention periodic revaluations or expert enquiry were defeated, while tacit acceptance and imposition by majority vote were felt to challenge some of the more sacred notions of international law and national sovereignty.

5. ENTRY INTO FORCE

The Convention was designed to enter into force twelve months after the lodging by twelve states of instruments of ratification or accession.[18] The original proposal from the committee on Final Clauses had required 20 ratifications, at least five of which should be from states with a tonnage equal to or greater than one million gross tons. The 1957 Convention had required five out of ten ratifications to be from states holding similar tonnage. The Yugoslav representative on the Committee of the Whole proposed that the tonnage criterion should be deleted, in order to reflect more adequately the changes which had taken place in the world community since 1957, so that states with large fleets should not have the privilege of making entry into force of the Convention dependent on their ratification of it. It was pointed out by the Greek delegate that a tonnage criterion was not a question of discrimination but had been introduced in the past to ensure that treaties coming into force involved the participation of major maritime states rather than others alone. The CLC asked for five ratifications out of eight to have similar tonnage in tankers. Nonetheless, states were not in favour of a tonnage condition and the sentence was deleted. Immediately following this, a United Kingdom proposal to reduce the necessary ratifications from 20 to 12 was adopted.

The 1976 Convention, which may be denounced after one year of its entry into force for a contracting party,[19] replaces and abrogates for ratifying States both the 1924 and the 1957 Conventions.[20]

The United Kingdom was the second state to ratify the 1976 Convention preceded by North Yemen. By mid-1984 there were 11 Contracting States. Although Poland had announced its intention to ratify at the IMO Legal Committee in October 1985, it was in fact the State of Benin which became the twelfth Contracting State on November 1, 1986. As a result the 1976 Limitation Convention will enter into force on December 1, 1986.

The United Kingdom Merchant Shipping Act 1979, ss.17–19 and Scheds. 4 and 5 will incorporate the Convention into British Law. Part I of Schedule 4 sets out the the relevant text of the Convention and Part II provides for a number of supplementary provisions concerned with interpretation and implementation in the United Kingdom. Schedule 5 lists consequential amendments to other legislation. The British legislation and the denunciation

---

[18] Strictly, Art. 17 is more specific and refers to "the first day of the month following one year after the date" of the 12th ratification. As this in fact took place on November 1, 1985, the entry into force period was 13 months, i.e. to December 1, 1986.

[19] Art. 19.

[20] Art. 17(4).

of the 1957 Convention will take effect on the same day as the new régime enters force internationally.[21-23]

[21-23] On commencement of the new régime, the following orders will be required:
  (1) Order presenting interest rates (Sched. 4, Pt. II para. 8(1)).
  (2) Tonnage Order (Sched. 4, Pt. I, Art. 6(5).
  (3) Hovercraft Order (Sched. 5, para. 4).
  (4) Standard "Parties-to-conventions" Order (Sched. 4, Pt. II para. 13).

IX

The Insurance Viewpoint

R. C. Seward*

It is fashionable to treat limitation as an anachronism, the remains of an outmoded system now suitable only as a game for lawyers to play. It has long been the practice in the United States to try and find evermore fanciful reasons for breaking limitation by pinning "privity" on the shipowner and it now seems that the same trend has reached the United Kingdom with the decision of the House of Lords in the *Marion*.[1] It is no doubt one of the strengths of the common law that it moves with the times, but is it really the task of judges to impose unrealistic standards on shipowners so as to enable the court to do "justice" and force the shipowner to abandon his limitation defence? It was Lord Denning who said in the *Bramley Moore*[2]:

> "Limitation of liability is not a matter of justice. It is a rule of public policy which has its origin in history and its justification in convenience."

By way of contrast Griffiths LJ in the *Garden City No. 2*[3]:

> "(Limitation of liability) . . . is of long standing and generally accepted by the trading nations of the world. It is a right given to promote the general health of trade and in truth is no more than a way of distributing the insurance risk."

Is there still a valid policy behind the shipowner's right to limit his liability or is it now a concept which should be relegated to historical footnotes?

1. THE PRINCIPLE OF LIMITATION OF LIABILITY

The original rationale for enabling shipowners to limit their liability was the unusually risky nature of shipping and the need to encourage people to go into the business. It was clear at the very beginnings of maritime commerce in Italy in the eleventh century,[4]

* Britannia Steamship Insurance Association Ltd.
[1] [1984] 2 Lloyd's Rep. 1.
[2] [1964] P. 200.
[3] [1984] 2 Lloyd's Rep. 37.
[4] See Tables of Amalfi—4 Black Book of the Admiralty 3.

as it is clear now, that a shipowner stood to lose a great deal more than his investment as a result of liabilities which might arise as part of the same incident which ruined the voyage (for example, a sinking). Whilst a man might be prepared to risk a proportion of his wealth on shipping, very few would be willing to risk the loss of their whole fortune on an adventure with such uncertain prospects.

The growth of maritime trade was closely paralleled by that of the concept of limitation and it seems to have been well established throughout Europe by the end of the seventeenth century. The Marine Ordinance of Louis XIV of France of 1681 which became incorporated in one form or another in most civil jurisdictions provided that "the owners of the ship shall be answerable for the deeds of the master; but shall be discharged, abandoning their ship and freight."[5]

The United Kingdom was relatively late in legislating to provide for shipowners' rights to limit and a shipowners' petition of 1733 to Parliament illustrates the problem:

" . . . the insupportable and unreasonable hardship to which our laws in this case subject them; and to which no owners of ships are exposed in other trading nations. . . . Unless some provision be made for their relief, trade and navigation will be greatly discouraged, since owners of ships find themselves without any fault on their part, exposed to ruin. . . . "

The statute which followed this in 1734[6] was aptly entitled "An act to settle how far owners of ships shall be answerable for the acts of the masters or mariners; and for giving further relief to the owners of ships."

In the early days limitation was usually based on the entirely rational basis of the value of the ship, being the capital involved in the adventure, and it is perhaps interesting to note that the P and I Clubs, who today cover about 85 per cent. of international shipowners' liability insurance, owe their origin to the first United Kingdom legislation which exposed shipowners to potential liabilities larger than the value of the ship plus pending freight. This legislation was The Merchant Shipping Act of 1854, which provided for a limitation fund based on a sterling multiple of the ship's tonnage and made it impossible to provide for liability coverage as part of the normal hull insurances. The present day system of shipowner's liability insurance is therefore literally built on concepts of limitation.

It is said that the need to encourage shipowners to invest is no

---

[5] See the Hanseatic Ordinances of 1614 and 1644, the Statutes of Hamburg 1603, the Maritime Codes of Sweden 1667 and the Marine Ordinance of Louis XIV—1681.
[6] 7 Geo. 2, c. 15.

longer a valid reason for limitation, despite the currently parlous financial position of shipping and the potentially vast liability exposure as evidenced by the *Amoco Cadiz*[7] case or the less famous (infamous) but equally expensive *Betelgeuse* explosion in Bantry Bay in 1979. The modern theory is that insurance is available and that this removes the danger of disaster from the shipowner.

This ability to insure applies, of course, as much to others likely to be damaged in a marine incident as it does to the shipowner himself. The jetty owner and the cargo owner both can and do insure their property, and life insurance is available for individuals. Indeed, insurance by the jetty owner is much more likely to reflect his potential exposure to loss than reliance on the vagaries of tort law since he is free to choose a form and extent of insurance cover to meet his needs.

This points to a modern justification for limitation. It provides a mechanism for sharing costs between all those involved in, and benefiting from, the maritime adventure. A certain number of accidents are inevitable and there would seem to be a very strong case for sharing the cost of these rather than imposing all the losses on the shipowner, particularly in cases where there was no real fault on his part.

Limitation has another highly important function under a modern insurance based system, which is that it makes the shipowner's liabilities insurable. The structure of shipowners' liability insurance is founded on the right of the shipowner to limit his liability and thus to bring a degree of comparability between different ships trading in different areas and exposed to different risks. The existence of the right to limit makes it possible for a shipowner to obtain cover for his total exposure and not just some proportion, limited instead by reference to a figure in his contract of insurance. This means that the shipowner is not "exposed to ruin," because he can insure the whole and not just part of his exposure. Finally the shipowner's right to limit introduces a highly necessary element of predictability into an area which would otherwise be devoid of guidelines.

2. SUB-STANDARD SHIPS

One of the criticisms of limitation is that it encourages shipowners not to maintain their ships properly on the basis that they will not be paying in full for the resultant claims. This theory notably fails to take account of the fact that this very lack of maintenance may well cause limitation to be broken, thus defeating the supposed object. If there is any lack of maintenance it will be as a result of attempts to cut costs, not to cheat limitation claimants.

[7] (1984) A.M.C. 2123.

Ship standards are best controlled by establishing internationally accepted norms for the design and building of ships and for training their crews. Enforcement can then be achieved by inspections, both by port authorities and by the authorities of the relevant flag state. The International Maritime Organisation (IMO) and the United States Coast Guard are both now active in this area and the recent decline in casualties may well be at least in part due to their efforts.

Limitation is highly relevant to the insurance of shipowners' liabilities but it has little or no influence on ship standards; rather these are affected by changes in the international consensus on how ships should be run and the attitude of the particular owner.

3. THE IMPORTANCE OF LIMITATION IN P AND I INSURANCE

The hull underwriter always knows the maximum amount of his exposure to a risk, namely the insured value, and whatever happens he will not be paying more than this and any legal fees associated with the claim.

He is even protected from the case which takes a long time to resolve since the hull policy limit is usually an absolute one inclusive of any interest. The international P and I insurer is not in such a happy position since his cover is best described as "unlimited coverage of a shipowner's legal liabilities." It is important to emphasise that the cover is for legal liabilities only and that all the P and I Club Rules require an owner to limit his liability where possible.

The existence of a secure right to limit removes an important element of uncertainty from shipowners' liability insurance and enables premiums to be both lower and more certain (a significant consideration in a mutual organisation which raises premiums to cover losses and does not operate on a fixed premium or profit making basis). In today's highly competitive shipping market the benefit of the lower premiums is passed to the consumer in reduced freight rates.

It is sometimes suggested that the substantial reinsurance cover which is currently purchased by the International Group of P and I Clubs means that limitation is no longer necessary. The real position is that the existence of limitation makes the extent of the cover possible. The reinsurers at the higher levels do not expect to pay claims and their premium rates reflect this. Still more importantly, the reinsurance available today might simply not be there in the future in the event of significantly large claims coupled with the demise of the right to limit. This volatility of the reinsurance market is well illustrated by the problems currently being experienced in obtaining general liability cover even at considerably increased rates. Many insurers have simply left the liability market and lawyers, doctors, accountants, engineers and even insurance brokers are finding trouble in buying the insurance necessary to protect their businesses.

4. EXPANDING LIABILITIES FOR SHIPOWNERS

Indeed, far from becoming less necessary, limitation is ever more important for shipowners as the impact and range of their potential liabilities expands.

Modern legislation often provides for no fault liability. Oil pollution legislation is an example, or the attempts by certain port authorities around the world to make a shipowner liable for accidents which occur as a result of the presence of the ship, rather than as a result of any fault by the ship. In both instances the shipowner can find himself liable to pay for incidents over which he had no control and could not have prevented. Another example is the classic problem of the compulsory pilot; the shipowner is forced to put his ship in the hands of a pilot over whom he has no power of selection and little real control and is then compelled to take responsibility for the pilot's errors. It is clear that the modern test of liability for the shipowner has moved a long way from negligence or even vicarious liability.

The range of shipowners' liabilities is also growing with the tendency of modern courts to expand the ambit of consequential loss claims. In this, shipping is not unique, but it does seem to be peculiarly affected. For example, the first major oil pollution of modern times the *Torrey Canyon*[8] in 1976, foreshadowed the development of a major head of potential liability from an area which had always been covered by liability insurers but never regarded as particularly serious.

The sheer measure of consequential losses can also be frightening; for example a supply vessel worth perhaps $4 million on hire to an oil rig operator (value $100 million) at a rate of maybe $4000 per day causes relatively minor damage to the oil rig and finds itself faced with claims for loss of production and down time running at $100,000–$200,000 per day; without limitation this does not make economic sense.

5. LIMITATION FOR SHIPOWNERS

It may be argued that shipping is not exceptional and why should shipowners have a special form of protection? Shipowners are in fact not alone in being protected and most professional transporters have some form of limit to their liability either by contract or

---

[8] In *Re Barracuda Tanker Corp.* (S/T *Torrey Canyon*) 281 F Supp. 228 S.D.N.Y. (1968) mod. 409 F2d 1013 (2 C.N. 1969).

statute (for example road hauliers, railways and airlines), as do others responsible for safeguarding the property of third parties without the means to know what the property consists of (for example hotel keepers). In addition there are certain special factors relevant to shipowners.

First, there is the near inevitability of a relatively high number of routine accidents coupled with the likelihood of occasional, but regular, serious incidents; the phrase "perils of the sea" is not an idle one and the degree of control exercisable over a fully loaded merchant ship in crowded waters is a great deal less than precise.

Secondly, there is the complexity of most incidents and the difficulty of sorting out ownership and responsibilities for various cargoes and damages on a voyage which may involve a multitude of different parties in many countries.

Thirdly, the shipowner is peculiarly exposed in that he owns or controls a highly visible and valuable asset, which is notoriously easy to arrest. There is a very real temptation, therefore, on both courts and legislatures to throw more and more responsibility onto the shipowner simply because there is a substantial asset which can be seized within the jurisdiction and he can thus be forced to pay.

Finally, the international shipowner is by definition dealing with many different countries and by reason of the trading pattern of his ships he may well find himself subject to the jurisdiction of almost any maritime nation, possibly even for alleged misconduct which has nothing whatever to do with that country. It is therefore highly desirable that there should be an international code of maritime law which is as uniform as possible, both as to the type of liabilities imposed and as to the quantum of those liabilities. Forum shopping or even forum scattering may be a highly profitable game for lawyers but it hardly helps to oil the wheels of international commerce.

6. ALTERNATIVES TO LIMITATION

It is sometimes suggested that shipowners do not need the protection of limitation since they can use the normal corporate structure of limited liability companies. This ploy is itself possibly ineffective, given the propensity of courts nowadays to consider "piercing the corporate veil"; but assuming for the moment this strategem would be effective, is it desirable?

The logic of the one-ship company would be such that it would have minimal insurance cover, since it would be cheaper, in the event of a serious incident, to abandon the ship and wind up the company, leaving claimants with no assets at all. The insurance cover would be for low levels and might well be exhausted by the costs of crew repatriation and suchlike and the third party claimants would be considerably worse off than they are now. As regards the protection of the insurer himself in the absence of shipowners' limitation, the obvious move would be towards much lower insurance limits and higher premiums. This would raise the costs of running ships and thus ultimately the cost to the consumer, but, more seriously, it would leave the shipowner exposed to bankruptcy in the event of a large claim significantly in excess of his insurance policy cover. In the words of the 1733 petition " ... owners of ships (would) find themselves without any fault on their part exposed to ruin. ... " The effect of either of these strategems would therefore be the very thing which those pressing for the abolition of limitation are seeking to avoid: a reduced amount of compensation available for claimants and an encouragement to irresponsible shipowning.

7. THE CURRENT LAW: A GAMBLING GAME

In the light of the genuine and continuing importance of the principle of shipowners' limitation it is worth examining the maze into which the courts have been leading those wishing to make use of it.

The theoretical test of a shipowners' right to limit his liability around the world may be considered as that introduced into English law by the 1894 Merchant Shipping Act and still preserved by the 1958 Merchant Shipping Act, which brought into English law the terms of the "International Convention Relating to the Limitation of Liability of Owners of Sea-Going Ships" (the 1957 Brussels Convention). There are in fact three basic systems currently in operation for deciding on the shipowner's right to limit. The 1924 Convention ("International Convention for the Unification of Certain Rules Relating to the Limitation of the Liability of Owners of Sea-Going Vessels"—Brussels), the 1957 Convention, and the American-style system enshrined in 46 USC §181–189 (1976). The two Conventions use a system of tonnage multiples in calculating the relevant fund, while the United States system uses the value of the ship and pending freight at the end of the voyage in question as the measure of the limitation fund. However, all three systems purport to apply the same test of the owner's ability to limit; that of the actual fault of the shipowner himself. The test therefore is to see if the owner's own fault caused the accident or whether it was due to the mistake of one of the subordinate staff in the operation of the ship. The rationale of this famous "fault or privity" rule lay in the fact that shipowners might reasonably be expected to answer for their own errors but could not be expected to respond on an unlimited basis for the fault of those over whom the owner might have little or no direct control.

The principle of this test is relatively straightforward, seems logical and involves a series of classic legal steps following an incident for which the shipowner seeks to limit his liability.

The claimant must establish the liability of the owner for the incident in question; this is done by proving the cause of the incident and that this cause was the responsibility of the shipowner either as a result of a negligent act, or because of an absolute liability. The burden then shifts to the shipowner (under current law) for him to demonstrate that there was no "fault or privity" on the part of the shipowner himself which contributed to the "cause" of the accident.

There are two traditional areas of difficulty in the search for "fault or privity"; first, whose actions can be considered to be those of the shipowner himself in the modern day of corporate ownership and secondly, how much investigation does the owner have to do into the detailed running of his ships and how much can safely be delegated to the staff concerned with the operation.

8. THE DILEMMA

It is worth examining these problem areas as a matter of general principle before seeing how different legal systems have attempted to resolve them.

It is important to choose proper staff for a job. At its simplest this may mean no more than ensuring that all the ship's officers and crew are correctly certified, but a determined court may extend this responsibility so as to oblige a shipowner to provide extensive courses of supplementary training.

It is clearly necessary to delegate authority together with responsibility, but how much instruction should a competent ship's master be given? If a shipowner leaves the master to deal with emergencies on the basis of his experience and seamanship, he is in danger of being accused of running away from his responsibilities. If, on the other hand, the master carries with him instructions for dealing with every situation, inevitably they won't cover the particular problem which arises, or, if they do, they will be wrong. Alternatively the master who spends all his time on the radio telephone to his head office is involving senior management in decisions which should properly be made by the man on the spot in the light of the circumstances on which he is best placed to decide. This has the very important psychological effect of undermining the confidence of the master and also his authority on board ship. He is placed in the invidious position of having considerable responsibility and no authority. The dangers of this were well illustrated by the unwillingness of the master of the *Amoco Cadiz*[9] to sign Lloyd's Open Form of Salvage Agreement

[9] See n. 7, *supra.*

without reference to his senior management, a lack of actual or perceived authority which might have been fatal. The instruction dilemma is therefore one of "damned if you do and damned if you don't." The modern court has added another twist to this screw by requiring an owner to prove not only that he employed adequate crew and gave them proper instructions, but also that he had a system of supervision such as to ensure that the master was actually acting properly and obeying instructions.

The second problem area is to decide who is responsible in the sense of making the shipowner responsible; if the ship's master is regarded as the owner's representative, the whole purpose of limitation may be defeated, but in a modern corporation it may be very difficult to find the person or persons actually exercising the central functions of the shipowner.

English law

The English legal definition of "actual fault or privity" is generally seen as that used by Buckley LJ in *Asiatic Petroleum Co.* v. *Lennard Carrying Co. Ltd.*[10]:

> "The words 'actual fault or privity' ... infer something personal to the owner, something blameworthy in him, as distinguished from constructive fault or privity such as the fault or privity of his servants or agents. But the words 'actual fault' are not confined to affirmative or positive acts by way of fault. If the owner be guilty of an act or omission to do something which he ought to have done, he is no less guilty of an 'actual fault' than if the act had been one of commission. To avail himself of the statutory defence, he must show that he himself is not blameworthy for having either done or omitted to do something or been privy to something. If he has means of knowledge which he ought to have used and does not avail himself of them, his omission so to do may be a fault, and, if so, it is an actual fault and he cannot claim the protection."

The test is objective; that is, how did this particular shipowner measure up to the standards of reasonably prudent comparable shipowners in the management and control of their vessels? The difficulty comes with the degree of management control, and more particularly supervision, which the shipowner is expected to exercise over those actually doing the job. There are several recent English cases where shipowners have been denied the right to limit even for what would appear to be navigational errors.[11]

[10] (1914) I K.B. 419 (C.A.)
[11] The *Norman* [1960] 1 Lloyd's Rep. 1; *Rederij Erven H. Groen and Groen* v. *England, The (Owners)* [1973] 1 Lloyd's Rep. 373; The *Lady Gwendolen* [1965] P. 294; The *Dayspring* [1968] 2 Lloyd's Rep. 204.

The classic test of the person exercising the central function of the shipowner in English law, is to be found in the speech of Viscount Haldane also from *Lennard's Carrying Co. Ltd.* v. *Asiatic Petroleum*[12] where he said:

> "(A company) is an abstraction. It has no mind of its own . . . , its active and directing will must consequently be sought in the person of somebody who for some purposes may be called an agent, but who is really the directing mind and will of the corporation, the very ego and centre of the personality of the corporation."

The "fault or privity" of the company is therefore:

> "the fault or privity of somebody who is not merely a servant or agent for whom the company is liable upon the footing of respondent superior, but somebody for whom the company is liable because his action is the very action of the company itself."

This suggests that a proper delegation of responsibility to a reputable management should be sufficient to protect the shipowner from losing his right to limit. The courts have however been reluctant to follow this logical route and have instead sought to find the "alter ego" much lower in the chain of command.

The difficulty of finding the right person was well illustrated in the case of the *Lady Gwendolen*[13] where the Guinness brewing company was running a "beer tanker" from their manufacturing plant in Ireland to Liverpool. The evidence was that this tanker habitually sailed at full speed regardless of weather conditions, relying entirely on radar. It was claimed that this must have been known to senior management since the sailing schedule was adhered to and no allowance made for fog. The inevitable collision in fog occurred and the question centred on who exercised the shipowning function of a brewing company so as to make their "actual fault or privity" the matter at issue. The court eventually fixed on the marine superintendent as being at fault since he was the most senior man in the company with any knowledge of shipping, despite the fact that he exercised no executive function. It was held that the superintendent should have checked the ship's log in order to see how the ship was being navigated in fog and the lack of any management control over the superintendent was sufficient to pin "actual fault or privity" on the shipowners. The court further suggested that they would also have found "actual fault" of the shipowner on the basis of the failure of the traffic

[12] [1915] A.C. 705.
[13] [1965] P. 294.

manager to supervise or even on the basis of the fault of the marine superintendent.

It would seem however that the English courts have now returned to the more traditional test of in the cases of the *Garden City*[14] and the *Marion*[15] where the responsibility is placed firmly back at director level and arguably even at managing director level, at least in the case of a genuine shipping company. This approach seems to be right since the search is really for the "ego" of the company not the "alter ego" and it was expressly approved by the House of Lords in *Tesco Supermarkets* v. *Nattrass*,[16] which although it was a case on the interpretation of a criminal statute is likely to be persuasive.

The *Marion*[17] however appears to have made a remarkable extension of the test on the other half of the limitation question which now involves a stringent investigation into office systems of supervision. In the case of the *Marion*, the master anchored on and damaged a submarine pipeline because he was not using up-to-date charts. The claims were of the order of US $25 million, of which a large part was consequential loss. The owners were able to show that the correct charts were actually on board the *Marion* and that they had a perfectly adequate system of ensuring that updates reached their ships. However, the House of Lords decided that this was not enough and that the owners also had to show that they had a system for ensuring that the correct charts were actually used. This meant a rigorous system of on-board investigations by marine superintendents and detailed study of the log books combined with a chain of command which ensured reports reaching the responsible director. To the innocent eye this seems to get perilously close to saying that the responsibility of the shipowner is to ensure that mistakes do not happen. The "catch 22" runs as follows; if there is an adequate system in good working order, it will not fail and therefore any failure leads by definition to an allegation of negligence by senior management. This theory flies in the face of proper management practice on the delegation of authority and leads to "gelded" ships' masters frightened to take decisions. The dangers of lack of sufficient authority and trust in a master being well illustrated by the *Amoco Cadiz*.[18]

There is another important result of this decision. The uncertainties inherent in any limitation action have been significantly increased, since it is now open to the lawyer investigating the right-to-limit to conduct detailed investigation into the internal procedures of the head office—the object of this

---

[14] [1982] 2 Lloyd's Rep. 382.
[15] See n. 1, *supra*.
[16] [1972] A.C. 153.
[17] See n. 1, *supra*.
[18] See n. 7, *supra*.

investigation being to show the personal fault of a member of the board of directors. This is hardly a practice likely to make for good commercial relations, and which company can say that their office systems are perfect? It is rumoured that even the Lords of the Admiralty were reluctant to disclose their practice with regard to reviewing log books in a recent collision case involving one or Her Majesty's ships.

The Commonwealth

It is difficult to be precise on the attitude of Commonwealth Courts towards limitation due to the paucity or even absence of reported cases. However it is probably safe to say that current practice in Commonwealth countries is modelled on English precedent, but that there is not as yet the same inclination to carry the search for "actual fault or privity" to the ridiculous lengths of the *Marion*.[19] It is probable that the test of "alter ego" will also remain potentially below boardroom level, though the English case of *Tesco Supermarkets* v. *Nattrass*[20] might persuade a Commonwealth court to look higher in the organisation. The principle therefore remains that limitation is most probably available for fault occurring on board ship and will only be called into question if the cause of the incident in the true proximate sense can be shown to be the fault of the head office, for example a failure to provide necessary equipment.

The civil law countries—Europe

Again the paucity of reported cases makes authority hard to come by; but the law of limitation in civil law countries, being based on a code, has not been subject to the same judge made glosses as are to be found in England. The result of this is that the 1957 Brussels Convention tends to be applied in its original pure form and the "actual fault or privity" has to be genuine before limitation will be denied.

This difference perhaps illustrates one of the main reasons for the modern tendancy towards uncertainty in limitation actions in common-law countries. The problem centres on money values and there is no doubt that in certain circumstances the right of a shipowner to limit his liability, if upheld, can lead to injustice. Some of the limitation fund values under the 1957 Brussels Convention do not provide for a fair distribution of risk between those parties involved in a modern maritime adventure. This comment applies with still more force in the United States where

[19] See n. 1, *supra*.
[20] See n. 16, *supra*.

existing law may lead to a limitation fund of almost nothing in the case of the total loss of the ship.

The United States

The governing statute in the United States is 9 Stat. 635 (1851) as amended by 46 USC §§181–189 (1976), "The Limitation Act," which owed its origins to pleas from shipowners very similar to those found as reasons for the English statutes in the previous century and which incorporated a similar doctrine. Most English lawyers would recognise the definition of "actual faulty or privity" as being the same as that used in *Lord* v. *Goodall*[21] to define the American test:

> "As used in the statute, the meaning of the words "privity or knowledge,' evidently, is a personal participation of the owner in some fault, or act of negligence, causing or contributing to the loss, or some personal knowledge or means of knowledge, of which he is bound to avail himself, of a contemplated loss, or of a condition of things likely to produce or contribute to the loss, without adopting appropriate means to prevent it. There must be some personal concurrence, or some fault or negligence on the part of the owner himself, or in which he personally participates, to constitute such privity, within the meaning of the act, as will exclude him from the benefit of its provisions."

Equally the reasoning behind the exemption of the shipowner from the normal doctrine of vicarious liability was put in a way immediately recognisable to an English lawyer in the case of "In *re Phoenix Sand & Gravel Co*"[22]:

> "The philosophy of shipowners' limitation seems to me this: There are so many things which shipowners must do by deputy, and must have done at great distances and under circumstances where human fallibility is peculiarly prone to produce error, that they have long been saved by statute from the consequences of their agents' acts."

However American courts have now put so many interpretative glosses on the Limitation Act that it is scarcely recognisable. They have done this both by enlarging the duties imposed on the shipowner and also by bringing the level at which those duties have to be discharged lower in the company hierarchy. There is little doubt that the dislike of the American judiciary for the concept of limitation has been strongly influenced by the ludicrous way in which the United States fund is calculated. This leads to the crazy

[21] 15 F.Cas. 884 aff'd. 102 U.S. 451 (1881).
[22] (1940) A.M.C. 508.

situation that the limitation fund is at its lowest when the disaster is greatest, for instance the *Titanic*[23] limit of the value of the one lifeboat recovered, or the *Morro Castle*[24] where the residual value was tiny and the injuries very serious.

The United States courts have attacked limitation on a broad front. The concept of "managing officer" has been expanded to include marine superintendents, port engineers and even ships' officers who are entrusted with supervisory duties. The test now seems to be not the position held by the individual in the company structure, but rather the scope of his authority and might be described as the individual whose duty includes: " . . . supervision of the phase of the business out of which the loss or injury occurred," *Coryll* v. *Phillips*.[25] The American courts have also required a remarkable degree of supervision, as for instance in *Spencer Kellogg & Son* v. *Hicks*,[26] where despite an express prohibition on sailing when there was ice in the river and no knowledge that a sailing was taking place when ice was present, a shipowner was held unable to limit his liability because a local plant manager did not "by inquiries or by personal inspection" assure himself that the launch did not operate. The mere presence of "senior staff" in the area of the incident may even be sufficient. The test seems therefore again to be very close to the absolute one of ensuring that accidents do not happen. Indeed the United States courts have also used the doctrine of the non-delegable duty (illegitimately imported from the United States COGSA despite express statutory language to the contrary[27]) to deny a shipowner the right to limit even when he has done everything reasonable to ensure safety, *Tug Ocean Queen Inc.* v. *The Tanker Four Lakes*.[28]

The English Courts have also been invited to deny limitation on the grounds of the non-delegable duty, but have resisted the temptation to do so. In the *Truculent*[29] Willmer J expressed the difference as:

> "(The non delegable duty) goes only to liability. . . . The question of limitation only arises after liability has been determined and it by no means follows that because liability cannot be evaded the right of limitation is lost."

The illogicality and injustice of the normal rules for calculation of the United States limitation fund on the basis of the value of the ship at the end of the voyage caused them to be amended by 49

[23] *Oceanic Steam Navigation Co.* v. *Mellor* 233 U.S. 724.
[24] (1939) A.M.C. 895 S.D.N.Y.
[25] 312 U.S. 406 (1943).
[26] 285 U.S. 502 (1932).
[27] 46 U.S. 1308 (1976).
[28] 598 F.Supp. 1062 (1974).
[29] [1952] P. 1.

Stat. 960 and 1479 of 1935 and 1936 following a fire on board the passenger ship *Morro Castle* in 1934[30] where there was a very low limitation fund (based on the damaged value of the ship) and considerable loss of life. The provision for constituting a limitation fund for personal injury is now based on a tonnage measurement similar to that of the international conventions and provides for a minimum fund of $60 per gross ton available to personal injury claimants only. This has recently been raised to $420 per gross ton.[31]

This same statute also amended the test which was to be applied in personal injury cases so that the level of responsibility was moved much lower and:

> "the privity or knowledge of the Master of a seagoing vessel or of the superintendent or managing agent of the owner thereof, at or prior to the commencement of each voyage, shall be deemed conclusively the privity or knowledge of the owner of such vessel."

It is perhaps not unfair to say that American courts have displayed such a wilful ability to ignore the plain statutory language in their search for excuses to break limitation that some of the spirit of Justice Black must have inspired them, for in his dissenting judgment in the case of *Maryland Gas Co.* v. *Cushing*[32] which was concerned with the loss of life of seamen and the question of whether the Limitation Act included an insurer sued directly—he said:

> "Judicial expansion of the Limited Liability Act at this date seems especially inappropriate. Many of the conditions in the shipping industry which induced the 1851 Congress to pass the Act no longer prevail. And later Congresses, when they wished to aid shipping, provided subsidies paid out of the public treasury rather than subsidies paid by injured persons. If shipowners really need an additional subsidy, Congress can give it to them without making injured seamen bear the cost."

The recent case of the *Summit Venture*[33] again shows the lengths to which a court will go in order to break limitation, particularly in a case involving the deaths of innocent third parties. All the facts suggested negligent navigation by a compulsory pilot, who was heavily criticised by the court, and yet limitation was denied on the basis that the ship's officers had not been adequately instructed on their responsibilities when a pilot was on board. The company manual was clear but the court found that it was not followed and

---

[30] See n. 24, *supra*.
[31] 46 U.S.C. S.183(b) as amended October 19, 1984.
[32] 347 U.S. 40 (1954).
[33] 566 F.Supp. 962.

the ship's officers concept of their rights and duties was very different from that laid down in the company manual. Once again it was held to be the duty of the owner not only to issue adequate instructions but also to ensure that they were followed.

The court also decided that an owner has a non-delegable duty to provide a competent crew and that the crew had been negligent and were therefore not competent. This concept is very close to completely vitiating the entire theory of limitation; the owner must ensure that the crew is competent, the crew made a mistake, ergo they were not competent and the owner had therefore failed in his duty. This finding was made despite the fact that the two lookouts were most aptly named Sit and Lok. The real reason for the decision can perhaps be found in the words of the court:

> "It is beneficial (sic) to recognise that limited liability is not favoured under the law. The development of the corporate form of business and the universal use of insurance has undercut the underlying historical basis of the Limitation Act . . .
> . . . The Limitation of Liability Act is an antiquated statute. It is time for Congress to take the wheel and re-examine the policies which led to the legislation. Granted there is little or no actual injustice when the statute is applied to a purely maritime case such as a collision between vessels. But how can a motorist who is unfamiliar with the maritime industry, customs and law, insure himself or herself against the risk of such a tragic encounter?" (Several cars and a Greyhound bus were involved when the bridge collapsed).

These comments show again that the judicial attack on limitation is fuelled by a dislike of the present application of principles which in themselves may remain valid. There is a danger of throwing out the baby with the bath water.

9. DIRECT ACTION AGAINST INSURERS

The judicial attack on fundamental concepts relating to limits of liability is well illustrated by the approach of the United States courts to direct action against the liability insurer.

In most jurisdictions there are insurance provisions which provide for a direct right of recovery by a third party claimant from the liability insurer in cases where the shipowner assured goes bankrupt. However the basic principle is that the third party "stands in the shoes of" the assured and can recover from the insurer the same amount as the assured himself would have received. The insurer can therefore avail himself of all the terms of the policy, including deductibles and policy conditions. The most recent English judicial expression of this was by Leggatt J. in

Socony Mobil Oil Co. Inc. v. *West of England Shipowners Mutual Insurance Association*[34] where he said:

> "The Act of 1930 transfers to the Plaintiffs not the claim but the contractual rights of the insured"

or putting it another way:

> "... (the phrase) the third party stepping into the shoes of the insured and (the phrase) the third party not being entitled to have the plums without the duff conveniently denote two points of principle. First, there can be transferred to the third party no more than the rights formerly vested in the insured. Secondly, the rights which are transferred are subject to the same incidents as when vested in the insured ..."

In *Post Office* v. *Norwich Union Fire Insurance Society Ltd.*,[35] Denning MR had clearly expressed the position and also the difference between a liability policy and an indemnity policy when he said:

> "Under that section the injured person steps into the shoes of the wrongdoer. There are transferred to him the wrongdoer's 'rights against the insurers under the contract.' What are those rights? When do they arise? So far as the 'liability' of the insured is concerned, there is no doubt that his liability to the injured person arises at the time of the accident, when negligence and damage coincide. But the 'rights' of the insured person against the insurer do not arise at that time. The policy says that 'the company will indemnify the insured against all sums which the insured shall become legally liable to pay as compensation in respect of loss of or damage to property.' It seems to me that the insured only acquires a right to sue for the money when his liability to the injured person has been established so as to give rise to a right of indemnity. His liability to the injured person must be ascertained and determined to exist, either by judgment of the court or by an award in arbitration or by agreement."

It is worth noting that the English Third Parties (Rights Against Insurers) Act 1930 only applies in the event of the insolvency of the insured against whom the third party has his claim. There is no question of a true direct action against the insurer. However United States courts have not necessarily followed this logical route and in Louisiana the direct action statute has been given such an interpretation as to allow full recovery by a third party from the insurer even when the shipowner assured is able to limit his liability, thus vitiating the principle of limitation and rewriting

[34] [1984] 2 Lloyd's Rep. 408.
[35] [1967] 2 Q.B. 363.

177

the contract of insurance. The logic of the fifth circuit court of Appeals in *Olympic Towing Corp.* v. *Nebel Towing Corp.*[36] was trenchently criticised in the dissenting judgment of Judge Brown:

> "As long as the Direct Action Statute subjects the insurer to no greater liability than the assured would have, it fulfills the Louisiana policy of public protection and avoids troublesome questions of conflict between state and federal maritime law. The court's reading rewrites the contract, imposes liability beyond that of the assured and ignores substantive limitations on liability under maritime principles. The essential uniformity of the Admiralty is at an end when for a like casualty across the line in Texas the 'liability' of the shipowner is less—by the amount of total damages and the policy limits—than it is in Louisiana."

The situation in non-direct action States such as New York remains true to normal principles and the comments of the New York Court in *Miller* v. *American S.S. Owners Mutual Protection and Indemnity Co.*[37] on the position in Louisiana are perhaps relevant:

> "The Fifth Circuit has construed insurance contracts . . . in the decision in *Cushing* v. *Maryland Casualty Co.* That opinion reflects a fundamental misunderstanding, or a determination to ignore, the difference between liability and indemnity insurance."

Despite this trenchant criticism, the Fifth Circuit continues to rewrite insurance policies and the recent case of *Crown Zellerback Corporation* v. *London S.S. Owners Mutual Insurance Association*[38] suggests that the most generous interpretation of that court's position must be a "determination to ignore." This case also contains a powerful dissent from Judge Brown based this time on the fact that the court chose to ignore a fundamental term of the insurance policy in question; a clause on which the whole insurance was based and which had been contained in one form or another in the policies issued by the P and I Association concerned since 1881. The clause read:

> "When a Member (shipowner) for whose account a ship is entered in this class, is entitled to limit his liability, the liability of this class (insurer) shall not exceed the amount of such limitation. . . . "

and the relevant section of the Louisiana Direct Action Statute read:

[36] 419 F. 2 d. 230.
[37] 509 F.Supp. 1047—S.D.N.Y. (1984).
[38] 745 F. 2 d. 995 (1984); A.M.C. 305 (1985).

"any action brought hereunder shall be subject to . . . the defences which could be urged by the insurer to a direct action brought by the insured. . . ."

Despite the clear wording of the clause and of the Statute the Fifth Circuit succeeded in deciding that because limitation was a defence personal to the owner (*per Nebel Towing* [39]) it was also invalid if incorporated into a policy of insurance. A curious decision which is now under appeal.

All insurance policies contain certain restrictions and standards of behaviour which the assured is expected to follow and on which the policy and the premiums are based. The whole basis is undermined, particularly in the context of mutual insurance, if courts simply ignore the plain words of the policy.

10. THE INSURER'S RIGHT TO DENY COVER

There is sometimes confusion between the right of a shipowner to limit his liability to third parties and the right of the shipowner's liability insurer to restrict his cover of the shipowner. Equally it is sometimes thought that if the shipowner loses his right to limit his liability, he will also lose his insurance cover or at least any cover in excess of the amount of his relevant limitation fund. The correct position is that the question of insurance cover is quite separate and different from issues of shipowner's limitation and the only link is that the insurer only covers a shipowner's legal liabilities. This means that if a shipowner is legally entitled to limit his liability, he must do so, and he has no cover in excess of the amount of the relevant limitation fund. This requirement may be subsumed within the general phrase that P and I policies are policies of indemnity and exist to reimburse shipowners for legal liabilities incurred and paid by them. In addition, as in any other insurance, the P and I policy may incorporate certain restrictions on the rights of the shipowner to recover, but these are matters of contract rather than general law.

The general law which enables an insurer to deny cover to a shipowner on the basis of his behaviour is to be found in the English Marine Insurance Act 1906 and similar statutory provisions in most countries with an insurance industry (for example the effect of the New York code is very similar). The sections of the Marine Insurance Act which deal with losses other than deliberate scuttling are sections 39(4) and 39(5) which read as follows:

39(4)   "A ship is deemed to be seaworthy when she is reasonably fit in all aspects to encounter the ordinary perils of the seas of the adventure assured."

[39] See n. 36, *supra*.

39(5)   "In a time policy there is no implied warranty that the ship
          shall be seaworthy at any stage of the adventure, but,
          when, with the privity of the assured, the ship is sent to sea
          in an unworthy state, the insurer is not liable for any loss
          attributable to unseaworthiness."

It is important that these clauses should not be read in isolation
and without knowledge of the way in which the English courts have
interpreted them, which is very restrictively. The test may again be
taken in stages: first proof of a defect; secondly proof that the
defect caused the loss; thirdly that the existence of the defect was
known or ought to have been known; and finally, and most
importantly, proof of knowledge by the assured shipowner that
the defect rendered the ship unseaworthy in the sense of it being
unlikely to complete the voyage. A definite element of recklessness
is required and probably the best definition is:

> "An act intentionally done or a deliberate omission by the
> assured, with knowledge that the performance will probably
> result in injury, or an act done or omitted in such a way as to
> allow an inference of reckless disregard of the probable
> consequences."

This is supported by the most recent English case on the subject,
Goldman v. *Thai Airways Ltd*[40] which was concerned with limitation
of liability under the Warsaw Convention 1955 (Aircraft) where
the relevant Article 25 talks of "an act or omission . . . done with
intent to cause damage or recklessly and with knowledge that
damage would probably result."

It is clear that the knowledge and the recklessness have to be at a
very senior level in the company and there is a definite implication
of personal fault though not of fraud. Equally the hope that the
ship will arrive safely does not excuse the fault if all the other
elements are there.

As would be expected, the insurer is also relieved from his
liability to pay if a ship is deliberately sunk or for other deliberate
acts of the assured.

Section 55(2) "The insurer is not liable for any loss attributable
          to the wilful misconduct of the assured, but unless the
          policy otherwise provides, he is liable for any loss
          proximately caused by a peril insured against, even
          though the loss would not have happened but for the
          misconduct or negligence of the master or crew."

[40] [1983] 3 All E.R. 693 C.A.

The leading modern English case on the application of these sections to P and I insurance is *The Eurysthenes*.[41] The case must, however, be read with extreme care since it went to the Court of Appeal on a most unusual interlocutory motion as a series of questions on assumed facts.

A recent case before the full court of the Supreme Court of Queensland suggests strongly that the modern approach to the denial of cover is very similar in the United Kingdom, the United States and the Commonwealth countries. The relevant statute was identical in wording to section 55(2) of the English Marine Insurance Act 1906 and the case turned on the question of whether "wilful misconduct" meant something less than intention to cause the loss. The Court found that the shipowners did not intend to cause the loss of the vessel but that they recklessly disregarded that probable result of their conduct and that such recklessness constituted "wilful misconduct"—*Wood* v. *Associated National Insurance Co. Ltd.* (The *Isothel*).[42] In reaching this decision the Court quoted with approval the American decision of *Orient Insurance Co.* v. *Adams*[43] where "wilful misconduct" was defined as "reckless exposure of the vessel to the perils of navigation knowing that she was not in a position to counter them." It would seem most likely that an English Court would reach a very similar result relying on what appears to be the ratio of *The Eurysthenes*. An insurer can therefore deny cover for misconduct falling short of deliberate scuttling, but the test is nonetheless subjective and very different from the test of "actual fault or privity" under the various limitation statutes. In addition the burden of proving the fault of the shipowner lies on the insurer, the reverse of the situation when the shipowner is trying to establish his right to limit his liability.

11. ADVANTAGES OF THE LONDON LIMITATION CONVENTION 1976

This Convention was drafted with a view to removing the anomalies of existing limitation law and producing a reasonable and logical system appropriate to modern conditions. This approach was expressly stated in the summary of the discussions which had taken place in the Legal Committee of IMO provided to the London Conference:

> "The earlier concept of limitation held that a shipowner should be able to free himself from liabilities which exceeded his total interest in a venture subject to marine perils. The

[41] [1976] 2 Lloyd's Rep. 171 (C.A.)
[42] L.M.L.N. 1985.
[43] 123 U.S. 67 (1887).

more modern view is that the shipowner should be able to free himself from liabilities which exceed amounts coverable by insurance at reasonable costs."

Like the 1924 and 1957 Conventions, the 1976 Convention does not deal with the factors which create liability but only with those which limit it. Indications are that it has, to a large degree, solved at least the insurance problems.

The limitation figures have been increased very substantially, both as a result of using higher monetary figures and minimum tonnages and also because of the changes in tonnage measurements introduced as a result of the incorporation of the 1969 Tonnage Measurements Convention. These changes have meant that the anomalous very low limitations for small tonnage ships have been removed and there is a better relationship between different types of ships. This reinforces the theory that modern limitation is intended to provide for an equitable distribution of risk between those participating in the maritime adventure and should end the perception of limitation as being somehow "unfair."

These higher figures were agreed by insurers and shipowners in exchange for greater certainty of the right to limit. The test for breaking limitation is now under Article 4:

"A personal act or omission committed with the intent to cause the loss, or recklessly and with knowledge that such loss would probably result."

The burden of proving this is on the claimant, a reversal of the present law; this seems to follow naturally from the change in the test and also reflects the theory of limitation as a right rather than a privilege. It is worth remarking that this test seems to approximate very closely to that used in English, Commonwealth and American law as the test for deciding whether a shipowner should be denied cover under his marine insurance policy. There seems therefore to be a very strong chance that the same set of facts which would enable a claimant to break the shipowner's limit would also be sufficient to deny the shipowner his insurance cover. Presumably this will considerably reduce the enthusiasm of claimants for attempting to break limits. It is also entirely in keeping with the theory that modern limitation is about insurance cover.

The scope of limitation has also been extended so that it should cover all those likely to be taking part in the maritime adventure. In particular it covers the owner, manager or operator of the ship, all charterers and the master and crew. This would end the current American game of searching for some party within the shipping organisation who is not within the body of those entitled to limit their liability, but who at the same time can be held responsible, to some degree, for the incident which caused the loss. This will assist in making limitation apply to the incident rather than the individual, an essential feature of an insurance based system.

Salvors are given the specific right to limit their liability, thus removing from them the problems created by the *Tojo Maru*[44] decision. Again this is a move which is clearly to the advantage of all concerned since salvors perform an important service for everybody affected by the business of shipping (this despite the general view of them as vultures). The risks necessarily taken by salvors are quite sufficient, without the additional danger of bankruptcy imposed by potentially unlimited liability for acts performed in emergency situations. Finally, the right to limit liability is specifically extended to insurers thus avoiding the effects of any attempt to make insurers liable in situations where their insured are not by means of "long arm" statutes. This provision expressly acknowledges the importance of insurance in the modern theory of limitation.

The 1976 Convention also attempts to cast its net wide enough to ensure that all types of damage are within it. It thus includes delay, wreck removal (optional) and physical damage, together with any consequential losses. Again this is important if the limitation fund is to include all the consequences of a particular incident. The interaction with other liability conventions is dealt with by preserving the separate liability provisions and limits for oil pollution set out in the 1969 Civil Liability Convention[45] and by including the 1974 Athens Passenger Convention within its ambit.[46] The Athens Convention expressly preserves the overall limits set out in the 1976 Convention (or other limitation conventions) by Article 19 which reads:

> "This Convention shall not modify the rights or duties of the carrier, and their servants or agents, provided for in international conventions relating to the limitation of liability of owners of seagoing ships."

The position is therefore that there are two potential funds, one for overall tonnage limitation and one for oil pollution liabilities. This splintering of risks and creation of separate funds for special types of risk is highly undesirable from an insurance point of view since it leads to a number of separate exposures arising out of the same incident. This naturally makes underwriters nervous and contracts the capacity of the overall market at the same time as increasing the cost. This factor is the more serious since the same

---

[44] [1971] 1 Lloyd's Rep. 341 (H.L.)
[45] See Art. 3 of the 1976 Convention.
[46] See Art. 7 of the 1976 Convention.

reinsurance market is likely to be involved on all risks and indeed on all ships involved in an incident. If limitation is to be based on modern concepts of insurability it is important to look at the overall costs of an incident and not treat each head of liability separately.

The 1976 Convention also deals with the difficulties posed by the use of poincare gold francs in older conventions. This could lead to considerable differences between limitation amounts in different countries purely as a result of using different methods of exchange calculation. The 1976 Convention provides for the use of Special Drawing Rights (SDR) which act as an international currency with daily published rates of exchange into all the OECD currencies. This should reduce the temptation for forum shopping since limitation funds should have a similar value in all countries; the insurance exposure is therefore also the same.

The problem of monetary inflation is dealt with in the 1976 Convention by means of a provision which provides for a new conference to be called purely on the question of raising limits.[47] This provision would seem to be the solution for those countries, such as the United States, which complain that the limits in the present 1976 Convention are too low. They can ratify the Convention and immediately move for revision of the figures. This criticism of the 1976 Convention completely fails to take account of the fact that even at its present values it is a great deal better than any of the current alternatives.

Finally, the 1976 Convention provides all the advantages of consensus on an international scale which limitation law provides within a country and should make it much more likely that only one limitation action will be held in one country.[48] There will be no incentive to go forum shopping if there is no financial advantage and the different effective tests for breaking limitation are standardized on an international basis. This would mean a uniform treatment of claimants in the distribution of the limitation fund and considerable cost savings by concentrating all proceedings in one court.

There is however one problem area relating to the cover required by an owner for collision liabilities which will be created by the 1976 Convention. The present rule is that P and I Clubs will provide excess collision liability cover above the excess of either the proper open market value of the ship or the 1957 Brussels Convention limit, whichever is the higher. This poses few problems since the market value is known for hull insurance purposes and is generally in excess of the 1957 Convention limit, which is in any event easily calculated. However, the advent of the

<hr>

[47] See Art. 21 of the 1976 Convention.
[48] See Art. 13 of the 1976 Convention.

1976 Convention will mean that the convention limit is usually (or at least very often in the present state of the market) in excess of the market value and moreover, will be a difficult figure to calculate, relying as it does on a different method of tonnage measurement.

12. CONCLUSION

Shipowners' limitation is not just an amusing game for lawyers to play, it is an integral and important part of the international liability insurance scheme. It can be justified as a means of achieving an equitable distribution of the risks inevitably attached to a maritime adventure and this is particularly relevant with the modern tendency towards *de jure* or *de facto* absolute liability on the part of the shipowner. It is also the case that ship standards have little or no connection with limitation but are on the other hand closely linked with appropriate internationally agreed criteria for shipbuilding and equipment and necessary crew training and qualification.

There is no doubt that the 1957 Convention figures are too low, and the American arrangements capricious, but the answer is not the present judicial free-for-all with judges straining the law and statutory language to try to give claimants larger compensation. The solution is higher limits and certainty as to what those limits are. It is not only insurers who benefit from certainty since if the figures are clear and not contested it is possible to get the compensation into the hands of the claimants quickly. The mere elimination of most attempts to break limitation would of itself enormously speed up the process and reduce the cost.

The public will also benefit from the fact that shipowners have reliable liability cover at a reasonable cost, since the savings will be reflected in freight rates. An effective system of limitation will make it possible to continue the present arrangements whereby insurance costs broadly reflect earnings capacity. The Convention provides for a sensible relationship between earnings capacity and the risks run (for example the supply boat is protected from the consequences of damaging an oil rig).

In summary, the 1976 Convention gives a substantial increase in limits to a fair and reasonable level and in return it gives a much greater degree of certainty that the limit is effective. The Convention attempts to give protection to all those involved in the maritime adventure and for every type of claim that might arise as a result of an accident. It provides a uniform financial measure and the vital consensus of forum. The criticism of the 1976 Convention seems to be that it is not perfect, that it reflects a compromise; however there is no doubt that it is better than the existing law and certainly it is better than nothing at all.

The 1976 Convention is to be welcomed from an insurance point of view; it re-confirms an important principle and will form a code which is largely clear and uniform. It should speed settlements and give both insurers and shipowners a greater degree of certainty. Maybe it will even cut legal costs.

PART B

NATIONAL PERSPECTIVES ON LIMITATION AND THE 1976 LIMITATION CONVENTION

X

Argentina and the 1976 Convention

Dr. Marcial J. Mendizábal*

1. SYSTEM OF LIMITATION OF LIABILITY UNDER ARGENTINE LAW

Description

The limitation of liability for maritime claims is governed by the Navigation Act (Law No. 20.094) which came into force in 1973.

(a) The persons entitled to limit liability are the shipowner, the disponent owner, the carrier, their servants and the master and members of the crew.

The claims against the master or a crewmember are subject to limitation when the event from which these claims derive had been caused by their personal fault, except when it is proved that the damage was a result of an act or omission incurred by them with the intention of producing the damage or when they had acted recklessly.

Lastly, when the master or crewmember is at the same time the owner, disponent owner, carrier or manager of the ship, he can only limit his liability when the fault derives from his functions as master or crewmember.

(b) The following claims are subject to limitation:–

(i) Loss of life or personal injuries;

(ii) Loss of, or damage to, property and loss of rights;

(iii) Liability derived from the raising or removal of a ship which is sunk or grounded or from damage caused to harbour works and waterways, except in the case of abandonment of the ship in favour of the State when the shipowner or the disponent owner had incurred personal fault or had acted recklessly and the damage was caused by such fault or reckless conduct.

The limitation can be invoked even when the liability derives from the property, possession, custody or control of the ship, unless it is proved that it was caused by the fault or privity of the person who invokes the limitation, or that of his servants other than the crew.

(c) In accordance with the law, the claims for salvage,

* Edye, Roche, De la Vega & Ray, Buenos Aires.

contribution in general average, those of the master, crewmember or their respective heirs derived from the contract of services, and those of other servants of the owner whose duties are connected with the ship, are excepted from limitation.

(d) The law establishes a system under which the persons mentioned in it are entitled to limit their liability to the value of the ship at the end of the voyage during which the events that gave rise to the claim or claims have occurred, plus the amount of the gross freights, that of the passage monies collected, or to be collected, for the same voyage and that of the credits which had originated during the voyage.

When the person limiting his liability is the shipowner the law gives him the option of placing the ship at the disposal of the claimants, through the competent Court, adding the other amounts mentioned above and starting limitation proceedings in Court within three months from the date of the conclusion of the voyage.

In the case of claims in respect of loss of life or personal injury the law provides that if the total amount, consisting of the value of the ship plus the other values mentioned above, is not sufficient to cover all the corresponding losses up to the sum of 13 Argentine Pesos gold per ton, the difference must be added in order to reach this sum, which will be exclusively earmarked for the payment of such compensation.

The claims against hull underwriters and the compensation paid by them are not included in the total amount of the limitation but they must be included, as well as any other asset of the person who invokes the limitation, in the amounts that must be added to reach 13 Argentine Pesos gold in cases of loss of life or personal injury.[1]

Background

Before the enactment of the Navigation Act in 1973, the limitation of liability of shipowners was governed by the Code of Commerce, which came into force in 1862. Under the old system, only shipowners were entitled to limit liability and exclusively in the case of claims derived from acts or omissions of the master. The limitation consisted in placing the ship at the disposal of the claimants, together with the freights earned or to be collected corresponding to the voyage on which the events that gave rise to the claims occurred. The system established by the Code of Commerce was in later years considered unfair in view of the evolution of the concept of liability, mainly with reference to

---

[1] The quotation of the Argentine Peso gold is established by the Government. In the absence of an official quotation at the time when the amount of the limitation is fixed, the value to be taken is that of the gold content of the Argentine Peso gold (7.258 grammes) and not that of its numismatic value.

compensation in cases of loss of life and personal injury. The abandonment of a ship at the end of the voyage left all creditors unprotected when, as happened in many cases, the ship was sunk or had lost most of her value.

Argentina did not accede to the 1957 Convention, not because of an essential disagreement with the system established by the Convention, but because the limit per ton fixed by it was considered too high in the case of our merchant fleet, whose ships had an average value lower than that of the limits of liability established by the Convention.

For that reason, our present Act adopted a system similar to that of the United States, adding the option in favour of the shipowner of placing the ship at the disposal of the claimants, plus the other values mentioned in paragraph (1)(d). That option is exclusively applicable to claims for damage to property, as in the case of claims for loss of life or personal injury the shipowner must add the amount required to reach the limit of 13 Argentine Pesos gold.

Scope of application

As Argentina has neither ratified nor acceded to any International Convention on Limitation of Liability for Maritime Claims, the Navigation Act is applicable to all cases in which, irrespective of the flag of the vessel, the persons entitled to limit their liability under Argentine Law invoke the limitation before an Argentine Court where a claim against them is pending.

2. QUESTIONS RELATED TO A POSSIBLE ADHERENCE TO THE 1976 CONVENTION

The substitution of the limitation of liability system established by the 1976 Convention for the one at present in force in Argentina would probably meet with the approval of the majority of the local maritime entities, including the Argentine Maritime Law Association, as the Convention's system eliminates the uncertainty on the actual amount of limitation, at least as regards claims for loss of, or damage to, property.

In view of the substantial difference between both systems of limitation and the scope of application of the Convention the accession of Argentina would require a modification of the domestic Law, as otherwise cases would inevitably appear in which it would be difficult to decide which system should be applied.

The decision whether to accede or not to the 1976 Convention will of course be a political one, based mainly on considerations of the economic effects that the Convention could have on the development of the country's merchant fleet and on its international trade, Argentina being at present basically a shipper country.

When the project of the present Navigation Act was drafted, its author, Dr. Atilio Malvagni, considered that the United States' system of limitation was preferable to that of the 1957 Convention because the limits per ton established by the Convention were too high in respect of the average value of Argentine merchant ships.[2]

A different criterion was held by another Argentine specialist, Dr. José Domingo Ray, when commenting on the Project and before the Navigation Act came into force.[3] He maintained that the limitation per ton system had the advantage of fixing limits of liability known by all beforehand and not linked to the uncertain value of the ship and that the amounts of those limits could be established in the law taking into consideration the interests of shipowners as well as those of the creditors.

It seems, consequently, that objections to Argentina's access to the 1976 Convention would be mainly founded on arguments referred to the economic effect it could produce on the shipping industry and on cargo interests in the present circumstances.

---

[2] Atilio Malvagni, *Proyecto de Ley General de la Navegación*, (Ministry of Education and Justice, 1962), at pp. 49 *et seq.*

[3] José Domingo Ray, *Derecho de la Navegación*, (Abeledo-Perrot, 1964), at pp. 291 *et seq.*

XI

France and the 1976 Convention

*Dr. Gerard Auchter**

During nearly three centuries, French Maritime Law contained an original system of limitation of shipowner's liability, based on the abandonment of ship and freight by the shipowner. Even after the enforcement of the 1924 Convention, the French system of limitation provided for in article 216 of the Commercial Code still survived for a few more decades. When a general revision and modernisation of French Maritime Law was undertaken in the 1966–1969 period, it was decided to introduce the system of limitation of liability contained in the 1957 Convention into the domestic legislation. A brief background and some comments about the history of limitation in French Maritime Law appears useful.

A detailed examination of the legal provisions relating to the limitation of shipowner's liability will not be undertaken within the framework of the present chapter. The main features of the 1967 Law and Decree may be examined however. From the examination of some particular problems raised in the interpretation of the 1957 Convention and the 1967 Law and Decree it clearly appears that the system of limitation of liability contained in these texts does not always work in a satisfactory way; about fifteen years after its enforcement, the new French legislation on the subject has to meet some criticisms. One, amongst others, is that the system of limitation of liability based on a value obtained by multiplying the ship's tonnage by a monetary figure does not appear satisfactory in all respects.

France was in 1976 one of the eight countries which signed the London Convention on the Limitation of Liability for Maritime Claims. This signature, which was followed by the approval of the Convention in 1981, did not mean at the time that the new international convention was well received in France, in fact it met some objections in Maritime Law doctrine. It does not appear, however, that the criticisms expressed towards the new IMO Convention were always justified. The recent developments in French Maritime legislation provide confirmation for this opinion. By the end of 1984, Parliament amended the existing

* Mulhouse University.

legislation relating to the limitation of shipowner's liability in order to bring it in accordance with the provisions contained in the 1976 Convention.

1. BRIEF BACKGROUND AND HISTORY OF LIMITATION

Justification for limitation

Examining the problem of the limitation of the shipowner's liability, Georges Ripert[1] observed that the system of the abandonment of ship and freight was the solution adopted in French legislation to give effect to a limitation of the shipowner's liability which existed in the maritime law of nearly all countries. Such a limitation was, in Georges Ripert's opinion, one of the basic principles of maritime law. The practical implementation of the principle may differ from one country to another, however, the limitation of liability remains a "keystone" of Maritime Law. And the justifications thereof given in French doctrine hardly differ from those expressed in the doctrine of other maritime countries. According to some authors, moral considerations are sometimes mentioned.

Professor Emmanuel du Pontavice[2] refers both to the considerable risks incurred by capital involved in a maritime business and the necessity to support an activity having the character of public services. But he mainly insists on the two following reasons for maintaining limitation of shipowner's liability in maritime law:

> it is of paramount importance, on the one hand, for all participants in maritime operations to prevent the retaining of a ship and her cargo in a port until it has been decided what compensation she may have to pay and what securities she may have to furnish; and, on the other hand, it is very difficult—and practically impossible—to get liability insurance for a shipowner when no limit of liability may be assessed and fixed in advance.

The latter argument was sharply critized by René Rodière[3] who considered that a system of liability based only on a calculation taking into account the ship's tonnage was open to criticism. In his opinion, such a system was contrary to both:

> moral standards: because the liability of the shipowner is limited to an amount which may be insured and not only assessed according to his fault or neglect, and also to general

---

[1] G. Ripert, *Traitè de droit maritime* (4th ed., 1952) Vol. 2, pp. 139–140, Ed. Rousseau, Paris.

[2] E. du Pontavice, *Le Statut des navires*, Libr. Tech., Paris, (1976), pp. 227–231.

[3] R. Rodière, *Traité Général de droit maritime, Introduction—L'armement*, (Ed. Dalloz, Paris, 1976), pp. 595–600.

principles of maritime law: ships are still exposed to many risks when they are navigating, the perils of the sea concept only applies to carriage of goods or passengers by sea, and a shipowner should, therefore, benefit from a limitation of his liability just when he is at fault and not, more generally, when he had the possibility to insure his liability.

Paul Chauveau[4] almost expressed similar views and insisted on the priority to be given in the matter to a system of liability of the shipowner based on his fault or neglect. Paul Chauveau also mentioned the specificity of the risks incurred in navigation at sea and the necessity for the shipowner to limit his liability when involving his ship in a maritime business; he considered that the possible risks of land activities were less significant and the limitation of a shipowner's liability was therefore justified.

Some authors in French doctrine, however, expressed doubts about the legal justifications given for maintaining the limitation in domestic maritime law. René Rodière noted that such a limitation was in some respects inconvenient for passengers who were not insured and thus often were practically deprived from any legal recourse against the shipowner.[5] The strongest criticisms came from the Ports Authorities who considered that the limitation of the shipowner's liability represented in fact a privilege which was not suited to recent developments of maritime law.[6]

History of limitation of shipowner's liability

(i) Commercial Code of 1807

The limitation of shipowner's liability was first provided for in a Royal Decree of 1681, and in 1807 the rule was inserted in article 216 of the Commercial Code. It was provided that the shipowner was liable for all damages resulting from acts of the master or from commitments he may have taken as regards the ship and maritime activities undertaken in his use. And it was added in the same text that the shipowner was entitled in every case to claim an exemption from his liabilities by the abandonment of the ship and the freight.

In his comments on the Royal Decree of 1681, René-Josué Valin who published toward the end of the Seventeenth Century a

---

[4] P. Chauveau, "Quelques réflexions sur la limitation de la responsabilité de l'armateur," Annuaire de droit maritime et aérien, Vol. II (1975), pp. 11–19, (Ed. A. Pedone, Paris).

[5] R. Rodière, *Précis de droit maritime*, Dalloz (9th Ed., 1982), Paris, pp. 121–124.

[6] P. Siré, "Un dialogue de sourds," D.M.F. (1975), pp. 387–392;—A. Pagès, "Le risque de mer et le facteur humain," D.M.F. (1975), pp. 451–457.

detailed commentary on the Decree, explained[7] at the time that it was fair to grant the shipowner the benefit of the limitation of his liability up to a limit consisting of his ship and the freight, because otherwise he might have risked the ruin caused by an irresponsible or dishonest master. In fact, when interpreting the provisions of article 216 of the French Commercial Code, the Courts, as well as French doctrine, did not take this justification into consideration and generally considered that the possibility for the shipowner to decide on the abandonment of ship and freight was justified because, at each voyage at sea he undertook, he was risking his ship and, at the same time, the shippers were risking their cargoes and the master and crew their lives and wages. A voyage at sea was then defined as a partnership involving common risks and profits, each partner engaging only a part of his assets. Because of the perils of the sea incurred, such a voyage therefore appeared as an undertaking with limited liability. The concept of a "maritime estate" accepted over two centuries in French Maritime Law was perfectly adapted to a system of limitation of the shipowner's liability based on the abandonment of ship and freight. But when the 1924 Convention and, later on, the 1957 Convention came into force, it appeared that the system of limitation contained in the French Commercial Code had become obsolete.

(ii) The 1924 and 1957 Conventions

France ratified the 1924 Convention on August 23, 1935. The French Government also ratified, on July 7, 1959, the Brussels Convention of 1957, but did not at the same time denounce its ratification of the 1924 Convention. This denunciation was only made on October 26, 1976 and became effective from October 26, 1977.

Neither the 1924 Convention nor the 1957 Convention have been considered as satisfactory in French Maritime Law doctrine. Both conventions often were found to be too greatly influenced by English legal notions on the subject. Some of the criticisms expressed against the two conventions are also made concerning French Law and Decree of 1967 relating to the legal status of sea-going ships. They will be examined in sub-paragraph (iii) hereunder.

---

[7] Quoted by R. Rodière, Traité Général de droit maritime, Introduction—L'armement, pp. 594–595.

(iii) *Law and Decree of 1967*

The rules and principles relating to the limitation of shipowner's liability, as contained in the 1957 Convention, have been adopted in Law nos. 67–5 of January 3, 1967[8] on the legal status of sea-going ships and other structures used in maritime activities. It may be noted, however, that Law nos. 67–5 does not deal with shipowner's liability alone. The matter is governed by Articles 58 to 69 of the Law, these provisions being gathered in Chapter VII—"Liability of the shipowner". The other Chapters of Law nos. 67–5 are devoted to registration of ships, shipbuilding, joint ownership, liens and mortgages and arrest of ships.

According to French constitutional practice in commercial law matters the Law only contains the basic principles on the subject dealt with in that Law and the provisions relating to the practical measures and application of the principles defined in the Law are contained in a Decree. Consequently, Law nos. 67–5 is completed by Decree nos. 67–967 of October 27, 1967[9] on the legal status of seagoing ships and other structures used in maritime activities. The Decree is subdivided in the same way as Law nos. 67–5, *i.e.* its Chapter VII only contains provisions relating to the limitation of shipowner's liability. In fact, Articles 59 to 87 of Decree nos. 67–967 exclusively deal with the limitation fund (constitution of the fund, proving and listing of claims, distribution of the fund and appeals); these provisions have been enacted pursuant to Article 4 of the 1957 Convention which provides for that the rules relating to the constitution and distribution of the limitation fund and all rules of procedure shall be governed by the national law of the State in which the fund is constituted.

Although Chapter VII of law nos. 67–5 and Chapter VII of Decree nos. 67–967 are supposed, according to their title, to be devoted to the "shipowner's liability," they actually only contain provisions relating to different aspects of the limitation of that liability. And, in addition to that, some provisions of Law nos. 67–5 also relate to the limitation of liability of persons other than the shipowner: charterer, managing owner or operator of the ship, master and members of the crew. Professor du Pontavice indicates[10] that during the revision work of the provisions contained in the French Commercial Code, it was first decided to repeal Article 216 of the Code and to replace it by a set of provisions intended to introduce the rules and principles of the 1957 Convention in French Maritime Law. Finally, it was decided to revise some parts of French Maritime Law by means of

---

[8] Text in J.O. of January 4, 1967.
[9] Text in J.O. of November 4, 1967.
[10] E. du Pontavice, *op.cit.*, pp. 233–235.

particular laws repealing some provisions of the Commercial Code, but not introduced in that Code. In the end, when the draft provisions relating to the shipowner's liability came under discussion, only those concerning the limitation of liability were introduced in Chapter VII of Law nos. 67–5.

It should be observed that Chapter VII of Law nos. 67–5 does not contain just a copy of the provisions of the French official translation of the 1957 Convention. It was considered that the 1957 Convention was an "English conceived" Convention and that its French official translation was drafted in a manner which did not appear fitted for the French legal language.[11] A "translation" into appropriate French language was therefore necessary, but at the same time any misrepresentation of the legal concepts contained in the 1957 Convention had to be avoided.

2. INTERPRETATION OF THE 1957 CONVENTION AND THE FRENCH 1967 LAW AND DECREE—PARTICULAR PROBLEMS

Law nos. 67–5 is based on the rules and principles contained in the 1957 Convention, and several of the Law's provisions, therefore, are closely inspired by those of the Convention. Thus, Articles 58 to 69 of Law nos. 67–5 do not deserve here a thorough examination. However, brief comments will be made about some legal provisions the interpretation of which have given rise to some discussions in the French Courts and doctrine. The following items will be examined; first, the application of the 1967 Law to other structures than seagoing ships; secondly, the right to limitation, and thirdly, the extent to which damages may be limited—the basis of calculation and the Gold Franc.

Application of Law nos. 67–5 to wrecks, ships under construction and pleasure boats

According to its title, Law nos. 67–5 concerns the legal status of seagoing ships and other structures used in maritime activities. It should be noted, however, that Chapter VII of the Law, containing the provisions relating to the limitation of the shipowner's liability, only refers to the owner of "a ship" and does not mention other structures. Some cases and decisions, however,

---

[11] R. Rodière, *Précis de droit maritime*, p. 131; P. Chauveau, *op.cit.* This sort of argument is used from time to time in France by some authors, especially when they are reluctant to accept fundamental changes in Maritime Law. More recently, and similarly, other international Maritime Conventions have been considered as badly drafted in their French official version or as not being in accordance with some traditional maritime law principles, especially when it was noted simultaneously that these Conventions had been signed under the "pressure" of developing countries.

have been decided on wrecks, ships under construction and pleasure boats and are examined below.

(a) Wrecks

In relation to the possibility of an owner pleading the limitation of his liability in cases where he owns a wreck that caused damages, René Rodière suggested making a distinction between three different cases[12]:

(i) where the owner is liable for damages caused by his ship before she sinks and becomes a wreck he may plead the limitation of his liability and constitute a limitation fund;

(ii) where the ship has become a wreck and causes damages thereafter one of the conditions required for the constitution of a limitation fund does not exist and the owner may not plead the limitation of his liability as the damages have not been caused by a ship,

(iii) where there are claims in respect of the raising or the removal of a ship which is wrecked and these operations are undertaken by the Administration the shipowner may plead the limitation of his liability, pursuant to Article 59 of Law nos. 67–5.

Prior to the coming into force of Law nos. 67–5, owners of sunken ships often were in conflict with the Administration (in fact, the Ports Authorities), the latter denying them the right to plead the limitation of their liability. The Administration claimed the reimbursement of all expenses incurred in the raising, removal or destruction of sunken ships, whereas the shipowner pleaded the right to abandon the ship which had become a wreck. And the Administrative Supreme Court sometimes decided in favour of the Authorities, although a sound interpretation of the relevant provision of the Commercial Code (art. 216 C.Com.) should have led the Court to give a decision in favour of shipowners.

(b) Ships under construction

When a ship under construction causes damage, her owner (shipyard or shipowner) may be brought to plead the limitation of his liability. Pursuant to Article 58 of Law nos. 67–5, such a possibility will be given only when the ship's registered tonnage has been calculated in accordance with the appropriate regulations and she has also been registered. A lack of ship's registration and tonnage registration therefore means for the owner an obligation to bear an unlimited liability for the damages caused by

[12] R. Rodière, *Traité Général de droit maritime, Introduction—L'armement*, pp. 629–630; *Précis de droit maritime*, pp. 133–134.

his ship.[13] Professor du Pontavice fully agrees with that interpretation, and he points out that, from an historical point of view, the limitation of the shipowner's liability is closely tied with maritime navigation, the perils of the sea and, more recently, with the practical impossibility to insure a ship which owner may not limit his liability. All these arguments do not appear relevant in the case of a ship still under construction.

(c) Pleasure boats

Law nos. 67–5 does not specify for which category of ships an owner may plead the limitation of his liability. Section 58 only considers the case of the owner of "a ship" and provides for the limitation of the owner's liability when damages occurred on board that ship or in a direct connection with its navigation or its use. Consequently, the limitation of a pleasure boat owner's liability seems indisputable.[14] Furthermore, Law nos. 67–522 of July 3, 1967, relating to Marine Insurance[15] provides for, in section 63, that its provisions do not apply to pleasure boats, as contracts for the insurance of such boats are subject to the provisions contained in a Law of July 13, 1930, which applies generally to all contracts of insurance in civil law and commercial law matters. But section 63 of Law nos. 67–522 also adds that an application of the provisions of the Law of July 13, 1930, does not prevent the constitution of a limitation fund.

Thus, the limitation of liability may be requested not only by the owner of a pleasure boat, but also by a charterer, a manager or an operator of such a boat. It has been suggested that, more generally, any person using a pleasure boat should be allowed to plead the limitation of his liability.[16]

The right to limitation—Some particular problems

Several problems should be examined under this heading, and many of them are of a controversial nature; this subparagraph will only contain some particular developments relating to the following items: the optional nature of limitation of liability, the persons entitled to limit their liability, the loss of the right to limit liability.

---

[13] R. Rodière, *Traité Général de droit maritime, Introduction—L'armement*, p. 631;—E. du Pontavice, *op.cit.*, pp. 239–240.
[14] E. du Pontavice and P. Cordier, "Navires et autres bâtiments de mer," Juris-Classeur Commercial (1984), Fascicule No. 1050, pp. 22–23.
[15] Text in J.O. of July 4, 1967.
[16] E. du Pontavice and P. Cordier, *op.cit.*, at p. 23.

(a) Optional nature of limitation of liability

Section 58 of Law nos. 67–5 clearly specifies that the limitation of the shipowner's liability is of an optional nature ("... the shipowner *may* limit his liability ...). The Government bill contained a provision drafted as follows: "The shipowner shall be liable only ... within the following limits. ... " When the bill was discussed in Parliament, it was explained during the proceedings that the limitation of his liability was optional for a shipowner, and the bill was amended accordingly.[17]

(b) Persons entitled to limit their liability

Another significant amendment to the Government bill concerned the persons entitled to constitute a limitation fund. The bill provided for the constitution of the fund without giving any indication about the persons allowed to constitute such a fund. The bill was amended and Law nos. 67–5 therefore expressly provides that the limitation fund is constituted by the shipowner "or by any other person substituted for him" (section 62). In accordance with section 62 of Law nos. 67–5, an insurer may therefore constitute a limitation fund.

As concerns the persons entitled to limit their liability, section 69 of Law nos. 67–5 provides that a charterer, a managing owner or an operator of the ship, as well as the master and their other servants at sea or on land when they are in the course of their duties, are entitled to limit their liability, in accordance with the rules contained in Chapter VII of the Law. The French Supreme Court recently delivered a decision in which some useful information is given about the persons who may plead limitation of their liability.[18] The Court held that the limitation of liability provided for in Law nos. 67–5 may be pleaded only by the persons listed in section 69, and noted that the insurer was not mentioned among these persons. The decision thus delivered by the Supreme Court has been sharply criticized in the French doctrine.

In another decision, the Supreme Court proposed an interesting construction of Article 1 of the 1957 Convention and Sections 58 and 59 of Law nos. 67–5.[19] The Court of Appeal of Rouen refused to grant limitation of liability to the master and shipowner on the ground that only claims caused by a peril of the sea were subject to limitation of liability. In the particular case, the damages

---

[17] E. du Pontavice, *op.cit.*, pp. 251–256.
[18] C. Cass. (ch.com.), December 7, 1982, (*The Jep*), D.M.F. 1983, pp. 595–601, comments by Y. M. Le Jean.
[19] C. Cass. (ch.com.), November 18, 1980, D.M.F. 1981, pp. 535–538, comments by Cl. Legendre.

resulted from the mixing of peanut oil with tallow, contained in two different tanks, following an incorrect operation of the pumping fittings during the discharging of the cargo. The Supreme Court rescinded the Court of Appeal's decision, considering that the possibility of a master or a shipowner limiting their liabilities is not granted subject to the requirement of a peril of the sea. It may be noted here that Article 1(1)(b) of the 1957 Convention expressly provides for the limitation of liability in respect of claims arising from loss or damage to any property caused by the act of any person on board the ship which occurs in the loading, carriage or discharge of the cargo.

(c) The loss of the right to limit liability

The provisions of Article 1(1) of the 1957 Convention and section 58 of Law nos. 67–5, relating to the loss of the right to limit liability, have also given rise to some interesting decisions. Both texts provide for the loss of the right to limit liability when the occurrence giving rise to the claim resulted from "the actual fault or privity of the owner"; but neither the 1957 Convention nor the French Law of January 3, 1967, give a definition of these terms. The Court of Appeal of Aix-en-Provence held that the actual fault of the shipowner has to be appreciated according to the practical circumstances in a concrete case.[20] The Court did not consider as an actual fault the collision of the ship with a wharf which was damaged. The owner of the wharf alleged a fault in the manoeuvre of the ship, saying that she was unable to navigate in a channel with the necessary precision because her steering equipment did not work properly; the ship was therefore unseaworthy and her owner had to be prevented from pleading the limitation of his liability. The appeal was dismissed on the ground that, in the Court's opinion, the shipowner proved that he had exercised due diligence in making the ship seaworthy and so maintaining her and, consequently, he had to be allowed to plead the limitation of his liability.

The Court of Appeal of Rouen likewise held that a shipowner may not be deprived of the limitation of his liability on the assertion only that the master and officers of his ship were incompetent, and that the actual fault of the owner was therefore proven.[21] Following a collision at sea in which one of the ships was at fault, her owner pleaded limitation; the owner of the opposing ship claimed there was actual fault or privity arguing the incompetence of the master, first mate and officers of the ship at

---

[20] C. App. Aix-en-Provence, March 18, 1977, (*The Beni Saf*), D.M.F. 1979, pp. 72–77.

[21] C. App. Rouen, August 1, 1979, (*The Ifni*), D.M.F. 1980, pp. 200–204.

fault, their lack of experience and the excessive speed of the ship at the time of the collision. The Court considered that in fact no proof of a fault or of negligence of the shipowner, related with the collision, had been found by the experts appointed by the Court.

It seems that French Courts seldom decide to deprive the shipowner of the right to limit liability on the basis of evidence of his actual fault or privity. Some cases may be mentioned and it is interesting to note that they more often concern owners of pleasure boats. Thus, the Court of First Instance of Marseille held that the owner of a pleasure boat was not entitled to plead limitation of his liability, on the ground of his actual fault, when serious negligence in the navigation of the boat had been proved.[22] The judges so decided in the following circumstances: the master (the son of the owner) was navigating in the Bay of Cassis (France) with two passengers on board who were possibly interested in the purchase of the boat; while in discussion with his passengers (he was "singing the praises of the boat" said the judgment), the master navigated at a speed of 15 or 16 knots (the authorized speed in the Bay was 3 knots), he did not notice a dinghy, collided with it and the owner of that small boat was killed. The Court considered that the owner of the pleasure boat was not entitled to plead limitation, after it had found a serious offence "committed with a profit seeking character."

The Court of Appeal of Montpellier also decided on a loss of the right to limit liability in a case where, during a sailing trip, a passenger was killed after the sailing boat capsized.[23] The Court considered that the master was inexperienced and that the sailing school, the owner of the boat, had acted with negligence by authorising the master to undertake a sailing initiation cruise in spite of the alarming weather forecasts. The owner of the sailing boat was therefore held fully liable for its punishable abstention.

Extent to which damages may be limited: basis of calculation, the Gold Franc

The 1957 Convention contains a limitation of liability expressed in "francs"; according to Article 3(6) of the Convention, the Franc mentioned in this provision shall be deemed to refer to a unit consisting of sixty five and a half milligrams of gold of millesimal fineness nine hundred. In France the Gold Franc is generally called the "Franc Poincaré." René Rodière had already mentioned ten years ago the difficulties encountered in France in the

---

[22] Trib.Gr.Inst. Marseille, June 1, 1977, D.M.F. 1978, pp. 99–113, comments by R. Rodière.

[23] C. App. Montpellier, October 7, 1982 (Sailing boat *Corail 7*), D.M.F. 1984, pp. 397–406, comments by H. de Richemont.

conversion of Francs Poincaré into French Francs[24]; these difficulties were met not only in the application of the 1957 Convention, but also when the Courts applied the Gold Franc provisions of the Hague-Visby Rules or of the 1929 Warsaw Convention. The French Law of January 3, 1967, provides (in section 61) that the shipowner shall not be liable beyond the limits contained in the 1957 Convention. Some recent decisions show that the problem of the conversion of Francs Poincaré into French Francs still raises many difficulties in the judicial construction of Article 3(1) and 3(6) of the 1957 Convention and section 61 of Law nos. 67.5.

In a dispute brought before the Court of Appeal of Paris in 1980[25], the judges had to decide on the value of the Franc Poincaré when converted into French Francs. In the case at issue, they examined and discussed at length the provisions of Article 22 of the 1929 Warsaw Convention, the subsequent developments in international air law (Guatemala Protocol of 1971, replacement of the Franc Poincaré by the S.D.R., Resolution of the ICAO Legal Committee of October 1974 rejecting the conversion of Francs Poincaré into national currencies on the basis of the value of gold on the free market, etc.). The Court finally came to the conclusion that in France a conversion of Francs Poincaré into French Francs had become impossible since 1978 and, considering that it was not possible for the Court to decline to decide a case, on the ground that the applicable legislation was inadequate or obscure, it was decided that a Franc Poincaré was equivalent to a French Franc. Concerning the application of the Franc Poincaré provisions contained in the 1957 Convention, the Court of Appeal of Rennes,[26] on the other hand, held that the only available legal basis was the official gold parity of 1969 and that the basis of the value of gold on the free market could not be used owing to the many hazards of the gold price on that market. Practically, the main result of the two Court decisions was a significant difference in their conversion of the Franc Poincaré into French Francs (100 Fr. Poincaré = 100 French Fr. in the first case, Court of Paris, and 100 Fr. Poincaré = 36,84 French Fr. in the second case, Court of Rennes).

An appeal against the decision of the Court of Paris was brought before the Supreme Court in 1983,[27] the decision was rescinded and the case transferred again to the Court of Appeal of Paris. The Supreme Court based its decision on the following grounds: the

[24] R. Rodière, *Traité Général de droit maritime, Introduction, L'armement,* pp. 638–639.

[25] C. App.Paris, January 31, 1980, Bull. Transp. 1980, pp. 315–318.

[26] C. App.Rennes, February 10, 1983, D.M.F. 1983, pp. 429–436.

[27] C. Cass. (ch.com.), March 7, 1983, D.M.F. 1983, pp. 602–605, Bull. Transp. 1983, pp. 482–483.

judges of appeal imposed a way of converting Francs Poincaré into French Francs which was different from the method of conversion provided for in Article 22 of the 1929 Warsaw Convention. However, the Court of Appeal should have given in its decision a construction consistent with the provisions contained in the international convention and, moreover, it should have requested also from the Governmental Authorities an official construction of these provisions. The Court of Appeal therefore re-examined the case[28] and decided to stay the judgment until the Governmental Authorities propose an appropriate construction of the Gold Francs provisions contained in the 1929 Warsaw Convention. In the meantime, some uncertainties still remain concerning the problem of the conversion of Francs Poincaré into French Francs, and especially in maritime law when the Gold Franc provision of the 1957 Convention is applicable.

3. IMPLEMENTATION OF THE 1976 CONVENTION IN FRENCH LAW

When the 1976 Convention was adopted at the IMCO Conference held in London in November 1976, the French delegation abstained from the vote. Nevertheless, France was among the first States ratifying or adhering to the new Convention on the Limitation of Liability for Maritime Claims. The French Government signed the Convention in 1976 subject to approval, the latter was given on July 1, 1981; the approval instrument contained a reservation relating to the right to exclude the application of Article 2(1)(d) and (e) of the Convention (concerning claims in respect of the raising, removal, destruction or rendering harmless of a ship which is sunk, wrecked, stranded or abandoned, or of the cargo of the ship).

Some of the particular problems examined in Part 2 of this Chapter may be solved when the provisions of the 1976 Convention come into force. The Convention met some criticisms in French doctrine. Apparently they were not convincing and it was decided in 1984 to amend the present legislation on the limitation of a shipowner's liability and to insert the Convention's rules and principles into the domestic legislation.

General attitude towards the 1976 Convention

It does not appear that, at the time of its signature, the new Convention on the Limitation of Liability for Maritime Claims gave rise to many comments, either of a negative or of a positive nature. P. Chauveau[29] gave a brief commentary on the Convention

[28] C. App. Paris, December 5, 1984, Bull. Transp. 1985, pp. 64–65.
[29] Paul Chauveau, "Rétrospective d'actualités," D.M.F. 1977, pp. 68–70.

and concluded with some general observations about the lack of a substantial connection between the different legal principles contained in it. R. Rodière also considered that the 1976 Convention was not satisfactory[30]; in his opinion, the new Convention showed all the failings of the 1957 Convention and, especially, concerning the replacement of the Gold Franc Unit by the S.D.R., the setting up of a particular limitation fund for loss of life or personal injury, and the possibility given to the shipowner to limit his liability even when the loss resulted from his personal act or omission, unless it was committed with the intent to cause loss or recklessly and with knowledge that loss would probably result from that personal act or omission.

The comments of P. Chauveau and R. Rodière may be compared with those of Claire Legendre[31] who undertook in 1977 a detailed review of the different legal problems dealt with in the new Convention on the Limitation of Shipowner's Liability for Maritime Claims. The author examined carefully the preparatory work undertaken during the years preceding the signature of the 1976 Convention, its different provisions and the discussions which took place during the Conference about some of them, and she concluded by considering that the 1976 Convention seems better suited to recent technical developments and that in many respects it brings an answer to some unresolved legal problems, especially as concerns salvage,[32] or the carriage of passengers by sea.

Implementation of the 1976 Convention in French Legislation

It seems that the French Government shared Claire Legendre's opinion on the improvements that the 1976 Convention was able to bring if its principles and rules were transposed into French Maritime Law. Two Government bills were prepared in 1984 and passed by Parliament after some minor changes; the two laws were promulgated by the end of the year and published in the "Journal Officiel" as Law nos. 84–1151 of December 21, 1984,[33] and Law nos. 84–1173 of December 22, 1984,[34] both texts have been

---

[30] R. Rodière, Mise à jour au Juin 10, 1978 du *Traité Général de droit maritime*, pp. 22–23; *Précis de droit maritime*, pp. 130–131, 137.

[31] C. Legendre, "La Conférence internationale de 1976 sur la limitation de la responsabilité en matière de créances maritimes," D.M.F. 1977, pp. 195–203.

[32] English law does not distinguish between "assistance" and "sauvetage," but would refer to both as salvage.

[33] Text in J.O. of December 22, 1984, pp. 3944–3945.

[34] Text in J.O. of December 27, 1984, p. 3985.

commented briefly in French doctrine.[35] Law nos. 84–1151 and Law nos. 84–1173 do not contain a set of new provisions relating to the limitation of the shipowner's liability, they just provide for the amendment of the existing legislation presently in force.

Law nos. 84–1151 of December 21, 1984, provides for the amendment of Sections 58, 59, 61, 64 and 66 of Law nos. 67–5 of January 3, 1967. The five Sections are contained in Chapter VII ("Liability of the shipowner") of Law nos. 67–5 relating to the legal status of seagoing ships. The main features of Law nos. 84–1151 are the following:

(i) the shipowner may limit his liability for claims in respect of measures taken in order to avert or minimize a loss, or for a loss caused by such measures (section 58 as amended by Law nos. 84–1151);

(ii) the shipowner is not entitled to limit his liability if it is proved that the loss resulted from his personal act or omission, committed with the intent to cause such loss, or recklessly and with knowledge that such loss would probably result (section 58 as amended);

(iii) the limits of liability mentioned in section 58 (amended) of Law nos. 67–5 shall be calculated as provided for in the 1976 Convention (section 61 as amended). The fund of limitation provided for in section 62 of Law nos. 67–5 shall comprise three parts assigned respectively to the payment of:
 – claims for loss of life or personal injury of passengers,
 – claims for loss of life or personal injury of persons other than passengers,
 – other claims (section 64 as amended);

(iv) the shipowner will not be entitled to limit his liability for claims by the State or by any other legal person having a public law nature and acting for and on behalf of the shipowner, in respect of the raising, removal, destruction or the rendering harmless of a ship which is sunk, wrecked, stranded or abandoned, including anything that is or has been on board such ship (section 59 as amended);

(v) for the implementation of the provisions contained in section 61 (as amended) of Law nos. 67–5, the ship's tonnage shall be the gross tonnage calculated as provided for in Article 6 of the 1976 Convention;

(vi) after section 69 of Law nos. 67–5, a new section 69(a) will be inserted in the amended law, containing the provisions provided for in Article 3(b), (c) and (d) of the 1976 Convention.

[35] Chronique juridique—Droit maritime commercial, J.M.M. 1985, pp. 508–509; Modification de la loi no. 67–5 du janvier 3, 1967, portant statut des navires et autres bâtiments de mer, J.M.M. 1985, p. 76; Un rapport complétant la loi no. 67–545 du juillet 7, 1967, relative aux évènements de mer, J.M.M. 1985, p. 148.

Law nos. 84–1173 of December 22, 1984, provides for one amendment only to Law nos. 67–545 of July 7, 1967, relating to collisions, salvage and general average. Sections 9 to 21 of Law nos. 67–545 are contained in Chapter II relating to salvage; the Chapter is now completed, according to Law nos. 84–1173, by section 21(a) providing that the salvor may also limit his liability in respect of loss of life or personal injury or loss of or damage to property occurring in direct connection with salvage operations, in accordance with the rules contained in Chapter VII (as amended) of Law nos. 67–5 of January 3, 1967. Section 21(a) further contains some other provisions of the 1976 Convention relating to the limitation of the salvor's liability (for example, servants of the salvor are also entitled to limit their liability).

As concerns the enforcement of Law nos. 84–1151 and Law nos. 84–1173, both texts provide that they will come into force at the same time as the 1976 Convention. Consequently, when the new Convention of 1976 on the Limitation of Liability for Maritime Claims is in force, there will be no real difference between international maritime law and French maritime law on the subject. Recent French maritime legislation in this respect greatly contributes to the international unification of maritime law.

XII

The German Democratic Republic and the 1976 Convention

Dr. Norbert Trotz*

1. GENERAL REMARKS ON THE EXISTING LAW

At present the German Democratic Republic (G.D.R.) has not yet acceded to the 1976 Limitation Convention. It is not the intention of this paper to utter prophecies on the question of whether or when the accession to the 1976 Convention will take place. Lawyers should be modest and stick to facts, and indeed, facts are not available in this respect. There is no formal decision, activity or any other sign which indicates that competent bodies or authorities have already a certain attitude towards the 1976 Convention. That can change overnight depending, for instance, on international developments (membership, entry into force of the 1976 Convention).

This state of affairs should not prevent us from trying to analyse particular aspects of the 1976 Convention from a national viewpoint based on the present law of limitation in the G.D.R. Some general remarks on the existing limitation system will provide the background for detailed comments.

In 1976 a new Merchant Shipping Code[1] was enacted in the G.D.R. replacing the fourth book of the *Handelsgesetzbuch* of 1896. Due to the incorporation of the 1957 Limitation Convention the new Code has led to a drastic change in the limitation law. The "fortune de mer" system in its classical continental version (*Sachhaftung*) contained in the *Handelsgesetzbuch* was abolished and is now history in the G.D.R. Surprisingly the formal accession to the 1957 Convention was only effected in 1979. The time difference between the introduction of the national Act and the accession was only for technical reasons. However it is impossible to take the year of the accession (1979) as a decision against the 1976 Limitation Convention. The accession to the 1957 Conven-

---

* Academy of Political Science and Law, Institute of Foreign Law and Comparative Law, Potsdam.
[1] See Handelsschiffahrtsgesetz (Merchant Shipping Code) of February 5, 1976, Gesetzblatt der D.D.R. (Official Gazette of the G.D.R.) part I (1976) 7, p. 109.

tion can rather be considered as a positive prejudice in favour of a future decision on the ratification of the 1976 Convention, because in this way the G.D.R. has already made the basic change from the old regime to a tonnage linked limitation system that is very similar to the system of the 1976 Convention. That may at least facilitate the preparation of the ratification of that Convention.

In connection with the deposit of the instrument of accession to the 1957 Convention the G.D.R. has made reservations in accordance with the Protocol of Signature. These reservations concern paragraph 2(a) (*wreck removal*) and 2(c) (*form of introduction into national law*). The reservation on wreck removal has not been extended to liability for damage to harbour works, basins and navigable waterways.

According to the reservation on wreck removal limitation under the Convention is not applicable to any claim arising from the removal or the demolition of wrecks, sunken or abandoned ships (including all property on board) in the territorial and inland waters of the G.D.R.[2] Several reasons may have caused this reservation, but apparently the main concern was to retain the existing national regime on wreck removal[3] which is not compatible with the limitation system of the Convention. Since the 1976 Convention allows for the same reservation (Article 18(1)), this problem cannot cause any difficulty for its ratification.

According to paragraph 2(c) of the Protocol of Signature the declaration says, that the G.D.R. "gives effect to the Convention by including in its national legislation the provisions of this Convention in a form which is appropriate to such legislation."[4] The relevant legislation for this purpose is the Merchant Shipping Code (sections 111–115) and the Decree on Procedures in Shipping Matters (sections 1–28).[5] Thus this part of the Code and the Decree are the applicable form of the 1957 Convention in the G.D.R.

The 1976 Convention does not grant a right for a similar reservation. The absence of such a right apparently sets certain

[2] For the wording of the declaration see Gesetzblatt der D.D.R. (Official Gazette of the G.D.R.) part II (1980) 7, p. 113. The English version: C.M.I.—News Letter, May 1979, p. 9.
[3] Verordnung über die Rettung von Menschenleben und Fahrzeugen aus Seenot und die Behandlung von Strandgut of August 29, 1972, Gesetzblatt der D.D.R. (Official Gazette of the G.D.R.) part I (1972) p. 633. See D. Richter-Hannes, R. Richter, N. Trotz, *See Handelsrecht—Grundriß*, (Berlin, 1977), p. 104.
[4] See n. 2, *supra.*
[5] Verordnung über zivilrechtliche Verfahren in Schiffahrtssachen (Decree on Civil Proceedings in Maritime Affairs) of May 27, 1976, Gesetzblatt der D.D.R. (Official Gazette of the G.D.R.) part I (1976) 21, p. 290 as revised by the Second Decree on Civil Proceedings in Maritime Affairs of November 28, 1978, Official Gazette of the G.D.R., part I (1980) 21, p. 207.

restrictions on the way of introducing the Convention into national law. At least it should be impossible for States to change the structure and wording in order to suit the Convention to their national legislative system. This is a reasonable course followed by the majority of recent conventions. In fact the right of States to adapt the structure and the wording of conventions to their national legal system has, in the past, adversely affected the unification of maritime law. The Hague Rules are an example of such an undesirable result.[6] Since the procedure adopted by the 1976 Convention is in general useful and in the interest of unification, it should not be an obstacle to the ratification of that Convention.

As mentioned above a special decree on procedural questions has been enacted in connetion with the Merchant Shipping Code. This decree also contains provisions on limitation procedure (constitution of the fund, the effect of constitution, the distribution of the fund, etc.).[7]

2. THE SCOPE OF THE RIGHT OF LIMITATION

Persons entitled to limit liability

The provisions of the Merchant Shipping Code of the G.D.R. (hereafter cited as M.S.C.) mirror only the corresponding rules of the 1957 Convention. Thus the owner, operator, and charterer on the one hand and the master, crew, and other servants of the aforementioned persons on the other hand have a right to limit liability.

In the 1976 Convention some additional provisions have been included extending the limitation right to other persons: (a) salvors, (b) persons mentioned in Article 1(4) and (c) insurers.

(a) It is well known that the special provision for the salvor in Article 1(3) of the 1976 Convention is a "*lex Toju Maru.*" In most cases the 1957 Convention should already cover the limitation right of the salvor. His right to limit liability can only be questioned in some exceptional situations which are very often the result of technical developments in salvage operations. Article 1(3) of the 1976 Convention should not be considered a real change of the existing law, but a means to solve a marginal problem and to adapt the law of limitation to modern technical developments. For this reason, the provision cannot create a serious problem in any national legislation.[8]

---

[6] See D. J. Markianos, *Die Übernahme der Haager Regeln in die nationalen Gesetze über die Verfrachterhaftung,* (Hamburg, 1960).

[7] For comments, see n. 3, "Limitation Procedure," *infra.*

[8] The special case of salvage of ships carrying dangerous cargo cannot be considered in this context.

(b) In comparison with the corresponding provision of the 1957 Convention, Article 1(4) of the 1976 Convention extends the personal scope of limitations, although the Conference in 1976 did not go so far as originally proposed by the Comité Maritime International.[9]

One might be permitted to say that the law of the G.D.R. is well prepared for the application of this provision of the 1976 Convention. The M.S.C. defines in paragraph 105, at least for the liability in tort, the persons for whose acts the shipowner is liable, namely "persons employed in the operation of the ship." This definition does not only cover the master, the crew, and the servants of the owner, but also any other persons rendering service for the ship including, to some extent, independent contractors.[10]

(c) The right of insurers to invoke limitation is at present recognized in the maritime law of the G.D.R. for claims in connection with pollution damage (M.S.C. s.116(4)). That provision is derived from the CLC 1969, but the extension to the general law of limitation should not cause any problem.

Claims subject to limitation

The definition of claims subject to limitation in Article 1(1)(a) and (b) of the 1957 Convention is casuistic and intricate. Besides, the reference to "infringement of any right" has caused problems in connection with the incorporation into the law of the G.D.R. In order to evade that problem and to bring the wording more in line with the national legal tradition both subparagraphs have been transformed into general language. Section 111(1) of the M.S.C. reads as follows:

"(a) personal injury or loss of life to persons who were on board the ship for carriage, or from the loss of or damage to property on board,

(b) other damage resulting from the operation of the ship, whatever the basis of liability may be."

This language at least comes fairly close to Article 2(1)(a) of the 1976 Convention. It is obvious that in this respect the provision of the 1976 Convention cannot give rise to any reservation; on the contrary, it is more acceptable for the legal system of the G.D.R. than the corresponding rule of the 1957 Convention.

But in Article 1(1)(c) the 1976 Convention refers also to "infringements of rights." In the light of the problem that arose in connection with the 1957 Convention it might be a question whether the corresponding rule of the 1976 Convention could

---

[9] Compare the C.M.I. Maxi Draft, Article 1.2, C.M.I.-Documentation (1974) II, p. 304.

[10] Richter-Hannes, Richter, Trotz, *op. cit.* n. 3.

cause similar difficulties. The answer requires some comments on the provision concerned in the 1957 Convention.

Article 1(1)(b) of the 1957 Convention refers to "infringements of rights" without any additional qualification. The interpretation of this part of the Convention has caused difficulties on account of the uncertain meaning of the word "rights."[11] For this reason it has not been included in the M.S.C, but the general wording in section 111(1)*(b)* of the M.S.C., quoted above, is broad enough to cover claims which are only conceivable as a result of an infringement of a right and not as loss consequential on physical damage. For instance, claims for loss caused by delay should come under that rule. But it was just an open question of interpretation whether the "rights" cover contractual rights, or non-contractual rights, or both. In case of contractual rights this rule would have the drastic effect of making the limitation applicable even to claims for loss resulting from a breach of a contract.

The method applied in the M.S.C. is to avoid the specific word but to cover the possible contents by a broad formula. This, of course, does not solve the problem, but it gives more room to manoeuvre and allows for reasonable results of interpretation because there is no need or pressure to search for the meaning of the particular word "rights."

Article 2(1)(c) of the 1976 Convention at least makes it clear that contractual rights are excluded. That solves a part of the problem but, nevertheless, it is still uncertain which claims come under this rule.[12] Since losses resulting from personal injury and from damage to property, including consequential losses, are already covered by Article 2(1)(a), it seems that (c) is only of certain value for claims resulting from pure economic loss. These represent, to say the least, a very limited category of claims. It can therefore be assumed that Article 1(1)(c) has been included in the 1976 Convention as "safety net" in order to make the limitation provisions water-tight.

Taking into account the reservation which prevails in the G.D.R. towards the corresponding provision of the 1957 Convention, it is difficult to foresee the position in respect of Article 2(1)(c) of the 1976 Convention. However, it can be said that the exclusion of contractual rights has considerably reduced the difficulties by eliminating the main risk of this rule, namely the intervention of global limitation into the field of the law of contract.

The inclusion of a specific type of contractual claim in Article 2(1)(b) of the 1976 Convention (loss resulting from delay) is necessary in the light of the Hamburg Rules. The application of

[11] See P. K. Sotiropoulos, *Die Beschränkung der Reederhaftung*, (Berlin, 1962), p. 263.

[12] See N. Trotz, *Zur internationalen Konvention von 1976 über die Haftungsbeschränkung für Forderungen aus der Seeschiffahrt*, (Potsdam-Babelsberg 1980), p. 36.

global limitation to this particular category of claims has never been disputed or refused in the G.D.R.; it was always the general nature of the rule in the 1957 Convention which caused discussions.

Claims in respect of wreck removal and similar operations in the law of the G.D.R. are excluded from limitation on account of the reservation made in connexion with the accession to the 1957 Convention.[13] The provision of the M.S.C. concerning this exclusion refers to claims resulting from the obligation of the owner to remove wrecks in the territorial sea, internal waters and inland waters of the G.D.R.[14] It is very likely that the G.D.R. would make the same reservation in respect of the 1976 Convention, Article 2(1)(d) and (e).

A new limitation right has been provided for in Article 2(1)(f) of the 1976 Convention. It has been copied from the CLC 1969 with the exception that the owner who may claim against his own fund in accordance with the CLC 1969, is not allowed to do so under the 1976 Convention. Since the G.D.R. is a member of the CLC 1969 the limitation for claims in respect of preventive measures is already recognized within the framework of pollution. The extension of this approach to global limitation is of practical importance if, in international or national law, a particular rule grants a right to a third person who has taken preventive measures to claim for compensation or the costs incurred. In such a case the limitation may become useful for both sides; the third person would have the possibility of making a claim against the fund and the owner would be protected against any payment outside the fund for damage in respect of which he can normally invoke limitation. It should be mentioned that the G.D.R. civil law, under certain circumstances, gives third persons a right to claim for expenses incurred in connexion with preventive measures.[15]

Claims excluded from limitation

In the M.S.C. of the G.D.R., (section 112), the following claims are excluded from limitation:
  (a) claims for salvage or contribution to general average,
  (b) claims arising from wreck removal,
  (c) claims of servants and agents,
  (d) claims for nuclear damage caused by nuclear ships or nuclear material,
  (e) claims for legal costs.
No comment is necessary on (a) and (c) because these provisions are identical with the corresponding rules in Article 1(4) of the

[13] See, *1. "General Remarks on the Existing Law," supra.*
[14] M.S.C., s.112(1)(b).
[15] Civil Code, s.326.

1957 Convention and Article 3(a) and (e) of the 1976 Convention. The reference to wreck removal in (b) is a consequence of the reservation made by the G.D.R.[16]

The exclusion of claims for nuclear damage from limitation goes further than the 1957 Convention which does not even mention this type of claim. The question is whether or not such an addition to the exceptions made in the 1957 Convention is in line with the provisions of that Convention. An answer would not be easy and would depend on the interpretation of the general scope of the global limitation of that Convention. The opinion has been expressed that the risk of nuclear damage is not a typical shipping risk and therefore is not covered by the global limitation in maritime law.[17] If that opinion is correct, the nuclear risk falls outside the scope of the 1957 Convention. The silence of the 1957 Convention in this respect can, of course, be invoked as evidence for and against this proposition because the absence of any provision has no particular reason. In 1957, apparently, it was not felt necessary to include a rule for a problem which was not relevant at that time. However, the Convention Relating to Civil Liability in the Field of Maritime Carriage of Nuclear Materials 1971 perhaps would support the view that nuclear risk is not a typical shipping risk. That Convention exonerates, under certain circumstances, any person liable in accordance with maritime law from the liability for nuclear damage, channelling the liability to the operator of the nuclear installation. It is clearly the intention of this Convention to exclude the application of maritime law and to ensure the exclusive application of the provisions on liability for nuclear damage.

The 1976 Convention fortunately has removed this uncertainty and has, in Article 3(c) and (d), excluded claims for nuclear damage from the scope of application of that Convention. Article 3(d) (nuclear ships) is a plain exception clause, whereas Article 3(c) sets some conditions. The 1976 Convention shall not apply to claims for nuclear damage, if they are subject to international or national rules governing or prohibiting limitation. These conditions will be met in most cases, because States are normally either a member of a nuclear convention or have national rules which channel the liability to the nuclear operator. In that case the claim would be subject to the nuclear provisions concerned, including the limitation rules which are part of such provisions.

Since the G.D.R. has not acceded to any nuclear convention on civil liability the national law would be applicable. In accordance with the Atomenergiegesetz (Nuclear Energy Law) and the Civil

---

[16] See p. 208, *supra.*
[17] Trotz, *op. cit.* n. 12, *supra*, p. 51 and R. Freise, *Die Reform der Reederhaftung und das allgemeine Haftpflichtrecht, Versicherungsrecht* (1972) 5, pp. 126 and 127.

Code the operator of the nuclear installation is liable for damage without limitation.[18]

The exception rule in Article 3(b) of the 1976 Convention has no equivalent in the 1957 Convention. This new provision is necessary in order to solve the conflict between the global limitation and the limitation under the CLC 1969. The CLC 1969 contains special limitation rules for claims which are at the same time subject to global limitation in accordance with the 1957 Convention. This conflict between both Conventions causes problems in countries which are parties to both instruments, like the G.D.R. That is particularly the case where a court in a State party to both Conventions wants to apply the CLC 1969 to a ship flying the flag of a country party to the 1957 Convention only. The contractual rules of public international law would not allow the application of the CLC 1969 in such a case. There is, therefore, no question about the need for a solution of this conflict.

The positive attitude which can be expected in the G.D.R. towards this provision of the 1976 Convention should not be affected by the position of the G.D.R. delegation at the London Conference in 1976 and by the dispute on the interpretation of Article 3(b) in the Legal Committee of I.M.O. after the Conference.

In fact, in 1976 the G.D.R. delegation was not satisfied with the draft finally adopted by the Conference because of the unforeseeable consequences of the wording chosen. Article 3(b) in its present version not only regulates the relationship between the two Conventions concerned but also the relationship between the 1976 Convention and undetermined national legislation on liability for oil pollution damage.[19] The G.D.R. delegation made a proposal which aimed at a more limited draft, covering only the relationship between the two Conventions in question.[20] That proposal was not accepted by the Conference. Since we have now to live with the wording in the 1976 Convention it is justified to say that a bad solution is better than no solution at all.

But one should be aware of the interpretation risk caused by the broad wording of Article 3(b). The risk involved became obvious in a debate of the Legal Committee of I.M.O. on the interpretation of that rule. At the 48th and the 49th meeting of the Legal

---

[18] Law on Nuclear Energy of December 8, 1983, Official Gazette of the G.D.R., part I (1983) 34, p. 325 and ss.343 and 344 of the Civil Law Code of 1975.

[19] See on the meaning of the provision E. Selvig, "The Limitation Convention 1976 and Oil Pollution Damage," [1979] 1 L.M.C.L.Q. p. 21.

[20] LEG/CONF. 5/C.1/WP 73 (November 11, 1976) and LEG/CONF. 5/C.1/WP 83, (November 15, 1976), the last mentioned document was made together with Liberia, the Netherlands and Poland.

Committee[21] the view was expressed that Article 3(b) of the 1976 Convention excludes any claim for oil pollution damage from limitation even though the claim is outside the personal scope of the CLC 1969 and could not be based on its provisions.

The victim of this interpretation could be the bareboat charterer who is not liable under the CLC 1969 but whose liability can arise under national law. The main concern of the discussion in the Legal Committee was whether the wording "claims for oil pollution damage within the meaning of. . . ." covers (a) the definitions of oil, of damage etc., only, or also (b) the person against whom a claim can be made.

(a) In that case *any* claim for oil pollution damage covered by the definitions of the CLC 1969 would be excluded from limitation in accordance with the 1976 Convention and the bareboat charterer could not invoke the global limitation rules. Since he is not liable on the basis of the CLC 1969 the limitation rules of that Convention would not apply either. The result would be unlimited liability.

(b) In this case Article 3(b) of the 1976 Convention would not exclude claims against the bareboat charterer because they were not claims "in the meaning of" the CLC 1969. Thus he could invoke limitation in accordance with the 1976 Convention.

The majority of delegations participating in the debate at the Legal Committee were in favour of an interpretation which allows for the application of the limitation rules of the 1976 Convention to oil pollution claims which cannot be based on the CLC 1969.[22] But the dispute, of course, could not be settled in the Legal Committee. A solution is now offered by the channelling provisions of the Protocol of 1984 to the CLC 1969.[23]

Conduct barring limitation

Traditionally the right of the shipowner to limit his liability has been considered the rule in the law of the G.D.R. and the breaking of limitation, in the case of fault of the owner, the exception, accordingly. Thus, the burden of proof has rested with the claimant in accordance with the rule that a person invoking an exceptional clause has to establish the application of the clause in the particular case by the evidence required. Consequently the claimant had to prove that the incident causing the damage in question resulted from the fault of the owner.

---

[21] See the report of the 48th and 49th session LEG 48/6 of March 19, 1982, pp. 22–23 and LEG 49/8 of November 1, 1982, pp. 25–26. In addition the U.K. document LEG 49/7 of July 12, 1982.

[22] LEG 49/6, p. 26.

[23] Protocol of 1984 to Amend the International Convention on Civil Liability for Oil Pollution Damage, 1969 LEG/CONF. 6/66. See, in particular, Art. 4.2.

This position has prevailed since the incorporation of the 1957 Convention into the law of the G.D.R. and the wording of section 111(3) of the M.S.C. is based on the principle. The effect resulting from this provision is in line with the 1957 Convention which leaves it to the *lex fori* to determine who bears the burden of proof.[24] Accordingly, States should be free to bind the national courts by a particular provision.

In general the formulation of section 111 of the M.S.C. shows the efforts made to keep this rule as narrow as possible and to retain the exceptional character. That concerns, for instance, the additional wording included in order to solve the problem of companies. It is expressly said that in the case of legal persons or associations only the fault of the "organs or partners appointed for representation" is relevant. The intention is to prevent an interpretation which enlarges the group of persons whose acts are considered acts of the "owner." The effectiveness of the restriction intended has not yet been tested in the courts of the G.D.R.[25]

The main difficulty in connection with the incorporation of the 1957 Convention was caused by the words "actual fault and privity," because there is no corresponding legal term in the German language. In the German translation of the text of the Convention the words *"persönliches Verschulden"* are used which can be retranslated as "personal fault." These words have been changed in the M.S.C. to "violation of duty by the owner himself." Both versions intend to preserve the limited scope of the rule. In any event they can already be considered a bridge to the corresponding provision in the 1976 Convention which speaks, in Article 4, of the "personal act or omission" of the owner.

3. LIMITATION PROCEDURE

Right of limitation and constitution of the fund

The 1957 Convention contains only some basic rules on the constitution and distribution of the fund. Therefore, national law mainly governs the limitation procedure and Article 4 of the 1957 Convention makes a specific reference to this effect. But even the few provisions on procedure in the Convention are not free from ambiguities. The national legislation, therefore, has to provide not only for a complete set of procedural rules but also has to ensure a clear interpretation of the provisions of the Convention.

One of the main questions is whether or not the constitution of the fund is a prerequisite for the exercise of the right of limitation. Whereas the 1976 Convention, in Article 10, leaves it clearly to the State Parties to decide that question, the 1957 Convention, in

[24] Art. 1(6).
[25] Official Gazette of the G.D.R. part II (1980) 7, p. 117.

Article 2(2) seems to be open to different interpretations in this respect. The law of the G.D.R. is based on the interpretation that the words "may be constituted" in Article 2(2) of the 1957 Convention do not introduce a condition for the exercise of the limitation right. Thus the owner may invoke limitation in a lawsuit where an action is brought against him even if he has not constituted a fund. But the owner would in such a case bear the risk that the claimant tries to secure his claim by arresting assets of the owner. That risk can only be avoided by the constitution of the fund.

The constitution of the fund

If the owner (or another person having a right to limit liability) wants to constitute a fund he has to apply for a special proceeding on limitation of liability.[26] The application for such a proceeding is admissible

(a) if a claim subject to limitation has been made against the owner either by an action in a court or outside legal proceedings, or

(b) if the owner can substantiate the future assertion of a claim.

The rights granted to the owner by these provisions are very wide; at any time after the occurrence giving rise to the claims he has the possibility to secure his limitation by the constitution of the fund. The first-mentioned case (where an action is brought against the owner in a court) covers the normal situation. The other cases (where a claim is made informally outside legal proceedings, or no claim is made but the owner alleged to be liable) go further and allow for protection against future actions of the claimant.

The limitation proceedings, under these circumstances are separated from the legal proceedings dealing with the claim itself and have an independent status without formal link to the action brought against the owner in a court. That is underlined by the exclusive competence of one court of the G.D.R. for any limitation proceeding.[27] The constitution of the fund with that court does not give jurisdiction for an action in respect of the claim itself. The court is, of course, competent for the distribution of the fund among the claimants and a claimant may file a claim at the court for participation in the distribution. But any dispute over the claim has to be settled by the court normally having jurisdiction over the case.[28] In any event, the special competence of a single court for limitation proceedings leaves the jurisdiction of other

[26] See s.1 of the Decree on Civil Proceedings in Maritime Affairs (MAP), and n. 5, *supra*.
[27] County Court of Rostock, M.S.C., s.115.
[28] With some exceptions in cases of actions of establishment in respect of claims which are already included in the limitation proceedings, M.A.P., ss.13, 22.

courts for actions in respect of the claim itself untouched. That is even the case where an arrest is made or a security is given to avoid the arrest and the owner later applies for a limitation proceeding and the transformation of the security into a limitation fund. In its new capacity as a fund the security comes then under the authority of the County Court of Rostock, but the jurisdiction of the court where the arrest was made remains effective in respect of the original action.

It is apparent that the separation of the limitation proceeding and the wide range of rights of the owner to apply for such proceedings can lead to intricate procedural situations. But Article 2(2) of the 1957 Convention allows for an interpretation which is broad enough to cover the above mentioned rights of the owner to apply for a limitation proceeding as provided for in the law of the G.D.R. It seems that the 1976 Convention is more restrictive in this regard. The first sentence of Article 11(1) of that Convention can be interpreted as such a restriction as it allows the constitution of the fund only when "legal proceedings are instituted in respect of claims subject to limitation." Even if this provision is in the first place a jurisdiction clause, it seems to bar the constitution of the fund before an action is brought in a court in respect of a claim. But that provision can also be regarded as "minimum standard" ensuring, at least in the case mentioned, the right of the owner to constitute the fund with the court in question. Thus States would have the duty to include such a right in their national law but they would be free to go even beyond that line. In that case Article 13(2) of the 1976 Convention would, in a certain way, restrict this freedom in the interest of the claimants. But that provision raises already the question of jurisdiction.

Jurisdiction

It has already been mentioned that within the G.D.R. the County Court of Rostock is exclusively competent for limitation proceedings. We have now to deal with the international jurisdiction for limitation proceedings. That question should not arise in States where limitation proceedings are always linked with legal proceedings instituted in respect of claims subject to limitation. The jurisdiction in respect of limitation proceedings could simply follow the normal jurisdiction of the court.

The system applied in the G.D.R. requires in any event, special rules on the international jurisdiction for limitation proceedings. The 1957 Convention is silent on jurisdiction; States are, therefore, free to enact their own provisions. They have only to take into account Article 5 of the 1957 Convention, which provides for mandatory effects of a security given at certain places. At least the courts mentioned in Article 5(2) should be competent in order to give the owner the possibility of using the benefits provided for.

The special provision on international jurisdiction in the law of the G.D.R. is contained in section 2 of the MAP. In accordance with that provision proceedings on limitation may be applied for in the following cases:

1. the person entitled to limitation or the claimant are citizens of the G.D.R., or have their residence or seat there;
2. the ship concerned is entered in the register of the G.D.R.;
3. the event giving rise to claims has occurred in the waters of the G.D.R.;
4. the ship has, after the event, called at a port of the G.D.R., or would have done so if the voyage had taken its normal course;
5. the passengers have left the ship in a port of the G.D.R., or the cargo is unloaded in such a port;
6. proceedings have been instituted at a court of the G.D.R. in respect of claims subject to limitation;
7. the shipowner has, because of an arrest of the vessel, given security at a court of the G.D.R. and has applied for the inclusion of that security in the limitation proceedings.

In the last mentioned case the court may reject the application for a limitation proceeding if none of the preconditions of cases 1 to 6 prevail and the implementation of the limitation proceeding in a court of the G.D.R. would be inexpedient. This right to refuse an application for limitation proceedings gives the necessary power to the court to take into account Article 5(2) of the 1957 Convention and to release the security when a security has already been given at a place in a contracting State mentioned in that provision of the Convention. It goes without saying that an application for a limitation proceeding cannot be rejected when the security is not released, or when the arrest leads to the institution of normal legal proceedings at a court of the G.D.R.

In the 1976 Convention the first sentence of Article 11(2) can be considered a jurisdiction clause. The effect of that clause depends on the interpretation which has already been discussed on p. 218, *supra*.

If Article 11 has to be understood as allowing the constitution of the fund only with the court where legal proceedings have been instituted in respect of claims subject to limitation, a special jurisdiction for limitation proceedings would be superfluous because the competence of courts for limitation proceedings is then governed by the normal jurisdiction of the courts. As to the present law of the G.D.R. this interpretation would have two consequences:

1. it would no longer be justified to give the shipowner the

right to constitute the fund outside or independent of legal proceedings in respect of claims subject to limitation;

2. the existing special provisions on jurisdiction of the court concerned for limitation proceedings would become superfluous.

But if that provision of the 1976 Convention can be regarded as a "minimum standard" giving the shipowner, at least in the case mentioned, the right to constitute a fund and leaving it to States to go even further, the G.D.R. could stay with the present law when the Convention becomes effective for this country.

Article 13(2) of the 1976 Convention provides, in any case, for a certain protection of the claimants against the constitution of the fund at an inconvenient place. Even if the shipowner would have a broader choice between places where the fund may be constituted, he is interested in the mandatory effect of exemption granted by Article 13(2)(a) to (d) and would, therefore, prefer the places mentioned in that provision.

XIII

The German Federal Republic and the 1976 Convention

*Prof. Dr. Rolf Herber**

1. HISTORY OF LIMITATION PROVISIONS

Before 1973, when the 1957 Convention relating to the Limitation of the Liability of Owners of Sea-going Ships was incorporated into German law, an entirely different system of limitation of liability was applicable in the Federal Republic of Germany.

In the second half of the last century the basis was laid for the actual provisions on maritime commercial law contained in book 4 of the Handelsgesetzbuch which to a large extent of its present contents came into force in 1900. The Handelsgesetzbuch and earlier laws of the Empire and of various states had rules not only on the liability of shipowners but on the limitation of this liability as well.

The principle of limitation of those times, valid until 1973, was simple, but different from the maritime law of most other countries. The shipowner[1] and the operator[2] were, according to these rules, personally liable for all claims arising out of the employment of the vessel, provided, however, that the claim was based on their own fault or privity. If the claim was based, to the contrary, on the fault or neglect of a member of the crew or someone else for whom the shipowner or operator was liable, there was limitation of his liability to the ship itself. The claimant in such a case, after having obtained a judgment against the shipowner, was able to enforce this judgment only *in rem* against the ship itself. No other assets of the shipowner were, in principle, exposed to his access.

To make that system somewhat clearer some remarks should be added. The object of the liability was the ship and the freight earned on a given voyage. The claims which were subject to this

---

* Institute of Maritime Law, Hamburg University.
[1] *"Reeder,"* who is under German law defined as a shipowner who uses the ship in his commercial interest.
[2] *"Ausrüster,"* who is defined as someone who uses a ship belonging to someone else—in practice by means of a bare-boat charter—in his own commercial interest.

limitation were mainly claims based on torts committed by members of the crew or other employees on the vessel. But there were also some claims arising out of contracts which the master, by authority of his legal powers to represent the shipowner abroad, had concluded in cases of emergency for the continuation of the voyage. Lastly, the shipowner (or operator) was personally liable—*i.e.*, the whole of his assets were exposed to the access of the claimant—if he was personally at fault as to the damage caused to the claimant or if he had authorized the master to conclude a given contract *in concreto*. And there was a replacing liability, limited in amount, where, after returning from the voyage in question, he had sent out the ship on a new voyage.

It should be mentioned that this system did limit the liability of the shipowner by law. There was, therefore, no need for any legal action or declaration of the shipowner or operator to limit his liability. The liability was limited from its very beginning by the law itself.

The system needed, in addition, corresponding rules on maritime liens. Because if the access of a claimant is limited to the ship itself it must be safeguarded by law; likewise he may be able to share in the value of the ship at least with a given ranking before mortgagees and those creditors who would be able to exercise their claims against other assets of the shipowner as well. So the *Handelsgesetzbuch* (section 754) set out a list of maritime liens providing protection to the claimants in relation to the claims for which the liability of the shipowner was limited accordingly.

This former limitation system was called the *Exekutions-System*,[3] because of its strict reduction of the right to execute a claim against ship and freight. It is still applicable in German Law for Inland Navigation[4] where all attempts to modernise the limitation system according to the developments in maritime law have failed until now.

There were obvious shortcomings of that limitation system. If the ship were lost as a consequence of the accident caused by his fault there was no liability whatsoever except with the wreck. And if a ship was badly maintained and therefore had a very low market value, the limitation sum, the countervalue of the ship's price (after the incident), was lower than in the case of a well-run vessel. These disadvantages and the need for international unification led to improvements.

In the international field, the International Maritime Committee (C.M.I.) had already tackled this topic at its Conferences in 1907, 1909 and 1922. The work led to a Convention in 1924 which, however, was not accepted by Germany. This Convention

---

[3] Execution System.
[4] *Binnenschiffahrtsgesetz.*

was based on a compromise between various systems other than the former German system. It did not meet support of many states. In particular, the United Kingdom and the United States—whose law had delivered the elements of the compromise—did not ratify it.

After the Second World War, in the light of previous experience and in view of a proceeding need to unify international maritime law, the work by the C.M.I. started again and led, after the C.M.I. Conference of 1955 in Madrid, to the adoption of the Brussels International Convention relating to the Limitation of the Liability of Owners of Sea-going Ships of October 10, 1957. This Convention contained a clear cut rule based on the lump sum system as, in principle, applicable in England since 1862. It was the basis of a wide-spread unification of limitation law which certainly contains some uncertainties and doubts. However, it has made it possible to rely on similar limitation principles all over the world, with the unfortunate exception of the limitation figures. This is not so much a consequence of shortcomings of the Convention but of developments in the international monetary system.

The Federal Republic of Germany ratified the 1957 Limitation Convention in 1972 where it entered into force on April 6, 1973. At the same time, the *Handelsgesetzbuch* was changed to some extent to incorporate the new rules. It is obvious, that the changes were rather fundamental, because the limitation system of the 1957 Convention was entirely different. The liability of the shipowner was no longer limited by law from the very beginning of the claim, but was subject to the right of the shipowner, or operator,[5] to limit his liability by depositing a limitation fund. These new principles required, at the same time, additional provisions on the constitution and distribution of the limitation fund as well as changes with regard to the list of maritime liens as mentioned above. In particular, the latter task of the German legislator caused some delay in ratification because there was an international Convention under work destined to simplify the law of maritime liens and mortgages. This Convention was adopted at a Brussels Diplomatic Conference in 1967, but did not, however, enter into force. The law of April 21, 1972, implementing the 1957 Limitation Convention, amended at the same time the rules on maritime liens and was almost completely based on the 1967 Maritime Liens and Mortgages Convention.

---

[5] Or, in addition, the charterer and the members of the crew.

2. EXISTING LEGAL SITUATION

Since April 6, 1973, therefore, the Federal Republic of Germany has been a party to the 1957 Limitation Convention.

The internal law of the Federal Republic of Germany has been amended by the incorporation of the principles of the said Convention and this has been done by means of a statute of June 21, 1972 (*Seerechtsänderungsgesetz*).[6] This Statute has adapted Section 486 *et.seq.* of the *Handelsgesetzbuch* to the principles of the 1957 Convention. In addition, the judicial procedure governing the establishment and distribution of the limitation fund has been laid down in a specific statute of the same date (*Seerechtliche Verteilungsordnung*).[7]

The principles of limitation on which this law is based need not be explained in detail because they correspond to the 1957 Convention. There are only a few features deviating or filling gaps which are particular to the law of the Federal Republic.

One of them is the treatment of the pilot's liability. Since the 1957 Convention does not provide for limitation of the liability of a pilot, a need was felt to provide for it in national law. Section 487(3) *Handelsgesetzbuch* provides for the pilot's right to invoke limitation to the extent that he is jointly liable with someone else who is entitled to do so. The rationale of this rule was that in these cases, as a rule, the shipowner or operator will be liable for the claim against the pilot also, so that a claimant may charge the limitation fund by this claim in any event. So it was possible, without contradicting the Convention and, in particular, without affecting the rights of competing claimants, to extend the benefit of limitation to the pilot under these circumstances.

One further element of the present legal situation may be mentioned. The rules of the Convention do not apply to claims by public authorities for wreck removal.[8] There are, it is true, similar provisions on limitation of these claims which, in fact, have been adapted to the new principles of limitation introduced into German law as a consequence of the 1957 Convention. However, they are not as watertight as the 1957 Convention provisions because they are part of administrative law and sometimes they care more about the public interest in recovering for expenses on wreck removal than of the interest of the shipowner in relying on limitation of liability in all cases. This is, incidentally, one of the shortcomings which will be remedied on the occasion of ratification of the 1976 Limitation Convention.

---

[6] *Bundesgesetzblatt* 1972 Teil I s.966.

[7] *Bundesgesetzblatt* 1972 Teil I s.953.

[8] Assuming that a state has exercised the right to make a reservation excluding the application of Art. 1(1)(c).

Of a purely national character is the limitation procedure as provided in the *Seerechtliche Verteilungsordnung*, mentioned above.

According to this the limitation fund, within the Federal Republic of Germany, can be established by invoking the limitation procedure (*Seerechtliches Verteilungsverfahren*). Jurisdiction lies exclusively with the Lower Court (*Amtsgericht*) in Hamburg.

The procedure requires a writ asking the Court to fix the limitation sum and to invoke the limitation procedure. The sum being fixed, any person liable out of the specific occurrence and entitled to limit his liability may deposit the limitation sum with the Court or—which is more frequent—provide for bail or security accepted expressly by the Court. Once the sum is paid, or security delivered, the Court starts the procedure. It announces to the public the invocation of the procedure and asks any claimant whose claim arises from the occurrence mentioned to present his rights to the Court. Thereafter, the claims announced to the Court will be discussed between claimants and debtors. To the extent that they remain controversial they have to be settled within ordinary proceedings. This division of powers between the Court of Distribution and the ordinary proceedings corresponds to the German system of bankruptcy procedure.

After the claims, or at least the majority of claims, have been fixed there will be a distribution of the limitation sum. To the extent that claims are still pending, or are not yet decidable, part of the sum can be retained by the Court for later distribution. During the procedure of limitation ordinary proceedings against the persons liable for claims subject to limitation are not admitted. The same goes for individual enforcement of claims or even judgments. The procedure has proved to be rather effective, as there have not been too many cases (about 50). The fact that most cases obviously are managed by settlement seems, however, due to the fact that there is an efficient and clearcut legal system of limitation for the event that the parties do not agree.

The system of limitation of liability, as in other countries, came into difficulties as a consequence of developments in the international monetary field. Since the limitation sum had been fixed in Poincaré Francs and the national currencies had lost their connection with the gold value, it was no longer possible to transfer the figures of the Convention, which had been incorporated into the *Handelsgesetzbuch*, into Deutsche Mark.

In the international field a Gold-Clause-Protocol to the 1957 Convention was not worked out. Because at the time, when this has been done for other international Conventions, the 1957 Limitation Convention was already under revision. Therefore, the national legislator has transformed the figures expressed in Poincaré Francs into Special Drawing Rights (SDR) and in this way taken them into the *Handelsgesetzbuch* (Section 487(3)). The limitation amount per ton thereafter is $206\frac{2}{3}$ SDR in case of occurrences giving rise to damage to property as well as to personal injury and $66\frac{2}{3}$ SDR in case of damage caused only to property. This change has been made by a statute of June 9, 1980.[9]

3. GENERAL ATTITUDE TOWARDS THE 1976 LIMITATION CONVENTION

The government of the Federal Republic of Germany has signed the Convention and is at present preparing draft legislation for approval and implementation.

Although, at the Conference, the delegation of the Federal Republic of Germany would have liked fewer changes to the 1957 Limitation Convention, preferably a simple protocol to that former Convention, it always agreed to the amendments performed to the system by the new Convention. Certainly, the 1976 Convention has shortcomings as well. But it meets some main objectives of necessary revision to the existing limitation system.

The most important element of modernisation is the fixing of higher amounts of the liability and the expression of these amounts in SDR. On the other hand, the system of calculating the amounts of limitation has become more complicated. Secondly, the new Convention solves the problem of limitation of liability of a salvor acting from outside a vessel. At the same time, the pilot gets the right to limit his liability. Not only are salvors and pilots covered by the limitation privilege, but also all other persons for whom the owner or charterer is liable. This contributes to a more watertight protection of owner and charterer, one of the original purposes of the Himalaya Clause.

The limitation amounts are less breakable than in the earlier Convention, namely only in the case where the person liable acted with intent or recklessly and with knowledge that loss would probably result. Further, the division of the limitation fund into three limitation funds—for personal injury other than passengers, for passengers and for damage to property—makes the Convention easier to apply in practice.

Lastly, a question of interpretation of the old Convention has been settled. It was clarified that the person liable may invoke limitation of liability even if no fund has been established. This was a solution, which did not conform to the wishes of the delegation of the Federal Republic of Germany, but which at least clarifies the situation.

The Convention solves, at the same time, the relationship of the

[9] *Gold frankenumrechnungsgesetz, Bundesgesetzblatt* 1980 Teil II, s.721.

226

general privilege of limitation of liability of the shipowner on one hand and the 1969 Convention on Civil Liability for Oil Pollution on the other hand. Unfortunately, it does not provide for the same relationship (*i.e.* preference of the later specific Convention) to a future Convention on liability for carriage of dangerous goods. Such a Convention was planned already in 1976. The I.M.O. Conference in 1984 failed to adopt it. But there will certainly be a need for rules of this kind in the forseeable future. Amendments by the delegation of the Federal Republic to provide for preference of such a later convention were, however, rejected by the Conference because of uncertainty as to the contents of these future rules. So a future revision or Protocol to the 1976 Convention may become necessary soon.

Altogether, the Convention is considered as well by the government as by commercial circles in Germany as a progress towards the actual legal situation and it is hoped that it will soon take the place of the 1957 Convention and provide a valuable basis for the limitation of the shipowner's liability worldwide.

4. DRAFT LAW TO IMPLEMENT THE 1976 LIMITATION CONVENTION

As already mentioned, a draft law aiming to approve the Convention and to implement its rules into the law of the Federal Republic of Germany is under preparation. It is likely[10] that the draft will be submitted to Parliament. In view of the normal duration of parliamentary proceedings this would mean that the corresponding law—if it is passed by Parliament and assuming no grave objections arise—may come into force at the beginning (and at the latest in the middle) of 1986. At that moment, the Federal Government would be able to deposit its instrument of ratification.

As to the form of *implementation* as provided by the present draft law there is a basic difference between the implementation of this Convention and that of the 1957 Convention. In 1972 the 1957 Convention was incorporated into German law by including the rules in an appropriate form into the *Handelsgesetzbuch*. Preparation of such a law was rather time-consuming and the interpretation might present a certain risk of deviation from that convention by the contracting countries. Therefore, the 1976 Convention will be applied as such and the additional provisions of national law will only refer to the text of the Convention. This is a change in the general attitude towards implementation of international conventions, which always presents a problem of legal techniques for countries in which neither the language nor the legal system corresponds to that of the Convention. The need, however, to

---

[10] As at May, 1985.

provide for uniform international interpretation to the extent possible conflicts with the interest of states with a developed codification system to keep coherent their internal legislation: at least in maritime law, which is mainly international.

The Draft Law, therefore, consists of three parts: the Draft Law of approval to the Convention; the Draft Law to amend the *Handelsgesetzbuch*; and the Draft Law to amend the *Seerechtliche Verteilungsordnung*.

As to the *contents of the law* there is no need to go into details of the Convention which have already been presented in Part A. I only would like to focus on the probable particularities of a future German incorporating law.

The Convention contains some blanks which have to be filled in by national law. The main ones are the following and they are, under the draft, being treated as follows:

(i) Article 2(1)(d) and (e), and Article 18 grant the possibility to Contracting States to make reservations as to limitation of claims with respect to wreck removal. The Draft Law provides for making use of this possibility. This was the same under the 1957 Convention and there, as well, the corresponding reservation has been made. To the earlier Convention, however, a different ruling in internal law was not issued so that, in fact, the rule of the Convention—at least in broad principles—applied.

Under the new régime it is intended to provide for a specific fund for wreck removal under national law. This safeguards, on the one hand, that the public authorities which normally benefit by these claims are not exposed to competition with other claimants. It limits, on the other hand, the risk of the shipowner so that he may only be held liable to a foreseeable amount from an incident, *i.e.*, in case of damage caused to property as well as to claims for wreck removal, which may, because of raising costs, reach double the amount of the Convention. This is an improvement towards the actual internal law, where in principle there is limitation of these claims, but this principle is not reliable because part of the claims are based on public law where the limitation does not apply. The Draft provides for limitation of all claims on whatever legal basis they are founded.

(ii) Article 6 provides for the possibility of Contracting States, within the distribution of the limitation fund for property claims, to grant preference for claims in respect of damage to harbour works, basins and waterways and aids to navigation over other claims for compensation of damage to property. The Draft Law makes use of this possibility, *i.e.* it provides for such a priority.

(iii) Article 15(2)(a) leaves the choice to contracting states to regulate by specific provisions of national law the system of limitation of liability for ships intended for navigation on inland waterways. This choice, which is not subject to an express reservation, is, of course, exercised by the Federal Republic of Germany. Inland navigation, in particular on the Rhine, plays an important role in German law of transport. The limitation system in inland transport law still is different from that in maritime law.[11] There have been moves, over a long period, to change the present limitation system to the system which is, since 1957, governing maritime law world-wide. A convention adopted by the ECE (CLN) in 1973, unfortunately did not enter into force.

(iv) Article 15(2)(d) leaves the possibility for national law to make rules for ships below 300 tons. The Draft Law makes use of this faculty by providing half the limitation sum for ships of 500 tons for all ships below 250 tons.

(v) Article 15(3) leaves freedom to Contracting States to except from the rules of the Convention claims arising in cases in which interests of persons who are nationals of other States Parties to the Convention are in no way involved. The Draft Law does not make use of this faculty. So the rules of the Convention will apply in all cases where the law of the Federal Republic as such is applicable under international private law.

There are some additional problems which need not, but may, be solved on the occasion of incorporation of the 1976 Limitation Convention. The most important of those is the *liability of a pilot*. It is true, that the pilot under the new Convention is able to limit his liability according to the same rules as are applicable for the shipowner. This means, however, that the pilot is protected against third-party claims only by amounts which are, in cases of great ships, much too high to safeguard his economic survival. German law until now does not provide for limitation of the pilot's liability in amount.

The Convention leaves freedom to national law to fix limitation sums for specific claims—similar to the limitation in amount foreseen, for example, in the Hague/Visby Rules or in national laws on the carriage of passengers by sea. The Draft Law provides for a limitation to an amount equivalent to a ship of 1,500 tons. This is the same amount which the Convention provides for the limitation of the salvor. And it is, perhaps, justifiable in the same manner as the latter: a ship, which the salvor or the pilot would use, might have this size. The law of the Federal Republic, thereby, for the first time provides for a protection of pilots against liability risks by fixing a ceiling. The amount is equivalent (in case of property damage) to 334,000 SDR. Beyond this ceiling, of course,

---

[11] See n. 2. *Existing Legal Situation, supra.*

the general limitation rule of the Convention is applicable to pilots; that means in practice, in particular, that the pilot benefits from a limitation fund established by the shipowner.

There are other rules provided for by the Draft Law which have only a slight connection with the 1976 Convention, *e.g.*, the introduction of mandatory liability rules for claims because of damages caused to passengers by sea. These rules do not exist until now, because the 1974 Athens Convention is not yet in force. It is still undecided whether the Federal Government will ask for authorisation to ratify this Convention. If they do so the main reason would be immediately to try to enter into a revision procedure in order to increase the amounts of liability under that Convention.

Finally the Draft Law will incorporate some elements of the Hague/Visby Rules to which the Federal Republic of Germany is not yet a party and, in particular, the liability rules (limitation per kg and the container clause) will be incorporated into German Law.

The limitation procedure will be changed in some respects because of modifications and clarifications in the 1976 Convention. The main difference is, as already mentioned, that the establishment of a limitation fund[12] will no more be an indispensable condition for invoking the limitation. The present German Law starts from this interpretation of the 1976 Convention. Minor changes to the procedure cannot be recorded in detail here. Basically the *Verteilungsverfahren* remains the same with regard to jurisdiction, procedure and results as it is at present.

Outlook

As already mentioned, it is likely that the Convention will be ratified by the Federal Republic of Germany in the beginning of 1986 and will get in force accordingly. The rules will be made applicable as internal German law as well. They will, however, in form not be incorporated into the German Commercial Code. Some supplementary provisions will be made as mentioned.

---

[12] In terms of German law: the introduction of the distribution procedure—*Verteilungsverfahren.*

XIV
Greece and the 1976 Convention

*Gerasimos M. Vlachos**

1. BRIEF BACKGROUND AND HISTORY OF LIMITATION PROVISIONS[1]

Greece adopted in 1835 the "Code de Commerce" system of law, *i.e.* cession of the ship *in natura* and of the freight to the creditors. In 1910 Greece adopted the Venice Conference 1907 system, *i.e.* at the option of the shipowner: cession of ship and freight, or payment of an amount—for each voyage—corresponding to 200 Drachmas per ton gross (net as from 1949). In 1910 200 Drachmas were equal to eight sovereigns. In 1949 an amount of 350,000 Drachmas (or 350 new Drachmas) was added to cover, specifically, loss of life and personal injury claims, if any.

2. PRESENT POSITION

The system now applicable as from 1958[2] is briefly as follows: The shipowner—or the operator registered in the Ships' Registry—has the right to limit liability by exercising the option of:
  either, a) ceding the ship and gross freight;
  —The value of any encumbrance (privilege or mortgage) in favour of other creditors and payable to them should be made good by the shipowner or operator exercising this option.
  —There is a specific right of cession in respect of damage caused in the territorial waters, at the roads or harbours by a wreck or damages to harbour installations or in respect of costs attached to the removal of the wreck.
  or, b) offering three tenths $(\frac{3}{10})$ of the ship's value at the commencement of the voyage plus an additional three tenths $(\frac{3}{10})$ to the satisfaction of loss of life and personal injury claims, if any.
  —If these additional three tenths $(\frac{3}{10})$ are not sufficient, the loss of

---

* Lawyer, Member of the Greek Maritime Law Association.
[1] For a basic bibliography in Greek (titles translated) see: J. Passias, *TheLimitation of Shipowners' Liability* (1948); Ph. G. Potamianos, *Principles of Maritime Law* (1966); C. N. Rokas, *Maritime Law* (1968); D. N. Kamvysis, *Maritime Law* (1982).
[2] Code of Maritime Law, Articles 84–106.

life and personal injury creditors are entitled to satisfy the balance of their claim by joining the creditors of the first three tenths ($\frac{3}{10}$).

—The loss of life and personal injury creditors, only, have a further right against the freight.

The option of cession cannot be exercised:

(a) on obligations created as a result of contracts on which the shipowner specifically consented or were approved by him;

(b) on obligations arising from contracts of employment of the master, officers and crew.

The option of three tenths ($\frac{3}{10}$) cannot be exercised for the limitation of salvage claims.

The cession of the ship does not transfer the ownership to the creditors. The owner is simply divested of the right of management or operation and the ship is a separated property destined to be sold. The sale proceeds are allocated among the creditors. The Greek Code of Maritime Law defines in detail the Court procedure following the declaration of cession in Articles 90–104.

The option of cession is perfectly legal even if the ship had sunk (but if sold the three tenths ($\frac{3}{10}$), only, could be offered) in which case the creditors all act against the gross freight, only, following the cession.

The total loss insurance proceeds do not replace the cession declared in case of creditors whose property is damaged and it is the loss of life and personal injury creditors exclusively (but not master, officers and crew) who are entitled to satisfy their claim by the insurance proceeds in case of cession declared of a sunken ship.

Another salient consequence of the existing system is that the servants are jointly and severally responsible *in integrum* with their shipowner and they are unable to limit their own personal liability. The servants' liability is a fundamental principle of provisions on tort of the civil law and it is explicitly established in collision cases.[3] In addition, personal detention in prison is applicable in Greece as an enforcement measure against those liable to pay a debt created as a result of a tort. It is seldom that such claims against shipowners' servants reach the Courts as normally the insurance or P & I cover of the ship would settle the creditors. The existing precedent of ordering the personal detention of servants (possibly the master or chief engineer) is, indeed, rare. The Thessaloniki Court Judgment No. 3310/83 is the most advanced in the exploration of this field, so far.

Under the present system the unbreakable right of limitation of the shipowner exists for the acts or omissions of the master in the exercise of his duties—and the torts of the master, officers, crew

---

[3] *Ibid.* Article 239.

or the pilot in the exercise of their duties. Greece is not a party to any of the conventions on limitation of shipowners liability (1924, 1957 or 1976). The International Convention on Tonnage Measurement of Ships 1969 has been ratified and is applicable as from November 19, 1983. Greece is also a member of the International Monetary Fund.

3. COMMENTS AND PROSPECTS OF IMPLEMENTATION OF LIMITATION PROVISIONS AS PER 1957 OR 1976 CONVENTION

The Greek system is completely different from the system of the Conventions. However it is restricted to claims presented in the Greek Courts involving Greek flag vessels. Foreign Courts are not bound to apply the law of the flag of the ship to blame and Courts of a member State of the 1957 or 1976 Conventions would apply the Convention. The vast majority of Greek flag ships engaged in international trading are therefore subject abroad to the limitation of liability systems applicable in other jurisdictions. The Greek system would continue to serve a very unimportant practical purpose.

The Greek Maritime Law Association recommended the ratification of the 1976 Convention or, at least, the 1957 Convention as amended by the Protocol of 1979. The matter is under the consideration of parties interested, but so far no positive step has been taken to any final decision. It is appreciated that the limits of 1976 Convention are high, particularly to ships up to 30,000 tons and exceedingly high in respect of claims for loss of life or personal injury in comparison with the prevailing low market value of ships. The rules of the Convention shall not apply to such claims by the master, officers and crew—*i.e.* the great majority of these claims—as according to Greek law governing their contract of service the shipowner is not entitled to limit his liability in respect of such claims, which would continue to be regulated by Greek law.

The limitation of shipowners' liability is closely connected with the insurance of the risks involved, the availability of cover and the cost attached to it. It is an element of ship's running cost. If, therefore, the traditional maritime countries with substantial tonnage become parties to the 1976 Convention the obligation of cherished competition on an even keel would make imperative the adoption of the Convention by Greece. Alternatively, lower premiums (if available) would gradually disappear as underwriters realise that the existing limitation system of Greek flag vessels does not reduce their shipowners' liability outside Greece.

Minor difficulties may arise regarding the corresponding provisions of Greek law which, if not expressly abolished, would become inapplicable as contrary to an international Convention constitutionally overruling national law. Probably, the consequences of the liability of servants would disappear in view of Article 1(4) of the 1976 Convention, unless the shipowner would pursue a recovery claim against the person for whose act, neglect or default he is responsible. The interpretation of Article 2(1)(c) might also involve reference to Greek legal provisions or precedents which are not exactly the same.

However the limitation status of the person liable as per article 4 of the 1976 Convention is secured by the absolute prerequisite of "intent," or reckless conduct "with knowledge." The burden of proof in charge of the plaintiff against the person liable is practically insuperable.

XV

Japan and the 1976 Convention

1. INTRODUCTION

In March, 1899, the Commercial Code which contains Maritime Laws was first enacted in Japan. This Code came into force from June 16, 1899. It introduced basically the German Commercial Code. In this Code it was provided that the shipowner could avoid any liability for claims resulting from an employee's negligence or misconduct in connection with the operation of the ship by abandoning the vessel herself and her freight to the claimants. However this abandonment system was revised in 1976.

On December 27, 1975, a new Act concerning limitation of shipowners' liability[1] was enacted separately from the Commercial Code and came into force from September 1, 1976, when the 1957 Brussels Convention became effective. This 1975 Act was made in order to introduce the 1957 Brussels Convention into Japan after Japan ratified that convention. This was a great change in our system of limitation of liability from an abandonment system to a monetary limitation system.

After the 1975 Act came into force, it was criticized for the smallness of the limitation amount. The criticism was especially severe in the case of claims for loss of life. Under the Act, the unit for the limitation amount (the gold franc) was fixed to equal ¥23. Supposing that the responsible ship was less than 300 limitation tons, the limitation amount would have been ¥21,390,000. Nowadays the size of a claim for loss of life has rapidly increased. It ranges from ¥50 million to ¥100 million per person, depending upon the income of the victim. The minimum limitation amount (¥21,390,000) when the vessel was less than 300 tons did not cover claims arising from a single loss of life. However, on January 26, 1978 the Court of Appeal of Tokyo stated that the amount of the limitation fund was not so low as to be improper, in handing down a judgment that the Limitation of

---

* Attorney, Fujii & Toda, Tokyo.
[1] The Act Relating to Limitation of Liability of Shipowners and Others, hereafter referred to as "the Limitation of Liability Act."

Liability Act was not unconstitutional.[2] This decision was upheld by the Supreme Court of Japan by its decision of November 5, 1980.[3]

2. THE 1976 CONVENTION

Criticism of the low level of the limitation amount mounted year after year. This caused an early ratification of the 1976 Limitation Convention. On May 21, 1982, the Limitation of Liability Act was revised in accordance with the 1976 Limitation Convention. Furthermore the date for the revised act to come into force was fixed to be within 2 years irrespective of the Convention itself being in force by that day. On May 20, 1984, the revised act in conformity with the 1976 Limitation Convention came into force in Japan. It was ahead of the Convention in coming into force.

Since then, Japanese laws concerning limitation of liability have been basically the same as the 1976 Limitation Convention with some exceptions and differences which are summarised below.

Claims in respect of wreck removal

In accordance with Article 18 of the London Convention, when ratifying it Japan reserved the right to exclude the application of Article 2,(1)(d), (e). Article 3(1) of the Limitation of Liability Act excludes claims in respect of wreck removal from the claims against which the shipowner can limit his liability. For example, if a ship is sunk, wrecked, stranded or abandoned in a harbour or fairway due to an accident and the Japanese Marine Safety Agency[4] orders the owner of the vessel to remove her to restore navigational safety, then the owner so ordered cannot limit his liability for the costs of the wreck removal. This order is directed only to the owner of the wrecked vessel even if that owner or his crew members were not at fault at all in causing the accident.[5]

If the owner does not comply with the order for wreck removal, then the M.S.A. removes the wreck and claims the costs from the owner. If the sinking of the ship was caused by a collision with another ship, the owner who paid the costs of wreck removal can recover the costs from the other ship to the extent that liability can be attributed to the other ship.

In such cases, there was heated debate over whether or not the owner of the other ship was entitled to limit his liability in respect of the indemnity claim for the costs of wreck removal which the

[2] 886 HANREI JIHO 89–94.
[3] 936 HANREI JIHO 105–107.
[4] "M.S.A.."
[5] Art. 27, Harbour Act (Kosoku-Ho); Art. 33(3) Marine Traffic Safety Act (Kaijo Kotsu Anzen-Ho).

owner of the sunken vessel had fully paid. This was resolved recently when the Supreme Court rendered judgment on April 26, 1985, that the owner of the other ship can limit his liability for such wreck removal indemnity claims from the sunken vessel owner.[6] It is criticised by some in that it will invite an owner, whose ship collides with a ship which sinks, to delay in settling the claim for wreck removal of the sunken ship. It is more favourable for him to wait until the owner of the sunken vessel has paid for the full costs of wreck removal with no limitation of liability, and then settle the portion of the costs for which he is found to be responsible, subject to his entitlement to limit his liability.

Limitation amount when tug and tow involved

There have been arguments on which amount should be the limitation amount: the amount calculated only on the tug's tonnage or the aggregate tonnage of the tug and the tow; and whether or not it should be affected by the tow being manned or unmanned.[7] On these points, we have recently had a very important precedent. The Court of Appeal of Osaka ruled on April 15, 1985, that the owner of a tug towing an unmanned barge could not limit his liability to an amount calculated only on the tug's tonnage and that the limitation amount should be calculated on the aggregate tonnage of the tug and the tow.[8] In this case the unmanned barge towed by the tug collided with and damaged a mine sweeper belonging to the Japanese Self Defence Naval Forces. The barge was not owned by the tugowner who was sued by the Japanese Government, the owner of the mine sweeper, in connection with the claims for repairs to the damaged mine sweeper. The tugowner appealed from the decision to the Supreme Court but the Supreme Court dismissed the appeal in December 1985.

Limitation of liability without constitution of a limitation fund

Article 10 of the 1976 Convention allows the right to limit liability to be invoked without constitution of a limitation fund. However under the Japanese Limitation of Liability Act, limitation of liability can be invoked only if the limitation fund has been deposited into the court in the form of cash or a letter of guarantee issued by a bank or an insurance company which has a registered office in Japan.[9]

[6] 1155 HANREI JIHO 296–299.
[7] See, *e.g.* C. Hill, *Maritime Law* (2nd edn., 1985), pp. 254–255.
[8] 1163 HANREI JIHO 139–143.
[9] Art. 25, Limitation of Liability Act.

Interest on the limitation amount

Before the revised Limitation of Liability Act came into force[10] interest was not required to be paid into the court with the limitation amount in applying for proceedings for limitation of liability. Further, there was no time limit for an application for limitation proceedings. Therefore, even if shipowners, or their underwriters, admitted that they had to pay the limitation amount to the claimants, it was their tendency to delay in payment since they did not need to pay any interest on the limitation amount. It was possible for them to earn interest on that amount for the period of delaying in payment to the creditors.

However, since the present provisions came into force from May 20, 1984, the situation has improved. Shipowners seeking limitation of liability have to deposit the limitation amount plus interest at 6 per cent. per annum from the date of the occurrence giving rise to the liability until the date of the constitution of the fund.[11]

A similar problem still exists though, in that the value of SDRs in terms of Japanese Yen has changed dramatically. If the exchange rate drops over 6 per cent. per annum, as it has recently, the above tendency would revive.

No consolidation of the limitation proceedings and other proceedings brought by creditors

In England or America I understand that the court having jurisdiction over the limitation proceedings can consolidate any other proceedings pending in other courts in which creditors are bringing actions against the shipowners in respect of which the shipowners claim limited liability.[12]

Further, in England or the United States, shipowners may raise defence in proceedings brought by a creditor, that they can limit liability.[13] But in Japan, the system is quite different. When an application for limitation proceedings is made by the shipowner to the competent court, the court may order commencement of the proceedings for the limitation of liability after the limitation amount plus interest has been deposited with the court. This decision is basically made without holding any hearings, by an *ex parte* procedure. It is a kind of declaration by the court that claimants who do not want to challenge the decision can file their claims to be paid in accordance with the court's distribution of the limitation fund. Of course a conditional filing is allowed in the case

---

[10] *i.e.*, before May 20, 1984.
[11] Art. 19, Limitation of Liability Act.
[12] McGuffie, Fugeman, Gray, *Admiralty Practice* (1964), para. 1219; *Benedict on Admiralty* (7th edn., 1983) s.52.
[13] *Admiralty Practice, op. cit.*, para. 1213.

of a creditor who intends to allege that his claims cannot be limited.[14]

For those who do not want to accept the decision to commence limitation proceedings, there are two choices. One is to appeal from the decision to the Court of Appeal. The other is to commence ordinary proceedings against the shipowners. The court in charge of the limitation proceedings does not have any power to discontinue those proceedings to consolidate all proceedings relevant to limitation of liability.[15] In the creditor's proceedings, the court has to hold hearings to decide on that case in the usual manner. Under this procedure the shipowner can argue that a limitation order has been made and the plaintiff's claims should be subject to the limitation proceedings. If the shipowner fails to raise this defence based upon the existence of the limitation order (or the judgment is made for the plaintiff before the limitation order is made) then the shipowner will lose the benefit of the limited liability conferred by the Limitation of Liability Act.

However, an important exception to the right of limitation of liability has been greatly changed, that is, the exception of "without the actual fault or privity" has been replaced by the more limited exception of "his personal act or omission committed with the intent to cause such loss, or recklessly and with knowledge that such loss would probably result."[16]

In addition to this change, since the amendment to the Limitation of Liability Act in accordance with the 1976 Limitations Convention brought about a considerable increase of the limitation amounts, the number of claimants who seek full recovery by alleging this exception is rapidly decreasing. Accordingly, the separation of proceedings as described above is not of as great importance as it was before.

[14] Art. 73, Limitation of Liability Act.
[15] Art. 64, Limitation of Liability Act.
[16] Art. 3(3), Limitation of Liability Act; Art. 4, 1976 Limitation Convention: see further, Chap. 4, *supra*.

XVI

The Nordic Countries and the 1976 Convention

*Professor Erling Selvig**

The Danish, Finnish, Norwegian and Swedish legislation which has implemented the 1976 Convention is uniform legislation prepared through Nordic cooperation.[1] The statutory provisions of all four countries are also nearly identical in form. This legislation falls in two parts, one reflecting the substantive provisions and the other containing new procedural rules on limitation funds and limitation actions.

In Denmark, Norway and Sweden the substantive provisions, mainly taken from the 1976 Convention, appear in the Maritime Codes (M.C.), sections 234–243a, and the procedural rules in sections 350–364 of the Codes. In Finland the relevant provisions are set out in the Maritime Code, sections 12–22, and in a separate statute on limitation funds and limitation actions relating to maritime claims.

On April, 1, 1984 the four countries deposited their documents of denunciation of the 1957 Convention. The denunciation became effective April 1, 1985 and the new legislation has entered into force in all the four countries as from that date. In the Nordic countries overdue law reforms are usually put into effect independently of the entry into force of the particular convention implemented by the new legislation. In 1984 Denmark, Finland, Norway and Sweden also deposited the documents of accession to the 1976 convention.

The provisions of the 1976 Convention Articles 1–9 have been reflected in the M.C. sections 234–238. Interest for late payment and legal costs are not subject to limitation. The option in Article 6(3) relating to claims in respect of damage to harbour works etc. has not been used. With respect to claims for oil pollution damage,[2] the Danish, Finnish and Swedish legislation only

---

* Scandinavian Institute of Maritime Law, University of Oslo.
[1] A commentary on the Swedish version of the new legislation has been prepared by Birgitta Blom, who served as chairman of the Committee of the Whole at the 1976 conference, see *Birgitta Blom*, Sjölagens bestämmelser om redaransvar, (Stockholm, 1985).
[2] Art. 3(b).

excludes claims "subject to" the national enactment of the 1969 Convention, while the corresponding Norwegian provisions exclude all claims for oil pollution damage "of the kind mentioned in" that Convention.[3]

Section 239 of the Maritime Code corresponds to Articles 10(2) and 12 and section 240 to Article 11. However, it is no condition for limitation that a limitation fund is established, and section 242 contains provisions as to the application of global limitation when the right to limit liability has been invoked in ordinary litigation. The provisions on bars to other actions[4] are set out in section 241.

The Nordic countries have not made use of the options contained in Article 15(2) and (3). Thus, the *minimum limit* established in the Convention[5] applies to all ships with a tonnage not exceeding 500 tons. However, the option relating to *drilling vessels*[6] has been used. The limits for such ships are 12 million SDR for personal claims and 20 million SDR for property claims irrespective of tonnage. These limits are equivalent to those applying to drilling rigs and similar moveable platforms used in off-shore activities.

The 1924 Convention Article 13 excluded warships and other ships used for governmental, non-commercial activity. This provision was not retained in the 1957 Convention, but in the Nordic countries this Convention has been understood not to have abandoned this principle. The right of limitation of liability for warships and other governmental ships would consequently be a matter for national law, and in the Nordic countries the prevailing view has been that the national enactments of the 1957 Convention applied correspondingly to such ships. Recent experiences with, *inter alia*, submarine accidents suggested that this might not be an entirely satisfactory approach, and now section 243(1) of the M.C. provides for two modifications. *First*, there is established a minimum limit for such ships calculated on the basis of 5,000 tons. *Secondly*, the right of limitation does not apply to claims in respect of loss or damage caused by the special qualities or use of such ships. In order to avoid misunderstanding, it is expressly stated that the new rules for warships and other governmental ships do not apply to icebreakers and salvage vessels.

As mentioned above, it is no condition for limitation that a limitation fund is established. However, according to M.C. s.240, a limitation fund may be established at the court where legal action,

[3] Norwegian M.C. sections 236(2) and 283(3), *cf.* Blom *op. cit.* pp. 82–83 and Er Selvig, "The 1976 Limitation Convention and Oil Pollution Damage" [1979] 1 LMCLQ 21.
[4] Art. 13.
[5] Art. 6(1).
[6] Art. 15(4).

arrest or the like has been instituted. When a fund has been established, the person establishing the fund, his liability insurer or any claimant may bring a limitation action for the purpose of determining the questions relating to the particular claims made, the right of limitation of liability, the limitation amount and the distribution of the fund among the claimants. When a limitation fund has been established, it constitutes a bar to separate legal actions before a domestic court relating to and of these matters.[7]

The procedure for limitation actions has been set out in M.C. ss.350 *et seq.* Claims which have not been made to the court where the action has been brought before the conclusion of the hearing regarding the distribution of the fund, will as a rule, be considered as discharged.[8] However, according to M.C. s.363 the court may, when determining the distribution of the fund, decide that a certain amount shall temporarily be set aside for claims not yet received.

The judgment in the limitation action is binding on all persons who would be entitled to make a claim against the fund irrespective of whether or not they have done so.[9] The consequences are: that the questions relating to the right to limitation and of the limitation amounts are finally decided; that the shipowner or other person entitled to global limitation cannot subsequently be held liable for any claim which could have been made against the fund; and that the distribution of the fund provided for in the judgment is final.

---

[7] s.240(3).
[8] M.C., s.357.
[9] M.C., s.364.

XVII

Poland and the 1976 Convention

Wejeiech Adamezak[*]

The adoption of the new convention by IMO put down the question of its ratification and the legal ramifications of such ratification in the internal law of all countries involved in maritime commerce, including Poland.

In Polish civil law the compensation for damage depends, first of all, upon the dimensions of such damage.[1] The provisions of the Polish civil code of 1964 implement the principle of total compensation. However, exceptions from this principle are recognised and amongst them is the limitation of the liability by virtue of the law. In the area of maritime law the principle of total compensation is restricted more often than in the civil law.[2] The Polish Maritime Code of 1961[3] contains the general principle that the ship's operator bears unlimited responsibility for his obligations,[4] but the same Code contains the exceptions from the cited principle giving the shipowner the privilege to limit his liability in many cases. The recognition of the unlimited responsibility of the shipowner as a general principle is of great importance because it justifies the narrow interpretation of the provisions governing the limitation of shipowner's liability.

In respect of shipowner's liability the provisions of the 1924 Convention on the Limitation of the Liability of Owners of Seagoing Ships[5] have been adopted in the Polish Maritime Code. So the liability of the ship's operator is limited according to Article 72

---

[*] Institute of Maritime Law, Gdańsk University.
[1] System prawa eywilnege, t. III, ez. I, Wrockaw-Warszawa-Krakow-Gdańsk-Lódź 1981, p. 290.
[2] J. Lopuski: Odpowiedzialnosć za szkodo w zegludze merskiej, Gdańsk 1969, p. 245.
[3] Formerly the maritime law in Poland was regulated by Book IV of the German Commercial Code of 1897. Extracts from *The Polish Maritime Code*—a translation by R. Adamski and J. Lopuski Wydawnietwe Merskie, Gdańsk 1973, are cited in this chapter.
[4] A ship's operator is the person who in his own name operates his own or somebody else's vessel in shipping. The provisions concerning limitation of liability by the ship's operator are *mutatis mutandis* applicable to the owner of the vessel and to the charterer.
[5] Ratified by Poland in 1936.

of the maritime code, in respect of obligations incurred under the heads of:

(i) compensation for damage caused to third parties by the acts or faults of the master, other members of the crew, pilot or any other person employed in the service of the vessel;

(ii) compensation for damage caused to cargo received for carriage, or to other property on board;

(iii) bill of lading;

(iv) compensation for damage caused by a nautical fault committed in the execution of contract;

(v) raising and removal of wreck, and any amounts due in connection therewith;

(vi) salvage remuneration;

(vii) general average contribution falling on the ship's operator;

(viii) contracts entered into, or legal acts done, by the master acting within the scope of his statutory authority while the vessel is away from her home port, where such contracts or acts are essential for the actual necessity of preserving the vessel or for continuing the voyage, unless such necessity has been caused by insufficiency or deficiency of the vessel's equipment or provisions at the beginning of the voyage.

The limitation of liability as laid down in the foregoing paragraph does not apply to obligations arising from a personal fault of the ship's operator, (as referred to in sub paragraph viii *supra,*) when the ship's operator has given the master a specific authority to contract such obligations or has ratified these, and the obligations in relation to members of the crew and other persons employed in the service of the vessel.

The ship's operator who at the same time is the master of the vessel cannot have the benefit of the limitation of liability in respect of his personal faults other than the nautical fault.

The limitation of the shipowner's liability means that in the cases cited above the shipowner is liable only up to the amounts defined in the Maritime Code. That is, under Article 73, he is liable only up to the amount equal to the aggregate value of:

(i) the vessel,

(ii) the freight, with which the money for the carriage of passengers and of their baggage is identified. Such freight, including the money for the carriage of passengers and of their baggage, is deemed to be a lump sum amounting to 10 per cent. of the vessel's value at the commencement of the voyage, even though no freight be earned by the vessel.

(iii) amounts due to the vessel by way of general average contribution and by way of compensation for damage to the vessel, sustained since the commencement of the voyage and not yet repaired, excluding, however, insurance indemnities.

In the cases enumerated above in Article 72(1), sub-paragraphs i–v the shipowner is liable, however, only up to the amounts calculated in conformity with the principle as laid down in this matter by International Convention. The Maritime Code does not indicate which Convention is the relevant one, but there is no doubt, that it is the 1924 Brussels Convention, cited above.

To persons entitled to compensation for damage caused by death or personal injuries, the ship's operator is liable in excess to the limits laid down in Article 73(1) or 73(2) up to an additional amount fixed and calculated in conformity with the principles of the International Convention. To a foreign creditor whose state has established a limit of liability lower than that determined by this International Convention, the ship's operator is liable only up to the lower limit.

In assessing the value of the vessel under Article 74 the following are conclusive:

(i) as regards the satisfaction of claims, including contractual claims, resulting from collision or other marine accidents, and from general average losses:

   (a) the condition of the vessel at the time of her arrival at the first port after the accident, disregarding, however, any diminution in value caused by a subsequent separate marine accident which has occurred before the arrival of the vessel at that port,

   (b) the condition of the vessel after the accident at the port at which the accident has occurred during the vessel's stay,

(ii) as regards the satisfaction of claims relating to the cargo or arising from a bill of lading, (but originating from other causes than those set in sub-paragraph (i)) the condition of the vessel at the port of destination of the cargo, or at the place where the voyage is broken, and where the cargo is destined to various ports—the condition of the vessel at the first of such ports,

(iii) in all other cases set out in Article 72(1)—the condition of thg vessel at the time of the termination of the voyage.

Under Article 75, claims originating from the same accident and, in the absence of an accident, claims in respect of which the value of the vessel is ascertained at the same port, participate in the division of the sum due from the ship's operator in proportion to the amount of each of such claims. Claims of persons entitled to compensation for damages resulting from death or personal injuries in consequence of the same accident, participate in the division of the additional amount provided for under the above provisions. Where such amount is not sufficient to satisfy those claims, the uncovered part thereof participates together with other claims in the division of the sum allocated for the satisfaction of the remaining damages. A bail arranged or security given by the ship's operator for an amount equal to the limit of his liability is available to all persons in respect of whom the ship's operator is entitled to limit his liability.

In 1972, Poland ratified the Brussels Convention of 1957 on the Limitation of the Liability of Owners of Sea-going ships. Nevertheless the Maritime Code has not been changed so far.[6]

The signing of the 1976 convention put down the question of its ratification and the eventual adoption into the internal law. The detailed analysis of the legal consequences of such a decision are not the purpose of this paper. Perhaps it would be more interesting to present some problems of particular importance from the point of view of the eventual incorporation of the 1976 Convention into the Polish law.

First, according to the text of the 1976 convention, it is necessary to examine who may limit his liability. The 1976 Convention establishes that the shipowners and salvers may limit their liability. The term shipowner shall mean the owner, charterer, manager and operator of a sea-going ship. Furthermore an insurer of liability for claims subject to limitation in accordance with the rules of the convention shall be entitled to the benefits of it to the same extent as the assured himself. Such regulation means that the old conception of the limitation of liability being a benefit of the shipowner only, as a person engaging his property in the marine enterprise, is finally rejected.[7] As noted above Article 77 of the Maritime Code gives the right to limit liability not only to the ship's operator, but also to the owner of the vessel and to the charterer. The adoption of the 1976 Convention would lead to the extension of the list of privileged persons entitled to limit liability. So it would mean new exceptions to the general principle of total compensation.

On the other hand, however, there are the strong arguments supporting the idea adopted in the 1976 Convention. The special situation of the salvor and the role which he plays in the shipping industry justifies giving him a right to limit his liability. Also, the giving of the benefit to the insurer should not be a serious obstacle to the ratification of the 1976 Convention by Poland. The claims subject to limitation in the 1976 Convention are more clearly

---

[6] Nevertheless, it would seem that a Polish Court ought to allow the ship of a country party to the 1957 Convention to limit liability in Poland according to the Rules of that Convention.

[7] J. Lopuski: *op. cit.*, p. 266.

constructed than in the 1957 Convention which makes them easier to adopt into Polish law.

From the point of view of Polish law one must emphasize the adoption of limitation of liability as to the claims in respect of loss resulting from delay in the carriage by sea of cargo, passengers, or their luggage and the claims in respect of other loss resulting from infringement of rights other than contractual rights occurring in direct connection with the operation of the ship or salvage operations.

The incorporation into Polish law of Article 3 of the 1976 Convention, enumerating the claims excepted from limitation could cause some difficulties. Among the said exceptions there are enumerated, *inter alia*, claims for oil pollution damage within the meaning of the International Convention on Civil Liability for Oil Pollution Damage of 1969. Poland has already ratified this convention, but its rules are not adopted so far in the Polish Maritime Code. So the adoption of the rules of the 1976 Convention has to be correlated with the relevant adoption into internal law of the rules of the 1969 Convention.

Article 4 of the 1976 Convention regulates conduct barring limitation: namely, a person liable shall not be entitled to limit his liability if it is proved that the loss resulted from his personal act or omission, committed with the intent to cause such loss, recklessly and with knowledge that such loss would probably result. The idea accepted in the said Article is not quite strange to the Polish law. Article 473(2) of the Civil Code has been based on a similar idea. Thus, according to this Article a contractual provision that the debtor will be not liable for a damage which he can do intentionally is invalid.

Article 8 of the 1976 Convention is of special importance from our point of view. The unit of account, adopted in the Convention, is the Special Drawing Right. Poland is not, so far, a member of the International Monetary Fund (IMF). However, the Convention contains special provisions in respect of States not being members of the IMF. The value of a national currency in terms of the Special Drawing Right, of a State Party which is not a member of the International Monetary Fund shall be calculated in a manner determined by that State Party. Nevertheless, those States which are not members of the Fund may use the solution contained in Article 8(2) of the 1976 Convention.

In such a situation Article 8 is no obstacle to the ratification of the 1976 Convention, more particularly as Poland has already ratified the 1979 Protocol to amend the International Convention Relating to the Limitation of the Liability of Owners of Sea-going Ships of 1957.

The principle adopted in Article 10 of the 1976 Convention that limitation of liability may be invoked notwithstanding that a limitation fund has not been constituted corresponds to the basic principles of the Polish law. Namely, limitation of liability is a question of the material law and Polish Law strongly stresses the distinction between the material and procedural law. The clear distinction between the rules governing limitation of liability and the provisions governing the constitution and distribution of the fund makes easier the adoption of the provisions of the 1976 Convention in Polish law.

In accordance with the above remarks it seems that no serious obstacles exist against the ratification by Poland of the 1976 Convention. Moreover, it is also quite possible to adopt its principles into the Polish law. Some of them clearly correspond to its principles.

The principles of the 1976 Convention correspond to the certain tendency which can be observed in the contemporary shipping relations towards limitation of the principle of total compensation and, at the same time, towards the objectivisation of liability.[8]

Of course the adoption of the principles of the 1976 Convention in the Polish law would cause the necessity of the change of almost the whole of Book II of the Maritime Code (Articles 72–77) devoted to the institution of the ship's operator and, furthermore, the determining by separate provisions of the rules governing the constitution and distribution of the limitation fund. On the other hand, it should be borne in mind that the adoption of the principles of the 1957 Convention in the Maritime Code would necessarily cause equal changes.

The problem of the ratification of the 1976 Convention was under discussion for some time. In my opinion there are no real obstacles to such ratification and the adoption of its principles into Polish law. Indeed at the IMO Legal Committee in October 1985 Poland announced its intention to ratify the 1976 Limitation Convention.

[8] J. Lopuski: op. cit., p. 245.

XVIII
Spain and the 1976 Convention

*Alejandro G. Sedano**

At present there are two situations in Spain in respect of limitation of liability, depending on whether the domestic Law or the 1957 Convention applies. Consequently they will be treated separately.

1. DOMESTIC LAW

In Spain the system of limitation of the Shipowner is *ad valorem* and, so, Article 837 of the Spanish Commercial Code states that "the shipowners' liability in case of collision is limited to the value of the vessel with her accessories and freights earned in the voyage."

This system, originally, was the cause of problems as to the way in which to fix the value of the vessel, *i.e.* whether the value in question should be considered before or after the collision.

The doubt was clarified by the Spanish Supreme Court in a decision of April 17, 1964, which established that for limitation purposes the value is that of the vessel immediately before the collision.

The Supreme Court based the decision on the following reasons: The contents of Article 837 should be interpreted in the most reasonable way to reach what the legislator had in mind, *i.e.* the limitation of liability, but not exoneration of liability which would occur if the vessel is totally lost. Similarly if the cost of repairs of the responsible vessel is deducted from the sound value, this would prejudice the innocent party.

Article 837 of the Commercial Code is referring to collision cases[1] and here we have to distinguish the situation when the collision is not with another vessel.

The Third Section of the Commercial Code[2] only refers to collisions between vessels and this was confirmed by the Spanish Supreme Court in a decision of December 6, 1929.

What, then, will happen when the collision is with installations ashore or other things which are not vessels? As Article 837 of the

* Estudio Juridico—Mercantil, Madrid.
[1] *Abordaje.*
[2] Arts. 826–839.

249

Commercial Code is not applicable, the liability of the shipowners falls within the scope of Article 902 of the Spanish Civil Code stating that: "The one that as a consequence of action or omission causes damages to another by any type of fault or negligence, is bound to repair the damages." This means that there is no limitation of liability for shipowners when damages caused by a vessel are not as a consequence of collision with another vessel.

2. THE BRUSSELS CONVENTION, 1957

This Convention, after being ratified by Spain, was published in the Official Bulletin of the State on January 30, 1971.[3] According to the Spanish Civil Code, Article 1, the Laws will be compulsory 20 days after their publication in the Official Bulletin and, consequently, one could think that the 1957 Convention was in force in Spain after the above publication. Nevertheless, Spain presented some reservations at the time of ratification. One of them was the following: "Reservation of the right to give force to the present Convention, either by giving it the same force as a Law, or incorporating it to the domestic legislation in a way applicable to the said Legislation." After that, no force has been given to the Convention nor have the dispositions of Article 96 of the Spanish Constitution been accomplished.

Article 96 of the Spanish Constitution states that: "The International Conventions properly celebrated once they have been published officially in Spain, will be part of the domestic legislation and that their dispositions can only be derogated, modified or suspended in the way foreseen in the Conventions themselves or in accordance with the general rules of International Law."

Article 94 of the same Constitution requires the previous authorisation of Parliament when the Conventions represent the modification or derogation of a Law or require legislative measures for their enforcement.

Evidently, if the 1957 Convention was in force and it could be applied not only to situations involving international interests but also to cases occurring in Spain and involving only Spanish interests, then there would have been derogation from articles of the Commercial Code and even the Civil Code. This, in accordance with Article 94 of the Spanish Constitution, requires the previous approval of Parliament.

Paragraph 5 of Article 1 of the Preliminary Title of the Civil Code declares that the dispositions of International Conventions will not be directly applicable in Spain until they have passed to form part of the domestic legislation by their publication in the

[3] Number 26/1971.

Official Bulletin. The Convention was not fully published as the reservations were omitted. They were published independently later and, on these reservations depends the effect and enforceability of the Convention.

This peculiar situation was raised quite recently by the leading Spanish Maritime Lawyer, Mr. Luis Perez del Molino, who questioned and rejected the application of the 1957 Convention in Spain.

Mr. Justice Gomez Chaparro,[4] in his decision of July 16, 1984, was in agreement with these arguments of Mr. Perez del Molino. He clearly stated that the 1957 Convention was not developed by the legislative power introducing the modifications to make possible its application by judges and Courts. Also that the requirements of Article 5 of the Civil Code and Article 96 of the Spanish Constitution had not been accomplished and he consequently denied the application of the Convention in spite of the arguments of the defendants in favour of its limitation of liability.

The above decision is now under appeal in the Court of Appeal of Madrid. It will take about a year to have a decision, which also can be appealed to the Supreme Court. This means that, at the moment, the value in Spain of the 1957 Convention is doubtful.

3. 1976 LIMITATION CONVENTION

The Convention was signed by the Spanish Ambassador in London on October 12, 1977, after the Board of Ministers' agreement of September 23, 1977.

The Ministry of Foreign Affairs proposed the ratification of the Convention to the Board of Ministers on November 18, 1980. The proposal was accepted in the Ministerial meeting held on December 4, 1980 and sent to the President of the Congress on January 31, 1981.

The Congress, in accordance with Article 94(1) of the Constitution, authorised the deposit of the instrument of ratification, and this was effected in the Office of the General Secretary of the I.M.O., on November 13, 1981.

The Spanish Association of Maritime Law consulted the Commission of Justice of Congress about the situation of the Convention and they were informed that the Convention will not be published in the Spanish Bulletin of the State until the Convention is internationally in force. As already noted for any law, decree or convention to be enforced in Spain it has to be published in advance in the said Bulletin of the State. The Ministry of Foreign Affairs on December 15, 1980, recommended the adoption of the 1976 Convention, as the 1957 Convention, to

---

[4] First Instance Court of Madrid, Number 11.

which Spain is a party, would be in force with subsidiary character, in connection with those States not being party to the new Convention.

There is no doubt that the intention of the legislator was to give force to the 1957 Convention when it was published in the Spanish Bulletin of the State, but due to a procedural defect there was an opportunity to dispute its enforceability in Spain. The way to avoid that problem in the future is simply to ratify the Convention without reservations or, if there is any reservation, to publish it in the Bulletin at the same time as the Convention. As to the application of the 1976 Convention in Spain to domestic cases, it only will be possible if the Spanish Government when ratifying the Convention expressly mentions it, or if it is done by means of a decree, stating clearly that such Convention will apply to disputes between nationals.

XIX

The United Kingdom and the 1976 Convention

*Steven J. Hazelwood**

1. IMPLEMENTATION

The 1976 Convention requires the United Kingdom, as a signatory, to adopt perhaps the most radical changes to its limitation regime in over a century. Yet the implementing provisions of this revolutionary change are to be found tucked away in sections 17 to 19 and Schedules 4 and 5 of the 1979 Merchant Shipping Act.[1] A statute with an innocuous and largely indescriptive title, the Act of 1979 contains a rag-bag of quite significant amendments to the maritime law of the United Kingdom. According to its long title it is an Act to make amendments to the law relating to pilotage, carriage by sea, liability of shipowners and salvors and pollution from ships and other amendments of the law relating to shipping, pollution and seamen.

Section 17(1) provides that the 1976 Convention, as set out in Part I of Schedule 4, shall have the force of law in the United Kingdom. Section 18(1) repeals section 502 of the Merchant Shipping Act 1894 and provides the owners of British ships with the same privilege of excluding liability for loss or damage by fire and loss or damage to undeclared valuables and by subsection (2) this privilege is extended to the Master and members of the crew.

Part I of Schedule 4 sets out the relevant text of the 1976 Convention and Part II contains supplementary provisions dealing with interpretation and implementation of the Convention in the United Kingdom. Schedule 5 contains the amendments to other relevant statutes consequential on the entering into force of the 1976 Convention.

As to the scope of the Convention, the Convention itself provides that it does not apply to air-cushioned vehicles nor to floating exploration platforms[2] but States are given various

---

* Centre for Marine Law and Policy, UWIST, Cardiff.
[1] 1979, c. 39.
[2] Art. 15(5).

options as to the precise scope of its operation. Following the pattern of the 1957 Convention, States are not mandatorily required to apply the new regime to either ships which are intended for navigation on inland waterways[3] or to ships below 300 g.r.t.[4] Also States may now exclude ships specially constructed for drilling.[5] According to Article 6 paragraph 3 States are entitled to give priority over other property claims to claims in respect of damage to harbour works and port installations.[6]

With regard to these options the United Kingdom has, consistent with existing arrangements, opted for the following provisions:

(i) continuing with present limitation provisions, the Convention regime will be applicable to vessels used on inland waterways as it is to seagoing vessels.[7]

(ii) the limit of liability for ships under 300 tons shall be half of that applicable to ships of 500 tons.[8]

(iii) the United Kingdom has not taken the option of promoting the claims of port installations and harbour authorities above others.

(iv) the new regime will not under United Kingdom law be applied to drilling vessels.

According to Article 10(1) of the Convention, States may provide that the benefits of limitation may only be obtained by a defendant who has previously constituted a limitation fund with the court in which legal proceedings against him have been commenced. The 1979 Act in Schedule 4 Article 10(1) provides simply that limitation of liability may be invoked notwithstanding that a limitation fund has not been so constituted.

One of the heads of claim subject to limitation under the Convention and contained in Schedule 4 of the 1979 Act includes claims in respect of raising, removal, destruction or the rendering harmless of a ship which is sunk, wrecked, stranded or abandoned, including anything that is or has been on board such ship.[9] The United Kingdom has made a reservation in respect of these wreck removal provisions and so liability continues to be unlimited in such cases.[10] It should be noted, however, that the position would be altered if and when a fund is established under Schedule 4 Part II in order to compensate harbour authorities for any loss of

[3] Art. 15(2)(a).
[4] Art. 15(2)(b).
[5] Art. 15(4).
[6] Art. 6(3).
[7] Sched. 4, Part II, para. 2.
[8] Sched. 4, Part II, para. 5.
[9] Sched. 4, Part I, Art. 2(1)(d).
[10] See, *The Millie* [1940] P. 1; *The Berwyn* [1977] 2 Lloyd's Rep. 99.

revenue.[11] Except for this provision relating to wreck removal, no other reservations were made by the United Kingdom.

2. ENTRY INTO FORCE

The 1976 Convention will enter into force one year after the end of the month in which the twelfth ratification has been made[12] and the United Kingdom will denounce the 1957 Brussels Convention and commence the 1979 Act to take effect on the same day as the new Convention enters into force internationally.

When the new regime commences, in order to give full effect to its provision in this country, the following Orders in Council will be required:

(i) an Order prescribing the rate of interest to be applied for the purposes of Article 11(1).[13] This provides that the limitation fund shall be constituted in the same of such of the amounts as provided for in Articles 6 and 7 as are applicable to claims for which the person may be liable together with interest thereon from the date of the occurrence giving rise to the liability until the date of the constitution of the fund.

(ii) a tonnage order. According to Schedule 4 Part II paragraph 5(2) a ship's tonnage shall be its gross tonnage calculated in such a manner as may be prescribed by an order made by the Secretary of State and by sub-paragraph (3) any order under this paragraph shall, so far as appears to the Secretary of State to be practicable, give effect to the regulations in Annex I of the International Convention on Tonnage Measurements of Ships 1976.[14]

(iii) a hovercraft order under Schedule 5, paragraph 4.

(iv) Schedule 4 Part I paragraph 13 provides that an Order in Council may be made declaring that any State specified in the Order is a party to the Convention and this would be conclusive evidence that the State is a party to the Convention.

As can be seen from the foregoing, the 1976 Convention is not self-sustaining and national legislative provisions are also required to cover a number of procedural aspects in implementing its provisions. Particular provisions made by the United Kingdom which have effect in connection with the Convention are contained in Part II of Schedule 4.

By Article 8 of the Convention a mechanism is required for the conversion from SDR's into the appropriate national currency and the United Kingdom has provided for this in paragraph 7(1) of Part II of Schedule 4. Under Article 7 of Part I of Schedule 4, in respect of claims arising for loss of life or personal injury to

[11] Sched. 4, Part II, para. 3(1).
[12] Art. 17.
[13] See, Sched. 4, Part II, para. 8(1).
[14] See further, Merchant Shipping Act 1983, (1983, c. 13).

passengers of a ship, the limit of liability of the shipowner is stated to be up to 25 million units of account, in the amount of 46,666 units of account multiplied by the number of passengers which the ship is authorised to carry according to the ship's certificate and in paragraph 6(1) of Part II of Schedule 4 it is provided that in the case of a passenger steamer within the meaning of Part III of the Merchant Shipping Act 1894 the "ship's certificate" shall be the passenger steamer's certificate issued under section 274 of the 1894 Act.[15]

Paragraph 11 of Part II of Schedule 4 provides that references in the Convention and the Schedule to a "court" means, in relation to England and Wales, the High Court, in relation to Scotland, the Court of Session and in relation to Northern Ireland, the High Court of Justice in Northern Ireland. Paragraph 12 states that references to a "ship" includes any structure (whether completed or in course of completion), launched and intended for use in navigation as a ship or part of a ship.[16]

3. REPEALS AND AMENDMENTS OF EXISTING LEGISLATION

In Schedule 5 of the 1979 Act can be found a set of consequential amendments. One of the amendments relates to the Merchant Shipping (Liability of Shipowners and Others) Act 1900 which, inter alia, allows the owners of docks, canals or a harbour or conservancy authority to limit liability. This is amended in section 2(1) so as to substitute the new break-clause and also by introducing the new method of calculating the limit of liability as well as applying the new provisions as to the constitution and distribution of the limitation fund to the 1900 Act. Schedule 5 also makes amendments in relation to Pilotage Authorities, The Crown Proceedings Act 1947, The Hovercraft Act 1968, The Carriage of Goods by Sea Act 1971 and the Merchant Shipping (Oil Pollution) Act 1971.

Schedule 7 of the Act contains the usual list of enactments which are repealed by the 1979 Act. The major casualty is that the whole of Part VIII of the 1894 Merchant Shipping Act, which contains the old familiar sections 502 and 503, is repealed. In the Merchant Shipping (Liability of Shipowners and Others) Act 1900, s.2(2), relating to tonnage measurements and s.2(3), relating to the definition of "owner" under the 1894 Act, are repealed. Other repeals include the whole of the Merchant Shipping (Liability of Shipowners and Others) Act 1958 except section 11 so far as applying to the 1900 Act.

---

[15] Sched. 4, Part II, para. 6(1).
[16] Cf. s.4(1) Merchant Shipping (Liability of Shipowners and Others) Act 1958.

4. THE REACTION OF THE UNITED KINGDOM

The major insurers of shipowners' liability claims are the Protection and Indemnity associations and a little over 92 per cent of the world's gross registered tonnage is entered in the clubs of the International Group of P. and I. Associations. Although the United Kingdom is now the home of very few shipowners it is the traditional home of the major P. and I. clubs and it may not be surprising, therefore, that this country was the second State to ratify the 1976 "London" Convention which is generally favourable to shipowners and their clubs.

It may be noted that the P. and I. clubs owe a certain amount to past limitation provisions for their very origin. In 1854 the Merchant Shipping Act[17] provided that the same limitations as had previously applied to cargo liabilities and collision liabilities would extend to responsibility in respect of any loss of life and personal injury claims. Liability was limited to a sum equal to the value of the vessel and freight but that the value of the ship was to be regarded as not less than £15 per registered ton, as the calculated average sound value per ton of British passenger ships in 1854. In fact, many vessels at this time were worth considerably less than this £15 limit and shipowners found themselves still paying more than their vessels were worth. One of the reasons for developing the P. and I. clubs was to protect shipowners against this eventuality of extra risks.

Whatever historical justifications[18] may have existed for introducing and persisting with the privilege of limitation of liability, the most plausible defence for its continued existence is that the concept is based not on justice but on convenience.[19] The convenience of the concept lies in the fact that limitation ensures the commercial insurability of claims against shipowners and certainly the 1976 Convention was devised very much with insurability in mind.

P. and I. clubs have grown up and their cover, underwriting, reinsurance arrangements and other practices have been developed against a background of limitation of liability and without such a facility the clubs would have to increase their premiums to possibly prohibitively high levels, radically alter the way in which they operate or even cease trading altogether. The raising of the global limitation figure[20] was traded off by the more strictly worded and almost unbreakable break-clause[21] in order to

---

[17] 17 & 18 Vict.c. 104.
[18] As to the history of limitation of liability in this country, see, *The Eurysthenes* [1976] 2 Lloyd's Rep. 171, 178, per Lord Denning, M.R.
[19] *The Bramley Moore* [1964] P. 200.
[20] Art. 6.
[21] Art. 4.

guarantee the insurability of shipowners' liability risks. The Chairman of the C.M.I. International Sub-Committee stated that "the limits that ultimately emerged—a decreasing amount per gross ton with increasing tonnage—were lower than the principle of insurability should have dictated."[22]

An oft repeated boast of the P. and I. clubs is that unlike traditional hull and cargo insurers the liability of the club is unlimited. In fact, numerous heads of cover are subject to some form of club limit, for example, liability in respect of pollution by oil or hazardous substances, charterers' liabilities and cover in respect of offshore exploration vessels. Many clubs can no longer indefinitely afford to give cover on a totally unlimited basis and some are adopting specific limits for specific risks under special contracts of entry and some clubs have recently been reviewing the efficacy of continuing to offer unlimited cover. Even in those cases where special contracts of entry are not agreed and members have "unlimited" cover then club rules always seek to ensure that the club will be liable only up to the owner's global limit of liability. Consistent with such practice the new Convention recognises the ability of insurers to take advantage of the shipowner's privilege of limitation of liability.[23]

The new limitation regime, although increasing the global limitation figure, may yet be more favourable to the shipowner and his club than the old regime. Where, under the old arrangements, a claim has arisen from the "actual fault or privity"[24] of the shipowner, both he and his P. and I. club would be deprived of the right to limit liability. Where the conduct of the shipowner has strayed beyond "actual fault or privity" into the more heinous activity of "wilful misconduct" the shipowner will fall within the club exception which relieves the club of the liability to indemnify its members in respect of liabilities arising from such

---

[22] See, Alex Rein, "International Variations on Concepts of Limitation of Liability," 53 *Tulane Law Review*, (1978–79), 1259, 1274. A study was undertaken by the Canadian government to assess the economic implications that would follow from the implementation of the new Convention, see: Canadian Transport Commission (Research Branch), The Convention on Limitation of Liability for Maritime Claims, 1976, Doc. 20–79–07, (1979), 138 as to commercial insurability, see pp. 35–49. See also, I.M.O. Legal Committee, 25th Session, Agenda item 2, I.M.C.O. document, LEG XXV/INF. 2, January 20, 1975.

[23] See, Merchant Shipping Act 1979, Sched. 4, Part I, Art. 1, para. 6 (as to the rights of an insurer of liability to limit his liability to the same extent as the assured); Art. 11(3) (as to the constitution of a limitation fund by an insurer); Art. 12(2) (as to settlement of claims by an insurer).

[24] Merchant Shipping Act 1894, ss. 502 and 503.

conduct. The position is, therefore, that P. and I. clubs are liable to indemnify their members in an unlimited amount only in respect of those few claims for which limitation is not available and also in respect of those rare instances where an otherwise "limitable" claim has arisen which is adjudged to have been caused by the actual fault or privity of a member but not as a result of his wilful misconduct.

Under the new regime,[25] although the global limitation figure has been raised, the P. and I. clubs should find that by virtue of the combination of the more heinous conduct required to break limitation[26] and the narrowing of the "unlimited-liability-gap," they will be required to indemnify far fewer cases of unlimited liability. The attitude of the clubs to the 1976 Convention may be gathered from a statement contained in a recent Directors' Report of one of the major clubs where it is stated[27]:

> "The Directors of the Association have expressed the desire that the Convention be brought into force and ratified by as many countries as possible. They acknowledge that the Convention is beneficial, not only to shipowners and those others who may limit their liability, but also to the Association itself, which needs to be able to have more confidence that claims against Members will be subject to limitation."

---

[25] See, Art. 4. For an account of the background to Art. 4, and the 1976 Convention in general, see Boal, "Effects to Achieve International Uniformity of Laws Relating to the Limitation of Shipowners' Liability," 53 Tulane Law Review, (1978–79) 1277, 1295. For similar wording see, The Athens Convention Relating to the Carriage of Passengers and Their Luggage by Sea (1974), Art. 13; United Nations Convention on the Carriage of Goods by Sea (The "Hamburg Rules") (1978), Art. 8; The Convention for the Unification of Certain Rules Relating to International Transportation by Air (The "Warsaw Convention") (1929), Art. 25 (as amended by the Hague Protocol, 1955); See also, *Goldman* v. *Thai Airways* [1983] 3 All E.R. 693 especially at p. 698–700 *per* Eveleigh, J.

[26] Art. 4.

[27] Directors' Report and Financial Statements of the United Kingdom Mutual Steam Ship Assurance Association (Bermuda) Limited, for the year ended February 20, 1983, p. 23.

XX

The U.S. and the 1976 Convention

*Alex L. Parks**

1. INTRODUCTION

It must be admitted, in all candour, that the United States has a
sorry history of failing to participate in international conventions.
The reasons are manifold, and not particularly relevant to this
discussion of the United States and the 1976 Convention, but
nonetheless must be kept in mind in order to understand the
apparent reluctance with which the United States has approached
adoption or ratification of the 1976 Convention.

Shipowners' limitation of liability in the United States had been
met, on more than one occasion, by ill-concealed judicial hostility.
As recently as 1970, one of the more active Circuit Courts of
Appeal in the United States noted that "in the vast majority of
cases limitation is denied for one reason or another."[1] In *Maryland
Casualty Co.* v. *Cushing*,[2] Mr. Justice Black suggested that if
Congress wishes to subsidise shipowners, the subsidy should be
done more directly than by limitation of liability at the expense of
injured seamen.

Notwithstanding such criticism, courts in the United States do
continue to grant limitation and from a statistical standpoint, it
may well be that limitation is becoming more popular than in prior
years. For example, during the period from 1973 to October
1976, limitation was granted in only 4 of 19 reported cases; from
November 1976 to December 1981, limitation was granted in 11
of 28 reported cases . . . an increase of from 21 per cent. to 39 per
cent.[3]

The difficulty is that the limitation of liability statutes in the
United States are an anachronism and until amended (as may be
devoutly hoped in light of currently pending legislation) litigants
and their attorneys must adjust and accommodate as best they can.

---

* Senior partner, Parks, Montague, Allen & Greif; Adjunct Professor, Willamette
  University.
[1] *Olympia Towing Corp.* v. *Nebel Towing Co.*, 419 F.2d 230 (1969); AMC 1571 (5th
  Cir. 1969), *cert. den.* 397 U.S. 989 (1970).
[2] 347 U.S. 409 (1954); AMC 837 (1954).
[3] D. Greenman, "Statistical Analysis of Limitation Cases, October 1953," December 1981, Mar. L. Ass'n of United States, Doc.No. 640 (1982).

The purpose of this chapter is to compare the existing United States law of shipowners' limitation with the 1976 Convention or adoption of national legislation to achieve the same result.[4]

2. BACKGROUND

The first codification of a law of shipowners' limitation of liability seems to have been the Marine Ordinance of 1681 during the reign of France's Louis XIV. It was not until 1734 that England enacted a statute relating to limitation of shipowners' liability.[5] The principal thrust of the English act was to limit the shipowner's liability by a calculation of the value of the vessel immediately *before* the casualty.

The first appearance of limitation in the United States was in state legislation of the states of Maine and Massachusetts. Both state acts were obviously influenced by the English act.[6]

National legislation with respect to limitation of liability was triggered in the United States by *New Jersey Steam Navigation Co.* v. *The Merchants' Bank of Boston (The Lexington).*[7] There, the steamship *Lexington* burned and sank. Aside from a heavy loss of life, a crate of commercial paper was also lost and it was the latter which precipitated the litigation. The Supreme Court refused to honor a contractual limitation of the shipowner's liability in the contract of affreightment. The Congress responded with the Limitation of Liability Act of 1851.

The 1851 Act has been called a composite: its framework was that of the English act; part of it was borrowed from the Maine and Massachusetts acts; the balance was a product of imaginative . . . some would disagree and call it unimaginative . . . draftsmanship. Although replete with ambiguities, necessitating the adoption by the Supreme Court of some equally imaginative rules, the Act did in a sense protect the American shipowner and created a rough parity with other maritime nations.[8]

The efficacy of the Act was first tested in *Norwich Co.* v. *Wright* in

---

[4] The author is deeply indebted to the numerous excellent papers, articles and reports on the subject which have recently appeared and have been of inestimable value. Among these are: D. Greenman, "Limitation of Liability: A Critical Analysis of United States Law in an International Setting," (1983) 57 Tul.L.R. pp. 1139–1207; C. Gunn, "Limitation of Liability: United States and Convention Jurisdictions," (1983) 8 Mar. Lawyer 29–68 (1983); Report of the Joint Committee of the Comite Maritime International and Limitation of Liability, Mar.L.Ass'n of United States, Doc.No. 619 (1979); Report of the Limitation of Liability Committee, Mar.L.Ass'n of the United States, Doc.-No. 653 (May, 1984); Report of the Committee on Limitation of Liability, Mar.L.Ass'n of the United States, Doc.No. 657 (November, 1984).

[5] 7 Geo. 2, c. 15 (1734).

[6] Interestingly, the Massachusetts Act was not repealed until 1902.

[7] 47 U.S. (6 How.) 344 (1848).

[8] *Norwich Co.* v. *Wright*, 80 U.S. (13 Wall.) 104, 121 (1871).

1871.[9] In that case, the steamer *City of Norwich* collided with the schooner *General S. Van Vliet* in Long Island Sound. Both vessels sank as a consequence of the collision with a loss of all cargo; however, the *City of Norwich* was later raised.

Important issues were resolved. The Supreme Court held that the value of the vessel seeking limitation was to be determined *after* the collision because the voyage on which the vessel was then engaged was automatically concluded when the vessel sank. Of equal importance was the holding that the insurance proceeds were not to be included in the limitation fund. It was quite apparent to the Supreme Court that the entire act was so poorly drafted and ambiguous that it was, for practical purposes, wholly unworkable. As a consequence, and without the slightest apparent authority, the Supreme court sought to fill in the interstices of the Act and render it workable by adopting, in 1872, its Admiralty Rules. Whether or not the Supreme Court really possessed the authority it arrogated to itself in adopting the Rules relating to limitation proceedings became a rather moot point because, as a practical matter, litigants and their counsel recognised the necessity for the Rules and chose to accede to them rather than contest the basic authority of the Supreme Court to adopt them. In any event, in 1966 the Federal Rules of Civil Procedure were amended and the former "Admiralty Rules" were "merged" so to speak, in the amendments. The rule relating to limitation proceedings is now found in Rule F, Supplemental Rules for Certain Admiralty and Maritime Claims.

The essential difference between the United States Act and the comparable acts of other major maritime nations lies in the computation of the amount to which liability can be limited. In the United States, if the loss is sustained without the privity or knowledge of the "owner," the liability of that owner does not exceed the amount or value of the interest of such owner in the vessel and her freight then pending. Except as to loss of life or bodily injury claims, the amount could be zero if the vessel is sunk or destroyed.

The exception as to loss of life or personal injury claims came about during the 1930's during which there were a series of maritime disasters. The most dramatic was that of the passenger vessel *Morro Castle* which burned in September, 1934. There was a loss of 135 lives and many personal injuries. In 1935 and 1936, Congress amended the Act by establishing a minimum limitation fund of $60 per registered gross ton to be applied to death and

[9] *Ibid.* n. 8.

personal injury claims.[10] However, the minimum fund applies only to "seagoing vessels" as defined in the Act.[11]

3. SYNOPSIS OF THE U.S. LIMITATION OF LIABILITY ACT

The Act generally is considered to be composed of nine statutory sections; *i.e.*, 46 U.S.C. 181 through 189.

46 U.S.C. s.181 provides essentially, that unless the shipper gives the carrier a written notice of the true character and value of certain commodities (such as precious metals, maps, writings, jewelry, etc.) and such information is entered on the bill of lading, the carrier is not liable whatsoever for any loss thereof. If entered on the bill of lading as specified, the carrier is only liable for the value and according to the character thereof so notified and entered. Little litigation has ensued under this section.

46 U.S.C. s.182 is the Fire Statute, discussed *infra*.

46 U.S.C. s.183 is the heart of the Act and necessarily must be quoted verbatim. It reads:

> "(a) The liability of the owner of any vessel, whether American or foreign, for any embezzlement, loss, or destruction by any person of any property, goods, or merchandise shipped or put on board of such vessel, or for any loss, damage, or injury by collision, or for any act, matter, or thing, loss, damage, or forfeiture, done, occasioned, or incurred, without the privity or knowledge of such owner or owners, shall not, except in the cases provided for in subsection (b) of this section, exceed the amount or value of the interest, of such owner in such vessel and her freight then pending.
>
> (b) In the case of any seagoing vessel, if the amount of the owner's liability as limited under subsection (a) of this section is insufficient to pay all losses in full, and the portion of such amount applicable to the payment losses in respect of loss of life or bodily injury is less than $60 per ton of such vessel's tonnage, such portion shall be increased to an amount equal to $60 per ton, to be available only for the payment of losses in respect of loss of life or bodily injury. If such portion so increased is insufficient to pay such losses in full, they shall be paid therefrom in proportion to their respective amounts.
>
> (c) For the purposes of this section the tonnage of a seagoing steam or motor vessel shall be her registered tonnage: Provided, that there shall not be included in such tonnage any space occupied by seamen or apprentices and appropriated to their use.
>
> (d) The owner of any such seagoing vessel shall be liable in

[10] 46 U.S.C. s.183(b).
[11] 46 U.S.C. s.183(f).

respect of loss of life or bodily injury arising on distinct occasions to the same extent as if no other loss of life or bodily injury had arisen.

(e) In respect of loss of life or bodily injury the privity or knowledge of the master of a seagoing vessel or of the superintendent or managing agent of the owner thereof, at or prior to the commencement of each voyage, shall be deemed conclusively the privity or knowledge of the owner of such vessel.

(f) As used in subsections (b), (c), (d), and (e) of this section and in section 183(b) of this title, the term "seagoing vessel" shall not include pleasure yachts, tugs, towboats, towing vessels, tank vessels, fishing vessels or their tenders, self-propelled lighters, nondescript self-propelled vessels, canal boats, scows, car floats, barges, lighters, or nondescript non-selfpropelled vessels, even though the same may be seagoing vessels within the meaning of such term as used in section 188 of this title."

46 U.S.C. s.183(b) relates to stipulations limiting the time for filing claims and commencing suit, making it unlawful for seagoing vessels to stipulate a shorter time than six months for giving notice of loss of life or bodily injury claims and a shorter time than one year for instituting suit on such claims.

46 U.S.C. s.183(c) forbids any vessel transporting passengers between ports of the United States or between any such port and a foreign port from contracting against liability for negligence.

46 U.S.C. s.184 seemingly relates to losses sustained by cargo owners and provides that if the whole value of the vessel and her freight for the voyage is not sufficient to make compensation to each cargo owner, the cargo owners receive compensation in proportion to their respective losses. It will be observed that this section refers only to cargo claims and not to other types of claims which are identified in 46 U.S.C. s.183(a). In *Butler* v. *Boston and Savannah S.S. Co.*,[12] the Supreme Court held, in effect, that the differences between the two sections were due to inadvertence and that the broader aspects of 46 U.S.C. s.183(a) should be read into 46 U.S.C. s.184. The last portion of 46 U.S.C. s.184 is rather ambiguous but appears to permit cargo owners (presumably all claimants) and the owner of the vessel to "take" appropriate proceedings for the purpose of apportioning the sum which may be divided among the parties.

46 U.S.C. s.185 permits a vessel owner, six months after a claimant shall have filed with the owner a written notice of claim, to petition a district court of the United States for limitation of liability and further requires that the owner either (a) deposit with

[12] 130 U.S. 527, 9 S.Ct. 612 (1889).

the court a sum equal to the value or amount of the interest of the owner of the vessel and freight, or approved security therefor,[13] or (b) at his option transfer to a trustee, to be appointed by the court, his interest in the vessel and freight. This section concludes, "upon compliance with the requirements of this section all claims and proceedings against the owner with respect to the matter in question shall cease."

Amendments made in 1936 to this section legitimised the procedure, long recognised by the Supreme court Admiralty Rules, that a bond could be posted in lieu of surrendering the vessel to a trustee. The last sentence, quoted above, has been the subject of much discussion and much litigation as it would appear to give to an Admiralty Court the authority to enjoin other lawsuits pending which might involve the subject matter of the limitation proceedings.

46 U.S.C. s.186 provides, in essence, that a bareboat charterer shall be deemed an "owner" within the meaning of the Act. This, of course, would exclude a time charterer or voyage charterer from petitioning for limitation.

46 U.S.C. s.187 preserves the remedies which any party might be entitled to, against the master, officers, or seamen on account of embezzlement, injury, loss, or destruction of merchandise, or property on board the vessel or on account of any negligence, fraud, or other malversation of such master, officers, or seamen, respectively. In a sense, the statute merely makes the agents of the vessel individually liable with respect to their own negligence or affirmative wrongs. This is true, whether or not an agent of the vessel may also be an owner or part owner of the vessel.

46 U.S.C. s.188, in essence, extends the provisions of the Act (with the exceptions of the loss of life amendments) to all seagoing vessels and all vessels used on lakes or rivers or in inland navigation, including canal boats, barges and lighters.[14] Thus, the Act effectively applies to all vessels whether on inland or international waters and regardless of their size. In the original version of the Act, it did not apply to any canal boat, barge, or lighter, or to any vessel of any description whatsoever, used in rivers or inland navigation. This exclusion was removed from the Act in 1886 by an appropriate amendment.

46 U.S.C. s.189 was not part of the original Act, having been

---

[13] Phrase "or approved security therefor" added in the 1936 amendment.
[14] The waters referred to must, of course, be "navigable" as that term is defined by the courts; *i.e.*, bodies of water, with or without tides, natural or artificial, navigable in fact, in interstate or foreign commerce. Landlocked bodies of water, located wholly within one state, and not communicating with rivers, channels or tributaries contiguous to interstate waters or the sea are not "navigable waters of the U.S." See *Johnson* v. *Wurthman*, 227 F.Supp. 135 (1964); AMC 1777 (D., Ore.).

adopted as a part of the Shipping Act of 1884, and its meaning is far from clear. It reads:

> "The individual liability of a shipowner shall be limited to the proportion of any or all debts and liabilities that his individual share of the vessel bears to the whole; and the aggregate liabilities of all the owners of a vessel on account of the same shall not exceed the value of such vessels and freight pending: *Provided,* That this provision shall not prevent any claimant from joining all the owners in one action; nor shall the same apply to wages due to persons employed by said shipowners."

In *Richardson* v. *Harmon,*[15] the Supreme Court attempted an explanation, stating:

> "Thus construed, this section harmonises with the policy of limiting the owner's risk to his interest in the ship in respect of all claims arising out of the conduct of the master and crew, whether the liability be strictly maritime or from a tort non-maritime, but leaves him liable for his own fault, neglect and contracts."

It will be observed that the last phrase of section 189 expressly provides that the section does not apply to wages due to persons employed by shipowners. Moreover, the language contained within the section relative to the words "individual share" indicates that the Act was intended to apply to joint ownership as well as sole ownership.

4. JUDICIAL CONSTRUCTION OF THE ACT

Persons entitled to limit

As noted above, limitation is available in the United States, generally speaking, only to an owner or demise charterer.[16] Ordinary time charterers are precluded from limiting.[17] Private owners of pleasure are entitled to limit even though contemporary

---

[15] 222 U.S. 96, 32 S.Ct. 27 (1911).

[16] *Admiral Towing Co.* v. *Woolen,* 290 F.2d 641 (1961); AMC 2333 (9 Cir., 1961); *Lanasse* v. *Travelers, Inc.,* [1972] AMC 818 (5 Cir.); *Flint* v. *Paladini,* 279 U.S. 59 (1929).

[17] *In Re Barracuda Tanker Corp.,* 409 F.2d 1013 (1969); AMC 1442 (2 Cir, 1969). Compare, however, *Petition of U.S. and Mathiasen's Tanker Industries, Inc.,* 259 F.2d 608, [1959] AMC 982 (3 Cir.), where a contractor managing a vessel owned by the United States was held entitled to claim limitation, although strictly speaking the contractor was neither an owner nor a demise charterer. See, also, *Calkins* v. *Graham,* 667 F.2d 1292 (1982); AMC 2433 (9 Cir.)(controlling shareholder of unpaid seller of a vessel not qualified either as owner or demise charterer to limit as the vessel was being manned, supplied, and victualled by the buyer).

thought finds little reason for allowing private owners to take advantage of the Act.[18] The demise charter need not be in writing nor even be identified as a "charter" so long as the agreement is express and embodies terms legally sufficient to establish the parties' relationship to the vessel.[19]

All vessel owners, whether foreign or domestic, who file petitions for limitation in United States courts, are entitled to limit.[20] Insurance companies, sued under a direct action statute, may not claim the benefit of the Limitation Act.[21]

What constitutes a "Ship" or "Vessel"

Under United States law, a vessel is broadly defined. 1 U.S.C. s.3 states[22]:

> "The word "vessel' includes every description of watercraft or other artificial contrivance used, or capable of being used as a means of transportation on water."

It should be noted, however, that s.183(f) of the Act expressly excludes from the definition of "seagoing vessel"—as respects the $60 per ton requirement as to loss of life or personal injury—such craft as pleasure yachts, tugs, towboats, towing vessels, tank vessels, barges, lighters, etc. even though the same might be considered as "seagoing vessels" within the meaning of such term as used in s.188 of the Act.

Surrender of entire flotilla in tug and tow situation

Under United States law, where the injury against which limitation is sought is to a third party, to whom the shipowner may

[18] *Gibboney* v. *Wright*, 517 F.2d 1054 (1975); AMC 2071 (5 Cir.); *Complaint of Rowley*, 425 F.Supp. 116 (1977); AMC 199 (D., Idaho); *Brown, Lim.Procs.*, 536 F.Supp. 750 (1983); AMC 1816 (N.D., Ohio)(owner of pleasure boat involved in a collision with a similar boat on a lake held entitled to limit; there is no requirement that the petitioner's vessel be engaged in "commercial activity"). And, see, *Foremost Ins.* v. *Richardson*, 102 S.Ct. 2654 (1982); AMC 2253 (1982), where the Supreme Court held that a collision between two pleasure boats came within admiralty jurisdiction in the United States.
[19] *Harbor Star*, 433 F.Supp. 854 (1977); AMC 1168 (D., Md.).
[20] *The Titanic*, 233 U.S. 718 (1914); *The Scotland*, 105 U.S. 24 (1882). The bare statement of the principle, however, does not address the convoluted problems which can arise under conflicts of laws concepts as to which law is to be applied. Compare, for example, *Black Diamond S.S. Corp.* v. *Robert Stewart & Sons, Ltd.*, 336 U.S. 386, 1949 AMC 393 (1949) with *In Re Chadade S.S. Co. (The Yarmouth Castle)*, 266 F.Supp. 517, 1967 AMC 1843 (S.D., Fla., 1967) and *In re Bethlehem Steel Corp.*, 631 F.2d 441 (1980); AMC 2122 (6 Cir., 1980).
[21] *Maryland Casualty* v. *Cushing*, 347 U.S. 409 (1954); AMC 837 (1954); *Olympic Towing Corp.* v. *Nebel Towing Co.*, 419 F.2d 230, [1969] AMC 1571 (5 Cir.).
[22] See, also, such decision as: *Texas Tower No. 4—Petition of U.S.*, 203 F.Supp. 215 (1962); AMC 1684 (S.D.N.Y.); *Offshore Company* v. *Robison*, 266 F.2d 769 (1959); AMC 2049; *Grimes* v. *Raymond Concrete Pile Company*, 356 U.S. 252 (1958).

owe no duty based upon contract or tort, the shipowner may limit his liability to the vessel against which a maritime lien would arise from the wrong.[23] Thus, the owner of a tug towing a barge belonging to a third party may claim limitation as to the tug when it was the "wrongdoer." The rule is different, of course, where the tug and barge are in common ownership and the vessel owner owes a duty, either in contract or tort, to the injured party.[24]

Privity or knowledge—actual fault or privity

In the United States, limitation will not be granted if the casualty can be attributed to the owner's privity or knowledge.[25] The phrase used in the Fire Statute (s.182) is owner's "design or neglect." Originally, it seems to have been thought that the two phrases were somehow different in degree but the more recent cases treat the terms as being essentially synonymous.[26]

Where corporate ownership is involved, privity or knowledge of the company's managerial and supervisory officers is attributed to their employing corporation. But the problem becomes acute in determining how high in the company hierarchy they must be in order to be denominated a "managerial" or "supervisory" employee.[27]

Burden of proof

In the United States, the burden of proof in limitation cases is upon the claimant to show negligence or fault while the burden is upon the petition for limitation to prove absence or lack of privity or knowledge. The importance of the burden of proof in such

[23] *Liverpool, Brazil and River Plate Steam Navigation Co.* v. *Brooklyn Eastern District Terminal*, 251 U.S. 48 (1919).
[24] See, *Standard Dredging Co.* v. *Kristensen*, 67 F.2d 548 (1933); AMC 1621 (2 Cir.); *Brown and Root Marine Operators, Inc.* v. *Zapata Off-Shore Company*, 377 F.2d 724 (1967); AMC 2684 (5 Cir.); *Allied Towing Lim.Procs.*, [1978] AMC 2484 (E.D., Va.).
[25] *Coryell* v. *Phipps*, 317 U.S. 406 (1943); AMC 18 (1943).
[26] *Complaint of Caldas*, 350 F.Supp. 566 (1973); AMC 1243 (E.D., Pa.); *Agrico* v. *Atlantic Forest*, 459 F.Supp. 638 (1979); AMC 801 (E.D., La.); *Cerro Sales* v. *Atlantic Marine*, 403 F.Supp. 562 (1976); AMC 375 (S.D.N.Y.).
[27] See such decisions as *The Buffalo Bridge Cases*, 338 F.2d 708 (1964); AMC 2503 (2 Cir.); *Greater New Orleans Expressway* v. *The Tug Claribell*, 222 F.Supp. 521 (1964); AMC 967 (E.D., La.); *Spencer Kellogg & Sons, Inc.* v. *Hicks (The Linseed King)*, 285 U.S. 502 (1932); AMC 503 (1932); *Marine Floridian Lim. Procs.*, [1980] AMC 983 (E.D., Va.) (limitation denied where shipowner failed to enforce company directives as to steering gear and periodic inspections); *Cargill* v. *Taylor Tow*, 483 F.Supp. 1094 (1980); AMC 2796 (E.D., Mo.) (tug owner denied limitation where it knew that only one of the tug's two engines was in working order); *Continental Oil* v. *Bonanza*, 706 F.2d 1365 (1983); AMC 2059 (5 Cir.) (oil supply boat's master held to be a managing agent whose privity and knowledge was imputed to the owning corporation). Compare the foregoing with *The Marion* [1983] 2 Lloyd's Rep. 52; [1984] 2 Lloyd's Rep. 1.

cases is underscored by such decisions as *Waterman S.S. Corp.* v. *Gay Cottons (The Chickasaw)*,[28] *The Marine Sulphur Queen*,[29] *Northern Trading & Fishing Co.* v. *Grabowki*,[30] and *Flota Mer. Gr. Lim. Procs.*[31]

The question in cases under the Fire Statute involving cargo loss or damage has become confused by conflicting decisions from the various circuits.[32]

"Personal contract" doctrine

Stated simply, in United States law one cannot limit against a liability growing out of his "personal obligation." Unfortunately, no one really knows what a "personal contract" really is. Certainly, charterparties are personal contracts.[33] Contracts of affreightment which include implied warranties of seaworthiness are personal contracts.[34]

In defining what contracts are personal, there appear to be two lines of authority (1) the contract was "personal" when made[35]; and (2) the nature of the owner's relationship to the breach of contract.[36]

Wreck removal and the anti-pollution statutes

The Wreck Statute (33 U.S.C. ss.408–415) imposes upon an owner a personal, non-delegable duty to mark the wreck. Liability arising from a failure to mark is therefore not subject to limitation.[37] Recovery for removal costs under the Rivers and Harbors Act cannot be limited against where the vessel is negligently sunk.[38] An owner's knowledge of the sinking of his vessel precludes limitation because it is within the owner's

---

[28] 414 F.2d 724 (1969); AMC 1682 (9 Cir.).

[29] 460 F.2d 89 (1972); AMC 1122 (2 Cir.).

[30] 477 F.2d 1267 (1973); AMC 1283 (9 Cir.).

[31] 440 F.Supp. 704 (1979); AMC 156 (S.D.N.Y.).

[32] Compare *Matter of Ta Chi Navigation (Panama) Corp. (The Euryplus)*, 677 F.2d 225 (1982); AMC 1710 (2 Cir., 1982) with *Sunkist Growers, Inc.* v. *Adelaide Shipping Lines, Ltd. (The Gladiola)*, 603 F.2d 1327 (1979); AMC 2782 (9 Cir., 1979), *cert. den.* 444 U.S. 1012 (1980).

[33] *Pendleton* v. *Bonner Line*, 246 U.S. 353 (1918).

[34] *Luckenbach* v. *McCahan Sugar Ref. Co.*, 248 U.S. 353 (1918).

[35] *Ibid.*, n. 33 and 34. See, also, *The Nat Sutton*, 62 F.2d 787, 1933 AMC 338 (2 Cir.); *The Temple Bar*, 45 F.Supp. 608 (1942); AMC 1125 (D., Md.).

[36] *Soerstad*, 257 F. 130 (S.D.N.Y., 1919); *The No. 34*, 25 F.2d 602 (1928); AMC 780 (2 Cir.).

[37] *The Snug Harbor*, 53 F.2d 407, *aff'd* 59 F.2d 984 (1932); AMC 964 (2 Cir.).

[38] *Wyandotte Transportation Co.* v. *U.S.*, 389 U.S. 191, [1967] AMC 2553.

knowledge and privity.[39] Nor does the Limitation Act apply to claims for damage to governmental works.[40]

Towage contracts—"personal" in nature?

In 1932, the Supreme Court in *Stevens* v. *The White City*[41] squarely held a towing situation is not a bailment and that negligence of the tower must be proved. Unfortunately, some recent decisions have apparently ignored or overlooked the *Stevens* decision and have held towing companies liable under the doctrine of breach of warranty of workmanlike service.[42] The warranty, although implied and not express, could be construed to be a "personal contract" against which the right to limit would be precluded. If, as was held in *The Cullen No. 32*,[43] an implied warranty of seaworthiness is a "personal contract," it is difficult to see why an implied warranty of workmanlike service in a towage contract would not equally be a "personal contract." It is to be hoped that this dichotomy will in due course be resolved.

Claims subject to limitation

The right to limit has been held available, *inter alia*, in the following classes of claims: death or personal injury of crewmen,[44] cargo losses,[45] salvage,[46] state anti-pollution statutes,[47] collision losses,[48] passengers' claims whether for loss of property or for personal injuries,[49] and non-maritime torts.[50] With respect to fire losses, see discussion, *supra*.

Cargo losses

A distinction must be drawn between liability of a common carrier for cargo losses incurred by reason of a failure to exercise

---

[39] *In re Chinese Maritime Trust, Ltd. (The Sian Yung)*, 478 F.2d 1357 (1973); AMC 1110.

[40] *U.S.* v. *Ohio Valley Co.*, 510 F.2d 1184 (1974); AMC 1477 (7 Cir.); *Hines* v. *U.S.*, 551 F.2d 717 (1977); AMC 380 (6 Cir.); *U.S.* v. *Federal Barge Lines*, 573 F.2d 993 (1978); AMC 2308 (8 Cir.).

[41] 285 U.S. 195 (1932); AMC 468 (1932).

[42] *Fairmont Shipping Corp.* v. *Chevron Int'l*, 551 F.2d 1252 (2 Cir.), *cert. den.* 423 U.S. 838 (1975); *Singer* v. *Dorr Towing Co.*, 272 F.Supp. 931 (1968); AMC 146 (E.D., La.); *Dunbar, Admx.* v. *H. Dubois Sons Co. and Bronx Towing Line, Inc.*, 275 F.2d 304 (1960); AMC 1393 (2 Cir.).

[43] 290 U.S. 82 (1933); AMC 1584 (1933).

[44] *Petition of East River Towing Co.*, 266 U.S. 355 (1925).

[45] *Earle & Stoddart* v. *Ellerman's Wilson Lines*, 287 U.S. 420 (1933); AMC 1 (1932).

[46] *The San Pedro*, 233 U.S. 365 (1912).

[47] See fns. 37–40, *supra*.

[48] *Norwich* v. *Wright*, 80 U.S. 104 (1872).

[49] *Butler* v. *Boston & Savannah S.S. Co.*, 130 U.S. 527.

[50] *The Atlas No. 7*, 42 F.2d 480 (1930); AMC 1029 (S.D.N.Y.); *The Brinton*, 48 F.2d 559 (1931); AMC 852 (2 Cir.).

due diligence to make the vessel seaworthy in all respects . . . a duty which is non-delegable . . . and the right of a shipowner to limit his liability for unseaworthiness. If the unseaworthy condition involves conditions which the owner ought to have corrected before the vessel departed, then limitation is denied. If, on the other hand, the unseaworthiness occurs during the course of a voyage due to the negligence of the master or crew in the navigation or management of the vessel, then limitation is granted.[51]

The limitation fund

Except as to claims for loss of life or personal injury, the limitation fund under United States law is comprised of the value of the vessel *after* the casualty, plus pending freight.[52]

What constitutes the value of the vessel

The custom under United States law is to include all that belongs to the vessel and which might be presumed to be the property of the owner, not merely the hull together with the boats, tackle, apparel and furniture, but all the appurtenances comprising whatever is on board for the object of the voyage, whatever that object might be. For example, oil tanks and reefer equipment temporarily installed by a charterer,[53] deck and engine stores and fuel oil on board,[54] portable and removable refrigerated cargo containers,[55] collision damage claim of the vessel owner,[56] and spare parts on board the vessel.[57]

Voyage rule

What is a voyage is a troublesome question. If the voyage is interrupted for repairs and the vessel afterwards resumes her onward course, without the owner notifying cargo that the voyage was abandoned, there is a single interrupted voyage and the value of the repairs are included in the fund.[58]

---

[51] Compare, *Comp. Nav. Epsilon, Lim. Procs.*, [1974] AMC 2608 (S.D.N.Y.) (limitation granted where stranding occurred due to negligence of the master) with *Irish Shipping Lim. Procs.*, [1975] AMC 2559 (S.D.N.Y.) (limitation denied for failure of the owner to obtain and airmail to the vessel the most recent radio beacon list).

[52] See, 2. "Background," *supra*.

[53] *The Paraiso*, 226 F. 966 (W.D., Wash., 1915).

[54] *Walter A. Luckenbach*, 14 F.2d 100 (1925); AMC 545, 1631 (9 Cir.).

[55] *In re Pacific Far East Line, Inc.*, 314 F.Supp. 1339 (1970); AMC 1592 (N.D., Cal.).

[56] *O'Brien* v. *Miller*, 168 U.S. 287 (1897).

[57] *The Black Eagle*, 87 F.2d 891 (1937); AMC 198 (2 Cir.).

[58] Compare, *The Frej*, 176 F.2d 401 (1949); AMC 1761 (2 Cir.) with *Pacific Bulk Carriers, Lim. Procs.*, [1975] AMC 1145 (S.D.N.Y.). In the former, because there was notification of abandonment repairs were not included; in the latter where there was no notice of abandonment, the value of the repairs was included.

Freight pending

Norwich v. *Wright, supra* clearly established that only freight money earned on the voyage is to be considered pending. If the voyage is terminated short of destination and freight is not prepaid, there is no freight pending. For example, in *La Bourgogne*,[59] it was held that where the casualty occurred on the latter half of a round trip voyage, only the freight on the latter portion of the voyage would be considered as pending.[60]

Multiple claims in the U.S.

Where there are multiple claims, and those claims exceed the limitation fund, the claims are consolidated into a single proceeding called a "concursus." There, the claimants file their claims, prove those claims in the limitation proceeding, the court makes the necessary adjustments and adjudications, and then distributes the fund *pro rata*.

Where there is only one claimant, the situation can become radically confused.[61] The procedure essentially is that the claimant brings an action against the shipowner in a state court. The shipowner then petitions for limitation of liability. The Federal court may then, in its discretion, dispose of the case, or, in the alternative, decline to exercise jurisdiction. Properly speaking, the Federal court should retain jurisdiction. If, in the state court action, the claimant challenges the right of the shipowner to limit, the Federal court may restrain the state court action. If, in the state court action, the claimant does not challenge the right to limit, the state court action may proceed. Any recovery in state court by the claimant would be subject to the limitation amount; *i.e.*, notwithstanding the amount of the state court judgment, the claimant cannot recover more than the limitation amount.

Practice and procedure

The petition for limitation must be filed within six months after date of receipt of written notice of a claim. The courts have adopted a most liberal attitude towards what is "written" notice. Almost any written communication, including letters, telegrams or memoranda can constitute "written notice." Preliminary communications, after a casualty, can be easily forgotten. Probably the only safe way to proceed is to file a petition to limit within six

---

[59] 210 U.S. 95 (1908).

[60] For additional cases involving freight, see the dissent in *Cross Contracting Co.* v. *Law*, 454 F.2d 408 (1972); AMC 1008 (5 Cir.), and *The Motomar*, 108 F.2d 755 (1940); AMC 476 (2 Cir.).

[61] *Langnes* v. *Green*, 282 U.S. 531 (1931); AMC 511 (1931); *Ex Parte Green*, 286 U.S. 437 (1932); AMC 802 (1932) (companion cases). See, also, *Petition of Red Star Barge Line, Inc.*, 160 F.2d 436 (1947); AMC 524 (2 Cir.).

months of the date of the casualty. This, however, has the disadvantage of alerting possible claimants that limitation will be claimed, and may serve as an actual invitation to present claims.

Petitions to limit by foreign shipowners

The filing by a foreign tugowner of a limitation proceeding in an United States court was held not to preclude it from relying on a provision in a towage contract requiring the owner of the tow to litigate all disputes in London courts, *M/S Bremen* v. *Zapata Offshore Co.*[62] In that case, involving a contract to tow an ocean-going drilling rig from Louisiana to a point off the coast of Italy, the drilling rig suffered damage while under tow in the Gulf of Mexico. Ignoring the "forum" clause in the towage contract the owner of the rig sued the towing company in a U.S. district court in Florida, asserting that the damage was due to negligent towage. The towing company moved to dismiss the action both on the ground of the forum clause and on the theory of *forum non conveniens*. In the alternative, it asked that the action be stayed pending submission of the dispute to the London courts. Before the court could rule, the towing company sued the drilling rig owner in the High Court in London. The drilling rig owner attacked the jurisdiction of the High Court but that court maintained its jurisdiction and upheld the validity of the forum selection clause. Meanwhile, the towing company (obviously as a defensive measure) filed a complaint in the United States district court in Florida seeking to limit its liability and reserving its rights under the forum selection clause. The drilling rig owner thereupon refiled its original claim in the limitation proceeding.

The trial court ruled, *inter alia*, that by filing its limitation proceeding, the towing company was obliged to do equity and refrain from pursuing its suit in London. The court of appeal upheld the trial court. The Supreme Court reversed, holding that the fact that the English courts would uphold the exculpatory language in the towage contract did not make enforcement of the forum selection clause invalid as against public policy. Moreover, the court also found no merit to the contention that the filing of a complaint in limitation by the towing company precluded it from insisting upon the forum selection clause.

A word of caution is in order. In the United States, an Admiralty Court has the power to permit parties to a limitation proceeding to crossclaim against each other for damages arising out of the same maritime casualty. Moreover, the court may retain jurisdiction to resolve the crossclaims even though the initial petitioner was granted exoneration or limitation.

---

[62] 407 U.S. 1 (1972); AMC 1407 (1972).

In *British Transport Commission* v. *United States*,[63] a Commission vessel collided with a U.S. transport in the North Sea. The United States petitioned for limitation and the Commission filed in the limitation action as a claimant. Other claimants also filed and sought to recover against the Commission and the U.S. At trial, the United States transport was exonerated and the Commission's vessel found solely at fault. On appeal, the Supreme Court held that an adjudication should have been made as to the crossclaims before the court. It will be seen that the ruling "trapped" an unsuspecting Commission. Had the Commission not entered the case and pursued its remedies in England, it would have had the benefit of the English limitation of liability and rather more favorable treatment with respect to its passenger contracts. Consequently, a foreign claimant must be prepared to run the risk of having to respond to the total loss if he files in a United States limitation action.

Direct action statutes

Historically, the relationship between assured and assurer under a liability policy has always been one of indemnification. Usually, the insurance contract requires the insurer to reimburse the insured after, but only after, the insured has paid the successful plaintiff. If, for any reason, the plaintiff could not recover against the insured, he had no better rights against the insurer; *e.g.*, if the insured became insolvent, the plaintiff could not avail himself of the insured's policy proceeds.

Unfortunately from the standpoint of P & I clubs, a direct action statute may change all the rules. For example, in *Olympic Towing Corp.* v. *Nebel Towing Co.*,[64] (following *Maryland Casualty Co.* v. *Cushing*, 347 U.S. 409 (1954)), the Fifth Circuit held that limitation of liability under the Federal statute is a personal defense available only to the shipowner, and not an insurer under the Louisiana Direct Action Statute. The court also held that the direct action statute becomes a part of every insurance policy, including P & I policies, having effect in Louisiana. That statute, by its terms, voids any policy clause requiring the injured person to obtain a judgment against the insured as a prerequisite to enforcing the contract obligation of the insurer. As the Fifth Circuit viewed it, any conflict between the direct action statute and the Federal limitation of liability statutes was so "minimal as to be insignificant."

The foregoing discussion of the judicial decisions construing the United States Limitation of Liability Act is intended to give only a broad overview of the status of the Act and its general interpreta-

[63] [1957] 2 Lloyd's Rep. 281.
[64] [1970] 1 Lloyd's Rep. 430.

tion as of this date. The purpose of the overview is to present the current law in order that it may be contrasted with ongoing efforts in the U.S. to persuade the Congress to enact domestic legislation which, if not totally in accord with the 1976 Limitation Convention, will bring the U.S. more in line with the other major maritime nations which have adopted or adhered to the 1976 Convention.

5. THE U.S. RESPONSE TO THE 1976 LIMITATION CONVENTION

It is a matter of common knowledge that the U.S. abstained from signing the Convention, principally for the reason that the United States delegation was of the belief that the amounts of the fund were not high enough.

Nonetheless, it is a fair statement that the vast majority of the maritime community in the U.S. were perfectly well aware that the current Act was woefully inadequate and anachronistic. The United States Maritime Law Association commendably undertook to prepare draft legislation to serve as a substitute for the present outmoded act. It was the goal of the proposed draft legislation to provide an adequate fund for claimants while preserving for claimants and shipowners alike the very substantial benefits of concursus and of a fair and equitable distribution of the fund after a major marine accident.

This task was undertaken by a Joint Committee consisting of members of the Committee on the Comite Maritime Internationale and the Committee on Limitation of Liability. The Joint Committee's work product was submitted to the Association at its May, 1979 meeting as Document No. 619. Although a cogent and penetrating minority report was subjoined, the Association as a whole enthusiatically approved the draft document.

Some time thereafter, Congress introduced legislation to change the current limitation act by increasing the fund available to death and personal injury claimants from $60 per ton to $400 per ton. Representatives of the MLA urged the pertinent Congressional committee to abandon such a "band-aid" approach and completely revise the existing act, using as a base the MLA draft legislation. The suggestion was adopted and on March 21, 1984 the House committee introduced a bill, H.R. 5207, purportedly modeled on the MLA draft.

H.R. 5207 did indeed follow the MLA draft, although there were some changes in phraseology with which the MLA was not particularly happy. The most notable was the language dealing with when limitation could be pleaded as a defense.

In the event, Congress adjourned without having taken action on H.R. 5207 although there appears to have been a total absence of any opposition to the bill. In the following session, the bill was reintroduced as H.R. 207 and that bill is currently pending before the Congress. Again, no opposition has surfaced.

Comparison of pending legislation with 1976 Convention

(i) Persons Entitled to Limit Liability

The current bill expands the list of parties entitled to limit, in three important categories: salvors; any type of charterer, manager or operator; and insurers. By contrast, the 1976 Convention would also allow limitation to "any person for whose act, neglect or default the shipowner or salvor is responsible." In the view of the MLA, such an extension was too broad to be acceptable as domestic legislation.

(ii) Conduct Barring Limitation

The pending bill places the burden of proof on the plaintiff seeking the right to limit. This is contrary to the Convention and follows the present United States rule.

(iii) Limitation Fund—General Limits

The tonnage concept of the Convention has been adopted under which, instead of one fund for the voyage, the party seeking limitation is required to deposit a fund for each "distinct occasion." And instead of measuring the fund by the value of the vessel plus freight, the Convention measures the fund by the gross tonnage of the vessel. However, the tonnage formula under the pending bill would produce higher amounts than would the tonnage scale under the Convention. Moreover, special consideration has been given to the amounts recoverable by crew members. The limitation fund for personal injury and death on the one hand and property on the other are separate and not interchangeable. Neither class can invade the other. The maximum liability to the party seeking limitation for any distinct occasion is $130,000,000, including the passenger claims, plus any supplemental amounts for crewmembers.

(iv) Limit of Liability—Passenger Claims

Passengers are protected by a fund equal to $100,000 multiplied by the authorised number of passengers with a minimum of $2,500,000 and a maximum of $50,000,000 for vessels of 500 or more authorised passengers.

(v) Constitution of the Fund

The pending bill changes the time limitation of six months after receipt of a claim in writing to six months after any distinct occasion which may give rise to a claim. Since the proposed legislation permits more persons than merely the owner and/or bareboat charterer to seek limitation, it is provided that each person seeking to limit must deposit the security required. At the end of the case where a number of parties seeking to limit have been held liable, the single fund ultimately constituted for distribution shall be contributed to by such parties or their sureties in proportion to their respective liabilities as fixed by the court.

(vi) Limitation Without Creating a Fund

Under the pending bill, a party may plead limitation as a defense without setting up a fund and even after the six months time limit. However, the person seeking to limit by way of such an affirmative defense does not thereby achieve a concursus of all claims in one jurisdiction since no injunction can issue without posting the required security. This procedure would, therefore, be of value only where one claimant is believed to exist.

(vii) Distribution of the Fund

Current principles of distribution are preserved in the pending bill as are the existing priorities. In addition, a party who settles a claim is given the right by subrogation to assert rights which the party so paid would have enjoyed under the Act. This provision was included to facilitate settlements of claims in limitation proceedings, particularly where the amount of the fund is substantially less than the total of the claims provable against the fund. Under current law, unless all claimants agree, voluntary settlements made by the party seeking the right to limit may be held to be outside the limitation fund.

(viii) Bar to Other Actions

The size of the limitation fund required under the pending bill is much larger than under current law. The purpose and philosophy behind these increases are twofold: (1) to afford greater recognition of the rights of persons sustaining injury and loss resulting from marine casualties, and (2) to set a minimum available fund in the event of shipowner liability, which will be sufficient in the vast majority of cases. To meet this goal, new formulae had to be developed which are completely unrelated to vessel value and the old concept of abandonment of the vessel by the owner as a measure of maximum liability. In exchange for this greater exposure, it is intended that the shipowner's liability would not be permitted to go above the prescribed limits unless, in effect, he has deliberately caused the loss.

The net result is that limitation will only very rarely be useful to the shipowner if such proceedings are considered useful only if the claims exceed the amount of the fund. The MLA report gives as an example, the loss of the *Andrea Doria*. If that loss were governed by the pending bill, the shipowner could not effectively limit because the Andrea Doria fund would greatly exceed the claims. In that case, all third party claims, including 44 deaths, were settled for approximately $6·2 million, whereas the funds required under the pending bill would total $56,400,000 with the possibility of an additional $100,000 for each crewmember killed or injured.

If the shipowner can invoke limitation only when claims exceed the fund then he will be denied concursus. Obviously, the simplest, most efficient and just method is to gather all such claims in a single forum. The pending bill therefore provides for preserving concursus even in situations where the fund will exceed all claims.

6. CONCLUSION

The present United States Limitation Act is antiquated, anachronistic and woefully inadequate. New legislation along the lines of the 1976 Convention is desperately needed. Such new legislation is now pending before the Congress. It is the consensus of those closest to the legislative scene that such new legislation will ultimately be enacted in the United States, hopefully in the near future.

XXI

Yugoslavia and the 1976 Convention

1. HISTORICAL BACKGROUND

Activity within the region of the Mediterranean Sea was governed by a certain concept of limitation of liability of shipowners through the principle of *Noxae Deditio* dating back as far as old Roman times. Thus, the principle *Noxae Deditio* implied a duty or obligation of the owner of a thing which caused the damage to deliver or surrender to the damaged party the thing by which the damage was done. In shipping, this principle had a special feature in situations where a wrong-doing ship, sunk as a consequence of an incident in which the sunken ship, prior to sinking, caused damage to another ship, property at sea or property along the shore. In colloquial and practical relations at sea, till recent times, a saying was very often used: "Ship sunk all claims settled."

The notion of limited liability was promulgated in the French Commercial Code of 1808 in an improved form and enacted in an explicit legal norm in Article 216, creating a special liberty or remedy to the shipowners, for acts of the master, to actually restrict its civil liability to the ship and relevant freight. As a consequence of Napoleon's invasion of the Eastern Adriatic area at the beginning of the 19th Century, application of the French Commercial Code 1808 (second part) was extended into the coastal region which today belongs to the Socialist Federal Republic of Yugoslavia.

It is interesting to note that the concept of limited liability in the form of abandoning ship and freight to creditors of shipowners survived as a governing applicable rule in the Yugoslav legal system[1] until the Sea and Inland Navigation Act, enacted in Yugoslavia on April 22, 1977, came into force on January 1, 1978.[2] Provisions of this Act, in detail, regulate substantial issues

---

* Dr. sc. iur. Attorney at law Professor, Dubrovnik.
[1] Judgment of the Commercial District Court Split, No. IX–P–617/80; Judgment of the High Commercial Court—Zagreb No. PZ 1936/82; Judgment of the Supreme Court of Croatia, No.Rev. 111/83 dated January 30, 1985.
[2] The Sea and Inland Navigation Act was published in the Official Gazette No. 22/1977.

of the legal concept of the operator's limited liability[3] and the relevant procedure for limitation of operator's liability.[4] The Sea and Inland Navigation Act has incorporated all the principles and provisions of the 1957 Convention, although Yugoslavia, having signed this Convention, did not ratify it.[5]

2. THE EXISTING SYSTEM OF LIMITATION

An operator of a shipowning activity, in Yugoslav Law, is a paramount feature and a legal concept which, in respect of global limitation of liability as per Article 391 of the Act, includes all persons entitled to the utilization of the ship *i.e.* the shipowner, the manager of the ship and the charterer. Subsequent provisions of the same Article extend application of the principle of limited liability to the master, members of the crew and the employees of the operator when responsible for maritime claims.

According to Article 379, the operator of a sea-going ship may limit his liability in respect of:
(a) personal claims for injury suffered by persons being carried in the ship and property claims relating to goods on board the ship;
(b) personal claims for injury suffered by persons on land or on water and property claims for damage to property not on board the ship, if such damage is caused by an act or omission, whether by default or not, of persons on board the ship for whose conduct the operator is responsible, and also of persons not being on board the ship for whose conduct the operator is responsible—- but only if an act or omission, whether by default or not, by these persons concerns navigation, management of the ship, loading, carriage or unloading of the cargo, or embarkation, carriage or disembarking of passengers;
(c) claims arising out of an ordered removal, raising or destruction of a ship which is sunk, stranded or abandoned including goods being on it, as well as compensation for damage caused by the ship to the sea or inland navigation port, port installations or waterways.

The operator may not limit his liability under Article 379 of this Act for obligations assumed if the occurence giving rise to the claim was caused by personal fault of the operator. The Act

---

[3] Arts. 379–396 inclusive.
[4] Arts. 397–423 inclusive.
[5] The documentation presented to the National Assembly in support of the adoption of the Sea and Inland Navigation Act contains a reference that Yugoslavia has intention to ratify the 1957 Convention as soon as preconditions are established for its applications, see p. 152 Apr. 1969. These preconditions are procedural provisions enacted by the Sea and Inland Navigation Act.

follows consequently the term of the 1957 Convention in French[6] as the corresponding version in English, "actual fault and privity," can not be introduced in the Yugoslav Law without some ambiguity which the concept of "privity" may create.

With due respect to Article 1(6) of the 1957 Convention which leaves it to the *lex fori* to determine the issue with whom lies the burden of proving whether or not the occurrence, giving rise to the claim, resulted from the actual fault or privity of the operator, the situation appears to be as follows.

The onus of proof of establishing that the operator is not entitled to derive the benefit of limitation of liability because the occurrence or casualty has been caused by personal fault of the operator lies with the claimant-creditor. Nevertheless, in a case where there is *prima facie* evidence, *e.g.* where certain defects of the ship or her equipment is a single or contributive cause of the incident, the onus shifts to the operator to prove that there was no fault on his part, *i.e.* that the operator exercised due diligence to make the ship seaworthy in all relevant aspects. The degree of fault is not material and any personal fault of the operator to any degree will be sufficient to deprive him of enjoying the benefit of limited liability. The standard of proof is on a balance of probabilities and concept of the criteria "beyond reasonable doubt" is not applicable in maritime law.

When the owner is a corporate body, personal fault means the fault on the *alter ego* or of the person entrusted with the management of or operation of the ship, *i.e.* the mind directing the operation.

A special category of victims, according to the Yugoslav Law, do have a special and privileged protection. These are the crew members and other persons employed by the operator for claims or damages resulting from loss of life or personal injury and such claims are not subject to limitation of the operator's liability.

Following solutions provided by the 1957 Convention, property claims are subject to lower limits and personal claims resulting from loss of life or personal injury to higher limits, whereas the upper limits are reserved for personal claims only.

However, in cases where the amounts exclusively appropriated (reserved) for the settlement of personal claims are insufficient to pay the personal claims in full, the unsettled balance of such claims, together with property claims, shall concur in the fund appropriated for the payment of property claims.

The fund of limited liability is expressed in Yugoslav dinars and

[6] The wording of the 1957 Convention in French language introduces the term "*Faute Personnelle*" translated into the Croatian language appropriately "*osobna krivnja.*"

is dependent on the size of the ship. It is calculated on the basis of each contributory ton.[7]

The figure in dinars used for establishing the amount of limited liability is subject to revision from time to time and the authority for amendment of the figure per ton is delegated to the Federal Executive Council by law.[8] The objective of this delegation of power is to avoid erosion of the fund because of inflation etc., and to maintain the limitation fund consistent with the figures as fixed in the 1957 Convention. At the request of the operator a limitation fund may be established in court, to be made available to the satisfaction of the creditor's claim. If there arises a significant material discrepancy between the actual value of the fund and the actual value conceived by the relevant provisions of the 1957 Convention, as a result of currency fluctuation, then it would be open to the creditors to raise this issue. There are fair prospects for the creditors to succeed with a claim that the equivalent of the actual value of the limitation fund as per the 1957 Convention be distributed among the creditors, on the basis that the legislators' intention for enactment of relevant provisions of the Yugoslav Law on limitation of operator's liability was to provide for a sufficiently high fund. Thus an actual value of the limitation fund, either for personal claims or property claims, should be maintained at the moment when the fund is constituted in conformity with the 1957 Convention, irrespective of the fact that Yugoslavia did not ratify the Convention, as the aim has been and should still prevail that all material issues and solutions, provided by the 1957 Convention, remain applicable.[9]

The amount by which the operator's liability, provided by the terms of the 1977 Act, is limited for sea-going ships, shall not be below the corresponding figure provided for 100 contributory tons. This means that if the ship which is involved in an incident for which the operator seeks limitation of liability is a small ship, according to whose characteristics contributory tonnage does not reach 100 tons, the minimum value of the limitation fund should

---

[7] The Federal Executive Council is authorised by the provisions of Art. 1036 s.1, para. 4 to revise the limitation figures in Dinars as per each contributing ton in accordance with Art. 380, in a case of change of Yugoslav currency.

[8] For mechanically propelled ships a contributory tonnage is calculated on ship's net tonnage increased for gross tonnage of the engine-room space. The tonnage Certificate will be accepted as *prima facie* evidence.

[9] There has been manifested in the past a tendency of Yugoslav judicial practice to respect solutions and principles of International Maritime Conventions, following as much as possible the approach "*in favorem Conventionis.*" Thus, *e.g.* prior to the ratification of the Hague Rules (Convention on Bills of Lading 1924) by S.F.R. Yugoslavia in 1959 and before the Law of Bill of Lading Convention was introduced into Yugoslav internal law, the Yugoslav Courts applied the principles of that Convention in resolving disputes on relevant matters.

correspond to the ship's size of not less than 100 contributory tons.

The constitution of a limitation fund shall not mean an admission of liability for claims for which it is constituted. In conformity with this well established principle, however, it is not considered that the claimant (creditor), by recording the claim in the procedure for limitation of liability, recognizes that the operator is entitled by law to limit his liability.

Claims for salvage remuneration and claims for general average contributions are not subject to global limitation at all. Furthermore, a separate system for limitation of liability is provided for claims arising out of nuclear incidents and for damages caused by oil pollution.

Articles 397–423 of the Act, enact procedural provisions for non-litigious proceedings presided over by a single judge of the court having jurisdiction over the case.

Court jurisdiction is dependent upon the territory within which the register of ships is kept for vessels flying the Yugoslav flag and, in a case of a foreign flag ship the jurisdiction is with the court in whose territory the ship has been arrested and, if not arrested, with the court in whose territory the amount of money for the constitution of the limitation fund has been deposited.

Article 398 of the Act lists particulars which should be included in the operator's submission for commencement of limitation of liability proceedings and these, in addition to the general data, are as follows:

(a) the description of the occurrence giving rise to the claim for which limitation of liability is proposed;

(b) the basis and the amount to which the liability is limited;

(c) the way in which the proposer intends to constitute the limitation fund (deposit of a sum or furnishing of other adequate security);

(d) the list of known claimants, stating the place of their seat or of their residence;

(e) information as to the kind and the probable amount of the claims of known claimants.

If formal requirements are satisfied, as provided by Article 398 of the Act, and the assets corresponding to the limitation fund can be freely disposed of to the benefit of the creditors, the court, by a decree, shall then approve the constitution of the limitation fund. The decree shall be published in the Official Gazette with a direct notice to all known potential creditors. The claimants must register their claims with the court within ninety days. The decree also contains the date and place for the hearing where the examination of the claims will take place.

If the operator does not satisfy the court of the assets being and remaining at the free disposal of the creditors, the court shall dismiss the petition for the constitution of a limitation liability fund.

Before or at the hearing, the creditors may challenge or contest the right of the operator to limit his liability. If that right is opposed, the court shall, by an additional decree, invite the creditor to bring action against the operator within thirty days of the date of service of the court's decree. Failing this, the creditor is estopped from contesting the operator's right to limit liability.

All disputes in litigious proceedings on issues of whether the operator is entitled or not to limit his liability should be brought before the same court with which the limitation fund has been constituted.

Jurisdiction of such a court is provided in an exclusive manner by virtue of Articles 410(1) and 1014(1), para. 2 of the Act, when issues are under dispute in connection with limitation procedure which has been conducted by a court in Yugoslavia. The legislators' reasons for the imposition of such a solution under exclusive jurisdiction, considered as one of the exceptions under the Yugoslav procedural system, appears to be that the national tribunals should keep and maintain control over non-litigious proceedings held previously before the Yugoslav courts.

The applicable law of Article 999 provides that matters of limitation of an operator's liability are governed by the substantive law of the country under which flag the vessel sails. Nevertheless, if such a substantive law is more favourable for the operator in comparison with the provisions of Yugoslav Law then Yugoslav Law shall apply.

3. THE 1976 CONVENTION

As already stated Yugoslavia, although a signatory, has never ratified the 1957 Convention, as it was expected it would follow together with the enactment of the same principle in its internal national law. Work on the preparation of the complete shipping code (which, in fact, is the 1977 Act) had been protracted over a decade by the time it was finally promulgated in April 1977. By that stage the I.M.O. 1976 Limitation Convention was already drafted and multinationally agreed upon. The S.F.R. of Yugoslavia is among the state signatories to the 1976 Convention. The 1976 Convention has attracted considerable interest in Yugoslavia and there is a wide scale support of industry concerned for the adherence and ratification of it.

Discussions so far held with the Yugoslav Maritime Law

Association[10] and within the circles of the Yugoslav Underwriting interests[11] have given overwhelming support for adherence to the 1976 Convention. There is no material reason, at least published so far, which may prevent Yugoslavia from adherence to the 1976 Convention, including its SDR formula and other improvements and solutions which have now been offered to the industry by the I.M.O. Nevertheless, the fact that legislative interventions require a considerable amount of time to accomplish the task of ratification of any new Convention still remains.

Now, besides the necessary adaptations to the new system of limitation of the operator's liability as provided by the 1976 Convention, it would also be necessary to introduce amendments and modifications in the legal system and solutions presently in force. This work is time consuming and one is hesitant to give any prediction as to when Yugoslavia will ratify the 1976 Convention but optimism may be shared that eventually the ratification of the 1976 Convention will take place by the S.F.R. of Yugoslavia as well, to the benefit of operators, shipowners and creditors and all other parties interested.

[10] A panel discussion that took place in Zagreb on December 14, 1984 on the issue of global limitation of Shipowners/Operators liability resulted with unanimous conclusion that Yugoslavia should ratify the 1976 Convention.
[11] A meeting held in Poreć on April 18 and 19, 1985 adopted a conclusion that the 1976 Convention should be ratified and that solutions of that Convention be introduced in Yugoslav internal law.

Appendix A

Conventions Relating to Limitation of Liability

INTERNATIONAL CONVENTION FOR THE UNIFICATION OF CERTAIN RULES RELATING TO THE LIMITATION OF THE LIABILITY OF OWNERS OF SEAGOING VESSELS. SIGNED AT BRUSSELS, AUGUST 25, 1924.

Article 1.—The liability of the owner of a seagoing vessel is limited to an amount equal to the value of the vessel, the freight, and the accessories of the vessel, in respect of:

1) Compensation due to third parties by reason of damage caused, whether on land or on water, by the acts or faults of the master, crew, pilot, or any other person in the service of the vessel;

2) Compensation due by reason of damage caused either to cargo delivered to the master to be transported, or to any goods and property on board;

3) Obligations arising out of bills of lading;

4) Compensation due by reason of a fault of navigation committed in the execution of a contract;

5) Any obligation to remove the wreck of a sunken vessel, and any obligations connected therewith;

6) Any remuneration for assistance and salvage;

7) Any contribution of the shipowner in general average;

8) Obligations arising out of contracts entered into or transactions carried out by the master, acting within the scope of his authority, away from the vessel's home port, where such contracts or transactions are necessary for the preservation of the vessel or the continuation of the voyage, provided that the necessity is not caused by any insufficiency or deficiency of equipment or stores at the beginning of the voyage.

Provided that, as regards the cases mentioned in Nos. 1, 2, 3, 4, and 5 the liability referred to in the preceding provisions shall not exceed an aggregate sum equal to 8 pounds sterling per ton of the vessel's tonnage.

Article 2.—The limitation of liability laid down in the foregoing article does not apply:

1) To obligations arising out of acts or faults of the owner of the vessel;

2) To any of the obligations referred to in No. 8 of article 1, when the owner has expressly authorized or ratified such obligation;

3) To obligations on the owner arising out of the engagement of the crew and other persons in the service of the vessel.

Where the owner or a part owner of the vessel is at the same time master, he cannot claim limitation of liability for his faults, other than his faults of navigation and the faults of persons in the service of the vessel.

Article 3.—An owner who avails himself of the limitations of his liability to the value of the vessel, freight, and accessories of the vessel must prove that value. The valuation of the vessel shall be based upon the condition of the vessel at the points of time hereinafter set out:

1) In cases of collision or other accidents, as regards all claims connected therewith, including contractual claims which have originated up to the time of arrival of the vessel at the first port reached after the accident, and also as regards claims in general average arising out of the accident, the valuation shall be according to the condition of the vessel at the time of her arrival at that first port.

If before that time a fresh accident, distinct from the first accident, has reduced the value of the vessel, any diminution of value so caused shall not be taken into account in considering claims connected with the previous accident.

For accidents occurring during the sojourn of a vessel in port, the valuation shall be according to the condition of the vessel at that port after the accident.

2) If it is a question of claims relating to the cargo, or arising from a bill of lading, not being claims provided for in the preceding paragraphs, the valuation shall be according to the condition of the vessel at the port of destination of the cargo, or at the place where the voyage is broken.

If the cargo is destined to more than one port, and the damage is connected with one and the same cause, the valuation shall be according to the condition of the vessel at the first of those ports.

3) In all the other cases referred to in article 1 the valuation shall be according to the conditions of the vessel at the end of the voyage.

Article 4.—The freight referred to in article 1, including passage money, is deemed, as respects vessels of every description, to be a lump sum fixed at all events at 10 per cent. of the value of the vessel at the commencement of the voyage.

That indemnity is due even though no freight be then earned by the vessel.

Article 5.—The accessories referred to in article 1 mean:

1) Compensation of material damage sustained by the vessel since the beginning of the voyage, and not repaired;

2) General average contributions in respect of material damage sustained by the vessel since the beginning of the voyage, and not repaired.

Payments on policies of insurance, as well as bounties, subventions, and other national subsidies, are not deemed to be accessories.

Article 6.—The various claims connected with a single accident, or in respect of which, in the absence of an accident, the value of a vessel is ascertained at a single port, rank with one another against the amount representing the extent of the owner's liability, regard being had to the order of the liens.

In proceedings with respect to the distribution of this sum the decisions given by the competent courts of the contracting States shall be evidence of a claim.

Article 7.—Where death or bodily injury is caused by the acts or faults of the captain, crew, pilot, or any other person in the service of the vessel, the owner of the vessel is liable to the victims or their representatives in an amount exceeding the limit of liability provided for in the preceding articles up to 8 pounds sterling per ton of the vessel's tonnage. The victims of a single accident or their representatives rank together against the sum constituting the extent of liability.

If the victims or their representatives are not fully compensated by this amount, they rank, as regards the balance of their claims, with the other claimants against the amounts mentioned in the preceding articles, regard being had to the order of the liens.

The same limitation of liability applies to passengers as respects the carrying vessel but does not apply to the crew or other persons in the service of that vessel whose right of action in the case of death or bodily injury remains governed by the national law of the vessel.

Article 8.—Where a vessel is arrested and security is given for an amount equal to the full limit of liability, it shall accrue to the benefit of all creditors whose claims are subject to this limit.

Where the vessel is subsequently again arrested, the court may order its release, if the owner, while submitting to the jurisdiction of the court, proves that he has already given security for an amount equal to the full limit of his liability, that the security so given is satisfactory, and that the creditor is assured of receiving the benefit thereof.

If the security is given for a smaller amount or if security is required on several successive occasions, the effect will be regulated by agreement between the parties, or by the court, so as to insure that the limit of liability be not exceeded.

If different creditors take proceedings in the courts of different States, the owner may, before each court, require account to be taken of the whole of the claims and debts so as to insure that the limit of liability be not exceeded.

The national laws shall determine questions of procedure and time limits for the purpose of applying the preceding rules.

Article 9.—In the event of any action or proceeding being taken on one of the grounds enumerated in article 1, the court may, on the application of the owner of the vessel, order that proceedings against the property of the owner other than the vessel, its freight and accessories shall be stayed for a period sufficient to permit of the sale of the vessel and distribution of the proceeds amongst the creditors.

Article 10.—Where the person who operates the vessel without owning it or the principal charterer is liable under one of the heads enumerated in article 1, the provisions of this convention are applicable to him.

Article 11.—For the purposes of the provisions of the present convention, "tonnage" is calculated as follows:

In the case of steamers and other mechanically propelled vessels, net tonnage, with the addition of the amount deducted from the gross tonnage on account of engine-room space for the purpose of ascertaining the net tonnage.

In the case of sailing vessels, net tonnage.

Article 12.—The provisions of this convention shall be applied in each contracting State in cases in which the ship for which the limit of responsibility is invoked is a national of another contracting State, as well as in any other cases provided for by the national laws.

Nevertheless the principle formulated in the preceding paragraph does not affect the right of the contracting States not to apply the provisions of this convention in favour of the nationals of a non-contracting State.

Article 13.—This convention does not apply to vessels of war, nor to government vessels appropriated exclusively to the public service.

Article 14.—Nothing in the foregoing provisions shall be deemed to affect in any way the competence of tribunals, modes of procedure, or methods of execution authorized by the national laws.

Article 15.—The monetary units mentioned in this convention mean their gold value.

Those contracting States in which the pound sterling is not a monetary unit reserve to themselves the right of translating the sums indicated in this convention in terms of pound sterling into terms of their own monetary system in round figures.

The national laws may reserve to the debtor the right of discharging his debt in national currency according to the rate of exchange prevailing at the dates fixed in article 3.

Article 16.—After an interval of not more than two years from the day on which the convention is signed, the Belgian Government shall place itself in communication with the Governments of the High Contracting Parties which have declared themselves prepared to ratify the convention, with a view to deciding whether it shall be put into force. The ratifications shall be deposited at Brussels at a date to be fixed by agreement among the said Governments. The first deposit of ratifications shall be recorded in a *procès-verbal* signed by the representatives of the powers which take part therein and by the Belgian Minister for Foreign Affairs.

The subsequent deposits of ratifications shall be made by means of a written notification, addressed to the Belgian Government, and accompanied by the instrument of ratification.

A duly certified copy of the *procès-verbal* relating to the first deposit of ratifications, of the notifications referred to in the previous paragraph, and also of the instruments of ratification accompanying them, shall be immediately sent by the Belgian Government through the diplomatic channel to the powers who have signed this convention or who have acceded to it. In the cases contemplated in the preceding paragraph the said Government shall inform them at the same time of the date on which it received the notification.

Article 17.—Nonsignatory States may accede to the present convention whether or not they have been represented at the International Conference at Brussels.

A State which desires to accede shall notify its intention in writing to the Belgian Government, forwarding to it the document of accession, which shall be deposited in the archives of the said Government.

The Belgian Government shall immediately forward to all the States which have signed or acceded to the convention a duly certified copy of the notification and of the act of accession, mentioning the date on which it received the notification.

Article 18.—The High Contracting Parties may at the time of signature, ratification, or accession declare that their acceptance of the present convention does not include any or all of the self-governing dominions, or of the colonies, overseas possessions, protectorates, or territories under their sovereignty or authority, and they may subsequently accede separately on behalf of any self-governing dominion, colony, overseas possession, protectorate, or territory excluded in their declaration. They may also denounce the convention separately in accordance with its provisions in respect of any self-governing dominion, or any colony, overseas possession, protectorate, or territory under their sovereignty or authority.

Article 19.—The present convention shall take effect, in the case of the States which have taken part in the first deposit of ratifications, one year after the date of the *procès-verbal* recording such deposit. As respects the States which ratify subsequently or which accede, and also in cases in which the convention is subsequently put into effect in accordance with article 18, it shall take effect six months after the notifications specified in article 16, paragraph 2, and article 17, paragraph 2, have been received by the Belgian Government.

Article 20.—In the event of one of the contracting States wishing to denounce the present convention, the denunciation shall be notified in writing to the Belgian Government, which shall immediately communicate a duly certified copy of the notification to all the other States informing them of the date on which it was received.

The denunciation shall only operate in respect of the States which made the notifications, and on the expiration of one year after the notification has reached the Belgian Government.

Article 21.—Any one of the contracting States shall have the right to call for a fresh conference with a view to considering possible amendments.

A State which would exercise this right should give one year advance notice of its intention to the other States through the Belgian Government, which would make arrangements for convening the conference.

Additional Article.—The provisions of article 5 of the convention for the unification of certain rules relating to collisions at sea, of September 23, 1910 (*British and Foreign State Papers*, Vol. 103, p. 434), the operation of which had been put off by virtue of the additional article of that convention, become applicable in regard to the States bound by this convention.

Done at Brussels, in a single copy, August 25, 1924.

PROTOCOL OF SIGNATURE

In proceeding to the signature of the International Convention for the unification of certain rules relating to the limitation of the liability of owners of seagoing vessels, the undersigned Plenipotentiaries adopted the present protocol which will have the same force and the same value as if the provisions were inserted in the text of the convention to which it relates:

I. The High Contracting Parties reserve to themselves the right not to admit the limitation of the liability to the value of the vessel, the accessories and the freight for damages done to works in ports, docks, and navigable ways and for the cost of removing the wreck, or the right only to ratify the treaty on those points on condition of reciprocity.

It is nevertheless agreed that the limitation of liability under the head of those damages will not exceed eight pounds sterling per ton of measurement, except as regards the cost of removing the wreck.

II. The High Contracting Parties reserve to themselves the right to decide that the owner of a vessel that is not used for the carriage of persons and measures not more than three hundred tons is liable as to claims arising from death or bodily injuries, in accordance with the provisions of the convention, but without there being occasion to apply to that liability the provisions of paragraph 1 of article 7.

Done at Brussels, in a single copy, August 25, 1924.

STATUS: Entered into force on June 2, 1931

Belgium	2. 6.30
Brazil	28. 4.31
Denmark	2. 6.30[1]
Dominican Rep.	23. 7.58
Finland	12. 7.34[1]
France	23. 8.35[2]
Hungary	2. 6.30
Malgache Republic	23. 8.35[3]
Monaco	15. 5.31[4]
Norway	10.10.33[1]
Poland	26.10.36
Portugal	2. 6.30
Spain	2. 6.30
Sweden	1. 7.38[1]
Turkey	4. 7.55

Note

(1) Convention denounced, with effect from June 30, 1963.
(2) Convention denounced, with effect from October 26, 1976.
(3) By the notification of France.
(4) Convention denounced, with effect from January 24, 1977.

INTERNATIONAL CONVENTION RELATING TO THE LIMITATION OF THE LIABILITY OF OWNERS OF SEA-GOING SHIPS. SIGNED AT BRUSSELS ON OCTOBER 10, 1957

The High Contracting Parties

Have recognised the desirability of determining by agreement certain uniform rules relating to the limitation of the liability of owners of sea-going ships:

Having decided to conclude a Convention for this purpose, and thereto have agreed as follows:

Article 1

1. The owner of a sea-going ship may limit his liability in accordance with Article 3 of this Convention in respect of claims arising from any of the following occurrences, unless the occurrence giving rise to the claim resulted from the actual fault or privity of the owner:

(a) loss of life of, or personal injury to, any person being carried in the ship, and loss of, or damage to, any property on board the ship;

(b) loss of life of, or personal injury to, any other person whether on land or on water, loss of or damage to any other property or infringement of any rights caused by the act, neglect or default of any person on board the ship for whose act, neglect or default the owner is responsible or any person not on board the ship for whose act, neglect or default the owner is responsible: Provided however that in regard to the act, neglect or default of this last class of person, the owner shall only be entitled to limit his liability when the act, neglect or default is one which occurs in the navigation or the management of the ship or in the loading, carriage or discharge of its cargo or in the embarkation, carriage or disembarkation of its passengers;

(c) any obligation or liability imposed by any law relating to the removal of wreck and arising from or in connection with the raising, removal or destruction of any ship which is sunk, stranded or abandoned (including anything which may be on board such ship) and any obligation or liability arising out of damage caused to harbour works, basins and navigable waterways.

2. In the present Convention the expression "personal claims" means claims resulting from loss of life and personal injury: the expression "property claims" means all other claims set out in paragraph (1) of this article.

3. An owner shall be entitled to limit his liability in the cases set out in paragraph (1) of this Article even in cases where his liability arises, without proof of negligence on the part of the owner or of persons for whose conduct he is responsible, by reason of his ownership possession, custody or control of the ship.

4. Nothing in this Article shall apply:

(a) to claims for salvage or to claims for contribution in general average;

(b) to claims by the Master, by members of the crew, by any servants of the owner on board the ship or by servants of the owner whose duties are connected with the ship, including the claims of their heirs, personal representatives or dependants, if under the law governing the contract of service between the owner and such servants the owner is not entitled to limit his liability in respect of such claims or if he is by such law only permitted to limit his liability to an amount greater than that provided for in Article 3 of this Convention.

5. If the owner of a ship is entitled to make a claim against a claimant arising out of the same occurrence, their respective claims shall be set off against each other and the provisions of this Convention shall only apply to the balance, if any.

6. The question upon whom lies the burden of proving whether or not the occurrence giving rise to the claim resulted from the actual fault or privity of the owner shall be determined by the *lex fori*.

Article 2

1. The limit of liability prescribed by Article 3 of this Convention shall apply to the aggregate of personal claims and property claims which arise on any distinct occasion without regard to any claims which have arisen or may arise on any other distinct occasion.

2. When the aggregate of the claims which arise on any distinct occasion exceeds the limits of liability provided for by Article 3, the total sum

representing such limits of liability may be constituted as one distinct limitation fund.

3. The fund thus constituted shall be available only for the payment of claims in respect of which limitation of liability can be invoked.

4. After the fund has been constituted, no claimant against the fund shall be entitled to exercise any right against any other assets of the shipowner in respect of his claim against the fund if the limitation fund is actually available for the benefit of the claimant.

Article 3

1. The amount to which the owner of a ship may limit his liability under Article 1 shall be:
   (a) where the occurrence has only given rise to property claims, an aggregate amount of 1,000 francs for each ton of the ship's tonnage;
   (b) where the occurrence has only given rise to personal claims, an aggregate amount of 3,100 francs for each ton of the ship's tonnage;
   (c) where the occurrence has given rise both to personal claims and property claims, an aggregate amount of 3,100 francs for each ton of the ship's tonnage, of which a first portion amounting to 2,100 francs for each ton of the ship's tonnage shall be exclusively appropriated to the payment of personal claims and of which a second portion amounting to 1,000 francs for each ton of the ship's tonnage shall be appropriated to the payment of property claims; provided however that in cases where the first portion is insufficient to pay the personal claims in full, the unpaid balance of such claims shall rank rateably with the property claims for payment against the second portion of the fund.

2. In each portion of the limitation fund the distribution among the claimants shall be made in proportion to the amounts of their established claims.

3. If before the fund is distributed the owner has paid in whole or in part any of the claims set out in Article 1 paragraph 1 he shall *pro tanto* be placed in the same position in relation to the fund as the claimant whose claim he has paid, but only to the extent that the claimant whose claim he has paid would have had a right of recovery against him under the national law of the State where the fund has been constituted.

4. Where the shipowner establishes that he may at a later date be compelled to pay in whole or in part any of the claims set out in Article 1 paragraph 1 the Court or other competent authority of the State where the fund has been constituted may order that a sufficient sum shall be provisionally set aside to enable the shipowner at such later date to enforce his claim against the fund in the manner set out in the preceding paragraph.

5. For the purpose of ascertaining the limit of an owner's liability in

accordance with the provisions of this article the tonnage of a ship of less than 300 tons shall be deemed to be 300 tons.

6. The franc mentioned in this article shall be deemed to refer to a unit consisting of sixty-five and a half milligrams of gold of millesimal fineness nine hundred. The amounts mentioned in paragraph 1 of this Article shall be converted into the national currency of the State in which limitation is sought on the basis of the value of that currency by reference to the unit defined above at the date on which the shipowner shall have constituted the limitation fund, made the payment or given a guarantee which under the law of that State is equivalent to such payment.

7. For the purpose of this Convention tonnage shall be calculated as follows:
—in the case of steamships or other mechanically propelled ships there shall be taken the net tonnage with the addition of the amount deducted from the gross tonnage on account of engine room space for the purpose of ascertaining the net tonnage.
—in the case of all other ships there shall be taken the net tonnage.

Article 4

Without prejudice to the provisions of Article 3, paragraph 2 of this Convention, the rules relating to the constitution and distribution of the limitation fund, if any, and all rules of procedure shall be governed by the national law of the State in which the fund is constituted.

Article 5

1. Whenever a shipowner is entitled to limit his liability under this Convention, and the ship or another ship or other property in the same ownership has been arrested within the jurisdiction of a contracting State or bail or other security has been given to avoid arrest, the Court or other competent authority of such State may order the release of the ship or other property or of the security given if it is established that the shipowner has already given satisfactory bail or security in a sum equal to the full limit of his liability under this Convention and that the bail or other security so given is actually available for the benefit of the claimant in accordance with his rights.

2. Where, in circumstances mentioned in paragraph 1 of this Article, bail or other security has already been given:
   (*a*) at the port where the accident giving rise to the claim occurred;
   (*b*) at the first port of call after the accident if the accident did not occur in a port;
   (*c*) at the port of disembarkation or discharge if the claim is a personal claim or relates to damage to cargo;
the Court or other competent authority shall order the release of the ship, bail or other security given, subject to the conditions set forth in paragraph 1 of this Article.

3. The provisions of paragraphs 1 and 2 of this Article shall apply likewise if the bail or other security already given is in a sum less than the

full limit of liability under this Convention: Provided that satisfactory bail or other security is given for the balance.

4. When the shipowner has given bail or other security in a sum equal to the full limit of his liability under this Convention such bail or other security shall be available for the payment of all claims arising on a distinct occasion and in respect of which the shipowner may limit his liability.

5. Questions of procedure relating to actions brought under the provisions of this Convention and also the time limit within which such actions shall be brought or prosecuted shall be decided in accordance with the national law of the Contracting State in which the action takes place.

Article 6

1. In this Convention the liability of the shipowner includes the liability of the ship herself.

2. Subject to paragraph 3 of this Article, the provisions of this Convention shall apply to the charterer, manager and operator of the ship, and to the master, members of the crew and other servants of the owner, charterer, manager or operator acting in the course of their employment, in the same way as they apply to an owner himself: Provided that the total limits of liability of the owner and all such other persons in respect of personal claims and property claims arising on a distinct occasion shall not exceed the amounts determined in accordance with Article 3 of the Convention.

3. When actions are brought against the master or against members of the crew such persons may limit their liability even if the occurrence which gives rise to the claims resulted from the actual fault or privity of one or more of such persons. If, however, the master or member of the crew is at the same time the owner, co-owner, charterer, manager or operator of the ship, the provisions of this paragraph shall only apply where the act, neglect or default in question is an act, neglect or default committed by the person in question in his capacity as master or as member of the crew of the ship.

Article 7

This Convention shall apply whenever the owner of a ship, or any other person having by virtue of the provisions of Article 6 hereof the same rights as an owner of a ship, limits or seeks to limit his liability before the Court of a Contracting State or seeks to procure the release of a ship or other property arrested or the bail or other security given within the jurisdiction of any such State.

Nevertheless, each Contracting State shall have the right to exclude, wholly or partially, from the benefits of this Convention any non-Contracting State, or any person who, at the time when he seeks to limit his liability or to secure the release of a ship or other property arrested or the bail or other security in accordance with the provisions of Article 5 hereof, is not ordinarily resident in a Contracting State, or does not have his principal place of business in a Contracting State, or any ship in respect of which limitation of liability or release is sought which does not at the time specified above fly the flag of a Contracting State.

Article 8

Each Contracting State reserves the right to decide what other classes of ship shall be treated in the same manner as sea-going ships for the purpose of this Convention.

Article 9

This Convention shall be open for signature by the States represented at the tenth session of the Diplomatic Conference on Maritime Law.

Article 10

This Convention shall be ratified and the instruments of ratification shall be deposited with the Belgian Government which shall notify through diplomatic channels all signatory and acceded States of their deposit.

Article 11

1. This Convention shall come into force six months after the date of deposit of at least ten instruments of ratification, of which at least five by States that have each a tonnage equal or superior to one million gross tons of tonnage.

2. For each signatory State which ratifies the Convention after the date of deposit of the instrument of ratification determining the coming into force such as is stipulated in paragraph 1 of this Article, this Convention shall come into force six months after the deposit of their instrument of ratification.

Article 12

Any State not represented at the tenth session of the Diplomatic Conference on Maritime Law may accede to this Convention.

The instruments of accession shall be deposited with the Belgian Government which shall inform through diplomatic channels all signatory and acceding States of the deposit of any such instruments.

The Convention shall come into force in respect of the acceding State six months after the date of the deposit of the instrument of accession of that State, but not before the date of entry into force of the Convention as established by Article 11, paragraph (1).

Article 13

Each High Contracting Party shall have the right to denounce this Convention at any time after the coming into force thereof in respect of such High Contracting Party. Nevertheless, this denunciation shall only take effect one year after the date on which notification thereof has been received by the Belgian Government which shall inform through diplomatic channels all signatory and acceding States of such notification.

Article 14

1. Any High Contracting Party may at the time of its ratification of or accession to this Convention or at any time thereafter declare by written notification to the Belgian Government that the Convention shall extend to any of the territories for whose international relations it is responsible. The Convention shall six months after the date of the receipt of such notification by the Belgian Government extend to the territories named therein, but not before the date of the coming into force of the Convention in respect of such High Contracting Party.

2. Any High Contracting Party which has made a declaration under paragraph 1 of this Article extending the Convention to any territory for whose international relations it is responsible may at any time thereafter declare by notification given to the Belgian Government that the Convention shall cease to extend to such territory. This denunication shall take effect one year after the date on which notification thereof has been received by the Belgian Government.

3. The Belgian Government shall inform through diplomatic channels all signatory and acceding States of any notification received by it under this article.

Article 15

Any High Contracting Party may three years after the coming into force of this Convention in respect of such High Contracting Party or at any time thereafter request that a conference be convened in order to consider amendments to this Convention.

Any High Contracting Party proposing to avail itself of this right shall notify the Belgian Government which shall convene the conference within six months thereafter.

Article 16

In respect of the relations between States which ratify this Convention or accede to it, this Convention shall replace and abrogate the International Convention for the unification of certain rules concerning the limitation of the liability of the owners of seagoing ships, signed at Brussels on the 25th of August 1924.

In witness whereof the Plenipotentiaries, duly authorized, have signed this Convention.

Done at Brussels, this tenth day of October 1957, in the French and English languages, the two texts being equally authentic, in a single copy, which shall remain deposited in the archives of the Belgian Government, which shall issue certified copies.

PROTOCOL OF SIGNATURE

1. Any State, at the time of signing, ratifying or acceding to this Convention may make any of the reservations set forth in paragraph 2. No other reservation to this Convention shall be admissible.

2. The following are the only reservations admissible:
(a) Reservation of the right to exclude the application of Article 1 paragraph 1 c);
(b) Reservation of the right to regulate by specific provisions of national law the system of limitation of liability to be applied to ships of less than 300 tons;
(c) Reservation of the right to give effect to this Convention either by giving it force of law or by including in national legislation, in a form appropriate to that legislation, the provisions of this Convention.

STATUS: Entered into force on May 31, 1968

RATIFICATIONS AND ACCESSIONS

Algeria	18. 8.64
Australia	30. 7.80[1]
Bahamas	21. 8.64[1][2]
Barbados	4. 8.65[1][3]
Belgium	31. 7.75
Belize	21. 8.64[1][3]
Denmark	1. 3.65[1][5]
Dominican Rep.	4. 8.65
Fiji	10.10.70
Finland	19. 8.64[1][5]
France	7. 7.59[1][6]
German Dem. Rep.	14. 2.79
Germany, Fed. Rep.	6.10.72[1]
Ghana	26. 7.61
Grenada	4. 8.65[1][2]
Guyana	25. 3.66[1]
Iceland	16.10.68
India	1. 6.71[1]
Iran	26. 4.66[1]
Israel	30.11.67[1]
Japan	1. 3.76[1]
Kiribati	21. 8.64[1]
Malgache Republic	13. 7.65
Mauritius	21. 8.64[1]
Monaco	24. 1.77
Netherlands	10.12.65[1]
Norway	1. 3.65[1][5]
Papua New Guinea	14. 3.80
Poland	1.12.72
Portugal	8. 4.68[1]
St. Lucia	4. 8.65[1][5]
St. Vincent Grenadines	4. 8.65[1][3]
Seychelles	21. 8.64[1][3]
Singapore	31. 5.68
Solomon Islands	21. 8.64[1][9]
Spain	16. 7.59[1]
Sweden	4. 6.64[1][5]
Switzerland	21. 1.66
Syrian Arab Rep.	10. 7.72
Tonga	13. 6.78
Tuvalu	21. 8.64[1][3]
United Arab Rep.	7. 9.65[4]
United Kingdom	18. 2.59[1][10]
Vanuatu	8.12.66[11]
Zaire	17. 7.67

Notes

(1) Declaration, reservation or statement issued at the time of deposit of the

301

instrument of acceptance, the text of which may be found by reference to the *CMI Yearbook* (1984/1985) at pp. 91–95.

(2) Originally by the accession of the United Kingdom, subsequently by succession on becoming an independent state.

(3) By the accession of the United Kingdom.

(4) Egypt denounced the Convention, with effect from May 8, 1985.

(5) Denmark, Finland, Norway and Sweden denounced the Convention, with effect from April 1, 1985.

(6) Extended to New Hebrides from December 8, 1966.

(7) Including Berlin (West).

(8) Japan denounced the Convention on May 19, 1983, with effect from May 20, 1984.

(9) By succession, maintaining the reservations originally formulated by the United Kingdom, subsequently by independent accession on July 7, 1978.

(10) United Kingdom acceded on behalf of: Isle of Man, November 18, 1960; Bermuda, British Antarctic Territories, Falkland Islands and Dependencies, Hong Kong, Gibraltar, British Virgin Islands, August 21, 1964; Guernsey and Jersey, October 21, 1964; Cayman Islands, Montserrat, Turks and Caicos Islands, August 4, 1965.

(11) United Kingdom denounced the Convention with effect from December 1, 1986.

(12) Reportedly as a consequence of the extension to the New Hebrides (see n. 6 above).

PROTOCOL OF 1979 AMENDING THE INTERNATIONAL CONVENTION RELATING TO THE LIMITATION OF THE LIABILITY OF OWNERS OF SEA-GOING SHIPS. DATED OCTOBER 10, 1957. AGREED IN BRUSSELS DECEMBER 21, 1979

1. Article 3, paragraph 1 of the Convention is replaced by the following:

"1. The amounts to which the owner of a ship may limit his liability under Article 1 shall be:

(a) where the occurrence has only given rise to property claims an aggregate amount of 66·67 units of account for each ton of the ship's tonnage;

(b) where the occurrence has only given rise to personal claims an aggregate amount of 206·67 units of account for each ton of the ship's tonnage;

(c) where the occurrence has given rise both to personal claims and property claims an aggregate amount of 206·67 units of account for each ton of the ship's tonnage, of which a first portion amounting to 140 units of account for each ton of the ship's tonnage shall be exclusively appropriated to the payment of personal claims and of which a second portion amounting to 66·6 units of account for each ton of the ship's tonnage shall be appropriated to the payment of property claims.

Provided however that in cases where the first portion is insufficient to pay the personal claims in full, the unpaid balance of such claims shall rank rateably with the property claims for payment against the second portion of the fund."

2. Article 3, paragraph 6 of the Convention is replaced by the following:

302

"6. The unit of account mentioned in paragraph 1 of this Article is the Special Drawing Right as defined by the International Monetary Fund. The amounts mentioned in that paragraph shall be converted into the national currency of the State in which limitation is sought on the basis of the value of that currency on the date on which the shipowner shall have constituted the limitation fund, made the payment or given a guarantee which under the law of that State is equivalent to such payment. The value of the national currency, in terms of the Special Drawing Rights, of a State which is a member of the International Monetary Fund, shall be calculated in accordance with the method of valuation applied by the International Monetary Fund in effect at the date in question for its operations and transactions. The value of the national currency, in terms of the Special Drawing Right, of a State which is not a member of the International Monetary Fund, shall be calculated in a manner determined by that State.

"7. Nevertheless, a State which is not a member of the International Monetary Fund and whose law does not permit the application of the provisions of the paragraph 6 of this Article may, at the time of ratification of the Protocol of 1979 or accession thereto or at any time thereafter, declare that the limits of liability provided for in this Convention to be applied in its territory shall be fixed as follows:

   (a) in respect of paragraph 1, a) of this Article, 1000 monetary units;

   (b) in respect of paragraph 1, b) of this Article, 3100 monetary units;

   (c) in respect of paragraph 1, c) of this Article, 3100, 2100 and 1000 monetary units, respectively.

The monetary unit referred to in this paragraph corresponds to 65·5 milligrammes of gold of millesimal fineness 900.

The conversion of the amounts specified in this paragraph into the national currency shall be made according to the law of the State concerned.

"8. The calculation mentioned in the last sentence of paragraph 6 of this Article and the conversion mentioned in paragraph 7 of this Article shall be made in such a manner as to express in the national currency of the State as far as possible the same real value for the amounts in paragraph 1 of this Article as is expressed there in units of account. States shall communicate to the depositary the manner of calculation pursuant to paragraph 6 of this Article or the result of the conversion in paragraph 7 of this Article, as the case may be, when depositing an instrument of ratification of the Protocol of 1979 or of accession thereto or when availing themselves of the option provided for in paragraph 7 of this Article and whenever there is a change in either."

3. Article 3, paragraph 7 of the Convention shall be renumbered Article 3, paragraph 9.

STATUS: Entered into force on October 6, 1984

Australia	30.11.83
Belgium	7. 9.83
Poland	6. 7.84
Portugal	30. 4.82
Spain	14. 5.82
United Kingdom	2. 3.82

(United Kingdom denounced Protocol with effect from December 1, 1986).

CONVENTION ON LIMITATION OF LIABILITY FOR MARITIME CLAIMS, 1976

The States Parties to this Convention,

HAVING RECOGNISED the desirability of determining by agreement certain uniform rules relating to the limitation of liability for maritime claims;

HAVE DECIDED to conclude a Convention for this purpose and have thereto agreed as follows:

CHAPTER I—THE RIGHT OF LIMITATION

Art. 1—Persons entitled to limit liability

1. Shipowners and salvors, as hereinafter defined, may limit their liability in accordance with the rules of this Convention for claims set out in Art. 2.

2. The term shipowner shall mean the owner, charterer, manager and operator of a sea-going ship.

3. Salvor shall mean any person rendering services in direct connection with salvage operations. Salvage operations shall also include operations referred to in Art. 2, para. 1(d), (e) and (f).

4. If any claims set out in Art. 2 are made against any person for whose act, neglect or default the shipowner or salvor is responsible, such person shall be entitled to avail himself of the limitation of liability provided for in this Convention.

5. In this Convention the liability of a shipowner shall include liability in an action brought against the vessel herself.

6. An insurer of liability for claims subject to limitation in accordance with the rules of this Convention shall be entitled to the benefits of this Convention to the same extent as the assured himself.

7. The act of invoking limitation of liability shall not constitute an admission of liability.

Art. 2—Claims subject to limitation

1. Subject to Arts. 3 and 4 the following claims, whatever the basis of liability may be, shall be subject to limitation of liability:

(a) claims in respect of loss of life or personal injury or loss of or damage to property (including damage to harbour works, basins and waterways and aids to navigation), occurring on board or in direct connection with the operation of the ship or with salvage operations, and consequential loss resulting therefrom;

(b) claims in respect of loss resulting from delay in the carriage by sea of cargo, passengers or their luggage;

(c) claims in respect of other loss resulting from infringement of rights other than contractual rights, occurring in direct connection with the operation of the ship or salvage operations;

(d) claims in respect of the raising, removal, destruction or the rendering harmless of a ship which is sunk, wrecked, stranded or abandoned, including anything that is or has been on board such ship;

(e) claims in respect of the removal, destruction or the rendering harmless of the cargo of the ship;

(f) claims of a person other than the person liable in respect of measures taken in order to avert or minimize loss for which the person liable may limit his liability in accordance with this Convention, and further loss caused by such measures.

2. Claims set out in para. 1 shall be subject to limitation of liability even if brought by way of recourse or for indemnity under a contract or otherwise. However, claims set out under para. 1(d), (e) and (f) shall not be subject to limitation of liability to the extent that they relate to remuneration under a contract with the person liable.

Art. 3—Claims excepted from limitation

The rules of this Convention shall not apply to:

(a) claims for salvage or contribution in general average;

(b) claims for oil pollution damage within the meaning of the International Convention on Civil Liability for Oil Pollution Damage, dated Nov. 29, 1969 or of any amendment or Protocol thereto which is in force;

(c) claims subject to any international convention or national legislation governing or prohibiting limitation of liability for nuclear damage;

(d) claims against the shipowner of a nuclear ship for nuclear damage;

(e) claims by servants of the shipowner or salvor whose duties are connected with the ship or the salvage operations, including claims of their heirs, dependants or other persons entitled to make such claims, if under the law governing the contract of service between the shipowner or salvor and such servants the shipowner or salvor is not entitled to limit his liability in respect of such claims, or if he is by such law only permitted to limit his liability to an amount greater than that provided for in Art. 6.

Art. 4—Conduct barring limitation

A person liable shall not be entitled to limit his liability if it is proved that the loss resulted from his personal act or omission, committed with the intent to cause such loss, or recklessly and with knowledge that such loss would probably result.

Art. 5—Counterclaims

Where a person entitled to limitation of liability under the rules of this Convention has a claim against the claimant arising out of the same occurrence, their respective claims shall be set off against each other and the provisions of this Convention shall only apply to the balance, if any.

CHAPTER II. LIMITS OF LIABILITY

Art. 6—The general limits

1. The limits of liability for claims other than those mentioned in Art. 7, arising on any distinct occasion, shall be calculated as follows:
   (*a*)   in respect of claims for loss of life or personal injury,
   - (i)   333,000 Units of Account for a ship with a tonnage not exceeding 500 tons,
   - (ii) for a ship with a tonnage in excess thereof, the following amount in addition to that mentioned in (i):
     for each ton from 501 to 3,000 tons, 500 Units of Account;
     for each ton from 3,001 to 30,000 tons, 333 Units of Account;
     for each ton from 30,001 to 70,000 tons, 250 Units of Account; and
     for each ton in excess of 70,000 tons, 167 Units of Account,
   (*b*)   in respect of any other claims,
   - (i)   167,000 Units of Account for a ship with a tonnage not exceeding 500 tons,
   - (ii) for a ship with a tonnage in excess thereof the following amount in addition to that mentioned in (i):
     for each ton from 501 to 30,000 tons, 167 Units of Account;
     for each ton from 30,001 to 70,000 tons, 125 Units of Account; and
     for each ton in excess of 70,000 tons, 83 Units of Account.

2. Where the amount calculated in accordance with para. 1(a) is insufficient to pay the claims mentioned therein in full, the amount calculated in accordance with para. 1(b) shall be available for payment of the unpaid balance of claims under para. 1(a) and such unpaid balance shall rank rateably with claims mentioned under para. 1(b).

3. However, without prejudice to the right of claims for loss of life or personal injury according to para. 2, a State Party may provide in its national law that claims in respect of damage to harbour works, basins and waterways and aids to navigation shall have such priority over other claims under para. 1(*b*) as is provided by that law.

4. The limits of liability for any salvor not operating from any ship or for any salvor operating solely on the ship to, or in respect of which, he is rendering salvage services, shall be calculated according to a tonnage of 1,500 tons.

5. For the purpose of this Convention the ship's tonnage shall be the gross tonnage calculated in accordance with the tonnage measurement

rules contained in Annex I of the International Convention on Tonnage Measurement of Ships, 1969.

Art. 7—The limit for passenger claims

1. In respect of claims arising on any distinct occasion for loss of life or personal injury to passengers of a ship, the limit of liability of the shipowner thereof shall be an amount of 46,666 Units of Account multiplied by the number of passengers which the ship is authorised to carry according to the ship's certificate, but not exceeding 25 million Units of Account.

2. For the purpose of this Article "claims for loss of life or personal injury to passengers of a ship" shall mean any such claims brought by or on behalf of any person carried in that ship:

(a) under a contract of passenger carriage, or

(b) who, with the consent of the carrier, is accompanying a vehicle or live animals which are covered by a contract for the carriage of goods.

Art. 8—Unit of account

1. The Unit of Account referred to in Arts. 6 and 7 is the Special Drawing Right as defined by the International Monetary Fund. The amounts mentioned in Arts. 6 and 7 shall be converted into the national currency of the State in which limitation is sought, according to the value of that currency at the date the limitation fund shall have been constituted, payment is made, or security is given which under the law of that State is equivalent to such payment. The value of a national currency in terms of the Special Drawing Right, of a State Party which is a member of the International Monetary Fund, shall be calculated in accordance with the method of valuation applied by the International Monetary Fund in effect at the date in question for its operations and transactions. The value of a national currency in terms of the Special Drawing Right, of a State Party which is not a member of the International Monetary Fund, shall be calculated in a manner determined by that State Party.

2. Nevertheless, those States which are not members of the International Monetary Fund and whose law does not permit the application of the provisions of para. 1 may, at the time of signature without reservation as to ratification, acceptance or approval or at the time of ratification, acceptance, approval or accession or at any time thereafter, declare that the limits of liability provided for in this Convention to be applied in their territories shall be fixed as follows:

(a) in respect of Art. 6, para. 1(a) at an amount of:

    (i) 5 million monetary units for a ship with a tonnage not exceeding 500 tons;

    (ii) for a ship with a tonnage in excess thereof, the following amount in addition to that mentioned in (i):

        for each ton from 501 to 3,000 tons, 7,500 monetary units;

        for each ton from 3,001 to 30,000 tons, 5,000 monetary units;

        for each ton from 30,001 to 70,000 tons, 3,750 monetary units; and

for each ton in excess of 70,000 tons, 2,500 monetary units; and
    (b)   in respect of Art. 6, para. 1(b), at an amount of:
        (i)   2·5 million monetary units for a ship with a tonnage not exceeding 500 tons;
        (ii) for a ship with a tonnage in excess thereof, the following amount in addition to that mentioned in (i):

for each ton from 501 to 30,000 tons, 2,500 monetary units;

for each ton from 30,001 to 70,000 tons, 1,850 monetary units; and

for each ton in excess of 70,000 tons, 1,250 monetary units; and

    (c)   in respect of Art. 7, para. 1, at an amount of 700,000 monetary units multiplied by the number of passengers which the ship is authorised to carry according to its certificate, but not exceeding 375 million monetary units.

Paragraphs 2 and 3 of Art. 6 apply correspondingly to subparas. (a) and (b) of this paragraph.

3. The monetary unit referred to in para. 2 corresponds to sixty-five and a half milligrammes of gold of millesimal fineness nine hundred. The conversion of the amounts specified in para. 2 into the national currency shall be made according to the law of the State concerned.

4. The calculation mentioned in the last sentence of para. 1 and the conversion mentioned in para. 3 shall be made in such a manner as to express in the national currency of the State Party as far as possible the same real value for the amounts in Arts. 6 and 7 as is expressed there in units of account. States Parties shall communicate to the depositary the manner of calculation pursuant to para. 1, or the result of the conversion in para. 3, as the case may be, at the time of the signature without reservation as to ratification, acceptance or approval, or when depositing an instrument referred to in Art. 16 and whenever there is a change in either.

Art. 9—Aggregation of claims

1. The limits of liability determined in accordance with Art. 6 shall apply to the aggregate of all claims which arise on any distinct occasion:
    (a)   against the person or persons mentioned in para. 2 of Art. 1 and any person for whose act, neglect or default he or they are responsible; or
    (b)   against the shipowner of a ship rendering salvage services from that ship and the salvor or salvors operating from such ship and any person for whose act, neglect or default he or they are responsible; or
    (c)   against the salvor or salvors who are not operating from a ship or who are operating solely on the ship to, or in respect of which, the salvage services are rendered and any person for whose act, neglect or default he or they are responsible.

2. The limits of liability determined in accordance with Art. 7 shall apply to the aggregate of all claims subject thereto which may arise on any distinct occasion against the person or persons mentioned in para. 2 of Art. 1 in respect of the ship referred to in Art. 7 and any person for whose act, neglect or default he or they are responsible.

Art. 10—Limitation of liability without constitution of a limitation fund

1. Limitation of liability may be invoked notwithstanding that a limitation fund as mentioned in Art. 11 has not been constituted. However, a State Party may provide in its national law that, where an action is brought in its courts to enforce a claim subject to limitation, a person liable may only invoke the right to limit liability if a limitation fund has been constituted in accordance with the provisions of this Convention or is constituted when the right to limit liability is invoked.

2. If limitation of liability is invoked without the constitution of a limitation fund, the provisions of Art. 12 shall apply correspondingly.

3. Questions of procedure arising under the rules of this Article shall be decided in accordance with the national law of the State Party in which action is brought.

CHAPTER III—THE LIMITATION FUND

Art. 11—Constitution of the fund

1. Any person alleged to be liable may constitute a fund with the court or other competent authority in any State Party in which legal proceedings are instituted in respect of claims subject to limitation. The fund shall be constituted in the sum of such of the amounts set out in Arts. 6 and 7 as are applicable to claims for which that person may be liable, together with interest thereon from the date of the occurrence giving rise to the liability until the date of the constitution of the fund. Any fund thus constituted shall be available only for the payment of claims in respect of which limitation of liability can be invoked.

2. A fund may be constituted, either by depositing the sum, or by producing a guarantee acceptable under the legislation of the State Party where the fund is constituted and considered to be adequate by the court or other competent authority.

3. A fund constituted by one of the persons mentioned in para. 1(*a*), (*b*) or (*c*) or para. 2 of Art. 9 or his insurer shall be deemed constituted by all persons mentioned in para. 1(*a*), (*b*) or (*c*) or para. 2, respectively.

Art. 12—Distribution of the fund

1. Subject to the provisions of paras. 1, 2 and 3 of Art. 6 and of Art. 7, the fund shall be distributed among the claimants in proportion to their established claims against the fund.

2. If, before the fund is distributed, the person liable, or his insurer, has settled a claim against the fund such person shall, up to the amount he has paid, acquire by subrogation the rights which the person so compensated would have enjoyed under this Convention.

3. The right of subrogation provided for in para. 2 may also be exercised by persons other than those therein mentioned in respect of any amount of compensation which they may have paid, but only to the extent that such subrogation is permitted under the applicable national law.

4. Where the person liable or any other person establishes that he may be compelled to pay, at a later date, in whole or in part any such amount

of compensation with regard to which such person would have enjoyed a right of subrogation pursuant to paras. 2 and 3 had the compensation been paid before the fund was distributed, the court or other competent authority of the State where the fund has been constituted may order that a sufficient sum shall be provisionally set aside to enable such person at such later date to enforce his claim against the fund.

Art. 13—Bar to other actions

1. Where a limitation fund has been constituted in accordance with Art. 11, any person having made a claim against the fund shall be barred from exercising any right in respect of such claim against any other assets of a person by or on behalf of whom the fund has been constituted.

2. After a limitation fund has been constituted in accordance with Art. 11, any ship or other property, belonging to a person on behalf of whom the fund has been constituted, which has been arrested or attached within the jurisdiction of a State Party for a claim which may be raised against the fund, or any security given, may be released by order of the court or other competent authority of such State. However, such release shall always be ordered if the limitation fund has been constituted:

(a) at the port where the occurrence took place, or, if it took place out of port, at the first port of call thereafter; or

(b) at the port of disembarkation in respect of claims for loss of life or personal injury; or

(c) at the port of discharge in respect of damage to cargo; or

(d) in the State where the arrest is made.

3. The rules of paras. 1 and 2 shall apply only if the claimant may bring a claim against the limitation fund before the court administering that fund and the fund is actually available and freely transferable in respect of that claim.

Art. 14—Governing law

Subject to the provisions of this chapter the rules relating to the constitution and distribution of a limitation fund, and all rules of procedure in connection therewith, shall be governed by the law of the State Party in which the fund is constituted.

CHAPTER IV—SCOPE OF APPLICATION

Article 15

1. This Convention shall apply whenever a person referred to in Art. 1 seeks to limit his liability before the court of a State Party or seeks to procure the release of a ship or other property or the discharge of any security given within the jurisdiction of any such State. Nevertheless, each State Party may exclude wholly or partially from the application of this Convention any person referred to in Art. 1, who at the time when the rules of this Convention are invoked before the courts of that State does not have his habitual residence in a State Party, or does not have his principal place of business in a State Party or any ship in relation to which

the right of limitation is invoked or whose release is sought and which does not at the time specified above fly the flag of a State Party.

2. A State Party may regulate by specific provisions of national law the system of limitation of liability to be applied to vessels which are:

(a) according to the law of that State, ships intended for navigation on inland waterways;

(b) ships of less than 300 tons.

A State Party which makes use of the option provided for in this paragraph shall inform the depositary of the limits of liability adopted in its national legislation or of the fact that there are none.

3. A State Party may regulate by specific provisions of national law the system of limitation of liability to be applied to claims arising in cases in which interests of persons who are nationals of other States Parties are in no way involved.

4. The Courts of a State Party shall not apply this Convention to ships constructed for or adapted to, and engaged in, drilling:

(a) when that State has established under its national legislation a higher limit of liability than that otherwise provided for in Art. 6; or

(b) when the State has become party to an international convention regulating the system of liability in respect of such ships.

In a case to which sub-para. (a) applies that State Party shall inform the depositary accordingly.

5. This Convention shall not apply to:

(a) aircushion vehicles;

(b) floating platforms constructed for the purpose of exploring or exploiting the natural resources of the seabed or the subsoil thereof.

CHAPTER V—FINAL CLAUSES

Art. 16—Signature, ratification and accession

1. This Convention shall be open for signature by all States at the headquarters of the InterGovernmental Maritime Consultative Organization (hereinafter referred to as "the Organization") from Feb. 1, 1977, until Dec. 31, 1977, and shall thereafter remain open for accession.

2. All States may become parties to this Convention by:

(a) signature without reservation as to ratification, acceptance or approval; or

(b) signature, subject to ratification, acceptance or approval followed by ratification, acceptance or approval; or

(c) accession.

3. Ratification, acceptance, approval or accession shall be effected by the deposit of a formal instrument to that effect with the Secretary-General of the Organization (hereinafter referred to as "the Secretary-General").

Art. 17—Entry into force

1. This Convention shall enter into force on the first day of the month

following one year after the date on which 12 States have either signed it without reservation as to ratification, acceptance or approval or have deposited the requisite instruments of ratification, acceptance, approval or accession.

2. For a State which deposits an instrument of ratification, acceptance, approval or accession, or signs without reservation as to ratification, acceptance or approval, in respect of this Convention after the requirements for entry into force have been met but prior to the date of entry into force, the ratification, acceptance, approval or accession or the signature without reservation as to ratification, acceptance or approval, shall take effect on the date of entry into force of the Convention or on the first day of the month following the 90th day after the date of signature or the deposit of the instrument, whichever is the later date.

3. For any State which subsequently becomes a Party to this Convention, the Convention shall enter into force on the first day of the month following the expiration of 90 days after the date when such State deposited its instrument.

4. In respect of the relations between States which ratify, accept, or approve this Convention or accede to it, this Convention shall replace and abrogate the International Convention relating to the Limitation of the Liability of Owners of Seagoing Ships, done at Brussels on Oct. 10, 1957, and the International Convention for the Unification of certain Rules relating to the Limitation of the Owners of Seagoing Vessels, signed at Brussels on Aug. 25, 1924.

Art. 18—Reservations

1. Any State may, at the time of signature, ratification, acceptance, approval or accession, reserve the right to exclude the application of Art. 2, para. 1(d) and (e). No other reservations shall be admissible to the substantive provisions of this Convention.

2. Reservations made at the time of signature are subject to confirmation upon ratification, acceptance or approval.

3. Any State which has made a reservation to this Convention may withdraw it at any time by means of a notification addressed to the Secretary-General. Such withdrawal shall take effect to the date the notification is received. If the notification states that the withdrawal of a reservation is to take effect on a date specified therein, and such date is later than the date the notification is received by the Secretary-General, the withdrawal shall take effect on such later date.

Art. 19—Denunciation

1. This Convention may be denounced by a State Party at any time after one year from the date on which the Convention entered into force for that Party.

2. Denunciation shall be effected by the deposit of an instrument with the Secretary-General.

3. Denunciation shall take effect on the first day of the month following the expiration of one year after the date of deposit of the instrument, or after such longer period as may be specified in the instrument.

1. A Conference for the purpose of revising or amending this Convention may be convened by the Organization.

2. The Organization shall convene a Conference of the States Parties to this Convention for revising or amending it at the request of not less than one-third of the Parties.

3. After the date of the entry into force of an amendment to this Convention, any instrument of ratification, acceptance, approval or accession deposited shall be deemed to apply to the Convention as amended, unless a contrary intention is expressed in the instrument.

Art. 21—Revision of the limitation amount and of unit of account or monetary unit

1. Notwithstanding the provisions of Art. 20, a Conference only for the purposes of altering the amounts specified in Arts. 6 and 7 and in Art. 8, para. 2, or of substituting either or both of the units defined in Art. 8, paras. 1 and 2, by other units shall be convened by the Organization in accordance with paras. 2 and 3 of this Article. An alteration of the amounts shall be made only because of a significant change in their real value.

2. The Organization shall convene such a Conference at the request of not less than one fourth of the States Parties.

3. A decision to alter the amounts or to substitute the units by other Units of Account shall be taken by a two-thirds majority of the States Parties present and voting in such Conference.

4. Any State depositing its instrument of ratification, acceptance, approval or accession to the Convention, after entry into force of an amendment, shall apply the Convention as amended.

Art. 22—Depositary

1. This Convention shall be deposited with the Secretary-General.

2. The Secretary-General shall:
(a) transmit certified true copies of this Convention to all States which were invited to attend the Conference on Limitation of Liability for Maritime Claims and to any other States which accede to this Convention;
(b) inform all States which have signed or acceded to this Convention of:
    (i) each new signature and each deposit of an instrument and any reservation thereto together with the date thereof;
    (ii) the date of entry into force of this Convention or any amendment thereto;
    (iii) any denunciation of this Convention and the date on which it takes effect;
    (iv) any amendment adopted in conformity with Arts. 20 or 21;
    (v) any communication called for by any Article of this Convention.

3. Upon entry into force of this Convention, a certified true copy

thereof shall be transmitted by the Secretary-General to the Secretariat of the United Nations for registration and publication in accordance with Art. 102 of the Charter of the United Nations.

Art. 23—Languages

This Convention is established in a single original in the English, French, Russian and Spanish languages, each text being equally authentic.

DONE AT LONDON this nineteenth day of November one thousand nine hundred and seventy-six.

IN WITNESS WHEREOF the undersigned being duly authorised for that purpose have signed this Convention.

STATUS: Entry into force on December 1, 1986 (2)

RATIFICATIONS AND ACCESSIONS

Bahamas	7. 6.83
Benin	1.11.85
Denmark	30. 5.84
Finland	8. 5.84
France	1. 7.81
Japan	6. 4.82
Liberia	17. 2.81
Norway	30. 3.84[3]
Poland	28. 4.86
Spain	13.11.81
Sweden	30. 3.84[3]
United Kingdom	31. 1.80[1][3]
Yemen Arab Rep.	6. 3.79

Note

(1) Declaration, reservation or statement issued with reference to the Convention (IMO. Misc. 85(1), "Status of Conventions," at pp. 251–252).
(2) As a result of the ratification of Benin.
(3) Notifications issued at the time of deposit, the text of which follow the text of the reservations or statements issued at the same time.
(4) Ratification by the United Kingdom was declared to be effective also in respect of Jersey, Guernsey, Isle of Man, Belize, Bermuda, British Virgin Is., Cayman Is., Falkland Is., Gibraltar, Hong Kong, Montserrat, Pitcairn, Saint Helena and Dependencies, Turks & Caicos Is., and the U.K. Sovereign Base Areas of Akrotiri and Dhekelia in Cyprus.
Belize has since become an independent state, to which it may be assumed the Convention will apply "provisionally," when it actually comes into force. Provisional application to Belize was not, however, explicitly referred to in the IMO "Status Report" to December 31, 1984.

CONVENTION OF THE LIABILITY OF OPERATORS OF NUCLEAR SHIPS 1962

Article III

1. The liability of the operator as regards one nuclear ship shall be limited to 1,500 million francs in respect of any one nuclear incident, notwithstanding that the nuclear incident may have resulted from any fault or privity of that operator; such limit shall include neither any interest nor costs awarded by a court in actions for compensation under this Convention.

    2. ...

    3. ...

    4. The franc mentioned in paragraph 1 of this Article is a unit of account constituted by sixty-five and one half milligrams of gold of millesimal fineness nine hundred. The amount awarded may be converted into each national currency in round figures. Conversion into national currencies other than gold shall be effected on the basis of their gold value at the date of payment.

STATUS: Not yet in force

RATIFICATIONS AND ACCESSIONS

Lebanon	3.6.75
Malagache Republic	13.7.65
Netherlands	20.3.74
Portugal	31.7.68
Suriname	20.3.74
Syrian Arab Rep.	1.8.74
Zaire	17.7.67

INTERNATIONAL CONVENTION ON CIVIL LIABILITY FOR OIL POLLUTION DAMAGE 1969. SIGNED AT BRUSSELS, NOVEMBER 29, 1969

Article V

1. The owner of a ship shall be entitled to limit his liability under this Convention in respect of any one incident to an aggregate amount of 2,000 francs for each ton of the ship's tonnage. However, this aggregate amount shall not in any event exceed 210 million francs.

    2. If the incident occurred as a result of the actual fault or privity of the owner, he shall not be entitled to avail himself of the limitation provided in paragraph 1 of this Article.

    3. For the purpose of availing himself of the benefit of limitation provided for in paragraph 1 of this Article the owner shall constitute a fund for the total sum representing the limit of his liability with the Court or other competent authority of any one of the Contracting States in which action is brought under Article IX. The fund can be constituted

either by depositing the sum or by producing a bank guarantee or other guarantee, acceptable under the legislation of the Contracting State where the fund is constituted, and considered to be adequate by the Court or another competent authority.

4. The fund shall be distributed among the claimants in proportion to the amounts of their established claims.

5. If before the fund is distributed the owner or any of his servants or agents or any person providing him insurance or other financial security has as a result of the incident in question, paid compensation for pollution damage, such person shall, up to the amount he has paid, acquire by subrogation the rights which the person so compensated would have enjoyed under this Convention.

6. The right of subrogation provided for in paragraph 5 of this Article may also be exercised by a person other than those mentioned therein in respect of any amount of compensation for pollution damage which he may have paid but only to the extent that such subrogation is permitted under the applicable national law.

7. Where the owner or any other person establishes that he may be compelled to pay at a later date in whole or in part any such amount of compensation, with regard to which such person would have enjoyed a right of subrogation under paragraphs 5 or 6 of this Article, had the compensation been paid before the fund was distributed, the Court or other competent authority of the State where the fund has been constituted may order that a sufficient sum shall be provisionally set aside to enable such person at such later date to enforce his claim against the fund.

8. Claims in respect of expenses reasonably incurred or sacrifices reasonably made by the owner voluntarily to prevent or minimize pollution damage shall rank equally with other claims against the fund.

9. The franc mentioned in this Article shall be a unit consisting of sixty-five and a half milligrams of gold of millesimal fineness nine hundred. The amount mentioned in paragraph 1 of this Article shall be converted into the national currency of the State in which the fund is being constituted on the basis of the value of that currency by reference to the unit defined above on the date of the constitution of the fund.

10. For the purpose of this Article the ship's tonnage shall be the net tonnage of the ship with the addition of the amount deducted from the gross tonnage on account of engine room space for the purpose of ascertaining the net tonnage. In the case of a ship which cannot be measured in accordance with the normal rules of tonnage measurement, the ship's tonnage shall be deemed to be 40 per cent. of the weight in tons (of 2240 lbs.) of oil which the ship is capable of carrying.

11. The insurer or other person providing financial security shall be entitled to constitute a fund in accordance with this Article on the same conditions and having the same effect as if it were constituted by the owner. Such a fund may be constituted even in the event of the actual fault or privity of the owner but its constitution shall in that case not prejudice the rights of any claimant against the owner.

STATUS: Entered into force on June 19, 1975

RATIFICATIONS AND ACCESSIONS

Algeria	14. 6.74
Australia	7.11.83[1]
Bahamas	22. 7.76
Belgium	12. 1.77[1]
Belize	[2]
Benin	1.11.85
Brazil	17.12.76
Cameroon	14. 5.84
Chile	2. 8.77
China Peoples Rep.	30. 1.80[1]
Denmark	2. 4.75
Dominican Rep.	2. 4.75
Ecuador	23.12.76
Fiji	15. 8.72
Finland	10.10.80
France	17. 3.75
Gabon	21. 1.82
German Dem. Rep.	13. 3.78[1]
Germany, Fed. Rep.	20. 5.75[1]
Ghana	20. 4.78
Greece	29. 6.76
Guatemala	20.10.82[1]
Hong Kong	1. 4.76[4]
Iceland	17. 7.80
Indonesia	1. 9.78
Italy	27. 2.79[1]
Ivory Coast	21. 6.73
Japan	3. 6.76
Kiribati	[2]
Korea, Republic	18.12.78
Kuwait	2. 4.81
Lebanon	9. 4.74
Liberia	25. 9.72
Maldives	16. 3.81
Monaco	21. 8.75
Morocco	11. 4.74
Netherlands	9. 9.75
New Zealand	27. 4.76
Nigeria	7. 5.81
Norway	21. 3.75
Oman	24. 1.85
Panama	7. 1.76
Papua New Guinea	12. 3.80
Poland	18. 2.76
Portugal	26.11.76
Senegal	27. 3.72
Seychelles	1. 4.76
Singapore	16. 9.81
Soloman Islands	[2]
South Africa	17. 3.76
Spain	8.12.75
Sri Lanka	12. 4.83
Sweden	17. 3.75
Syrian Arab Rep.	6. 2.75[1]

Tunisia	4. 5.76
Tuvala	(3)
United Arab Emirates	15.12.83
United Kingdom	17. 3.75[4]
USSR	24. 6.74[1]
Vanuatu	2. 2.83
Yemen Arab Rep.	6. 3.79
Yugoslavia	18. 6.76

Notes

(1) Declaration, reservation or statement issued in reference to the Convention (IMO MISC. (85)1, "Status of Conventions," at pp. 154–159).

(2) The Convention was originally extended to Belize, Gilbert Is. (now Kiribati) and the Solomon Is. (by the United Kingdom) on April 1, 1976, with effect from the same date. Since then, these dependencies have become independent states to which the Convention applies *provisionally* (*i.e.* they are not yet Contracting States in their own rights).

(3) The Convention was originally extended to Tuvalu (by the United Kingdom) on April 1, 1976, with effect from the same date. Since then, Tuvalu has become an independent state and a Contracting State to the Convention, with effect from October 1, 1978.

(4) The Convention was extended to Jersey, Guernsey, and the Isle of Man on March 1, 1976, with effect from February 1, 1976 (according to IMO Misc. (85)(1)).

The Convention was extended to Bermuda on March 1, 1976 with effect from February 3, 1976 (*ibid.*)

The Convention was extended to Anguilla May 8, 1984 with effect from September 1, 1984

The Convention was extended to British Indian Ocean Territory, British Virgin Islands, Caymans, Falkland Islands and Dependencies, Gibraltar, Hong Kong, Montserrat, Pitcairn, St. Helena and Dependencies, Turks and Caicos, United Kingdom Sovereign Base Areas of Akrotiri and Dhekelia in Island of Cyprus on April 1, 1976, with effect from the same date (*ibid.*)

PROTOCOL TO THE INTERNATIONAL CONVENTION ON CIVIL LIABILITY FOR OIL POLLUTION DAMAGE 1969. AGREED IN LONDON, NOVEMBER 19, 1976

Article II

Article V of the Convention is amended as follows:

(1) Paragraph 1 is replaced by the following text:

"The owner of a ship shall be entitled to limit his liability under this Convention in respect of any one incident to an aggregate amount of 133 units of account for each ton of the ship's tonnage. However, this aggregate amount shall not in any event exceed 14 million units of account."

(2) Paragraph 9 is replaced by the following text:

9(a). The "unit of account" referred to in paragraph 1 of this Article is the Special Drawing Right as defined by the International Monetary Fund. The amounts mentioned in paragraph 1 shall be converted into the national currency of the State in which the fund is being constituted on the basis of the value of that currency by reference to the Special Drawing Right on the date of the constitution of the fund. The value of the national currency, in terms

318

of the Special Drawing Right, of a Contracting State which is a member of the International Monetary Fund, shall be calculated in accordance with the method of valuation applied by the International Monetary Fund in effect at the date in question for its operations and transactions. The value of the national currency, in terms of the Special Drawing Right, of a Contracting State which is not a member of the International Monetary Fund, shall be calculated in a manner determined by that State.

9(b). Nevertheless, a Contracting State which is not a member of the International Monetary Fund and whose law does not permit the application of the provisions of paragraph 9(a) of this Article may, at the time of ratification, acceptance, approval of or accession to the present Convention, or at any time thereafter, declare that the limits of liability provided for in paragraph 1 to be applied in its territory shall, in respect of any one incident, be an aggregate of 2,000 monetary units for each ton of the ship's tonnage provided that this aggregate amount shall not in any event exceed 210 million monetary units. The monetary unit referred to in this paragraph corresponds to sixty-five and a half milligrammes of gold of millesimal fineness nine hundred. The conversion of these amounts into the national currency shall be made according to the law of the State concerned.

9(c). The calculation mentioned in the last sentence of paragraph 9(a) and the conversion mentioned in paragraph 9(b) shall be made in such a manner as to express in the national currency of the Contracting State as far as possible the same real value for the amounts in paragraph 1 as is expressed there in units of account. Contracting States shall communicate to the depositary the manner of calculation pursuant to paragraph 9(a), or the result of the conversion in paragraph 9(b) as the case may be, when depositing an instrument referred to in Article IV and whenever there is a change in either.

STATUS: Entered into force on April 8, 1981

RATIFICATIONS AND ACCESSIONS

Australia	7.11.83
Bahamas	3. 3.80
Belize	[3]
Cameroon	14. 5.84
Denmark	3. 6.81
Finland	8. 1.81
France	7.11.80
Germany, Fed. Rep.	28. 8.80[1][5]
Hong Kong	[2]
Italy	3. 6.83
Kuwait	1. 7.81
Liberia	17. 2.81
Maldives	14. 6.81
Netherlands	3. 8.82
Norway	17. 7.78
Oman	24. 1.85
Poland	30.10.85

Singapore	15.12.81
Spain	22.10.81
Sweden	7. 7.78
United Arab Emirates	14. 3.84
United Kingdom	31. 1.80[1][2]
Yemen Arab Rep.	4. 6.79

Notes

(1) Declaration or notification issued in reference to the Protocol (IMO Misc. (85)(1), "Status of Convention," at pp. 166–167).

(2) The Protocol was extended to Anguilla May 8, 1984, with effect from September 1, 1984.

The ratification by the United Kingdom has also been declared to be effective in respect of Jersey, Guernsey, Isle of Man, Belize, Bermuda, British Indian Ocean Territory, British Virgin Islands, Caymans, Falkland Islands and Dependencies, Gibraltar, Hong Kong, Montserrat, Pitcairn, St. Helena and Dependencies, Turks and Caicos, United Kingdom Sovereign Base Areas of Akrotiri and Dhekelia in Island of Cyprus. (N.B: no dates indicated by the IMO "Status Report" to December 31, 1984.)

(3) Belize has since become an independent state to which the Protocol applies *provisionally* (*ibid.*).

PROTOCOL OF 1984 TO AMEND THE INTERNATIONAL CONVENTION ON CIVIL LIABILITY FOR OIL POLLUTION DAMAGE, 1969. ADOPTED IN LONDON MAY 25, 1984

Article 6

Article V of the 1969 Liability Convention is amended as follows:

1. Paragraph 1 is replaced by the following text:

1. The owner of a ship shall be entitled to limit his liability under this Convention in respect of any one incident to an aggregate amount calculated as follows:

 (a) 3 million units of account for a ship not exceeding 5,000 units of tonnage;

 (b) for a ship with a tonnage in excess thereof, for each additional unit of tonnage, 420 units of account in addition to the amount mentioned in subparagraph (a);

provided, however, that this aggregate amount shall not in any event exceed 59·7 million units of account.

2. Paragraph 2 is replaced by the following text:

2. The owner shall not be entitled to limit his liability under this Convention if it is proved that the pollution damage resulted from his personal act or omission, committed with the intent to cause such damage, or recklessly and with knowledge that such damage would probably result.

3. Paragraph 3 is replaced by the following text:

3. For the purpose of availing himself of the benefit of limitation provided for in paragraph 1 of this Article the owner shall constitute a fund for the total sum representing the limit of his liability with the Court or other competent authority of any one of the Contracting States in which action is brought under Article IX or, if no action is brought, with

any Court or other competent authority in any one of the Contracting States in which an action can be brought under Article IX. The fund can be constituted either by depositing the sum or by producing a bank guarantee or other guarantee, acceptable under the legislation of the Contracting State where the fund is constituted, and considered to be adequate by the Court or other competent authority.

4. Paragraph 9 is replaced by the following text:

9(a). The "unit of account" referred to in paragraph 1 of this Article is the Special Drawing Right as defined by the International Monetary Fund. The amounts mentioned in paragraph 1 shall be converted into national currency on the basis of the value of that currency by reference to the Special Drawing Right on the date of the constitution of the fund referred to in paragraph 3. The value of the national currency, in terms of the Special Drawing Right, of a Contracting State which is a member of the International Monetary Fund, shall be calculated in accordance with the method of valuation applied by the International Monetary Fund in effect on the date in question for its operations and transactions. The value of the national currency, in terms of the Special Drawing Right, of a Contracting State which is not a member of the International Monetary Fund, shall be calculated in a manner determined by that State.

9(b). Nevertheless, a Contracting State which is not a member of the International Monetary Fund and whose law does not permit the application of the provisions of paragraph 9(a) may, at the time of ratification, acceptance, approval of or accession to this Convention or at any time thereafter, declare that the unit of account referred to in paragraph 9(a) shall be equal to 15 gold francs. The gold franc referred to in this paragraph corresponds to sixty-five and a half milligrammes of gold of millesimal fineness nine hundred. The conversion of the gold franc into the national currency shall be made according to the law of the State concerned.

9(c). The calculation mentioned in the last sentence of paragraph 9(a) and the conversion mentioned in paragraph 9(b) shall be made in such manner as to express in the national currency of the Contracting State as far as possible the same real value for the amounts in paragraph 1 as would result from the application of the first three sentences of paragraph 9(a). Contracting States shall communicate to the depositary the manner of calculation pursuant to paragraph 9(a), or the result of the conversion in paragraph 9(b) as the case may be, when depositing an instrument of ratification, acceptance, approval of or accession to this Convention and whenever there is a change in either.

5. Paragraph 10 is replaced by the following text:

10. For the purpose of this Article the ship's tonnage shall be the gross tonnage calculated in accordance with the tonnage measurement regulations contained in Annex I of the International Convention on Tonnage Measurement of Ships, 1969.

6. The second sentence of paragraph 11 is replaced by the following text:

Such a fund may be constituted even if, under the provisions of paragraph 2, the owner is not entitled to limit his liability, but its constitution shall in that case not prejudice the rights of any claimant against the owner.

STATUS: Not yet in force (1)

United Kingdom

Notes

(1) Article 13(1) of the CLC PROT 1984: "This Protocol shall enter into force twelve months following the date on which ten States including six States each with not less than one million units of gross tanker tonnage have deposited instruments of ratification, acceptance, approval or accession with the Secretary-General of the Organization."

INTERNATIONAL CONVENTION ON THE ESTABLISHMENT OF AN INTERNATIONAL FUND FOR COMPENSATION FOR OIL POLLUTION DAMAGE 1971. SIGNED IN BRUSSELS, DECEMBER 18, 1971

GENERAL PROVISIONS

Article 1

For the purposes of this Convention—

4. "Franc" means the unit referred to in Article V, paragraph 9 of the Liability Convention.

5. "Ship's tonnage" has the same meaning as in Article V, paragraph 10 of the Liability Convention.

Article 4

4. (a) Except as otherwise provided in sub-paragraph (b) of this paragraph, the aggregate amount of compensation payable by the Fund under this Article shall in respect of any one incident be limited, so that the total sum of that amount and the amount of compensation actually paid under the Liability Convention for pollution damage caused in the territory of the Contracting States, including any sums in respect of which the Fund is under an obligation to indemnify the owner pursuant to Article 5, paragraph 1, of this Convention, shall not exceed 450 million francs.

(b) The aggregate amount of compensation payable by the Fund under this Article for pollution damage resulting from a natural phenomenon of an exceptional, inevitable and irresistible character, shall not exceed 450 million francs.

5. Where the amount of established claims against the Fund exceeds the aggregate amount of compensation payable under paragraph 4, the amount available shall be distributed in such manner that the proportion between any established claim and the amount of compensation actually recovered by the claimant under the Liability Convention and this Convention shall be the same for all claimants.

6. The Assembly of the Fund (hereinafter referred to as "the Assembly") may, having regard to the experience of incidents which have occurred and in particular the amount of damage resulting therefrom and

to changes in the monetary values, decide that the amount of 450 million francs referred to in paragraph 4, sub-paragraphs (a) and (b), shall be changed, provided however, that this amount shall in no case exceed 900 million francs or be lower than 450 million francs. The changed amount shall apply to incidents which occur after the date of the decision effecting the change.

STATUS: Entered into force on October 16, 1978

RATIFICATIONS AND ACCESSIONS

Algeria	2. 6.75
Bahamas	22. 7.76
Belize	[2][3]
Benin	1.11.85
Cameroon	14. 5.84
Denmark	2. 4.75
Fiji	4. 3.83
Finland	10.10.80
France	11. 5.78
Gabon	21. 1.82
Germany, Fed. Rep.	30.12.76[1]
Ghana	20. 4.78
Hong Kong	[2]
Iceland	17. 7.80
Indonesia	1. 9.78
Italy	27. 2.79
Japan	7. 7.76
Kiribati	[3]
Kuwait	2. 4.81
Liberia	25. 9.72
Maldives	16. 3.81
Monaco	23. 8.79
Netherlands	3. 8.82
Norway	21. 3.75
Oman	10. 5.85
Papua New Guinea	12. 3.80
Poland	16. 9.85
Portugal	11. 9.85
Seychelles	[2][3]
Soloman Islands	[2][3]
Spain	8.10.81
Sri Lanka	12. 4.83
Sweden	17. 3.75
Syrian Arab Rep.	6. 2.75[1]
Tunisia	4. 5.76
Tuvalu	1.10.78[2][4]
United Arab Emirates	15.12.83
United Kingdom	2. 4.76[2]
Yugoslavia	16. 3.78

(1) Declaration, reservation or statement issued in reference to the Convention (IMO Misc. (85)1, "Status of Conventions," at p. 193).

(2) Ratification of the United Kingdom was declared at that time to be extended to Guernsey, Jersey, Isle of Man, Belize, Bermuda, British Indian Ocean Territory, British Virgin Is., Cayman Is., Falkland Is. and Dependencies, Gibraltar, Gilbert Is., (Kiribati), Hong Kong, Montserrat, Pitcairn Group, St. Helena and Dependencies, Seychelles, Solomon Is., Turks and Caicos Is., Tuvalu, U.K. Sovereign base areas of Akrotiri and Dhekelia in Cyprus, effective from October 16, 1978.
The Convention was extended to Anguilla, with effect from September 1, 1984.

(3) Belize, Kiribati, Seychelles and Solomon Is. have since become independent States to which it may be assumed the Convention applies "provisionally." (This "provisional" application is not, however, explicitly noted by the IMO "Status Report" to December 31, 1984).

(4) Tuvalu has since become an independent state and a Contracting State to the Conventions by the process of succession on the date of independence October 1, 1978.

PROTOCOL TO THE INTERNATIONAL CONVENTION ON THE ESTABLISHMENT OF AN INTERNATIONAL FUND FOR COMPENSATION FOR OIL POLLUTION DAMAGE 1971. AGREED IN LONDON, NOVEMBER 19, 1976

Article II

Article 1, Paragraph 4 of the Convention is replaced by the following text: "Unit of Account" or "Monetary Unit" means the unit of account or monetary unit as the case may be, referred to in Article V of the Liability Convention, as amended by the Protocol thereto adopted on 19 November 1976.

Article III

The amounts referred to in the Convention shall wherever they appear be amended as follows:

(a) Article 4:

  (i) "450 million francs" is replaced by "30 million units of account or 450 million monetary units";

  (ii) "900 million francs" is replaced by "60 million units of account or 900 million monetary units."

STATUS: Not yet in force. (4)

Bahamas	3. 3.80
Belize	(2)(3)
Denmark	3. 6.81
Finland	8. 1.81
France	7.11.80
Germany, Fed. Rep.	28. 8.80[1]
Hong Kong	31. 1.80[2]
Italy	21. 9.83
Liberia	17. 2.81
Netherlands	1.11.82
Norway	17. 7.78
Poland	3.10.85
Portugal	11. 9.85
Spain	5. 4.82
Sweden	7. 7.78
United Kingdom	31. 1.80[2]

Notes

(1) Declaration, reservation or statement issued in reference to the Convention (IMO Misc. (85)1, "Status of Conventions," at p. 200).

(2) Ratification of the United Kingdom was declared, at that time, to be extended to the Anguilla, Jersey, Guernsey, Isle of Man, Belize, Bermuda, British Indian Ocean Territory, British Virgin Is., Cayman Is., Falkland Is., Gibraltar, Hong Kong, Montserrat, Pitcairn, Saint Helena and Dependencies, Turks and Caicos Is., and to the U.K. Sovereign Base Areas of Akrotiri and Dhekelia in Cyprus.

(3) Belize has since become an independent state to which it may be assumed the Protocol will apply "provisionally," when it comes into force. (Provisional application is not, however, explicitly referred to in the IMO "Status Report" to December 31, 1984).

(4) "Entry into force" requirements are detailed in Art. VI of the Protocol. There are presently Contracting States representing approximately three quarters of the total quantity of "contributing oil" required for entry into force.

PROTOCOL OF 1984 TO AMEND THE INTERNATIONAL CONVENTION ON THE ESTABLISHMENT OF AN INTERNATIONAL FUND FOR COMPENSATION FOR OIL POLLUTION DAMAGE 1971. ADOPTED IN LONDON MAY 25, 1984

Article 2

Article 1 of the 1971 Fund Convention is amended as follows:

4. Paragraph 4 is replaced by the following text:

4. "Unit of account" has the same meaning as in Article V, paragraph 9, of the 1984 Liability Convention.

5. Paragraph 5 is replaced by the following text:

5. "Ship's tonnage" has the same meaning as in Article V, paragraph 10, of the 1984 Liability Convention.

Article 6

Article 4 of the 1971 Fund Convention is amended as follows:

3. Paragraph 4 is replaced by the following text:

4. (a) Except as otherwise provided in subparagraphs (b) and (c) of this

paragraph, the aggregate amount of compensation payable by the Fund under this Article shall in respect of any one incident be limited, so that the total sum of that amount and the amount of compensation actually paid under the 1984 Liability Convention for pollution damage within the scope of application of this Convention as defined in Article 3 shall not exceed 135 million units of account.

(b) Except as otherwise provided in subparagraph (c), the aggregate amount of compensation payable by the Fund under this Article for pollution damage resulting from a natural phenomenon of an exceptional, inevitable and irresistable character shall not exceed 135 million units of account.

(c) The maximum amount of compensation referred to in subparagraphs (a) and (b) shall be 200 million units of account with respect to any incident occurring during any period when there are three Parties to this Convention in respect of which the combined relevant quantity of contributing oil received by persons in the territories of such Parties, during the preceding calendar year, equalled or exceeded 600 million tons.

(d) Interest accrued on a fund constituted in accordance with Article V, paragraph 3, of the 1984 Liability Convention, if any, shall not be taken into account for the computation of the maximum compensation payable by the Fund under this Article.

(e) The amounts mentioned in this Article shall be converted into national currency on the basis of the value of that currency by reference to the Special Drawing Right on the date of the decision of the Assembly of the Fund as to the first date of payment of compensation.

4. Paragraph 5 is replaced by the following text:

5. Where the amount of established claims against the Fund exceeds the aggregate amount of compensation payable under paragraph 4, the amount available shall be distributed in such a manner that the proportion between any established claim and the amount of compensation actually recovered by the claimant under this Convention shall be the same for all claimants.

5. Paragraph 6 is replaced by the following text:

6. The Assembly of the Fund may decide that, in exceptional cases, compensation in accordance with this Convention can be paid even if the owner of the ship has not constituted a fund in accordance with Article V, paragraph 3, of the 1984 Liability Convention. In such case paragraph 4(e) of this Article applies accordingly.

STATUS: Not yet in force (1).

SIGNATORIES

Denmark	Norway
Finland	Poland
France	Portugal
Germany (Fed. Rep.)	Sweden
Morocco	United Kingdom
Netherlands	United States

Notes

(1) "Entry into force" requirements are detailed in Art. 30 of the Protocol.

DRAFT ARTICLES FOR A CONVENTION ON LIABILITY AND COMPENSATION IN CONNECTION WITH THE CARRIAGE OF NOXIOUS AND HAZARDOUS SUBSTANCES BY SEA. (FOR DIPLOMATIC CONFERENCE WHICH MET BETWEEN 30 APRIL–MAY 25, 1984)

LIMITATION OF LIABILITY OF THE SHIPOWNER

ALTERNATIVE A

Article 6

1. The limitation of the liability of the owner shall be determined by the provisions of the 1976 Convention, in so far as they are not incompatible with the present Convention.

2. All Contracting States shall apply the provisions of the 1976 Convention with respect to all claims arising in any distinct incident, including claims not covered by the present Convention. If the 1976 Convention has been revised or amended, a Contracting State shall apply the provisions of its most recent version having entered into force, unless such State has an obligation to apply an earlier version of that Convention.

[3. Contracting States shall apply Article 13 of the 1976 Convention only if a fund has been constituted in a Contracting State.]

4. This Article shall not affect the liability of a shipper under Articles 7 and 8 and of the owner under Article 12.

ALTERNATIVE B

Article 6

1. The limitation of the liability of the owner in respect of claims arising from any one incident and occasioned by damage covered by the present Convention shall be calculated as follows:

(*a*) in respect of claims for loss of life or injury,
- (i)   [ ] units of account for a ship with a tonnage not exceeding 500 tons,
- (ii)   for a ship with a tonnage in excess thereof, the following amount in addition to that mentioned in (i):
  for each ton from 501 to 3,000 tons, [ ] units of account;
  for each ton from 3,001 to 30,000 tons, [ ] units of account;
  for each ton from 30,001 to 70,000 tons, [ ] units of account; and
  for each ton in excess of 70,000 tons, [ ] units of account.

(*b*) in respect of any other claims,
- (i)   [ ] units of account for a ship with a tonnage not exceeding 500 tons,
- (ii)   for a ship with a tonnage in excess thereof, the following amount in addition to that mentioned in (i):
  for each ton from 501 to 30,000 tons, [ ] units of account;
  for each ton from 30,001 to 70,000 tons, [ ] units of account; and
  for each ton in excess of 70,000 tons, [ ] units of account.

2. Where the amount calculated in accordance with paragraph 1(a) is insufficient to pay the claims mentioned therein in full, the amount calculated in accordance with paragraph 1(b) shall be available for payment of the unpaid balance of claims under paragraph 1(a) and such unpaid balance shall rank rateably with claims mentioned under paragraph 1(b).

3. However, without prejudice to the right of claims for loss of life or personal injury according to paragraph 2, a State Party may provide in its national law that claims in respect of damage to harbour works, basins and waterways and aids to navigation shall have such priority over claims under paragraph 1(b) as is provided by that law.

4. For the purpose of this Article the ship's tonnage shall be the gross tonnage calculated in accordance with the tonnage measurement regulations contained in Annex I of the International Convention on Tonnage Measurement of Ships, 1969.

5. The provisions of this Article shall not apply to claims by servants of the owner or bareboat charterer whose duties are connected with the ship, including claims of their heirs, dependants or other persons entitled to make such claims, if under the law governing the contract of service between the owner or bareboat charterer and such servants the owner or bareboat charterer is not entitled to limit his liability in respect of such claims, or if he is by such law only permitted to limit his liability to an amount greater than that provided for in paragraph 1.

6. Where a person entitled to limitation of liability under the rules of the present Convention has a claim against the claimant arising out of the same occurrence and covered by the present Convention their respective claims shall be set off against each other, and the provisions of the present Convention shall only apply to the balance, if any. (It was observed that this provision might be included in a separate article.)

[7. The limits of liability determined in accordance with this Article shall apply to the aggregate of all claims covered by the present Convention which arise on any distinct occasion against the shipowner, charterer, manager and operator of the ship and any person for whose act, neglect or default he or they are responsible. Provided, however, that the preceding provision shall not affect the liability of a shipper according to Articles 7 and 8]. (This paragraph would be deleted if Article 3, paragraph 5, were to be retained.)

Article 6A

1. The owner shall not be entitled to limit his liability if it is proved that the damage resulted from his personal act or omission, committed with the intent to cause such damage or recklessly and with knowledge that such damage would probably result.

2. For the purpose of availing himself of the benefit of the limitation provided for in Article 6, the owner shall constitute a fund for the amounts provided for in Article 6, paragraph 1, with the court or other competent authority of any one of the Contracting States in which action is brought under Article 14. The fund can be constituted either by depositing the sum or by producing a bank guarantee or other guarantee, acceptable under the legislation of the Contracting State where the fund is constituted, and considered to be adequate by the court or another

competent authority. Any fund thus constituted shall be available only for the payment of claims in respect of which limitation of liability can be invoked.

[2a. A fund constituted by one of the persons mentioned in Article 6, paragraph 7, or his insurer or other person providing financial security shall be deemed constituted by all persons mentioned in that paragraph.] (This paragraph would have to be deleted if paragraph 7 of Article 6 were not retained.)

3. Subject to the provisions of Article 6, paragraphs 2 and 3, the fund shall be distributed among the claimants in proportion to the amounts of their established claims.

4. If before the fund is distributed the owner or any of his servants or agents or any person providing him with insurance or other financial security has as a result of the incident in question, paid compensation for damage, such person shall, up to the amount he has paid, acquire by subrogation the rights which the person so compensated would have enjoyed under the present Convention.

5. The right of subrogation provided for in paragraph 4 may also be exercised by a person other than those mentioned therein in respect of any amount of compensation for damage which he may have paid but only to the extent that such subrogation is permitted under the applicable national law.

6. Where the owner or any other person establishes that he may be compelled to pay at a later date in whole or in part an amount of compensation, with regard to which such person would have enjoyed a right of subrogation under paragraph 4 or 5, had the compensation been paid before the fund was distributed, the court or other competent authority of the State where the fund has been constituted may order that a sufficient sum shall be provisionally set aside to enable such person at such later date to enforce his claim against the fund.

7. An owner who has taken preventive measures shall, in respect of the costs of those measures, have the same rights against the fund as any other claimant.

8. The insurer or other person providing financial security shall be entitled to constitute a fund in accordance with this Article on the same conditions and having the same effect as if it were constituted by the owner. Such fund may be constituted even in the event that according to paragraph 1 the owner shall not be entitled to limit his liability, but its constitution shall in that case not prejudice the rights of any claimant against the owner.

Article 6B

1. Where the owner, after an incident, has constituted a fund in accordance with Article 6A, and is entitled to limit his liability,

(a) no person having a claim for damage arising out of that incident shall be entitled to exercise any right against any other assets of the owner in respect of such claim;

(b) the court or other competent authority of any Contracting State shall order the release of any property belonging to the owner which has been arrested or seized in respect of a claim for damage arising out of that incident, and shall similarly release any bail or other security furnished to avoid such arrest or seizure.

2. The foregoing shall, however, only apply if the claimant has access to the court administering the fund and the fund is actually available and freely transferable in respect of his claim.

Article 6C

Articles 6–6B shall not affect the liability of the owner under Article 12.

Appendix B

British Statutes and Statutory Instruments Relating to Limitation

The Merchant Shipping Act 1854

(17 & 18 Vict. c. 104)

s.504 No owner of any sea-going ship or share therein shall in cases where all or any of the following events occur without his actual fault or privity; (that is to say.)

(1) Where any loss of life or personal injury is caused to any person being carried in such ship;

(2) Where any damage or loss is caused to any goods, merchandise, or other things whatsoever, on board any such ship;

(3) Where any loss of life or personal injury is, by reason of the improper navigation of such sea-going ship as aforesaid, caused to any person carried in any other ship or boat;

(4) Where any loss or damage is, by reason of any such improper navigation of such sea-going ship as aforesaid, caused to any other ship or boat, or to any goods, merchandise, or other things whatsoever, on board any other ship or boat;

Be answerable in damages to an extent beyond the value of his ship, and the freight due or to grow due in respect of such ship during the voyage which at the time of the happening of any such events as aforesaid is in prosecution or contracted for, subject to the following proviso; (that is to say,) that in no case where any such liability as aforesaid is incurred in respect of loss of life or personal injury to any passenger, shall the value of any such ship and the freight thereof be taken to be less than £15. per registered ton.

The Merchant Shipping Act Amendment Act 1862

(25–26 Vict. c. 63)

s.54. The owners of any ship, whether British or foreign, shall not in cases where a or any of the following events occur without their actual fault or privity; (that is to say,)

(1.) Where any loss of life or personal injury is caused to any person being carried in such ship;

(2.) Where any damage or loss is caused to any goods, merchandise, or other things whatsoever on board any such ship;

(3.) Where any loss of life or personal injury is by reason of the improper navigation of such ship as aforesaid caused to any person carried in any other ship or boat;

(4.) Where any loss or damage is by reason of the improper navigation of such ship as aforesaid caused to any other ship or boat, or to any goods, merchandise, or other thing whatsoever on board any other ship or boat;

be answerable in damages in respect of loss of life or personal injury, either alone or together with loss or damage to ships, boats, goods, merchandise, or other things, to an aggregate amount exceeding £15 for each ton of their ship's tonnage; nor in respect of loss or damage to ships, goods, merchandise, or other things, whether there be in addition loss of life or personal injury or not, to an aggregate amount exceeding £8 for each ton of the ship's tonnage; such tonnage to be the registered tonnage in the case of sailing ships, and in the case of steam ships the gross tonnage, without deduction on account of engine room.

In the case of any foreign ship which has been or can be measured according to British law, the tonnage as ascertained by such measurement shall, for the purposes of this section, be deemed to be the tonnage of such ship.

In the case of any foreign ship which has not been and cannot be measured under British law, the surveyor-general of tonnage in the U.K., and the chief measuring officer in any British possession abroad, shall, on receiving from or by direction of the court hearing the case, give evidence concerning the dimensions of the ship as it may be found practicable to furnish, give a certificate under his hand, stating what would in his opinion have been the tonnage of such ship if she had been duly measured according to British law, and the tonnage so stated in such certificate shall, for the purposes of this section, be deemed to be the tonnage of such ship.

Merchant Shipping Act 1894, s.503

[Note. The English Limitation provisions have been through a number of transformations as described earlier in this book and in *Marsden* (11th ed.) Chapter 7, and *Temperley* (7th ed.), paras. 427 *et seq*. For convenience of reference section 503 is reproduced below in three versions. First, the original unamended version; secondly, the version which existed after the coming into force of the Merchant Shipping (Liability of Shipowners and Others) Act 1958; thirdly, the final version before its repeal by the Merchant Shipping Act 1979, taking account of the Merchant Shipping Acts 1979, 1981, 1984.

502. The owner of a British sea-going ship, or any share therein, shall not be liable to make good to any extent whatever any loss or damage happening without his actual fault or privity in the following cases: namely,—

(i.) Where any goods, merchandise, or other things whatsoever taken in or put on board his ship are lost or damaged by reason of fire on board the ship; or

(ii.) Where any gold, silver, diamonds, watches, jewels, or precious stones taken in or put on board his ship, the true nature and value of which have not at the time of shipment been declared by the owner or shipper thereof to the owner or master of the ship in the bills of lading or otherwise in writing, are lost or damaged by reason of any robbery, embezzlement, making away with, or secreting thereof.

Merchant Shipping Act 1894, s.503

I. The Original Version

503.—(1.) The owners of a ship, British or foreign, shall not, where all or any of the following occurrences take place without their actual fault or privity; (that is to say,)

(a.) Where any loss of life or personal injury is caused to any person being carried in the ship;

(b.) Where any damage or loss is caused to any goods, merchandise, or other things whatsoever on board the ship;

(c.) Where any loss of life or personal injury is caused to any person carried in any other vessel by reason of the improper navigation of the ship;

(d.) Where any loss or damage is caused to any other vessel, or to any goods, merchandise, or other things whatsoever on board any other vessel, by reason of the improper navigation of the ship;

be liable to damages beyond the following amounts; (that is to say,)

(i.) In respect of loss of life or personal injury, either alone or together with loss of or damage to vessels, goods, merchandise, or other things, an aggregate amount not exceeding fifteen pounds for each ton of their ship's tonnage; and

(ii.) In respect of loss of, or damage to, vessels, goods, merchandise, or other things, whether there be in addition loss of life or personal injury or not, an aggregate amount not exceeding eight pounds for each ton of their ship's tonnage.

(2.) For the purposes of this section—

(a.) The tonnage of a steam ship shall be her gross tonnage without deduction on account of engine room; and the tonnage of a sailing ship shall be her registered tonnage:

Provided that there shall not be included in such tonnage any space occupied by seamen and apprentices or appropriated to their use which is certified under the regulations scheduled to this Act with regard thereto.

(*b*.) Where a foreign ship has been or can be measured according to British law, her tonnage, as ascertained by that measurement shall, for the purpose of this section, be deemed to be her tonnage.

(*c*.) Where a foreign ship has not been and cannot be measured according to British law, the surveyor-general of ships in the United Kingdom, or the chief measuring officer of any British possession abroad, shall, on receiving from or by the direction of the court hearing the case, in which the tonnage of the ship is in question, such evidence concerning the dimensions of the ship as it may be practicable to furnish, give a certificate under his hand stating what would in his opinion have been the tonnage of the ship if she had been duly measured according to British law, and the tonnage so stated in that certificate shall, for the purposes of this section, be deemed to be the tonnage of the ship.

(3.) The owner of every sea-going ship or share therein shall be liable in respect of every such loss of life, personal injury, loss of or damage to vessels, goods, merchandise, or things as aforesaid arising on distinct occasions to the same extent as if no other loss, injury, or damage had arisen.

Merchant Shipping Act 1894, s.503

II. THE 1958 VERSION

[Note: what remains of section 503 is set out in plain print; provisions substituted by the Merchant Shipping (Liability of Shipowners and Others) Act 1958 are shown in italics without square brackets; italics in square brackets denote, in the form of a paraphrase, the additions which the Act of 1958 has, in effect, made to section 503.][1]

s.503(1) The owners of a ship, British or foreign, shall not, where all or any of the following occurrences take place without their actual fault or privity; (that is to say,)

(*a*) Where any loss of life or personal injury is caused to any person being carried in the ship;

(*b*) Where any damage or loss is caused to any goods, merchandise, or other things whatsoever on board the ship;

(*c*) *where any loss of life or personal injury is caused to any person not carried in the ship through the act or omission of any person (whether on board the ship or not) in the navigation or management of the ship or in the loading, carriage or discharge of its cargo or in the embarkation, carriage or disembarkation of its passengers, or through any other act or omission of any person on board the ship*[2];

(*d*) *where any loss or damage is caused to any property (other than any property mentioned in paragraph (b) of this subsection) or any rights are infringed through the act or omission of any person (whether on board the ship or not) in the navigation or management of the ship, or in the*

[1] Reference should be made to the Act of 1958, *infra*, for its exact terms and it should be read in conjunction with s.503 paraphrasing from *Marsden, op. cit.*
[2] The 1958 Act, s.2(1).

loading, carriage or discharge of its cargo or in the embarkation, carriage or disembarkation of its passengers, or through any other act or omission of any person on board the ship[2];

be liable to damages beyond the following amounts; (that is to say,)

(i)   In respect of loss of life or personal injury, either alone or together with *such loss, damage or infringement as is mentioned in paragraphs (b) and (d) of this subsection,*[3] an aggregate amount not exceeding *an amount equivalent to three thousand one hundred gold francs,*[4] for each ton of their ship's tonnage; and

(ii) In respect of *such loss, damage or infringement as is mentioned in paragraphs (b) and (d) of this subsection,*[3] whether there be in addition loss of life or personal injury or not, an aggregate amount not exceeding *an amount equivalent to one thousand gold francs,*[5] for each ton of their ship's tonnage;

[*and the number by which the amount equivalent to three thousand one hundred gold francs mentioned in this section is to be multiplied shall be three hundred in any case where the tonnage concerned is less than three hundred tons.*].[6]

[*For the purposes of this section a gold franc shall be taken to be a unit consisting of sixty-five and a half milligrams of gold of millesimal fineness nine hundred.*][7]

[*The Minister of Transport may from time to time by order made by statutory instrument specify the amounts which for the purposes of this section are to be taken as equivalent to three thousand one hundred and one thousand gold francs respectively.*][8]

[*Where money has been paid into court (or, in Scotland, consigned in court) in respect of any liability to which a limit is set as aforesaid, the ascertainment of that limit shall not be affected by a subsequent variation of the amounts specified under the immediately preceding paragraph unless the amount paid or consigned was less than that limit as ascertained in accordance with the order then in force under that paragraph.*][9]

[*For the purposes of subsection (1) of this section where any obligation or liability arises—*

(a)   *in connection with the raising, removal or destruction of any ship which is sunk, stranded or abandoned or of anything on board such a ship, or*

(b)   *in respect of any damage (however caused) to harbour works, basins or navigable waterways,*

the occurrence giving use to the obligation or liability shall be treated as one of the occurrences mentioned in paragraphs (b) and (d) of subsection (1) of this section and the obligation or liability as a liability to damages.][10]

[*The provisions of sub-paragraph (a) supra, relating to an obligation or liability arising in connection with the raising, removal or destruction of any ship which is sunk, stranded or abandoned or of anything on board such ship shall not*

---

[2] The 1958 Act, s.2(1).

[3] *Ibid.*

[4] *Ibid.* s.1(1)(a).

[5] The 1958 Act, s.1(1)(b).

[6] The 1958 Act, s.1(1).

[7] *Cf. Ibid.* s.1(2).

[8] *Cf. Ibid.* s.1(3).

[9] *Cf. Ibid.* s.1(4).

[10] *Cf. Ibid.* s.2(2).

come into force until such day as the Minister of Transport may by order made by statutory instrument appoint.][11]

[The Minister of Transport may by order make provision for the setting up and management of a fund to be used for the making to harbour or conservancy authorities of payments needed to compensate them for the reduction, in accordance with sub-paragraph (a) supra, of amounts recoverable by them in respect of the obligations and liabilities mentioned in that paragraph, and to be maintained by contributions from such authorities raised and collected by them in respect of vessels in like manner as other sums so raised by them; and any such order may contain such incidental and supplementary provisions as appear to the Minister to be necessary or expedient.][12]

[The power to make an order under the preceding paragraph of this section shall include power to vary or revoke any such order by a subsequent order and any such power shall be exercisable by statutory instrument, which shall be subject to annulment in pursuance of a resolution of either House of Parliament.][13]

[The application of this section to any liability shall not be excluded by reason only that the occurrence giving rise to the liability was not due to the negligence of any person.][14]

[Nothing in this section shall apply to any liability in respect of loss of life or personal injury caused to, or loss of or damage to any property or infringement of any right of a person who is on board or employed in connection with the ship under a contract of service with all or any of the persons whose liabilities are limited by that section, if that contract is governed by the law of any country outside the United Kingdom and that law either does not set any limit to that liability or sets a limit exceeding that set to it by that section.][15]

2. For the purposes of this section—

(a) The tonnage of a steam ship shall be her registered tonnage, with the addition of any engine room space deducted for the purpose of ascertaining that tonnage; and the tonnage of a sailing ship shall be her registered tonnage[16]:

Provided that there shall not be included in such tonnage any space occupied by seamen or apprentices and appropriated to their use which is certified under the regulations scheduled to this Act with regard thereto.

(b) Where a foreign ship has been or can be measured according to British law, her tonnage, as ascertained by that measurement shall, for the purpose of this section, be deemed to be her tonnage.

(c) Where a foreign ship has not been and cannot be measured according to British law, the surveyor-general of ships in the United Kingdom, or the chief measuring officer of any British possession abroad, shall, on receiving from or by the direction of the court hearing the case, in which the tonnage of the ship is in question, such evidence concerning the dimensions of the ship as it may be practicable to furnish, give a certificate under his hand stating what would in his opinion have been the tonnage of the ship

[11] Cf. Ibid. s.2(5).
[12] Cf. Ibid. s.2(6).
[13] Cf. Ibid. s.2(7).
[14] Cf. Ibid. s.2(3).
[15] Cf. Ibid. s.2(4). Note the effect of Merchant Shipping Act 1979, s.35(1).
[16] As amended by the Merchant Shipping Act 1906, s.69.

336

if she had been duly measured according to British law, and the tonnage so stated in that certificate shall, for the purposes of this section, be deemed to be the tonnage of the ship.

(3) *The limits set by this section to the liabilities mentioned therein shall apply to the aggregate of such liabilities which are incurred on any distinct occasion, and shall so apply in respect of each distinct occasion without regard to any liability incurred on another occasion.*[17]

The persons whose liability in connection with a ship is excluded or limited by Part VIII of the Merchant Shipping Act, 1894, shall include any charterer and any person interested in or in possession of the ship, and, in particular, any manager or operator of the ship.

In relation to a claim arising from the act or omission of any person in his capacity as master or member of the crew or (otherwise than in that capacity) in the course of his employment as a servant of the owners or of any such person as is mentioned in subsection (1) of this section,—

(a) *the persons whose liability is excluded or limited as aforesaid shall also include the master, member of the crew or servant, and, in a case where the master or member of the crew is the servant of a person whose liability would not be excluded or limited apart from this paragraph, the person whose servant he is; and*

(b) *the liability of the master, member of the crew or servant himself shall be excluded or limited as aforesaid notwithstanding his actual fault or privity in that capacity, except in the cases mentioned in paragraph (ii) of section five hundred and two of the said Act of 1894.*[18]

Merchant Shipping Act 1894, s.503

III: The Final Version

[Note: Section 503 is reproduced as amended and paraphrased above in II: The 1958 Version, but with further amendments made by the Merchant Shipping Act 1981 shown in square brackets, by the Merchant Shipping Act 1984 shown in italics and by the Merchant Shipping Act 1979 in italics inside square brackets.]

s.503.—(1) The owners of a ship, British or foreign, shall not, where all or any of the following occurrences take place without their actual fault or privity; (that is to say,)

(a) Where any loss of life or personal injury is caused to any person being carried in the ship;

(b) Where any damage or loss is caused to any goods, merchandise, or other things whatsoever on board the ship;

(c) where any loss of life or personal injury is caused to any person not carried in the ship through the act or omission of any person (whether on board the ship or not) in the navigation or management of the ship or in the loading, carriage or discharge of its cargo or in the embarkation, carriage or disembarkation of its passengers, or through any other act or omission of any person on board the ship;

(d) where any loss or damage is caused to any property (other than any

---

[17] M.S. (Liability of Shipowners and Others) Act 1958, s.8(2).
[18] *Ibid.* s.3.

property mentioned in paragraph (*b*) of this subsection) or any rights are infringed through the act or omission of any person (whether on board the ship or not) in the navigation or management of the ship, or in the loading, carriage or discharge of its cargo or in the embarkation, carriage or disembarkation of its passengers, or through any other act or omission of any person on board the ship;

be liable to damages beyond the following amounts; (that is to say,)

(i) In respect of loss of life or personal injury, either alone or together with such loss, damage or infringement as is mentioned in paragraphs (*b*) and (*d*) of this subsection, an aggregate amount not exceeding an amount equivalent to 206·67 special drawing rights for each ton of their ship's tonnage; and

(ii) In respect of such loss, damage or infringement as is mentioned in paragraphs (*b*) and (*d*) of this subsection, whether there be in addition loss of life or personal injury or not, an aggregate amount not exceeding an amount equivalent to 66·67 special drawing rights for each ton of the ship's tonnage.

[The special drawing rights referred to above are the special drawing rights as defined by the International Monetary Fund, and their equivalent shall be determined on the basis of the value of sterling—

(*a*) if a limitation action is brought, on the date on which the limitation fund is constituted; and

(*b*) in any other case, on the date of the judgment in question.][19]

[(1) The value on a particular day of one special drawing right shall be treated as equal to such a sum in sterling as the International Monetary Fund have fixed as being the equivalent of one special drawing right—

(*a*) for that day; or

(*b*) if no sum has been so fixed for that day, for the last day before that day for which a sum has been so fixed.

(2) A certificate given by or on behalf of the Treasury stating—

(*a*) that a particular sum in sterling has been fixed as aforesaid for a particular day; or

(*b*) that no sum has been so fixed for a particular day and that a particular sum in sterling has been so fixed for a day which is the last day for which a sum has been so fixed before the particular day.

shall be conclusive evidence of those matters for the purposes of subsection (1) above; and a document purporting to be such a certificate shall in any proceedings be received in evidence and, unless the contrary is proved, be deemed to be such a certificate.

(3) The Treasury may charge a reasonable fee for any certificate given in pursuance of subsection (2) above, and any fee received by the Treasury by virtue of this subsection shall be paid into the Consolidated Fund.][20]

For the purposes of subsection (1) of this section where any obligation or liability arises—

(*a*) in connection with the raising, removal or destruction of any ship

[19] Merchant Shipping Act 1981, s.1(3).
[20] Merchant Shipping Act 1981, s.3.

which is sunk, stranded or abandoned or of anything on board such a ship, or

(b) in respect of any damage (however caused) to harbour works, basins or navigable waterways,

the occurrence giving use to the obligations or liability shall be treated as one of the occurrences mentioned in paragraphs (b) and (d) of subsection (1) of this section and the obligation or liability as a liability to damages.

The provisions of sub-paragraph (a) supra, relating to an obligation or liability arising in connection with the raising, removal or destruction of any ship which is sunk, stranded or abandoned or of anything on board such ship shall not come into force until such day as the Minister of Transport may by order made by statutory instrument appoint.

The Minister of Transport may by order make provision for the setting up and management of a fund to be used for the making to harbour or conservancy authorities of payments needed to compensate them for the reduction, in accordance with sub-paragraph (a) supra, of amounts recoverable by them in respect of the obligations and liabilities mentioned in that paragraph, and to be maintained by contributions from such authorities raised and collected by them in respect of vessels in like manner as other sums so raised by them; and any such order may contain such incidental and supplementary provisions as appear to the Minister to be necessary or expedient.

The power to make an order under the preceding paragraph of this section shall include power to vary or revoke any such order by a subsequent order and any such power shall be exercisable by statutory instrument, which shall be subject to annulment in pursuance of a resolution of either House of Parliament.

The application of this section to any liability shall not be excluded by reason only that the occurrence giving rise to the liability was not due to the negligence of any person.

Nothing in this section shall apply to any liability in respect of loss of life or personal injury caused to, or loss of or damage to any property or infringement of any right of a person who is on board or employed in connection with the ship under a contract of service with all or any of the persons whose liabilities are limited by that section, if that contract is governed by the law of any country outside the United Kingdom and that law either does not set any limit to that liability or sets a limit exceeding that set to it by that section.

[*Nothing in section 503 of the Merchant Shipping Act 1894 (which relates to the limitation of liability in certain cases of loss of life, injury or damage) shall apply to any liability in respect of loss of life or personal injury caused to, or loss of or damage to any property of, a person who is on board or employed in connection with the ship in question if—*

(a) *he is so on board or employed under a contract of service governed by the law of any part of the United Kingdom; and*

(b) *the liability arises from an occurrence which took place after the coming into force of this subsection and before the coming into force of the following subsection;*

and in this subsection "ship" has the same meaning as in the said section 503.][21]

[21] This paragraph is Merchant Shiping Act 1979, s.35(1).

(2) *For the purposes of this section the tonnage of a ship shall be ascertained as follows:*

    (a)   *where the register tonnage of the ship has been or can be ascertained in accordance with the tonnage regulations of this Act, the ship's tonnage shall be the register tonnage of the ship as so ascertained but without making any deduction required by those regulations of any tonnage allowance for propelling machinery space;*

    (b)   *where the tonnage of the ship cannot be ascertained in accordance with paragraph (a) above, a surveyor of ships shall, if so directed by the court, certify what, on the evidence specified in the direction, would in his opinion be the tonnage of the ship as ascertained in accordance with that paragraph if the ship could be duly measured for the purpose; and the tonnage stated in his certificate shall be taken to be the tonnage of the ship.*

(3) The limits set by this section to the liabilities mentioned therein shall apply to the aggregate of such liabilities which are incurred on any distinct occasion, and shall so apply in respect of each distinct occasion without regard to any liability incurred on another occasion.

The persons whose liability in connection with a ship is excluded or limited by Part VIII of the Merchant Shipping Act 1894, shall include any charterer and any person interested in or in possession of the ship, and, in particular, any manager or operator of the ship.

In relation to a claim arising from the act or omission of any person in his capacity as master or member of the crew or (otherwise than in that capacity) in the course of his employment as a servant of the owners or of any such person as is mentioned in subsection (1) of this section,—

    (a)   the persons whose liability is excluded or limited as aforesaid shall also include the master, member of the crew or servant, and, in a case where the master or member of the crew is the servant of a person whose liability would not be excluded or limited apart from this paragraph, the person whose servant he is; and

    (b)   the liability of the master, member of the crew or servant himself shall be excluded or limited as aforesaid notwithstanding his actual fault or privity in that capacity, except in the cases mentioned in paragraph (ii) of section five hundred and two of the said Act of 1894.

[Amendments made by the Merchant Shipping (Liability of Shipowners and Others) Act 1958 are in square brackets]

504. Where any liability is alleged to have been incurred by the owner of a British or foreign ship [[22]in respect of any occurrence in respect of which his liability is limited under section five hundred and three of this Act], and several claims are made or apprehended in respect of that liability, then, the owner may apply in England and Ireland to the High Court, or in Scotland to the Court of Session, or in a British possession to any competent court, and that court may determine the amount of the owner's liability and may distribute that amount rateably among the several claimants, and may stay any proceedings pending in any other court in relation to the same matter, and may proceed in such manner and subject to such regulations as to making persons interested parties to the proceedings, and as to the exclusion of any claimants who do not come in

[22] Words substituted by Merchant Shipping (Liability of Shipowners and Others) Act 1958, s.8(3).

within a certain time, and as to requiring security from the owner, and as to payment of any costs, as the court thinks just.

Rules of the Supreme Court, Order 75

[Extracts relevant to Merchant Shipping Acts 1894 to 1971]

ADMIRALTY PROCEEDINGS

Application and interpretation (O.75, r. 1)

(2) In this Order—
"limitation action" means an action by shipowners or other persons under the Merchant Shipping Acts 1894 to 1971 for the limitation of the amount of their liability in connection with a ship or other property;

Limitation action: parties (O.75, r. 37)

37.—(1) In a limitation action the person seeking relief shall be the plaintiff and shall be named in the writ by his name and not described merely as the owner of, or as bearing some other relation to, a particular ship or other property.

(2) The plaintiff must make one of the persons with claims against him in respect of the casualty to which the action relates defendant to the action and may make any or all of the others defendants also.

(3) At least one of the defendants to the action must be named in the writ by his name but the other defendants may be described generally and not named by their names.

(4) The writ must be served on one or more of the defendants who are named by their names therein and need not be served on any other defendant.

(5) In this rule and rules 38, 39 and 40 "name" includes a firm name or the name under which a person carries on his business, and where any person with a claim against the plaintiff in respect of the casualty to which the action relates has described himself for the purposes of his claim merely as the owner of, or as bearing some other relation to, a ship or other property, he may be so described as defendant in the writ and, if so described, shall be deemed for the purposes of the rules aforesaid to have been named in the writ by his name.

Limitation action: summons for decree or directions (O.75, r. 38)

38.—(1) Within 7 days after the acknowledgment of issue or service of the writ by one of the defendants named therein by their names or, if none of them acknowledges issue or service, within 7 days after the time limited for acknowledging service the plaintiff, without serving a statement of claim must take out a summons returnable in chambers before the registrar or district registrar, as the case may be, asking for a decree limiting his liability or, in default of such a decree, for directions as to the further proceedings in the action.

(2) The summons must be supported by an affidavit or affidavits proving—

    (*a*) the plaintiff's case in the action, and

    (*b*) if none of the defendants named in the writ by their names has acknowledged service, service of the writ on at least one of the defendants so named.

(3) The affidavit in support of the summons must state—

    (*a*) the names of all the persons who, to the knowledge of the plaintiff, have claims against him in respect of the casualty to which the action relates, not being defendants to the action who are named in the writ by their names, and

    (*b*) the address of each of those persons, if known to the plaintiff.

(4) The summons and every affidavit in support thereof must, at least 7 clear days before the hearing of the summons, be served on any defendant who has acknowledged issue or service of the writ.

(5) On the hearing of the summons the registrar, if it appears to him that it is not disputed that the plaintiff has a right to limit his liability, shall make a decree limiting the plaintiff's liability and fix the amount to which the liability is to be limited.

(6) On the hearing of the summons the registrar, if it appears to him that any defendant has not sufficient information to enable him to decide whether or not to dispute that the plaintiff has a right to limit his liability, shall give such directions as appear to him to be appropriate for enabling the defendant to obtain such information and shall adjourn the hearing.

(7) If on the hearing or resumed hearing of the summons the registrar does not make a decree limiting the plaintiff's liability, he shall give such directions as to the further proceedings in the action as appear to him to be appropriate including, in particular, a direction requiring the taking out of a summons for directions under Order 25 and, if he gives no such direction, a direction fixing the period within which any notice under Order 38, rule 21, must be served.

(8) Any defendant who, after the registrar has given directions under paragraph (7) ceases to dispute the plaintiff's right to limit his liability must forthwith file a notice to that effect in the registry or district registry, as the case may be, and serve a copy on the plaintiff and on any other defendant who has acknowledged issue or service of the writ.

(9) If every defendant who disputes the plaintiff's right to limit his liability serves a notice on the plaintiff under paragraph (8) the plaintiff may take out a summons returnable in chambers before the registrar or district registrar, as the case may be, asking for a decree limiting his liability; and paragraphs (4) and (5) shall apply to a summons under this paragraph as they apply to a summons under paragraph (1).

Limitation action: proceedings under decree (0.75, r. 39)

39.—(1) Where the only defendants in a limitation action are those named in the writ by their names and all the persons so named have either been served with the writ or acknowledged the issue thereof, any decree in the action limiting the plaintiff's liability (whether made by a registrar or on the trial of the action)—

(a) need not be advertised, but

(b) shall only operate to protect the plaintiff in respect of claims by the persons so named or persons claiming through or under them.

(2) In any case not falling within paragraph (1) any decree in the action limiting the plaintiff's liability (whether made by a registrar or on the trial of the action)—

(a) shall be advertised by the plaintiff in such manner and within such time as may be provided by the decree;

(b) shall fix a time within which persons with claims against the plaintiff in respect of the casualty to which the action relates may file their claims, and, in cases to which rule 40 applies, take out a summons if they think fit, to set the order aside.

(3) The advertisement to be required under paragraph (2)(a) shall, unless for special reasons the registrar or judge thinks fit otherwise to provide, be a single advertisement in each of three newspapers specified in the decree, identifying the action, the casualty and the relation of the plaintiff thereto (whether as owner of a ship involved in the casualty or otherwise as the case may be) stating that the decree has been made and specifying the amounts fixed thereby as the limits of the plaintiff's liability and the time allowed thereby for the filing of claims and the taking out of summonses to set the decree aside.

The plaintiff must within the time fixed under paragraph (2)(b) file in the registry or district registry, as the case may be, a copy of each newspaper in which the advertisement required under paragraph 2(a) appears.

(4) The time allowed under paragraph 2(b) shall, unless for special reasons the registrar or judge thinks fit otherwise to provide, be not less than 2 months from the latest date allowed for the appearance of the advertisements; and after the expiration of the time so allowed, no claim may be filed or summons taken out to set aside the decree except with the leave of the registrar.

(5) Save as aforesaid, any decree limiting the plaintiff's liability (whether made by a registrar or on the trial of the action) may make any such provision as is authorised by section 504 of the Merchant Shipping Act 1894.

Limitation action: proceedings to set aside decree (O.75, r. 40)

40.—(1) Where a decree limiting the plaintiff's liability (whether made by a registrar or on the trial of the action) fixes a time in accordance with rule 39(2) any person with a claim against the plaintiff in respect of the casualty to which the action relates, who—

(a) was not named by his name in the writ as a defendant to the action, or

(b) if so named, neither was served with the writ nor has acknowledged the issue thereof,

may, within that time, after acknowledging issue of the writ, take out a summons returnable in chambers before the registrar or district registrar, as the case may be, asking that the decree be set aside.

(2) The summons must be supported by an affidavit or affidavits showing that the defendant in question has a bona fide claim against the plaintiff in respect of the casualty in question and that he has sufficient

prima facie grounds for the contention that the plaintiff is not entitled to the relief given him by the decree.

(3) The summons and every affidavit in support thereof must, at least 7 clear days before the hearing of the summons, be served on the plaintiff and any defendant who has acknowledged issue or service of the writ.

(4) On the hearing of the summons the registrar, if he is satisfied that the defendant in question has a bona fide claim against the plaintiff and sufficient prima facie grounds for the contention that the plaintiff is not entitled to the relief given him by the decree, shall set the decree aside and give such directions as to the further proceedings in the action as appear to him to be appropriate including, in particular, a direction requiring the taking out of a summons for directions under Order 25.

Merchant Shipping (Liability of Shipowners and Others) Act 1900

[Note: Provisions in italics are those repealed, or to be rendered inoperative, on the coming into force of the Merchant Shipping Act 1979. The provisions in square brackets are paraphrases of the provisions which will then be substituted by the 1979 Act]

2. (1) The owners of any dock or canal, or a harbour authority or a conservancy authority, as defined by the Merchant Shipping Act 1894, shall not, where *without their actual fault or privity* any loss or damage is caused to any vessel or vessels, or to any goods, merchandise, or other things whatsoever on board any vessel or vessels, [unless it is proved that the loss resulted from the personal act or omission of the owners or authority, committed with the intent to cause such loss, or recklessly and with knowledge that such loss would probably result,] be liable to damages beyond an aggregate amount [ascertained by applying the method of calculation specified in paragraph 1(*b*) of Article 6 of the 1976 Limitation Convention read with paragraph 5(1) and (2) of Part II of Schedule 4 to the Merchant Shipping Act 1979 to] *"equivalent to 66·67 special drawing rights"*[23] *for each ton of the tonnage of* the largest registered British ship which, at the time of such loss or damage occurring, is, or within the period of five years previous thereto has been, within the area over which such dock or canal owner, harbour authority, or conservancy authority, performs any duty or exercises any power. A ship shall not be deemed to have been within the area over which a harbour authority or a conservancy authority performs any duty, or exercises any powers, by reason only that it has been built or fitted out within such area, or that it has taken shelter within or passed through such area on a voyage between two places both situate outside that area, or that it has loaded or unloaded mails or passengers within that area.

(2) *For the purpose of this section the tonnage of ships shall be ascertained as provided by section five hundred and three, subsection two, of the Merchant Shipping Act 1894, and the register of any ship shall be sufficient evidence that*

[23] Words and figures in quotation marks substituted by virtue of Merchant Shipping (Liability of Shipowners and Others) Act 1958, s.1(1)(*b*), (2), and the Merchant Shipping Act 1981, s.1(4). See also s.3 of the 1981 Act, *infra.*

the gross tonnage and the deductions therefrom and the registered tonnage are as therein stated.

(3) *Section five hundred and four of the Merchant Shipping Act 1894, shall apply to this section as if the words "owner of a British or foreign ship" included a harbour authority, and a conservancy authority, and the owner of a canal or of a dock.*

[The Limitation Fund shall be constituted and distributed according to Articles 11 and 12 of the 1976 Limitation Convention in Part I of Schedule 4 to the Merchant Shipping Act 1979 and paragraphs 8 and 9 of Part II of that Schedule.]

(4) For the purpose of this section the term "dock" shall include wet docks and basins, tidal docks and basins, locks, cuts, entrances, dry docks, graving docks, gridirons, slips, quays, wharves, piers, stages, landing-places, and jetties.

(5) For the purpose of this section the term "owners of a dock or canal" shall include any person or authority having the control and management of any dock or canal, as the case may be.

(6) Nothing in this section shall impose any liability in respect of any such loss or damage on any such owners or authority in any case where no such liability would have existed if this Act had not passed.

3. The limitation of liability under this Act shall relate to the whole of any losses and damages which may arise upon any one distinct occasion, although such losses and damages may be sustained by more than one person, and shall apply whether the liability arises at common law or under any general or private Act of Parliament, and notwithstanding anything contained in such Act.

Dangerous Vessels Act 1985

Application of Merchant Shipping (Liability of Shipowners and Others) Act 1900

2. Where—

(a) a harbour authority is liable for any loss or damage occurring outside the harbour of that authority in consequence of directions given by a harbour master in purported exercise of his powers under section 1 above,[24] and

(b) the provisions of the Merchant Shipping (Liability of Shipowners and Others) Act 1900 would apply so as to limit that liability if the loss or damage in question had occurred in that harbour;

then, for the purposes of that Act, that loss or damage shall be deemed to have occurred in that harbour.

Merchant Shipping (Liability of Shipowners and Others) Act 1958

[Sections 1–3 have been incorporated into the Merchant Shipping Act 1894, s.503, II: The 1958 Version, above]

[24] These relate to prohibiting the entry to or requiring the removal from, harbour of dangerous vessels.

4.—(1) Part VIII of the Merchant Shipping Act 1894, shall apply to any structure, whether completed or in course of completion, launched and intended for use in navigation as a ship or part of a ship, and the expression "ship" in the said Part VIII and in this Act shall be construed accordingly.

(2) The said Part VIII shall apply to any British ship notwithstanding that it has not yet been registered.

(3) The tonnage of any ship or structure to which the said Part VIII applies by virtue of this section shall, for the purposes of that Part, be ascertained as provided by subsection (2) of section five hundred and three of the said Act of 1894 with regard to foreign ships.

5.—(1) Where a ship or other property is arrested in connection with a claim which appears to the court to be founded on a liability to which a limit is set by section five hundred and three of the Merchant Shipping Act 1894, or security is given to prevent or obtain release from such an arrest, the court may, and in the circumstances mentioned in subsection (3) of this section shall, order the release of the ship, property or security, if the conditions specified in subsection (2) of this section are satisfied; but where the release is ordered the person on whose application it is ordered shall be deemed to have submitted to the jurisdiction of the court to adjudicate on the claim (or, in Scotland, to have prorogated that jurisdiction).

(2) The said conditions are—

(*a*) that security which in the opinion of the court is satisfactory (in this section referred to as "guarantee") has previously been given, whether in the United Kingdom or elsewhere, in respect of the said liability or any other liability incurred on that same occasion and the court is satisfied that, if the claim is established, the amount for which the guarantee was given or such part thereof as corresponds to the claim will be actually available to the claimant; and

(*b*) that either the guarantee is for an amount not less than the said limit or further security is given which, together with the guarantee, is for an amount not less than that limit.

(3) The circumstances mentioned in subsection (1) of this section are that the guarantee was given in a port which, in relation to the claim, is the relevant port (or, as the case may be, a relevant port) and that that port is in a Convention country.

(4) For the purposes of this section—

(*a*) a guarantee given by the giving of security in more than one country shall be deemed to have been given in the country in which security was last given;

(*b*) any question whether the amount of any security is (either by itself or together with any other amount) not less than any limit set by section five hundred and three of the Merchant Shipping Act 1894, shall be decided as at the time at which the security is given;

(*c*) where part only of the amount for which a guarantee was given will be available to a claimant that part shall not be taken to correspond to his claim if any other part may be available to a claimant in respect of a liability to which no limit is set as mentioned in subsection (1) of this section.

(5) In this section—

"Convention country" means any country in respect of which the Convention is in force (including any country to which the Convention extends by virtue of Article 14 thereof);

"relevant port"—

(a) in relation to any claim, means the port where the event giving rise to the claim occurred or, if that event did not occur in a port, the first port of call after the event occurred; and

(b) in relation to a claim for loss of life or personal injury or for damage to cargo, includes the port of disembarkation or discharge.

"the Convention" means the International Convention relating to the Limitation of the Liability of Owners of Seagoing Ships signed in Brussels on the tenth day of October, nineteen hundred and fifty-seven.

(6) If Her Majesty by Order in Council declares that any country specified in the Order is a Convention country within the meaning of this section, the Order shall, while in force, be conclusive evidence that the country is a Convention country; but any Order in Council under this section may be varied or revoked by a subsequent Order in Council.

(7) In the application of this section to Scotland the references to arrest shall be construed as referring to arrestment on the dependence of an action or in rem and for references to release from arrest or to the ordering of such a release there shall be substituted references to the recall of an arrestment.

6.—(1) No judgment or decree for a claim founded on a liability to which a limit is set by section five hundred and three of the Merchant Shipping Act 1894, shall be enforced, except so far as it is for costs (or, in Scotland, expenses), if security for an amount not less than the said limit has been given, whether in the United Kingdom or elsewhere, in respect of the liability or any other liability incurred on the same occasion and the court is of opinion that the security is satisfactory and is satisfied that the amount for which it was given or such part thereof as corresponds to the claim will be actually available to the person in whose favour the judgment or decree was given or made.

(2) For the purposes of this section—

(a) any question whether the amount of any security is not less than any limit set by section five hundred and three of the Merchant Shipping Act 1894, shall be decided as at the time at which the security is given;

(b) where part only of the amount for which security has been given will be available to the person in whose favour the judgment or decree was given or made that part shall not be taken to correspond to his claim if any other part may be available to a claimant in respect of a liability to which no limit is set as mentioned in subsection (1) of this section.

7.—(1) In making any distribution in accordance with section five hundred and four of the Merchant Shipping Act 1894, the court may, if it thinks fit, postpone the distribution of such part of the amount to be distributed as it deems appropriate having regard to any claims that may later be established before a court of any country outside the United Kingdom.

(2) No lien or other right in respect of any ship or property shall affect the proportions in which under the said section five hundred and four any amount is distributed amongst several claimants.

Merchant Shipping (Oil Pollution) Act 1971

[Note: Provisions in italics are those repealed or ceasing to have effect by virtue of the Merchant Shipping Act 1979, s.38 and Sched. 7. Provisions in square brackets are those substituted by the 1979 Act.]

Limitation of liability under s.1

4. (1) Where the owner of a ship incurs a liability[25] under section 1 of this Act by reason of a discharge or escape which occurred without his actual fault or privity—

(a) *section 503 of the Merchant Shipping Act 1894 (limitation of liability) shall not apply in relation to that liability; but*[26]

(b) he may limit that liability in accordance with the provisions of this Act, and if he does so his liability (that is to say, the aggregate of his liabilities under section 1 resulting from the discharge or escape) shall not exceed *2,000 gold francs* [133 special drawing rights][27] for each ton of the ship's tonnage nor (where the tonnage would result in a greater amount) *210 million gold francs* [14 million special drawing rights][27]

(2) For the purposes of this section the tonnage of a ship shall be ascertained as follows:–

(a) if the ship is a British ship (whether registered in the United Kingdom or elsewhere) or a ship to which an Order under section 84 of the Merchant Shipping Act 1894 applies, its tonnage shall be taken to be its registered tonnage increased, where a deduction has been made for engine room space in arriving at that tonnage, by the amount of that deduction;

(b) if the ship is not such a ship as is mentioned in the preceding paragraph and it is possible to ascertain what would be its registered tonnage if it were registered in the United Kingdom, that paragraph shall apply (with the necessary modifications) as if the ship were so registered;

(c) if the ship is not such a ship as is mentioned in paragraph (a) of this subsection and is of a description with respect to which no provision is for the time being made by regulations under section 1 of the Merchant Shipping Act 1965 (tonnage regulations) its tonnage shall be taken to be 40 per cent. of the weight (expressed in tons of 2,240 lbs.) of oil which the ship is capable of carrying;

[25] For oil pollution damage: see Chapter 7, generally.

[26] The repeal of this paragraph will take place when s.503 ceases to have effect. See then Art. 3(b) of the 1976 Limitation Convention and para. 4(1), Sched. 4, Part II, Merchant Shipping Act 1979.

[27] The gold franc references were replaced on the coming into force of the CLC Protocol 1976 (see Appendix A.6, *supra*) on March 8, 1981; Merchant Shipping Act 1979, s.38(1).

(d) if the tonnage of the ship cannot be ascertained in accordance with the preceding paragraphs the Chief Ship Surveyor of the Department of Trade and Industry shall, if so directed by the court, certify what, on the evidence specified in the direction, would in his opinion be the tonnage of the ship if ascertained in accordance with those paragraphs, and the tonnage stated in his certificate shall be taken to be the tonnage of the ship.

(3) For the purposes of this section a gold franc shall be taken to be a unit of sixty-five and a half milligrams of gold of millesimal fineness nine hundred.[27]

4. The Secretary of State may from time to time by order made by statutory instrument specify the amounts which for the purposes of this section are to be taken as equivalent to 2,000 gold francs and 210 million gold francs respectively.[27]

(5) Where the amounts specified by an order under the preceding subsection are varied by a subsequent order the variation shall not affect the limit of any liability under section 1 of this Act if, before the variation comes into force, an amount not less than that limit (ascertained in accordance with the order then in force) has been paid into court (or, in Scotland, consigned in court) in proceedings for the limitation of that liability in accordance with this Act.[27]

Limitation actions

5.—(1) Where the owner of a ship has or is alleged to have incurred a liability under section 1 of this Act he may apply to the court for the limitation of that liability to an amount determined in accordance with section 4 of this Act.

(2) If on such an application the court finds that the applicant has incurred such a liability and is entitled to limit it, the court shall, after determining the limit of the liability and directing payment into court of the amount of that limit,—

(a) determine the amounts that would, apart from the limit, be due in respect of the liability to the several persons making claims in the proceedings; and

(b) direct the distribution of the amount paid into court (or, as the case may be, so much of it as does not exceed the liability) among those persons in proportion to their claims, subject to the following provisions of this section.

(3) No claim shall be admitted in proceedings under this section unless it is made within such time as the court may direct or such further time as the court may allow.

(4) Where any sum has been paid in or towards satisfaction of any claim in respect of the damage or cost to which the liability extends,—

(a) by the owner or the person referred to in section 12 of this Act as "the insurer"; or

(b) by a person who has or is alleged to have incurred a liability, otherwise than under section 1 of this Act, for the damage or cost

---

[27] The gold franc references were replaced on the coming into force of the CLC Protocol 1976 (see Appendix A.6, *supra*) on March 8, 1981; Merchant Shipping Act 1979, s.38(1).

and who is entitled to limit his liability in connection with the ship by virtue of *the Merchant Shipping (Liability of Shipowners and Others) Act 1958*[28] [the Merchant Shipping Act 1979];

the person who paid the sum shall, to the extent of that sum, be in the same position with respect to any distribution made in proceedings under this section as the person to whom it was paid would have been.

(5) Where the person who incurred the liability has voluntarily made any reasonable sacrifice or taken any other reasonable measures to prevent or reduce damage to which the liability extends or might have extended he shall be in the same position with respect to any distribution made in proceedings under this section as if he had a claim in respect of the liability equal to the cost of the sacrifice or other measures.

(6) The court may, if it thinks fit, postpone the distribution of such part of the amount to be distributed as it deems appropriate having regard to any claims that may later be established before a court of any country outside the United Kingdom.

Restriction on enforcement of claims after establishment of limitation fund

6.—(1) Where the court has found that a person who has incurred a liability under section 1 of this Act is entitled to limit that liability to any amount and he has paid into court a sum not less than that amount—

(a) the court shall order the release of any ship or other property arrested in connection with a claim in respect of that liability or any security given to prevent or obtain release from such an arrest; and

(b) no judgment or decree for any such claim shall be enforced, except so far as it is for costs (or, in Scotland, expenses);

if the sum paid into court, or such part thereof as corresponds to the claim, will be actually available to the claimant or would have been available to him if the proper steps in the proceedings under section 5 of this Act had been taken.

(2) In the application of this section to Scotland, any reference (however expressed) to release from arrest shall be construed as a reference to the recall of an arrestment.

Concurrent liabilities of owners and others

7. Where, as a result of any discharge or escape of persistent oil from a ship, the owner of the ship incurs a liability under section 1 of the Act, and any other person incurs a liability, otherwise than under that section, for any such damage or cost as is mentioned in subsection (1) of that section, then, if—

(a) the owner has been found, in proceedings under section 5 of this Act, to be entitled to limit his liability to any amount and has paid into court a sum not less than that amount; and

(b) the other person is entitled to limit his liability in connection with

---

[28] Words in italics will be substituted by those in square brackets on the coming into force of the 1976 Limitation Convention; Merchant Shipping Act 1979, Sched. 5.

the ship by virtue of *the Merchant Shipping (Liability of Shipowners and Others) Act 1958*[29] [the Merchant Shipping Act 1979];
no proceedings shall be taken against the other person in respect of his liability, and if any such proceedings were commenced before the owner paid the sum into court, no further steps shall be taken in the proceedings except in relation to costs.

Establishment of limitation fund outside United Kingdom

8. Where the events resulting in the liability of any person under subsection 1 of this Act also resulted in a corresponding liability under the law of another Convention country sections 6 and 7 of this Act shall apply as if the references to sections 1 and 5 of this Act included references to the corresponding provisions of that law and the references to sums paid into court included references to any sums secured under those provisions in respect of the liability.

8A.[30]*—(1) Sections 4 to 8 of this Act shall not apply to a ship which at the time of the discharge or escape was registered in a country—*

(a) which was not a Convention country, and

(b) which was a country in respect of which the 1957 Convention was in force.

(2) In this section "the 1957 Convention" means the International Convention relating to the Limitation of the Liability of Owners of Seagoing Ships signed in Brussels on October 10, 1957.

(3) If Her Majesty by Order in Council declares that any country—

(a) is not a Convention country within the meaning of this Act, and

(b) is a country in respect of which the 1957 Convention is in force,

or that it was such a country at a time specified in the Order, the Order shall, while in force, be conclusive evidence of the facts stated in the Order.

Liability for cost of preventive measures where s.1 does not apply

15.—(1) Where,—

(a) after an escape or discharge of persistent oil from a ship, measures are reasonably taken for the purpose of preventing or reducing damage in the area of the United Kingdom which may be caused by contamination resulting from the discharge or escape; and

(b) any person incurs, or might but for the measures have incurred, a liability, otherwise than under section 1 of this Act, for any such damage;

then, notwithstanding that subsection (1)(b) of that section does not apply, he shall be liable for the cost of the measures, whether or not the person taking them does so for the protection of his interests or in the performance of a duty.

(2) For the purposes of section 503 of the Merchant Shipping Act 1894 (limitation of liability) any liability incurred under this section shall be deemed to be a liability to damages in respect of such loss, damage or infringement as is mentioned in subsection (1)(d) of that section. (s.15(2) will be substituted by

[29] *Ibid.*

[30] Inserted by the Merchant Shipping Act 1974, s.9: repeal will coincide with the introduction of the 1976 Limitation Convention.

the following subsection on the coming into force of the 1976 Limitation Convention: Merchant Shipping Act 1979, Sched. 5.)

[(2) For the purposes of section 17 of the Merchant Shipping Act 1979 (limitation of liability) any liability incurred under this section shall be deemed to be a liability in respect of such damage to property as is mentioned in paragraph 1(*a*) of article 2 of the Convention in Part I of Schedule 4 to that Act.]

[(2A) (s.2A inserted by the Merchant Shipping Act 1979, s.38(2).) A payment into court of the amount of a limit determined in pursuance of this section shall be made in sterling; and—

(*a*) for the purpose of converting such an amount from special drawing rights into sterling one special drawing right shall be treated as equal to such a sum in sterling as the International Monetary Fund have fixed as being the equivalent of one special drawing right for—

  (i) the day on which the determination is made, or
  (ii) if no sum has been so fixed for that day, the last day before that day for which a sum has been so fixed;

(*b*) a certificate given by or on behalf of the Treasury stating—

  (i) that a particular sum in sterling has been so fixed for the day on which the determination was made, or
  (ii) that no sum has been so fixed for that day and that a particular sum in sterling has been so fixed for a day which is the last day for which a sum has been so fixed before the day on which the determination was made,

shall be conclusive evidence of those matters for the purposes of this Act;

(*c*) a document purporting to be such a certificate shall, in any proceedings, be received in evidence and, unless the contrary is proved, be deemed to be such a certificate.]

Merchant Shipping Act 1974

[The provisions in italics will be repealed by the Merchant Shipping Act 1979, s.38(4) on the coming into force of the Fund Protocol 1976 (see Appendix A.9, *supra*) and replaced by the provisions in square brackets.]

Part I—The International Oil Pollution Compensation Fund

Interpretation of Part 1

1.—(4) For the purposes of this Part of this Act a ship's tonnage shall be the net tonnage of the ship with the addition of the amount deducted from the gross tonnage on account of engine room space for the purpose of ascertaining the net tonnage.

If the ship cannot be measured in accordance with the normal rules, its tonnage shall be deemed to be 40 per cent. of the weight in tons (of 2240 lbs.) of oil which the ship is capable of carrying.

(5) For the purposes of this Part of this Act, where more than one discharge or escape results from the same occurrence or from a series of occurrences having the same origin, they shall be treated as one.

(6) In this Part of this Act a franc shall be taken to be a unit of 65½ milligrammes of gold of millesimal fineness 900.

(7) The Secretary of State may from time to time by order made by statutory instrument specify the amounts which for the purposes of this Part of this Act are to be taken as equivalent to any specified number of francs.

Liability of the Fund

4.—(10) The Fund's liability under this section shall be subject to the limits imposed by paragraphs 4, 5 and 6 of Article 4 of the Fund Convention which impose an overall liability on the liabilities of the owner and of the Fund, and the text of which is set out in Schedule 1 to this Act.

(12) For the purpose of giving effect to the said provisions of Article 4 of the Fund Convention a court giving judgment against the Fund in proceedings under this section shall notify the Fund, and—

(a) no steps shall be taken to enforce the judgment unless and until the court gives leave to enforce it,

(b) that leave shall not be given unless and until the Fund notifies the court either that the amount of the claim is not to be reduced under the said provisions of Article 4 of the Fund Convention, or that it is to be reduced to a specified amount, and

(c) in the latter case the judgment shall be enforceable only for the reduced amount.

[(13) Any steps taken to obtain payment of an amount or a reduced amount in pursuance of such a judgment as is mentioned in subsection (12) above shall be steps to obtain payment in sterling; and—

(a) for the purpose of converting such an amount from special drawing rights into sterling one special drawing right shall be treated as equal to a such a sum in sterling as the International Monetary Fund have fixed as being the equivalent of one special drawing right for—

(i) the day on which the judgment is given, or

(ii) if no sum has been so fixed for that day, the last day before that day for which a sum has been so fixed;

(b) a certificate given by or on behalf of the Treasury stating—

(i) that a particular sum in sterling has been so fixed for the day on which the judgment was given, or

(ii) that no sum has been so fixed for that day and that a particular sum in sterling has been so fixed for a day which is the last day for which a sum has been so fixed before the day on which the judgment was given,

shall be conclusive evidence of those matters for the purposes of this Act;

(c) a document purporting to be such a certificate shall, in any proceedings, be received in evidence and, unless the contrary is proved, be deemed to be such a certificate.

SCHEDULE 1

OVERALL LIMIT ON LIABILITY OF FUND

Article 4—paragraphs 4, 5 and 6

4. (*a*) Except as otherwise provided in sub-paragraph (b) of this paragraph the aggregate amount of compensation payable by the Fund under this Article shall in respect of any one incident be limited, so that the total sum of that amount and the amount of compensation actually paid under the Liability Convention for pollution damage caused in the territory of the Contracting States, including any sums in respect of which the Fund is under an obligation to indemnify the owner pursuant to Article 5, paragraph 1, of this Convention, shall not exceed *450 million francs*. [30 million special drawing rights].

(*b*) the aggregate amount of compensation payable by the Fund under this Article for pollution damage resulting from a natural phenomenon of an exceptional, inevitable and irresistible character shall not exceed *450 million francs*. [30 million special drawing rights].

5. Where the amount of established claims against the Fund exceeds the aggregate amount of compensation payable under paragraph 4, the amount available shall be distributed in such a manner that the proportion between any established claim and the amount of compensation actually recovered by the claimant under the Liability Convention and this Convention shall be the same for all claimants.

6. The Assembly of the Fund (hereinafter referred to as "the Assembly") may, having regard to the experience of incidents which have occurred and in particular the amount of damage resulting therefrom and to changes in the monetary values, decide that the amount of *450 million francs* [30 million special drawing rights] referred to in paragraph 4, sub-paragraph (a) and (b), shall be changed; provided, however, that this amount shall in no case exceed *900 million francs* [60 million special drawing rights] or be lower than *450 million francs* [30 million special drawing rights]. The changed amount shall apply to incidents which occur after the date of the decision effecting the change. (The amount has been increased to 675 million gold francs).

Nuclear Installations Act 1965, s.14

14. Protection for ships and aircraft. (1) A claim under this Act in respect of any occurrence such as is mentioned in section 7(2)(b) or (c), 10 or 11 of this Act which constitutes a breach of a person's duty under section 7, 8, 9, 10 or 11 of this Act shall not give rise to any lien or other right in respect of any ship or aircraft; and section 503 of the Merchant Shipping Act 1894 (which relates to the limitation of the liability of shipowners) shall not apply to that claim. *(Provisions in italics will be repealed by the Merchant Shipping Act 1979, Sched. 7, on the coming into force of the 1976 Limitation Convention: see Art. 3(c) and para. 4(2), Sched. 4, Part II, the Merchant Shipping Act 1979.)*

(2) Subsection (1) of this section shall have effect in relation to any claim notwithstanding that by reason of section 16 of this Act no payment for the time being falls to be made in satisfaction of the claim.

Hovercraft Act 1968

[Note: Provisions in italics are those to be repealed and replaced by those in square brackets by virtue of the Merchant Shipping Act 1979, Sched. 5]

Power to make Orders in Council with respect to hovercraft.

1. (1) Her Majesty may by Order in Council make such provision as she considers expedient—
   (i) For applying the following enactments, and any instrument made under them, in relation to the following matters respectively, that is . . . to say—
   (ii) in relation to the carriage of property by hovercraft (except baggage (See the Carriage by Air Act 1961, Carriage by Air (Supplementary Provisions) Act 1962, Carriage of Goods by Air and Road Act 1979.) . . .), . . . *Part VIII of the Merchant Shipping Act 1894* [Sections 17 and 18 of the Merchant Shipping Act 1979] so far as *that Part* [those sections] relates to property on board ship,
   (iii) in relation to loss of life or personal injury connected with a hovercraft which is caused to persons not carried by the hovercraft, in relation to loss or damage connected with a hovercraft which is caused to property not carried by the hovercraft and in relation to infringements of rights through acts or omissions connected with a hovercraft, *the said Part VIII* [the said sections of the Merchant Shipping Act 1979]

The Hovercraft (Civil Liability) Order 1986 (S.I. 1986, No. 1305) was made on July 25, 1986 and will come into operation on December 1, 1986

Merchant Shipping Act 1983

s.9 (2) For the purposes of section 503 of the 1894 Act and section 4 of the Merchant Shipping (Oil Pollution) Act 1971 (limitation of owner's liability by reference to tonnage), the tonnage of a registered ship measured for length or a ship registered under section 5 of this Act is her register tonnage ascertained in accordance with the tonnage regulations of the 1894 Act, but without making any deduction required by those regulations of any tonnage allowance for propelling machinery space.

(3) If the tonnage referred to in subsection (2) above cannot be so ascertained, a surveyor of ships shall, if so directed by the court, certify what on the evidence specified in the direction would in his opinion be that tonnage as so ascertained, and the tonnage stated in his certificate shall be taken for the purposes referred to in that subsection to be the tonnage of the ship.

42.—(1) A licensed pilot, a person authorised to act as the assistant of a licensed pilot by the authority who licensed the pilot and the pilotage authority who employ a licensed pilot or such an assistant shall not be liable—

(a) in the case of a pilot or assistant, for neglect or want of skill; and

(b) in the case of a pilotage authority, for neglect or want of skill by the pilot or assistant or by the authority in employing the pilot or assistant,

beyond the amount of £100 and the amount of the pilotage charges in respect of the voyage during which the liability arose.

(2) Where any proceedings are taken against a pilot, assistant or pilotage authority for any neglect or want of skill in respect of which liability is limited as provided by this section, and other claims are made or apprehended in respect of the same neglect or want of skill, the court in which the proceedings are taken may—

(a) determine the amount of the liability,

(b) upon payment by the pilot, assistant or pilotage authority of that amount into court, distribute that amount rateably among the several claimants,

(c) stay or, in Scotland, sist any proceedings pending in any other court in relation to the same matter,

(d) proceed in such manner and subject to such requirements—

    (i) as to making persons interested parties to the proceedings,

    (ii) as to the exclusion of any claimants who do not come in within a certain time,

    (iii) as to requiring security from the pilot, assistant or pilotage authority,

    (iv) as to payment of any costs,

as the court thinks just.

Limitation of liability

55.—(1) Where, without any such personal act or omission of theirs as is mentioned in Article 4 of the Convention in Part I of Schedule 4 to the Merchant Shipping Act 1979, any loss or damage is caused—

(a) to any vessel or vessels, or

(b) to any goods, merchandise or other things whatsoever on board any vessel or vessels, or

(c) to any other property or rights of any kind, whether on land or on water or whether fixed or movable,

a pilotage authority shall not be liable to damages beyond the amount of £100 multiplied by the number of pilots holding licences from the pilotage authority under section 12 of this Act for the pilotage district of the pilotage authority at the date when the loss or damage occurs.

(2) The limit of liability under subsection (1) above shall apply whether the liability arises at common law or under any public general or local Act of Parliament and notwithstanding anything contained in any such Act passed before July 16, 1936 (the date of the passing of the Pilotage Authorities (Limitation of Liability) Act 1936).

(3) Nothing in this section shall impose any liability in respect of any such loss or damage on any pilotage authority in any case where no such liability would have existed if this Part of this Act had not been enacted.

(4) Until such day as the Secretary of State may by order appoint, subsection (1) above shall have effect in the United Kingdom as if for the words from "any such" to "1979" there were substituted the words "their fault or privity".

56. The limit of liability under section 55 of this Act shall relate to the whole of any losses and damages which may arise upon any one distinct occasion although such losses and damages may be sustained by more than one person.

57.—(1) Where any liability is alleged to have been incurred by a pilotage authority in respect of any loss or damage to which section 55 of this Act applies and several claims are made or apprehended in respect of that liability, then the pilotage authority may apply to the court.

(2) On an application under subsection (1) above, the court may—

(a) determine the amount of liability of the pilotage authority,

(b) distribute that amount rateably among the several claimants,

(c) stay or, in Scotland, sist any proceedings pending in any other court in relation to the same matter,

(d) proceed in such manner and subject to such requirements—
    (i) as to making persons interested parties to the proceedings,
    (ii) as to the exclusion of any claimants who do not come in within a certain time,
    (iii) as to requiring security from the pilotage authority,
    (iv) as to the payment of any costs,
as the court thinks just.

(3) In this section, "the court" means—

(a) in England and Wales, the High Court,

(b) in Scotland, the Court of Session,

(c) in Northern Ireland, the High Court.

58.—(1) Where any pilotage authority are the owners of any ship, nothing in this Part of this Act shall affect any limitation of liability conferred on them or other rights to which they are entitled as such owners under section 17 or 18 of the Merchant Shipping Act 1979, and accordingly the foregoing provisions of this Part of this Act shall not apply to any loss or damage the liability of which can be limited under the said sections.

(2) Until such day as the Secretary of State may by order appoint, subsection (1) above has effect in the United Kingdom as if—

(a) for the words "under section 17 or 18 of the Merchant Shipping Act 1979" there were substituted the words "by or under Part VIII of the Merchant Shipping Act 1894, and the Merchant Shipping (Liability of Shipowners and Others) Act 1900",

(b) for the word "sections" there were substituted the word "enactments".

An order under this subsection may appoint different days for different purposes.

Appendix C

Merchant Shipping Act 1979 (Extracts)

[Note: the 1979 Act contains the provisions to enact the 1976 Limitation Convention into English law (see Chapter 18, *supra*). Although the 1979 Act incorporates the Convention in Schedule 4, Pt. I, it should be noted that this part of the Schedule only contains those parts of the Schedule directly relevant to British law. This has meant omitting some parts of the Convention. Articles 6(3), 8, 10(1), 12(1), 15 and 16–23 of the Convention (the full text of which is reproduced in Appendix A4, *supra*) may be contrasted with the text of Schedule 4, Pt. I. Schedule 4, Pt. II contains the special provisions of British law necessary to give full effect to the Convention: accordingly, Pt. I must be read subject to Pt. II.]

Liability of shipowners and salvors

17.—(1) The provisions of the Convention on Limitation of Liability for Maritime Claims 1976 as set out in Part I of Schedule 4 to this Act (hereafter in this section and in Part II of that Schedule referred to as "the Convention") shall have the force of law in the United Kingdom.

(2) The provisions of Part II of that Schedule shall have effect in connection with the Convention, and the preceding subsection shall have effect subject to the provisions of that Part.

18.—(1) Subject to subsection (3) of this section, the owner of a British ship shall not be liable for any loss or damage in the following cases, namely—

   (a) where any property on board the ship is lost or damaged by reason of fire on board the ship; or

   (b) where any gold, silver, watches, jewels or precious stones on board the ship are lost or damaged by reason of theft, robbery or other dishonest conduct and their nature and value were not at the time of shipment declared by their owner or shipper to the owner or master of the ship in the bill of lading or otherwise in writing.

(2) Subject to subsection (3) of this section, where the loss or damage arises from anything done or omitted by any person in his capacity as master or member of the crew or (otherwise than in that capacity) in the course of his employment as a servant of the owner of the ship, the preceding subsection shall also exclude the liability of—

   (a) the master, member of the crew or servant; and

   (b) in a case where the master or member of the crew is the servant of a person whose liability would not be excluded by that subsection apart from this paragraph, the person whose servant he is.

(3) This section does not exclude the liability of any person for any loss or damage resulting from any such personal act or omission of his as is

mentioned in article 4 of the Convention in Part I of Schedule 4 to this Act.

(4) In this section "owner", in relation to a ship, includes any part owner and any charterer, manager or operator of the ship.[1]

19.—(1) The enactments mentioned in Schedule 5 to this Act shall have effect with the amendments there specified (which are consequential on sections 17 and 18 of this Act).

(2) Her Majesty may by Order in Council provide that the said sections 17 and 18, the preceding subsection and Schedules 4 and 5 to this Act shall extend, with such modifications, if any, as are specified in the Order, to any of the following countries, namely—

    (a)   the Isle of Man;

    (b)   any of the Channel Islands;

    (c)   any colony;

    (d)   any country outside Her Majesty's dominions in which Her Majesty has jurisdiction in right of the government of the United Kingdom.

(3) Any statutory instrument made by virtue of the preceding subsection shall be subject to annulment in pursuance of a resolution of either House of Parliament.

(4) Nothing in the said sections 17 and 18 or the said Schedule 4 shall apply in relation to any liability arising out of an occurrence which took place before the coming into force of those sections, and subsection (1) of this section and Schedule 5 to this Act shall not affect the operation of any enactment in relation to such an occurrence.

Amendment of s.503 of Merchant Shipping Act 1894 etc.

35.—(1) s.35(1) related to s.503 and is reproduced earlier in this Appendix in the Merchant Shipping Act 1894, III The Final Version.

(2) The provisions having the force of law under section 17 of this Act shall not apply to any liability in respect of loss of life or personal injury caused to, or loss of or damage to any property of, a person who is on board the ship in question or employed in connection with that ship or with the salvage operations in question if—

    (a)   he is so on board or employed under a contract of service governed by the law of any part of the United Kingdom; and

    (b)   the liability arises from an occurrence which took place after the coming into force of this subsection;

and in this subsection "ship" and "salvage operations" have the same meaning as in those provisions.

Application of Merchant Shipping Acts to certain structures etc.

41.—(1) The Secretary of State may by order provide that a thing designed or adapted for use at sea and described in the order is or is not to be treated as a ship for the purposes of any provision specified in the order of the Merchant Shipping Acts or the Prevention of Oil Pollution Act 1971 or an instrument made by virtue of any of those Acts; and such an order may—

    (a)   make different provision in relation to different occasions;

[1] s.18 replaces the old Merchant Shipping Act 1894, s.502 in the same way that s.17 and Sched. 4 replaces s.503.

(b) if it provides that a thing is to be treated as a ship for the purposes of a provision specified in the order, provide that the provision shall have effect in relation to the thing with such modifications as are so specified.

(2) Where the Secretary of State proposes to make an order in pursuance of the preceding subsection it shall be his duty, before he makes the order, to consult such persons about the proposal as appear to him to represent the persons in the United Kingdom who he considers are likely to be affected by the order.

48.—The enactments and instruments with respect to which provision may be made by Order in Council in pursuance of section 1(1)(h) of the Hovercraft Act 1968 shall include this Act and any instrument made under it.

49.—(1) Any power to make an order or regulations conferred on the Secretary of State by this Act shall be exercisable by statutory instrument.

(2) Section 738 of the Merchant Shipping Act 1894 (which among other things provides for the publication in the London Gazette, the laying before Parliament and the alteration and revocation of Orders in Council made under that Act or any Act amending that Act) shall not apply to an Order in Council made under this Act.

(4) Any statutory instrument containing an order made by virtue of ... paragraph 3 ... or 5 of Part II of Schedule 4 to this Act ... shall be subject to annulment in pursuance of a resolution by either House of Parliament.

(5) Any statutory instrument containing an order made by virtue of paragraph 8(1) of Part II of Schedule 4 to this Act shall be laid before Parliament after being made.

SCHEDULE 3

CONVENTION RELATING TO THE CARRIAGE OF PASSENGERS AND THEIR LUGGAGE BY SEA[2]

PART I—TEXT OF CONVENTION

ARTICLE 19

Other conventions on limitation of liability

This Convention shall not modify the rights or duties of the carrier, the performing carrier, and their servants or agents provided for in international conventions relating to the limitation of liability of owners of seagoing ships.

---

[2] This Convention will be enacted fully when ss.14, 15 are brought into force. s.16 has given effect to the Convention domestically since 1981 (see Chapter 3, *supra*). Only the parts relevant to global limitation are reproduced here.

Interpretation

1. In this Part of this Schedule any reference to a numbered article is a reference to the article of the Convention which is so numbered and any expression to which a meaning is assigned by article 1 of the Convention has that meaning.

Application of ss.502 and 503 of Merchant Shipping Act 1894 and section 17 and 18 of this Act

12. Nothing in section 502 of the Merchant Shipping Act 1894 or section 18 of this Act (which among other things limit a shipowner's liability for the loss or damage of goods in certain cases) shall relieve a person of any liability imposed on him by the Convention.

13. It is hereby declared that nothing in the Convention affects the operation of section 503 of the Merchant Shipping Act 1894 or section 17 of this Act (which limit a shipowner's liability in certain cases of loss of life, injury or damage).

SCHEDULE 4

CONVENTION ON LIMITATION OF LIABILITY FOR MARITIME CLAIMS 1976

PART I—TEXT OF CONVENTION

CHAPTER I. THE RIGHT OF LIMITATION

ARTICLE I

Persons entitled to limit liability

1. Shipowners and salvors, as hereinafter defined, may limit their liability in accordance with the rules of this Convention for claims set out in Article 2.

2. The term "shipowner" shall mean the owner, charterer, manager or operator of a seagoing ship.

3. Salvor shall mean any person rendering services in direct connexion with salvage operations. Salvage operations shall also include operations referred to in Article 2, paragraph 1(*d*), (*e*) and (*f*).

4. If any claims set out in Article 2 are made against any person for whose act, neglect or default the shipowner or salvor is responsible, such person shall be entitled to avail himself of the limitation of liability provided for in this Convention.

5. In this Convention the liability of a shipowner shall include liability in an action brought against the vessel herself.

6. An insurer of liability for claims subject to limitation in accordance

with the rules of this Convention shall be entitled to the benefits of this Convention to the same extent as the assured himself.

7. The act of invoking limitation of liability shall not constitute an admission of liability.

ARTICLE 2

Claims subject to limitation

1. Subject to Articles 3 and 4 the following claims, whatever the basis of liability may be, shall be subject to limitation of liability;

(a) claims in respect of loss of life or personal injury or loss of or damage to property (including damage to harbour works, basins and waterways and aids to navigation), occurring on board or in direct connexion with the operation of the ship or with salvage operations, and consequential loss resulting therefrom;

(b) claims in respect of loss resulting from delay in the carriage by sea of cargo, passengers or their luggage;

(c) claims in respect of other loss resulting from infringement of rights other than contractual rights, occurring in direct connexion with the operation of the ship or salvage operations;

(d) claims in respect of the raising, removal, destruction or the rendering harmless of a ship which is sunk, wrecked, stranded or abandoned, including anything that is or has been on board such ship;

(e) claims in respect of the removal, destruction or the rendering harmless of the cargo of the ship;

(f) claims of a person other than the person liable in respect of measures taken in order to avert or minimize loss for which the person liable may limit his liability in accordance with this Convention, and further loss caused by such measures.

2. Claims set out in paragraph 1 shall be subject to limitation of liability even if brought by way of recourse or for indemnity under a contract or otherwise. However, claims set out under paragraph 1(d), (e) and (f) shall not be subject to limitation of liability to the extent that they relate to remuneration under a contract with the person liable.

ARTICLE 3

Claims excepted from limitation

The rules of this Convention shall not apply to:

(a) claims for salvage or contribution in general average;

(b) claims for oil pollution damage within the meaning of the International Convention on Civil Liability for Oil Pollution Damage dated November 29, 1969 or of any amendment or Protocol thereto which is in force;

(c) claims subject to any international convention or national legislation governing or prohibiting limitation of liability for nuclear damage;

363

(d) claims against the shipowner of a nuclear ship for nuclear damage;

(e) claims by servants of the shipowner or salvor whose duties are connected with the ship or the salvage operations, including claims of their heirs, dependants or other persons entitled to make such claims, if under the law governing the contract of service between the shipowner or salvor and such servants the shipowner or salvor is not entitled to limit his liability in respect of such claims, or if he is by such law only permitted to limit his liability to an amount greater than that provided for in Article 6.

ARTICLE 4

Conduct barring limitation

A person liable shall not be entitled to limit his liability if it is proved that the loss resulted from his personal act or omission, committed with the intent to cause such loss, or recklessly and with knowledge that such loss would probably result.

ARTICLE 5

Counterclaims

Where a person entitled to limitation of liability under the rules of this Convention has a claim against the claimant arising out of the same occurrence, their respective claims shall be set off against each other and the provisions of this Convention shall only apply to the balance, if any.

CHAPTER II. LIMITS OF LIABILITY

ARTICLE 6

The general limits

1. The limits of liability for claims other than those mentioned in Article 7, arising on any distinct occasion, shall be calculated as follows:

(a) in respect of claims for loss of life or personal injury,

    (i) 333,000 Units of Account for a ship with a tonnage not exceeding 500 tons,

    (ii) for a ship with a tonnage in excess thereof, the following amount in addition to that mentioned in (i):

for each ton from 501 to 3,000 tons, 500 Units of Account;

for each ton from 3,001 to 30,000 tons, 333 Units of Account;

for each ton from 30,001 to 70,000 tons, 250 Units of Account, and

for each ton in excess of 70,000 tons, 167 Units of Account,

(b) in respect of any other claims,

    (i) 167,000 Units of Account for a ship with a tonnage not exceeding 500 tons,

(ii) for a ship with a tonnage in excess thereof the following amount in addition to that mentioned in (i):

for each ton from 501 to 30,000 tons, 167 Units of Account;

for each ton from 30,001 to 70,000 tons, 125 Units of Account; and

for each ton in excess of 70,000 tons, 83 Units of Account.

2. Where the amount calculated in accordance with paragraph 1(a) is insufficient to pay the claims mentioned therein in full, the amount calculated in accordance with paragraph 1(b) shall be available for payment of the unpaid balance of claims under paragraph 1(a) and such unpaid balance shall rank rateably with claims mentioned under paragraph 1(b).

4. The limits of liability for any salvor not operating from any ship or for any salvor operating solely on the ship to, or in respect of which he is rendering salvage services, shall be calculated according to a tonnage of 1,500 tons.

ARTICLE 7

The limit for passenger claims

1. In respect of claims arising on any distinct occasion for loss of life or personal injury to passengers of a ship, the limit of liability of the shipowner thereof shall be an amount of 46,666 Units of Account multiplied by the number of passengers which the ship is authorised to carry according to the ship's certificate, but not exceeding 25 million Units of Account.

2. For the purpose of this Article "claims for loss of life or personal injury to passengers of a ship" shall mean any such claims brought by or on behalf of any person carried in that ship:

(a) under a contract of passenger carriage, or
(b) who, with the consent of the carrier, is accompanying a vehicle or live animals which are covered by a contract for the carriage of goods.

ARTICLE 8

Unit of Account

1. The Unit of Account referred to in Articles 6 and 7 is the Special Drawing Right as defined by the International Monetary Fund. The amounts mentioned in Articles 6 and 7 shall be converted into the national currency of the State in which limitation is sought, according to the value of that currency at the date the limitation fund shall have been constituted, payment is made, or security is given which under the law of that State is equivalent to such payment.

Aggregation of claims

1. The limits of liability determined in accordance with Article 6 shall apply to the aggregate of all claims which arise on any distinct occasion:
   (a) against the person or persons mentioned in paragraph 2 of Article 1 and any person for whose act, neglect or default he or they are responsible; or
   (b) against the shipowner of a ship rendering salvage services from that ship and the salvor or salvors operating from such ship and any person for whose act, neglect or default he or they are responsible; or
   (c) against the salvor or salvors who are not operating from a ship or who are operating solely on the ship to, or in respect of which, the salvage services are rendered and any person for whose act, neglect or default he or they are responsible.

2. The limits of liability determined in accordance with Article 7 shall apply to the aggregate of all claims subject thereto which may arise on any distinct occasion against the person or persons mentioned in paragraph 2 of Article 1 in respect of the ship referred to in Article 7 and any person for whose act, neglect or default he or they are responsible.

ARTICLE 10

Limitation of liability without constitution of a limitation fund

1. Limitation of liability may be invoked notwithstanding that a limitation fund as mentioned in Article 11 has not been constituted.

2. If limitation of liability is invoked without the constitution of a limitation fund, the provisions of Article 12 shall apply correspondingly.

3. Questions of procedure arising under the rules of this Article shall be decided in accordance with the national law of the State Party in which action is brought.

CHAPTER III. THE LIMITATION FUND

ARTICLE 11

Constitution of the fund

1. Any person alleged to be liable may constitute a fund with the Court or other competent authority in any State Party in which legal proceedings are instituted in respect of claims subject to limitation. The fund shall be constituted in the sum of such of the amounts set out in Articles 6 and 7 as are applicable to claims for which that person may be liable, together with interest thereon from the date of the occurrence giving rise to the liability until the date of the constitution of the fund. Any fund thus constituted shall be available only for the payment of claims in respect of which limitation of liability can be invoked.

2. A fund may be constituted, either by depositing the sum, or by producing a guarantee acceptable under the legislation of the State Party where the fund is constituted and considered to be adequate by the Court or other competent authority.

3. A fund constituted by one of the persons mentioned in paragraph 1(*a*), (*b*) or (*c*) or paragraph 2 of Article 9 or his insurer shall be deemed constituted by all persons mentioned in paragraph 1(*a*), (*b*) or (*c*) or paragraph 2, respectively.

ARTICLE 12

Distribution of the fund

1. Subject to the provisions of paragraphs 1 and 2 of Article 6 and of Article 7, the fund shall be distributed among the claimants in proportion to their established claims against the fund.

2. If, before the fund is distributed, the person liable, or his insurer, has settled a claim against the fund such person shall, up to the amount he has paid, acquire by subrogation the rights which the person so compensated would have enjoyed under this Convention.

3. The right of subrogation provided for in paragraph 2 may also be exercised by persons other than those therein mentioned in respect of any amount of compensation which they may have paid, but only to the extent that such subrogation is permitted under the applicable national law.

4. Where the person liable or any other person establishes that he may be compelled to pay, at a later date, in whole or in part any such amount of compensation with regard to which such person would have enjoyed a right of subrogation pursuant to paragraphs 2 and 3 had the compensation been paid before the fund was distributed, the Court or other competent authority of the State where the fund has been constituted may order that a sufficient sum shall be provisionally set aside to enable such person at such later date to enforce his claim against the fund.

ARTICLE 13

Bar to other actions

1. Where a limitation fund has been constituted in accordance with Article 11, any person having made a claim against the fund shall be barred from exercising any right in respect of such a claim against any other assets of a person by or on behalf of whom the fund has been constituted.

2. After a limitation fund has been constituted in accordance with Article 11, any ship or other property, belonging to a person on behalf of whom the fund has been constituted, which has been arrested or attached within the jurisdiction of a State Party for a claim which may be raised against the fund, or any security given, may be released by order of the Court or other competent authority of such State. However, such release shall always be ordered if the limitation fund has been constituted:

(*a*) at the port where the occurrence took place, or, if it took place out of port, at the first port of call thereafter; or

(*b*) at the port of disembarkation in respect of claims for loss of life or personal injury; or

(*c*) at the port of discharge in respect of damage to cargo; or

(*d*) in the State where the arrest is made.

3. The rules of paragraphs 1 and 2 shall apply only if the claimant may bring a claim against the limitation fund before the Court administering that fund and the fund is actually available and freely transferable in respect of that claim.

ARTICLE 14

Governing law

Subject to the provisions of this Chapter the rules relating to the constitution and distribution of a limitation fund, and all rules of procedure in connection therewith, shall be governed by the law of the State Party in which the fund is constituted.

CHAPTER IV. SCOPE OF APPLICATION

ARTICLE 15

This Convention shall apply whenever any person referred to in Article 1 seeks to limit his liability before the Court of a State Party or seeks to procure the release of a ship or other property or the discharge of any security given within the jurisdiction of any such State.

PART II—PROVISIONS HAVING EFFECT IN CONNECTION WITH CONVENTION

Interpretation

1. In this Part of this Schedule any reference to a numbered article is a reference to the article of the Convention which is so numbered.

Right to limit liability

2. The right to limit liability under the Convention shall apply in relation to any ship whether seagoing or not, and the definition of "shipowner" in paragraph 2 of article 1 shall be construed accordingly.

Claims subject to limitation

3.—(1) Paragraph 1(*d*) of article 2 shall not apply unless provision has been made by an order of the Secretary of State for the setting up and management of a fund to be used for the making to harbour or conservancy authorities of payments needed to compensate them for the reduction, in consequence of the said paragraph 1(*d*), of amounts recoverable by them in claims of the kind there mentioned, and to be maintained by contributions from such authorities raised and collected by them in respect of vessels in like manner as other sums so raised by them.

(2) Any order under sub-paragraph (1) above may contain such incidental and supplemental provisions as appear to the Secretary of State to be necessary or expedient.

(3) If immediately before the coming into force of section 17 of this Act an order is in force under section 2(6) of the Merchant Shipping (Liability of Shipowners and Others) Act 1958 (which contains provisions corresponding to those of this paragraph) that order shall have effect as if made under this paragraph.·

Claims excluded from limitation

4.—(1) The claims excluded from the Convention by paragraph (b) of article 3 are claims in respect of any liability incurred under section 1 of the Merchant Shipping (Oil Pollution) Act 1971.

(2) The claims excluded from the Convention by paragraph (c) of article 3 are claims made by virtue of any of sections 7 to 11 of the Nuclear Installations Act 1965.

The general limits

5.—(1) In the application of article 6 to a ship with a tonnage less than 300 tons that article shall have effect as if—
(a) paragraph (a)(i) referred to 166,667 Units of Account; and
(b) paragraph (b)(i) referred to 83,333 Units of Account.

(2) For the purposes of article 6 and this paragraph a ship's tonnage shall be its gross tonnage calculated in such manner as may be prescribed by an order made by the Secretary of State.

(3) Any order under this paragraph shall, so far as appears to the Secretary of State to be practicable, give effect to the regulations in Annex 1 of the International Convention on Tonnage Measurement of Ships 1969.

Limit for passenger claims

6.—(1) In the case of a passenger steamer within the meaning of Part III of the Merchant Shipping Act 1894 the ship's certificate mentioned in paragraph 1 of article 7 shall be the passenger steamer's certificate issued under section 274 of that Act.

(2) In paragraph 2 of article 7 the reference to claims brought on behalf of a person includes a reference to any claim in respect of the death of a person under the Fatal Accidents Act 1976, the Fatal Accidents (Northern Ireland) Order 1977 or the Damages (Scotland) Act 1976.

Units of Account

7.—(1) For the purpose of converting the amounts mentioned in articles 6 and 7 from special drawing rights into sterling one special drawing right shall be treated as equal to such a sum in sterling as the

International Monetary Fund have fixed as being the equivalent of one special drawing right for—

    (*a*)   the relevant date under paragraph 1 of article 8; or

    (*b*)   if no sum has been fixed for that date, the last preceding date for which a sum has been so fixed.

    (2) A certificate given by or on behalf of the Treasury stating—

    (*a*)   that a particular sum in sterling has been fixed as mentioned in the preceding sub-paragraph for a particular date; or

    (*b*)   that no sum has been so fixed for that date and that a particular sum in sterling has been so fixed for a date which is the last preceding date for which a sum has been so fixed,

shall be conclusive evidence of those matters for the purposes of those articles; and a document purporting to be such a certificate shall, in any proceedings, be received in evidence and, unless the contrary is proved, be deemed to be such a certificate.

Constitution of fund

    8.—(1) The Secretary of State may from time to time, with the concurrence of the Treasury, by order prescribe the rate of interest to be applied for the purposes of paragraph 1 of article 11.

    (2) Where a fund is constituted with the court in accordance with article 11 for the payment of claims arising out of any occurrence, the court may stay any proceedings relating to any claim arising out of that occurrence which are pending against the person by whom the fund has been constituted.

Distribution of land

    9. No lien or other right in respect of any ship or property shall affect the proportions in which under article 12 the fund is distributed among several claimants.

Bar to other actions

    10. Where the release of a ship or other property is ordered under paragraph 2 of article 13 the person on whose application it is ordered to be released shall be deemed to have submitted to (or, in Scotland, prorogated) the jurisdiction of the court to adjudicate on the claim for which the ship or property was arrested or attached.

Meaning of "court"

    11. References in the Convention and the preceding provisions of this Part of this Schedule to the court are—

    (*a*)   in relation to England and Wales, references to the High Court;

    (*b*)   in relation to Scotland, references to the Court of Session;

    (*c*)   in relation to Northern Ireland, references to the High Court of Justice in Northern Ireland.

12. References in the Convention and in the preceding provisions of this Part of this Schedule to a ship include references to any structure (whether completed or in course of completion) launched and intended for use in navigation as a ship or part of a ship.

Meaning of "State Party"

13. An Order in Council made for the purposes of this paragraph and declaring that any State specified in the Order is a party to the Convention shall, subject to the provisions of any subsequent Order made for those purposes, be conclusive evidence that the State is a party to the Convention.

SCHEDULE 5

LIABILITY OF SHIPOWNERS AND SALVORS: CONSEQUENTIAL AMENDMENTS

[Note: the relevant parts of the following amendments have already been included along with the statutes to which they relate earlier in this Appendix]

The Merchant Shipping (Liability of Shipowners and Others) Act 1900

1.—(1) In section 2(1) of the Merchant Shipping (Liability of Shipowners and Others) Act 1900 for the reference to the actual fault or privity of the owners or authority there shall be substituted a reference to any such personal act or omission of the owners or authority as is mentioned in article 4 of the Convention in Part I of Schedule 4 to this Act.

(2) The limit of liability under that section shall be ascertained by applying to the ship mentioned in subsection (1) the method of calculation specified in paragraph 1(*b*) of article 6 of the Convention read with paragraph 5(1) and (2) of Part II of that Schedule.

(3) Articles 11 and 12 of the Convention in Part I of that Schedule and paragraphs 8 and 9 of Part II of that Schedule shall apply for the purposes of that section.

The Pilotage Authorities (Limitation of Liability) Act 1936

(Paragraph 2 was repealed by the Pilotage Act 1983, Sched. 4.)

The Crown Proceedings Act 1947

3. For section 5 of the Crown Proceedings Act 1947, including that Act as it applies in Northern Ireland, there shall be substituted—
"5.—(1) The provisions of sections 17 and 18 of the Merchant Shipping Act 1979 and of Schedule 4 to that Act (liability of shipowners and salvors) shall apply in relation to His Majesty's ships as they apply in relation to other ships.

(2) In this section "ships" has the same meaning as in those provisions."

4. In section 1(1)(*i*) of the Hovercraft Act 1968 for the words "Part VIII of the Merchant Shipping Act 1894", "that Part" and "the said Part VIII" there shall be substituted respectively the words "sections 17 and 18 of the Merchant Shipping Act 1979", "those sections" and "the said sections of the Merchant Shipping Act 1979".

The Carriage of Goods by Sea Act 1971

5. In section 6(4) of the Carriage of Goods by Sea Act 1971 for the words from "section 502" to "1958" there shall be substituted the words "section 18 of the Merchant Shipping Act 1979 (which".

The Merchant Shipping (Oil Pollution) Act 1971

6.—(1) In sections 5(4)(*b*) and 7(*b*) of the Merchant Shipping (Oil Pollution) Act 1971 for the words "the Merchant Shipping (Liability of Shipowners and Others) Act 1958" there shall be substituted the words "the Merchant Shipping Act 1979".

(2) For section 15(2) of that Act shall be substituted—

"For the purpose of section 17 of the Merchant Shipping Act 1979 (limitation of liability) any liability incurred under this section shall be deemed to be a liability in respect of such damage to property as is mentioned in paragraph 1(a) of article 2 of the Convention in Part I of Schedule 4 to that Act."

SCHEDULE 7

Enactments Repealed

Part I—Enactments Relating to Liability of Shipowners and Salvors

Chapter	Short title	Extent of repeal
57 & 58 Vict. c. 60	The Merchant Shipping Act 1894.	Part VIII.
63 & 64 Vict. c. 32.	The Merchant Shipping (Liability of Shipowners and Others) Act 1900.	Section 2(2) and (3).
6 Edw. 7, c. 48.	The Merchant Shipping Act 1906.	Section 69.
1 & 2 Geo. 5, c. 42	The Merchant Shipping Act 1911.	Section 1(2).
11 & 12 Geo. 5, c. 29.	The Merchant Shipping Act 1921.	In section 1 the words "and VIII".

Chapter	Short title	Extent of repeal
6 & 7 Eliz. 2, c. 62.	The Merchant Shipping (Liability of Shipowners and Others) Act 1958.	The whole Act except section 11 so far as applying to the Merchant Shipping (Liability of Shipowners and Others) Act 1900.
1965 c. 47.	The Merchant Shipping Act 1965.	Section 5(2). In Schedule 1, the entry relating to the Crown Proceedings Act 1947.
1965 c. 57.	The Nuclear Installations Act 1965.	In section 14(1) the words from "and section 503" to "shipowners)."
1971 c. 59.	The Merchant Shipping (Oil Pollution) Act 1971.	Section 4(1)(a). Section 8A.
1974 c. 43.	The Merchant Shipping Act 1974.	Section 4(1) (c) (ii) together with the word "or" preceding it. Section 9.

PART II—OTHER ENACTMENTS

[Note: only those references to provisions in this Appendix are extracted]

Chapter	Short title	Extent of repeal
1971 c. 59.	The Merchant Shipping (Oil Pollution) Act 1971.	Section 4(3) to (5).
1974 c. 43.	The Merchant Shipping Act 1974.	Section 1(6) and (7).

Statutory Instruments made in order to give effect to the Limitation Convention in the United Kingdom

At time of going to press, three orders have been made:

(1) The Merchant Shipping Act 1979 (Commencement No. 10) Order 1986 (S.I. 1986 No. 1052 (c.28)), made on June 23, 1986, which brings into force from 1st December 1986 those provisions of the Merchant Shipping Act 1979 which relate to the 1976 Limitation Convention, viz., sections 17, 18, 19(1), 19(4), 50(4) in so far as it relates to the repeals enumerated in Part 1 of Schedule 7, Schedule 4 (the Convention), Schedule 5 (consequential amendments relating to the liability of salvors) and Schedule 7, Part 1 (repeals).

(2) The Pilotage Act 1983 (Appointed Day No. 1) Order (S.I. 1986 No. 1051), made on June 23 1986, which appoints December 1st 1986 as the day for giving effect to the provisions contained in sections 55(4) and 58(2) of the Pilotage Act 1983 which alter the rights of pilotage authorities to limit liability so as to give effect to the Convention.

(3) The Merchant Shipping (Liability of Shipowners and Others) (Calculation of Tonnage) Order 1986 (S.I. 1986 No. 1040), made on June 23, 1986 under powers contained in para. 5 of Schedule 4 Part II to the Merchant Shipping Act 1979, enacts that tonnage shall be calculated for the purpose of the Convention in accordance with the provisions of the Merchant Shipping (Tonnage) Regulations 1982 (S.I. 1982 No. 841)/. The 1982 Regulations implement the International Convention on Tonnage Measurement of Ships 1969. See p. 47 supra. This Order, too, comes into force on December 1, 1986.

One further order is expected. The Merchant Shipping (Liability of Shipowners and Others) (Rate of interest) Order 1986 will set the rate of interest to be applied to limitation funds established by defendants seeking to limit liability under the Convention. This order will also come into force on December 1, 1986.

No further orders are expected in respect of the United Kingdom.

Index

Global limitation, 5
Gold francs, 36, 201–203. *See also*
    Limitation unit.

Harbours. *See* Docks and harbours.
History, 4, 161–162
    Argentina, 118
    F.R.G., 221–223
    France, 191–193
    G.D.R., 207
    Greece, 231
    Japan, 235
    Nordic, 240
    U.K., 18–21, 257
    U.S.A., 260–262
    Yugoslavia, 279

I.M.O., 9, 152, 164, 214
Insurance. *See also* Insurer.
    1976 Convention, 151, 186
    deny cover, 179–180
    hull policy, 164
    limitation, 163
    third parties, 176–179
    unseaworthiness, 112
    U.S.A., 274
Interest on claims, 238, 255
Insurer. *See also* Insurance.
    deny cover, 179–181
    direct action against, 176–179
    France, 199
    G.D.R., 210
    limitation, 29–30, 121, 246
    U.S.A., 274

Judgment recognition, 126–127, 136
Jurisdiction,
    1968 Convention, 141–142
    agreements, 130–131
    choice of, 117–118, 132
    C.L.C., 146
    F.R.G., 225
    forum non conveniens, 132
    G.D.R., 218–219
    Greece, 233
    lex fori, 6, 138, 281
    national law, 134
    proceedings (limitation and liability),
        119, 127–129
    U.K., 31
    U.S.A., 273–274
    Yugoslavia, 283–284

L.O.F., 113
Limitation fund,
    actual figure, 12
    administration, 118
    bar, 122

Limitation fund—*cont.*
    constitution, 119, 122–123
    distribution, 121, 135
    examples, 85–86, 88–92
    F.R.G., 225
    France, 205
    G.D.R., 216–218, 220
    guarantee, 120
    Japan, 237
    limitation without constitution of, 119,
        237, 241
    monetary system, 4
    Nordic, 241–242
    option system, 4
    Poland, 248
    provisional, 121
    unit, 36
    U.K., 254
    U.S.A., 271, 276–277
    Yugoslavia, 281, 283
Limitation unit, 36–40. *See also* Gold
    francs and S.D.R.'s.
    1976 Convention, 184
    F.R.G., 225–226
    France, 201–203
    Japan, 235
    U.K., 255
    Yugoslavia, 281–282
Limits, 11–12, 40

Manager, 29. *See also* Shipowner.
Master,
    Argentina, 187
    Greece, 233
Mortgages and liens, 139–140, 222–223

Nuclear, 28, 213

Oil pollution. *See also* Conventions —
    C.L.C. 1969.
    1976 Convention, 149, 183, 215
    Nordic, 240–241
    separate limitation, 7, 27, 144, 147–148
Operator. *See also* Shipowner.
    definition, 29
    Poland, 244
Owner. *See* Shipowner.

Passengers, 53–57
    examples, 97–99
    U.S.A., 276
Personal claims, 10. *See also* Claims
    subject to limitation.
Persons entitled to limit, 29–31
    extension, 5
    Argentina, 187
    France, 199
    G.D.R., 209